Lonely Planet

Discover
Great
Britain

Experience the best
of Great Britain

This edit
Neil Wilson,
Oliver Berry, Fionn Davenport, Marc Di Duca, Belinda Dixon,
Peter Dragicevich, Damian Harper, Anna Kaminski,
Catherine Le Nevez, Andy Symington

Contents

On the Road

Contents

In Focus

Survival Guide

This is Great Britain

Few places pack so much into such a tiny space as Britain. It's barely 600 miles from England's south coast to Scotland's northern tip so you can cross the island in a day, but you could spend a lifetime exploring and only scratch the surface. This proportionally challenged island manages to cram more sights into each square mile than a country 10 times its size.

History is undoubtedly one of the major highlights of a visit here. From clifftop castles and medieval cathedrals to stone circles and Roman ruins, the British landscape recounts a story that stretches back 5000 years. On your journey, you'll encounter a collection of kings and courtiers, heroes and villains, engineers and inventors, not to mention a host of writers, poets, painters, architects and artistic visionaries.

The landscape is another jewel in the nation's crown. Encompassing everything from green fields to isolated islands, rolling plains to wild hills, and sandy beaches to snowcapped mountains, the British landscape is astonishingly varied. Iconic cities such as London, Manchester, York, Bath and Edinburgh are stuffed with amazing architecture, captivating culture and hundreds of historic sights. And beyond the metropolises are 15 stunning national parks which now cover over 10% of the landscape, as well as countless quaint villages, hamlets and market towns – all of which make exploring this green and pleasant land an unbridled pleasure.

Of course, Britain isn't actually one country at all – it's three rolled into one. Some of the differences between the nations of England, Wales and Scotland are obvious (particularly the accents of the people), but others are more subtle, and getting to grips with their individual quirks is a fundamental part of what makes travel here so fascinating. It's called Great Britain for a reason, you know – and you're about to find out why.

> 66
> *Few places pack so much into such a tiny space as Britain*
> 99

St Paul's Cathedral (p65), London
CHRIS HEPBURN/GETTY IMAGES ©

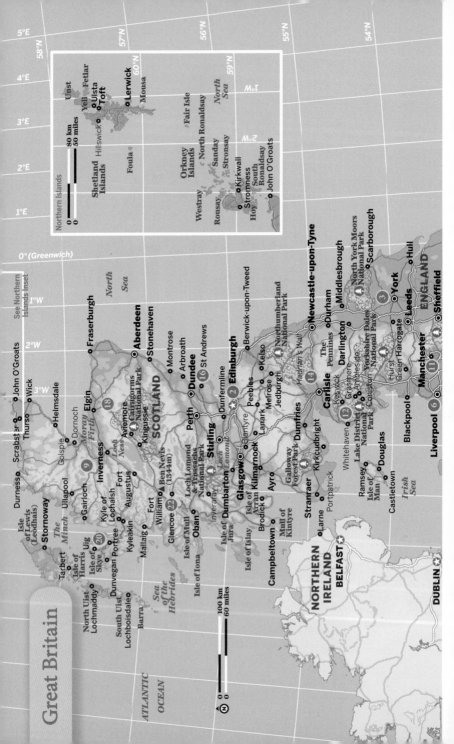

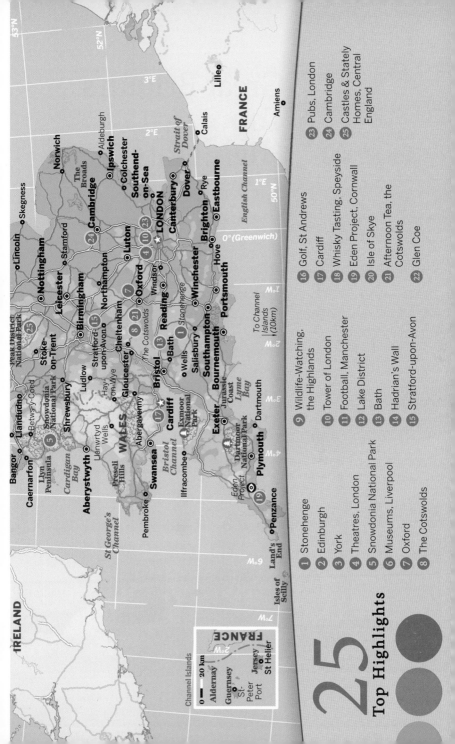

25 Top Highlights

1. Stonehenge
2. Edinburgh
3. York
4. Theatres, London
5. Snowdonia National Park
6. Museums, Liverpool
7. Oxford
8. The Cotswolds
9. Wildlife-Watching, the Highlands
10. Tower of London
11. Football, Manchester
12. Lake District
13. Bath
14. Hadrian's Wall
15. Stratford-upon-Avon
16. Golf, St Andrews
17. Cardiff
18. Whisky Tasting, Speyside
19. Eden Project, Cornwall
20. Isle of Skye
21. Afternoon Tea, the Cotswolds
22. Glen Coe
23. Pubs, London
24. Cambridge
25. Castles & Stately Homes, Central England

25 Great Britain's Top Highlights

Stonehenge

Mysterious and compelling, Stonehenge (p192) is Britain's most iconic ancient site. People have been drawn to this myth-rich ring of bluestones for the last 5000 years, and we're still not sure why it was built. Most visitors get to gaze at the 50-ton megaliths from behind the perimeter fence, but with enough planning you can book an early-morning or evening tour and walk around the inner ring. In the slanting sunlight, away from the crowds, it's an ethereal place – an experience that certainly stays with you.

PETER ADAMS/GETTY IMAGES ©

M. TURNER PHOTOGRAPHY/GETTY IMAGES ©

② Edinburgh

Scotland's capital city is famous for its summer festivals, but even outside festival time, this is a fascinating city to explore – full of winding lanes, hidden courtyards and architectural sights. The top draws are the city's clifftop castle and the palace of Holyroodhouse, but Edinburgh (p298) is a city of subtle pleasures, whether that means a picnic in the grounds of Holyrood Palace, a pint in an Old Town pub or a stroll along the Royal Mile. Edinburgh Castle (p308)

York

With its Viking heritage and maze of medieval streets, York (p220) is a showcase for English history. For a great introduction, join one of the city's many walking tours through the snickelways (narrow alleys), then admire the intricacies of York Minster, the biggest medieval cathedral in northern Europe, or explore the history of another age at the National Railway Museum. York Minster (p224)

The Best...
Cathedrals

ST PAUL'S CATHEDRAL
London's most beautiful cathedral, and Christopher Wren's masterwork. (p65)

YORK MINSTER
York's mighty minster is known for its ornate towers and medieval stained glass. (p224)

CANTERBURY CATHEDRAL
The mothership of the Anglican Church has centuries' worth of history. (p107)

SALISBURY CATHEDRAL
Has the tallest spire of any English cathedral, so you'll need a head for heights. (p190)

WINCHESTER CATHEDRAL
Gothic wonder with one of the longest medieval naves in Europe. (p188)

The Best...
Nightlife

LONDON
With its many clubs, pubs
and theatres, you'll never
be bored in the capital.
(p94)

BRIGHTON
South-coast town with
lively nightlife and the
biggest gay scene outside
London. (p114)

GLASGOW
Pubs and bars aplenty
ensure Scotland's second
city never sleeps. (p320)

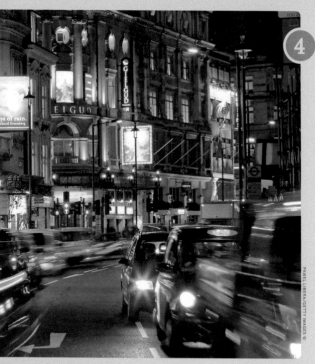

London's Theatre Scene

4

London has been famous for its shows ever since the days of William Shakespeare, and nothing much has changed. Theatre is still a major part of the capital's cultural life, and you should definitely find time to catch a show while you're in town – whether it's a musical in the West End, a bit of Shakespeare at the restored Globe Theatre, or a cutting-edge play at the National Theatre or Royal Court. Shaftesbury Ave, West End

PAWEL LIBERA/GETTY IMAGES ©

Snowdonia National Park

5

Wales' best-known national park (p277) has the most breathtaking scenery this side of the Scottish Highlands. The busiest part is around Snowdon itself, Wales' highest mountain, where hardy visitors hike to the summit, and everyone else lets the train take the strain by climbing aboard the historic Victorian railway. On a clear day, you can see clear to the Irish Sea.

MARK GREENWOOD LANDSCAPES/GETTY IMAGES ©

Liverpool's Museums

Liverpool (p237) will forever be associated with The Beatles, but this city now has even more to offer. After a redevelopment, the old Albert Dock has become a World Heritage Site, and has museums exploring the city's maritime past and murky slave-trading history. And fans of the Fab Four will find places to indulge, from the Cavern Club to the Beatles Story. Museum of Liverpool

MARI AVELLINO/GETTY IMAGES ©

PROJECT8/GETTY IMAGES ©

Oxford

For centuries the brilliant minds and august institutions of Oxford University (p134) have made this city famous across the globe. You'll get a glimpse of this revered world as you stroll hushed college quads and cobbled lanes roamed by cycling students and dusty academics. The beautiful buildings and archaic traditions have changed little over the years, leaving Oxford much as alumni such as Einstein or Tolkien would have found it. Christ Church college (p134)

The Cotswolds

The most wonderful thing about the Cotswolds (p142) is that no matter how lost you get, you'll still end up in an impossibly picturesque village complete with rose-clad cottages, a honey-coloured stone church and a cosy local pub serving a choice of real ales. It's easy to leave the crowds behind and find your very own slice of medieval England – and some of the best boutique hotels in the country. Church of St Mary the Virgin, Lasborough

The Best...
Stately Homes

CASTLE HOWARD
Baroque masterpiece that featured in *Brideshead Revisited*. (p227)

CHATSWORTH HOUSE
Known as the Palace of the Peaks, and stuffed with priceless treasures. (p161)

BLENHEIM PALACE
Winston Churchill's birthplace and the seat of the dukes of Marlborough. (p140)

STOURHEAD
Glorious southwest mansion, best known for its landscaped parkland. (p194)

CULZEAN CASTLE
The most impressive Scottish stately home, with antiques and artworks galore. (p321)

Wildlife-Watching in the Highlands

It might not be an untouched wilderness, but Britain still has a wealth of wildlife. From spotting red deer on Exmoor to spying ospreys in the Lake District, there are numerous opportunities to get acquainted with the island's animal inhabitants. The best place to discover this wild side is in the Highlands (p344), where you can take a boat trip in search of dolphins and whales, or spy eagles above snowy peaks. Red deer

The Best...
Castles

WINDSOR CASTLE
The largest and oldest occupied fortress in the world, and the Queen's country retreat. (p117)

WARWICK CASTLE
Perhaps the classic British castle, and still impressively intact. (p149)

CAERNARFON CASTLE
Moody castle and military stronghold on the Welsh coast. (p282)

EDINBURGH CASTLE
Edinburgh's fortress has enough to fill several visits. (p308)

STIRLING CASTLE
Perched on a volcanic crag, and quieter than Edinburgh. (p324)

10 Tower of London

With its battlements and turrets overlooking the Thames, the Tower of London (p66) is an icon of the capital. The walls are nearly 1000 years old, established by William the Conqueror in the 1070s. Since then, the Tower has been a fortress, royal residence, treasury, mint, arsenal and prison. Today it's home to the Crown Jewels, the famous red-coated Yeoman Warders (known as Beefeaters) and a flock of ravens which – legend says – must never leave. White Tower (p67)

Football

In some parts of the world it's called soccer, but here it's football. The English Premier League has some of the world's finest teams, including Arsenal, Liverpool and Chelsea, plus *the* most famous club on the planet: Manchester United. North of the border, Scotland's best-known teams are Glasgow Rangers and Glasgow Celtic, and their rivalry is legend. In Wales the national sport is most definitely rugby. Football at Old Trafford (p233), Manchester

DAVID C TOMLINSON/GETTY IMAGES ©

Lake District

William Wordsworth and his Romantic chums were the first to champion the charms of the Lake District (p243), and it's not hard to see what stirred them. With soaring mountains, whaleback fells, razor-edge valleys and – of course – glistening lakes (as well as England's highest hill), this craggy corner of northwest England has some of the country's finest vistas. Come for the comfortable lakeside hotels, or come for hardy hiking – whatever you choose, inspiration is sure to follow. Blea Tarn, Langdale Pikes

Bath

Britain boasts many great cities, but Bath (p176) is the belle of the ball. The Romans founded a huge bathhouse here to take advantage of the area's natural hot springs, which you can still visit to this day; but it's Bath's stunning Georgian archi-tecture that really makes a visit here special. The city was redeveloped on a grand scale during the 18th century and its streets are lined with fabulous buildings. Marlborough Buildings, Bath

Hadrian's Wall

Hadrian's Wall (p250) is Britain's most dramatic Roman ruin. Built almost 2000 years ago, this great barrier marked the division between the civilised lands of Roman Britain and the unruly territory of the Celts and Picts to the north. Though much has disappeared, you can still see many surviving sections of wall and several original forts.

14

The Best...
Wild Spots

YORKSHIRE DALES
Green and grand, made famous by James Herriot's novels. (p226)

GOWER PENINSULA
Beautiful coastal scenery within easy reach of Cardiff. (p270)

DARTMOOR NATIONAL PARK
These wild southwest moors stir the imagination. (p202)

ISLE OF MULL
Whale-watching trips run from this craggy Scottish island. (p353)

EXMOOR
Spot deer on a wildlife safari. (p188)

The Best...
Landmark Buildings

HOUSES OF PARLIAMENT
The seat of British
government. (p61)

BUCKINGHAM PALACE
The Queen's modest
London home. (p61)

GLOBE THEATRE
Shakespeare's original
'Wooden O'. (p72)

**PALACE OF
HOLYROODHOUSE**
Boasts centuries of
Scottish history. (p303)

SCONE PALACE
Where Scotland's kings
were crowned. (p325)

15

Stratford-upon-Avon

The pretty town of Stratford-upon-Avon (p150) is famed around the world as the birthplace of the nation's best-known dramatist, William Shakespeare. Today the town's tight knot of Tudor streets forms a map of Shakespeare's life and times, while crowds of fans enjoy a play at the theatre or visit the five historic houses owned by Shakespeare and his relatives, with a respectful detour to the old stone church where the Bard was laid to rest.

Left: Shakespeare's Birthplace (p150); Above: Prince Hal statue, Gower Memorial, Bancroft Gardens

LEFT: KATHY COLLINS/GETTY IMAGES © ABOVE: EPICS/GETTY IMAGES ©

Golf at St Andrews

It may be a 'good walk spoilt' but golf is one of the most popular sports in Britain, both with participants of all levels and thousands of spectators too (especially during major tournaments). With courses across the country, visitors to Britain with a penchant for the little white ball will surely want to try their skill. A highlight for aficionados is a round on the Old Course at St Andrews (p328), the venerable home of golf.

16

Cardiff

17

The exuberant capital of Wales, Cardiff (p264) has recently emerged as one of Britain's leading urban centres. After a mid-20th-century decline, the city entered the new millennium with vigour and confidence, flexing architectural muscles and revelling in a sense of style. From the historic castle to the ultramodern waterfront, lively street cafes to infectious nightlife, and Victorian shopping arcades to the gigantic rugby stadium, Cardiff is definitely cool. Cardiff Bay

CHRIS HEPBURN/GETTY IMAGES ©

Whisky Tasting in Speyside

If you fancy trying a wee dram or two, then Speyside (p331) in Scotland is the place to head. Some of the country's most prestigious whisky distilleries are dotted around this remote valley, many of which offer guided tours and tasting sessions. Before enjoying your tipple, remember a couple of tips: in Scotland, whisky is never spelled with an 'e' (that's the Irish variety); and when ordering at the bar, asking for 'Scotch' is something of a faux pas (ask for whisky). Glenfiddich Distillery (p332), Dufftown

The Best...
Museums

BRITISH MUSEUM
Delve into the vast collections at the nation's foremost museum. (p78)

NATURAL HISTORY MUSEUM
Giant dinosaurs and geological treasures in a Victorian landmark. (p73)

IMPERIAL WAR MUSEUM NORTH
The Manchester outpost of London's moving war museum. (p233)

KELVINGROVE ART GALLERY & MUSEUM
Quirky Glasgow museum full of Victorian curiosities. (p317)

Eden Project

Cornwall's coastline is well worthy of a trip in its own right, but the county's top attractions are the three space-age biomes of the Eden Project (p207), which re-create diverse habitats from around the world such as the humid Mediterranean and the tropical rainforest, and shed light on some of the environmental challenges facing the world in the 21st century. It's educational and inspirational, and is definitely one of the southwest's must-sees.

IMAGES ETC LTD/GETTY IMAGES ©

The Best...
Viewpoints

WHITE CLIFFS OF DOVER
Stroll along these celebrated chalk cliffs on England's south coast. (p111)

LAND'S END
The very end of Cornwall – and Britain. (p208)

SNOWDON
Stand on the roof of Wales. (p279)

BEN NEVIS
Enjoy glorious views over the Highland glens. (p350)

GLASTONBURY TOR
Enjoy 360-degree views over Somerset from this mythical hill. (p185)

20 Isle of Skye

Of all Scotland's islands, Skye (p355) is the best loved. Ringed by cliffs and beaches, cloaked with fields and moors, and framed by the rugged Cuillin Hills, Skye is a paradise for lovers of the Scottish landscape, and a popular getaway for thousands of people every year. The island is easily reached from the mainland by boat or bridge, which makes it a great add-on to any Scottish road trip. Make sure you pack the camera. Neist Point Lighthouse

Afternoon Tea

No one does tea quite like the British – it's not just a tradition here, it's a religion. To appreciate it at its best, head to a cafe, such as Huffkins (p144), or a country hotel that serves proper afternoon tea – a gourmet spread that includes cakes, sandwiches and a pot of loose-leaf tea, sipped (of course) from china tea cups. Even better, every region serves its own slightly different version. Scones with jam and cream

Glen Coe

In the Highlands of Scotland you're never far from a knock-out view, but the area around Glencoe (p347) still raises a gasp. This wild valley has perhaps the most iconic view of any Scottish glen, hemmed in by mountains towering above the snaking road. In summer it looks beautiful and benign, but in the depths of winter it's another story. Nearby lurks Ben Nevis, Britain's loftiest mountain, and the lively town of Fort William, dubbed the 'Outdoors Capital of the UK'.

Britain's Pubs

It's no secret that the Brits like a good drink, and the pub's still the place where most people do it. The classic pub has been the centre of British social life for centuries, and wherever you travel there'll be a local to discover: from ornate Victorian boozers in London to country pubs, hunkering under timber beams and warmed by a crackling hearth. The traditional drink is a pint of real ale – served warm and flat, and an acquired taste.

The Best...
Ruins

FOUNTAINS ABBEY
The remains of Britain's greatest abbey, torn down during Henry VIII's Dissolution of the Monasteries. (p228)

HOUSESTEADS
Wander among the ruins of this evocative fort on Hadrian's Wall. (p250)

TINTAGEL CASTLE
Dramatic clifftop ruins on the Cornish coast, with legendary connections to King Arthur. (p187)

GLASTONBURY ABBEY
Another mighty medieval abbey reduced to rubble. (p185)

The Best...
Historic Towns

CHESTER
Walk round Chester's medieval walls, the finest in England. (p236)

CANTERBURY
Stately town with an even statelier cathedral. (p106)

WINDSOR & ETON
Home to the Queen's second home and England's poshest public school. (p116)

BUXTON
Spa-town splendour in the middle of the Peak District. (p160)

BRISTOL
This southwest harbour city has a salty sea-faring past. (p185)

Cambridge

Abounding with exquisite architecture and steeped in tradition, Cambridge (p118) is a university town extraordinaire. The tightly packed core of ancient colleges, the picturesque riverside 'Backs' (college gardens) and the surrounding green meadows give Cambridge a more tranquil appeal than its historic rival Oxford. Highlights include the intricate vaulting of King's College Chapel, and no visit is complete without an attempt to steer a punt (flat-bottomed boat) along the river and under the quirky Mathematical Bridge. Bridge of Sighs

Castles & Stately Homes

Britain's turbulent history is nowhere more apparent than in the mighty castles that dot the landscape, from romantic clifftop ruins such as Corfe or sturdy fortresses such as Caernarfon, to formidable Stirling and still-inhabited Windsor. And when the aristocracy no longer needed castles, they built vast mansions known as 'stately homes' at the heart of their country estates – Chatsworth House (p161) and Castle Howard (p227) are among the finest.

Corfe Castle (p187), Dorset

Great Britain's
Top Itineraries

London to Bath
The Bare Essentials

5 DAYS

Five days is barely enough to get started, so we've picked out only the key stops for this whistle-stop itinerary.

BATH ④

STONEHENGE ③

WINDSOR ② LONDON ①

English Channel (La Manche)

① London (p60)

London simply has to be the start of any tour of England, but with only two days in the capital you'll need to work fast. On day one tick off **Trafalgar Square** plus **Buckingham Palace** and **Westminster Abbey**, followed by the **Houses of Parliament** and the tower of **Big Ben**. You'll just about have time for an afternoon at the **Tower of London**, and an evening ride on the **London Eye**. On day two, visit **St Paul's Cathedral** in the morning, spend the afternoon at the **British Museum**, and catch an evening show in the **West End** or at **Shakespeare's Globe**.

LONDON ⊙ WINDSOR
🚃 **One hour** Direct trains run from London Waterloo to Windsor Riverside; trains from London Paddington require a change at Slough.
🚗 **45 minutes** 25 miles via the M4.

② Windsor (p116)

The Queen's country getaway at **Windsor Castle** makes an ideal day trip from London, and is packed with priceless portraits and fascinating architecture.

Tower Bridge (p64), London
JOHNNY GREIG/GETTY IMAGES ©

WINDSOR ⊙ SALISBURY (FOR STONEHENGE)
🚃 **2½ hours** Take the train from Windsor Riverside and change at Clapham Junction
🚗 **90 minutes** Via the M3 and A303

③ Stonehenge (p192)

Salisbury is ideal for an afternoon excursion to **Stonehenge**, which lies about 10 miles to the north across Salisbury Plain. Back in Salisbury itself, the needlelike spire of **Salisbury Cathedral** is the tallest such tower in England, and affords glorious views across the medieval Cathedral Close and beyond.

SALISBURY ⊙ BATH
🚃 **One hour** Frequent trains to Bath Spa train station. 🚗 **One hour** Follow the main road (A36), detouring via Stonehenge.

④ Bath (p176)

West from Salisbury is the stunning city of **Bath**, a must-see for its incredible Georgian architecture and beautifully preserved **Roman Baths**. If time allows, relax in the naturally hot waters of the futuristic **Thermae Bath Spa**.

5 DAYS

London to Stratford-upon-Avon
English Idylls

This trip through the English countryside features the dreaming spires of Oxford and the quaint villages of the Cotswolds, and finishes in Shakespeare-central, Stratford-upon-Avon.

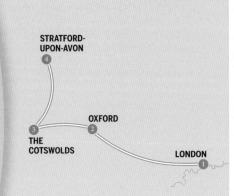

STRATFORD-UPON-AVON ④

OXFORD ②

③ THE COTSWOLDS

LONDON ①

① London (p60)

You could devote your two days in London to its top-ticket sights, or you could delve a little deeper and take in a few of the more out-of-the-way attractions: perhaps a river trip down the Thames to maritime **Greenwich**, a visit to one of London's bustling markets such as the ones on **Camden Lock** or **Portobello Road**, or a scenic stroll through **Hyde Park.** On day two focus your time on the capital's countless museums: the art-oriented **Victoria & Albert Museum** and **Tate Britain**, or the scientifically inclined **Science Museum** and **Natural History Museum**.

LONDON ● OXFORD

🚃 **One hour** From London's Paddington Station direct to Oxford. 🚗 **90 minutes** (traffic permitting) From central London to Oxford on the M40.

② Oxford (p134)

The city of Oxford is one of England's most famous university towns. Take your pick from the many colleges, but make sure to visit **Christ Church College** and **Magdalen College**. With a bit more time you could also take in a tour of the **Radcliffe Camera** and the **Ashmolean Museum**, and perhaps factor in a visit to the fabulous mansion of **Blenheim Palace**.

OXFORD ● THE COTSWOLDS

🚗 **30 minutes** Buses are limited, so you'll need your own wheels to explore. The quickest route from Oxford is the A40, which heads 20 miles west to Burford, one of the gateway villages.

③ The Cotswolds (p142)

With their country pubs and thatched cottages, the villages of the Cotswolds paint an idyllic vision of olde-worlde England. There are many to discover, but **Stow-on-the-Wold** and **Chipping Campden** are particularly photogenic. Many, such as **Broadway** and **Minster Lovell**, date back to the days of the Domesday Book. The surrounding countryside is littered with walks and bike rides, and there are lots of gorgeous boutique hotels and B&Bs to choose from.

THE COTSWOLDS ● STRATFORD-UPON-AVON

🚃 **One hour** Buses run regularly from Chipping Campden to Stratford-upon-Avon.
🚗 **30 minutes** From the northern edge of the Cotswolds to Stratford-upon-Avon.

④ Stratford-upon-Avon (p150)

Arguably England's most important literary town, Stratford-upon-Avon is awash with Shakespeare sights, including **Shakespeare's Birthplace**, his wife **Anne Hathaway's Cottage** and his grave at **Holy Trinity Church**. The town gets very busy in summer, so try to visit in spring or autumn to see it at its best. Whatever time of year you come, you'll need to book ahead if you want to catch a play courtesy of the renowned **Royal Shakespeare Company**.

Anne Hathaway's Cottage, Stratford-Upon-Avon (p152)
PETER SCHOLEY/GETTY IMAGES ©

10 DAYS

Brighton to St Ives
Go West

A tour along England's scenic southern coastline, veering via the cities of Brighton, Bristol, Bath and Plymouth, before finishing in style on the Cornish seaside.

Cardigan Bay

BRISTOL

Bristol Channel

③ ④ **BATH**

② **WINCHESTER**

① **BRIGHTON**

ST IVES ⑤

⑥

LAND'S END

PLYMOUTH

English Channel (La Manche)

1 Brighton (p111)

The buzzy seaside town of Brighton is only an hour from London and is known for its nightlife, eccentric shopping and excellent restaurants. One sight you definitely shouldn't miss is the bizarre **Brighton Pavilion**, designed in extravagant Oriental style for the Prince Regent, later George IV.

BRIGHTON ○ WINCHESTER

🚌 **2¼ hours** You'll need to change at Southampton. 🚗 **1¾ hours** Take the A27, then turn onto the M3.

2 Winchester (p188)

The former capital of England, Winchester has an enticing mix of history and architecture. The town's main landmark is its immense **cathedral**, which looks plain on the outside, but conceals a wonderland of soaring pillars and dazzling stained glass inside.

WINCHESTER ○ BRISTOL

🚌 **Two hours** Change again at Southampton. 🚗 **1¾ hours** On the A34 and M4.

3 Bristol (p185)

Once Britain's third-largest harbour, Bristol has reinvented itself as a creative city with a distinctly quirky side. It has some great galleries and museums – make time for the impressive **M-Shed** and the decks of the SS *Great Britain*, one of the greatest steamships of its day. Spend the afternoon exploring the genteel suburb of Clifton and its famous suspension bridge.

BRISTOL ○ BATH

🚌 **15 minutes** Two or three direct per hour. 🚗 **30 minutes** On the A4.

4 Bath (p176)

It's a half-hour drive from Bristol to Bath, but for fans of English architecture it's an essential detour. At **No 1 Royal Crescent**, you can step inside one of Bath's finest townhouses, restored using 18th-century techniques and materials. Another famous terrace, the **Circus**, is a short walk away.

BATH ○ PLYMOUTH

🚌 **2¾ hours** Change at Bristol or Westbury for Plymouth. 🚗 **Three hours** Direct via the M4 and M5, or cross-country via Wells.

5 Plymouth (p198)

Plymouth has a rich maritime history: the Pilgrim Fathers' *Mayflower* set sail for America from here in 1620, followed 150 years later by Captain Cook. Today the **Mayflower Steps** mark the point of departure. The wild national park of **Dartmoor** is also nearby.

PLYMOUTH ○ ST IVES

🚌 **2¼ hours** Change at St Erth for the scenic branch line. 🚗 **1¾ hours** Via the A38 and A30.

6 St Ives (p205)

Seaside St Ives makes a gorgeous base for exploring Cornwall. Galleries abound, including **Tate St Ives** and the **Barbara Hepworth Museum**. Further afield are the eco-domes of the **Eden Project**, the island abbey of **St Michael's Mount** and the sea-smashed cliffs at **Land's End**.

St Ives (p205), Cornwall

10 DAYS

London to the Peak District
Palaces & Peaks

Head west from London to take in Wales' top sights, before turning north for a day in medieval Chester, lively Liverpool and the picturesque Peak District.

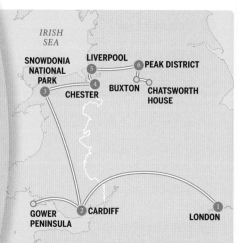

IRISH SEA

SNOWDONIA NATIONAL PARK

LIVERPOOL 5

PEAK DISTRICT 6

CHESTER

3

4 BUXTON

CHATSWORTH HOUSE

GOWER PENINSULA

2 CARDIFF

LONDON 1

1 London (p60)

Kick off this trip with a couple of the capital's outer attractions: the incredible botanical gardens of **Kew** and then **Hampton Court Palace**, perhaps the most glorious Tudor structure in England.

LONDON ➡ CARDIFF

🚃 **Two hours** Direct from London Paddington, or with a change at Bath. 🚗 **2½ hours** On the M4.

2 Cardiff (p264)

Then it's on from one capital to another. Seaside Cardiff has completely reinvented itself in recent years, and the waterfront is now awash with interest, including the **National Assembly Building** and the **Wales Millennium Stadium**. **Cardiff Castle** is another essential stop, as are the nearby **Gower Peninsula** and the moody ruins of **Tintern Abbey**.

CARDIFF ➡ BETWS-Y-COED

🚃 **Four hours** Cross-country to Llandudno, then change for the Conwy Valley line. 🚗 **3½ hours** Along the A470.

3 Snowdonia National Park (p277)

Wales is known for its knock-out scenery, but few places can top Snowdonia in terms of sheer spectacle. It's home to the country's highest mountain: dedicated hikers will want to walk to the top, but if you're short on time you could just take the **Snowdon Mountain Railway**.

BETWS-Y-COED ➡ CHESTER

🚃 **1½ hours** Change at Llandudno. 🚗 **1½ hours** A470 north towards Llandudno, then the A55.

4 Chester (p236)

For medieval atmosphere, Chester is definitely a must-see. Its rust red city walls and cobbled streets are full of charm, especially along the **Rows** – a photogenic tangle of galleried arcades that have hardly changed since the Middle Ages.

CHESTER ➡ LIVERPOOL

🚃 **45 minutes** Several trains per hour. 🚗 **45 minutes** Via the M53, A41 and Mersey Tunnel.

5 Liverpool (p237)

There are plenty of reasons to visit Liverpool, but there's no getting away from the fact that the Fab Four are still the major draw. Fans will find plenty to satisfy their fascination, especially among the memorabilia on show at the **Beatles Story**. Other highlights include the renowned **Walker Art Gallery**, the historic waterfront of **Albert Dock** and the moving **International Slavery Museum**.

LIVERPOOL ➡ BUXTON

🚃 **Two hours** Change in Manchester. 🚗 **1½ hours** Take the M62 and M60.

6 Peak District (p159)

This rugged range of valleys, hills and villages is one of northern England's most popular countryside getaways, and offers a wealth of opportunity for hiking and biking. Afterwards you can relax in the elegant spa town of **Buxton** or take a trip to **Chatsworth House**, a classic example of country-house extravagance.

Formal gardens, Hampton Court Palace (p83)
SIMON GREENWOOD/GETTY IMAGES ©

London to Edinburgh
The Full Monty

This long-distance adventure links Old London Town with Scotland's capital, taking in the historic towns of Cambridge and York and two of England's finest national parks en route.

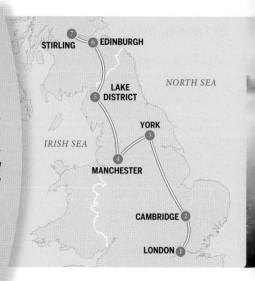

London (p60)

There's not much time to spare on this long-distance tour, so you'll probably have to limit yourself to just a day in London. Spend the morning browsing around the **British Museum**, head down to **Buckingham Palace** for the Changing of the Guard at 11.30am, whizz over to **St Paul's Cathedral**, cross the river to the **South Bank** and the **Tate Modern**, and finish in the West End via the **Palace of Westminster** and **Trafalgar Square**.

LONDON 〇 CAMBRIDGE
🚆 **1¼ hours** From London King's Cross or Liverpool St. 🚗 **1½ hours** Once you're clear of the London traffic, head to Cambridge on the M11.

② Cambridge (p118)

Arch rival to Oxford and England's second celebrated seat of academia, Cambridge is equally famous for its history and architecture. Key colleges to visit include **Trinity College**, the largest and arguably most impressive, as well as **King's College**, with its wonderfully ornate chapel. It's also well worth strolling along the **Backs** for their picturesque riverside scenery; look out for the wonderful **Mathematical Bridge**.

CAMBRIDGE 〇 YORK
🚆 **2½ hours** Change trains at Peterborough.
🚗 **Three hours** It's a long drive to York of around 160 miles via the A1.

③ York (p220)

It's easy to while away a full day in the graceful city of York. All streets in the centre lead to the mammoth **Minster**, but don't overlook the medieval street known as the **Shambles** and the smells-and-all re-creation of a Viking settlement at **Jorvik**. Northwest of York lie the **Yorkshire Dales**, a rugged landscape of peaks and valleys that are guaranteed to have you reaching for your camera.

YORK 〇 MANCHESTER
🚆 **One hour, 20 minutes** Direct to Manchester Piccadilly. 🚗 **1½ hours** Straight across via the A64 and M62; expect traffic around Leeds.

Lake Grasmere (p247), Lake District
PETER ADAMS/GETTY IMAGES ©

Wordsworth all lived here – but it's best known as one of England's best places for a hike. Trails wind out over the park's jagged hills, while vintage cruise boats chug out across the surface of **Windermere** and other nearby lakes.

WINDERMERE ⟶ EDINBURGH

🚆 **2½ hours** Change at Oxenholme for main-line services north. 🚗 **Three hours** You'll cover at least 150 miles along the M6, A74 and A702.

⑥ Edinburgh (p298)

You'll need at least a day in Edinburgh to cover all the must-sees, such as **Edinburgh Castle** and the **Palace of Holyroodhouse**, as well as the scenery of the **Royal Mile** and the shopping on **Prince's St**. If you have time, detours to the **Royal Yacht Britannia** and **Rosslyn Chapel** will reward the effort.

EDINBURGH ⟶ STIRLING

🚆 **One hour** Direct from Edinburgh's Waverley train station. 🚗 **One hour** Along the M9.

⑦ Stirling (p321)

From Edinburgh it is relatively straightforward to reach the historic **Stirling Castle** and the nearby **Wallace Monument**. With a bit of extra time, you could head onwards to visit scenic **Glen Coe** and legendary **Loch Ness**.

④ Manchester (p233)

Manchester is a lively metropolis with a wealth of cultural institutions and a cracking music scene. Make time for the **Imperial War Museum North**, the **Lowry** and the revitalised area around **Salford Quays**. Meanwhile football fans will want to make a pilgrimage to **Old Trafford**, Manchester United's home stadium, and the brand-new **National Football Museum**.

MANCHESTER ⟶ WINDERMERE

🚆 **1½ hours** From Manchester Piccadilly, you'll usually need to change at Oxenholme. 🚗 **1½ hours** Along the M6.

⑤ Lake District (p243)

Britain's favourite national park has numerous literary connections – Beatrix Potter, Arthur Ransome and William

Great Britain Month by Month

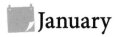 January

London Parade

A ray of light in the gloom, the New Year's Day Parade in London (to use its official title; www.londonparade.co.uk) is one of the biggest events of its kind in the world, featuring marching bands, street performers, classic cars, floats and displays winding their way through the streets, watched by over half a million people.

Up Helly Aa

Half of Shetland dresses up with horned helmets and battle axes in this spectacular re-enactment of a Viking fire festival (www.uphellyaa.org), with a torchlit procession leading the burning of a full-size Viking longship.

March

Six Nations Rugby Championship

Highlight of the rugby calendar (www.rbs6nations.com), with the home nations playing at London's Twickenham, Edinburgh's Murrayfield and Cardiff's Millennium Stadium.

University Boat Race

Annual race down the River Thames in London between the rowing teams from Cambridge and Oxford Universities (www.theboatrace.org), an institution since 1856 that still enthrals. the country.

 April

Grand National

Half the country has a flutter on the highlight of the three-day horse race meeting at Aintree

Top Events

- **Edinburgh Festivals**, August
- **Glastonbury**, late June
- **Notting Hill Carnival**, August
- **Braemar Gathering**, September
- **Hay Festival**, May

August Notting Hill Carnival (p44)
PHOTOGRAPHER: SIMON GREENWOOD/GETTY IMAGES ©

(www.aintree.co.uk) on the first Saturday of the month – a steeplechase with a testing course and notoriously high jumps.

London Marathon
Superfit athletes cover 26.22 miles in just over two hours, while others dress up in daft costumes and take considerably longer. (www.london-marathon.co.uk)

Spirit of Speyside
Based in Dufftown, this is a Scottish festival of whisky, food and music (www.spiritof speyside.com), with five days of art, cooking, distillery tours and outdoor activities.

May

FA Cup Final
Grand finale of the football (soccer) season for over a century. Teams from across England battle it out over the winter months, culminating in this heady spectacle at Wembley Stadium.

Brighton Festival
Lively three-week arts fest (www.brighton festival.org) taking over the streets of buzzy south-coast resort Brighton. Alongside the mainstream performances there's a festival fringe as well.

Chelsea Flower Show
The Royal Horticultural Society flower show at Chelsea (www.rhs.org.uk/ chelsea) is the highlight of the gardener's year.

Hay Festival
The ever-expanding 'Woodstock of the mind' (www.hayfestival.com) brings an intellectual influx to book-town Hay-on-Wye.

Glyndebourne
Famous festival (www.glyndebourne. com) of world-class opera in the pastoral surroundings of East Sussex, running until the end of summer.

June

Derby Week
Horse-racing, people-watching and clothes-spotting are on the agenda at this week-long meeting in Epsom, Surrey (www.epsomderby.co.uk).

Cotswold Olimpicks
Welly-wanging, pole-climbing and shin-kicking are the key disciplines at this traditional Gloucestershire sports day (www.olimpickgames.co.uk), held every year since 1612.

Trooping the Colour
Military bands and bear-skinned grenadiers march down London's Whitehall in this martial pageant to mark the monarch's birthday.

Royal Ascot
It's hard to tell which matters more, the fashion or the fillies, at this highlight of the horse-racing year in Berkshire (www. ascot.co.uk).

Wimbledon Tennis
The world's best-known grass-court tennis tournament (www.wimbledon.org) attracts all the big names, while crowds cheer or eat tons of strawberries and cream.

Glastonbury Festival
One of Britain's favourite pop and rock gatherings (www.glastonburyfestivals. co.uk), invariably muddy and still a rite of passage for every self-respecting British teenager.

Royal Regatta
Boats of every description take to the water for Henley's upper-crust river jamboree (www.hrr.co.uk).

August

Edinburgh Festivals

Edinburgh's most famous August happening is the International Festival and Fringe, but this month the city also has an event for anything you care to name – books, art, theatre, music, comedy, marching bands... (www.edinburghfestivals.co.uk)

Notting Hill Carnival

London's famous multicultural Caribbean-style street carnival in the district of Notting Hill (www.nottinghillcarnival. biz). Steel drums, dancers, outrageous costumes.

Reading Festival

Venerable rock and pop festival (www. readingfestival.com), always a good bet for big-name bands.

National Eisteddfod of Wales

The largest celebration of native Welsh culture, steeped in history, pageantry and pomp (www.eisteddfod.org.uk); held at various venues around the country.

Pride

Highlight of the gay and lesbian calendar, a technicolour street parade heads through London's West End.

July

T in the Park

World-class acts since 1994 ensure this major music festival (www.tinthepark. com) is Scotland's answer to Glastonbury.

Royal Welsh Show

Prize bullocks and local produce at this national farm and livestock event (www. rwas.co.uk) in Builth Wells.

Cowes Week

Britain's biggest yachting spectacular (www.aamcowesweek.co.uk) on the choppy seas around the Isle of Wight.

September

Bestival

Quirky music festival (www.bestival. net) on the Isle of Wight with a different fancy-dress theme every year.

Great North Run

Tyneside plays host to the one of the biggest half marathons in the world (www.greatrun. org), with the greatest number of runners in any race at this distance.

Abergavenny Food Festival

The mother of all epicurean festivals (www.abergavennyfoodfestival.co.uk) and the champion of Wales' burgeoning food scene.

 Braemar Gathering

The biggest and most famous Highland Games (www.braemargathering.org) in the Scottish calendar, traditionally attended by members of the royal family. Highland dancing, caber-tossing and bagpipe-playing.

 # October

 Dylan Thomas Festival

A celebration of the Welsh laureate's work with readings, events and talks in Swansea (www.dylanthomas.com).

 # November

 Guy Fawkes Night

Also called Bonfire Night (www.bonfire night.net), 5 November sees fireworks fill Britain's skies in commemoration of a failed attempt to blow up parliament way back in 1605.

 Remembrance Day

Red poppies are worn and wreaths are laid in towns and cities around the country on 11 November in commemoration of fallen military personnel (www.poppy.org.uk).

 # December

 New Year's Eve

Fireworks and street parties in town squares across the country. In London, crowds line the Thames for a massive midnight fireworks display.

Far left: September Traditional Scottish dancing at a Highland Games **Left: August** Reading Festival

What's New

For this new edition of Discover Great Britain, our authors hunted down the fresh, the transformed, the hot and the happening. Here are a few of our favourites. For latest recommendations, see lonelyplanet.com/great-britain.

1 STONEHENGE
A £27 million revamp of Britain's most famous prehistoric site has seen the area around the stones returned to grassland, and the opening of an impressive new visitor centre. (p192)

2 SHANGRI-LA AT THE SHARD
The first opening in the UK for the luxury Asian hotel chain, this is Europe's first elevated hotel, occupying levels 34 to 52 of London's Shard skyscraper. (p86)

3 THE MAKING OF HARRY POTTER
Prospective Hogwarts pupils can waggle their wands and practise their spells during this spectacular new tour at Warner Bros Studios, just outside London. (☑ 0845 084 0900; www.wbstudiotour.co.uk; Studio Tour Dr, Leavesden; adult/child £31/24; ⊙ 9am-9.30pm)

4 EDEN PROJECT
Cornwall's iconic eco-centre has an added attraction in the form of a new treetop walkway through the rainforest biome. (p207)

5 KING RICHARD III: DYNASTY, DEATH & DISCOVERY
The amazing story of the discovery of the skeletal remains of King Richard III beneath a Leicester car park in 2012 is celebrated in this new, high-tech visitor centre. (http://kriii.com; St Martin's Pl; adult/child £7.95/4.75; ⊙ 10am-4pm Mon-Fri, to 5pm Sat & Sun)

6 BLEAK HOUSE
Snooze in the very bedroom occupied for 12 productive summers by one Charles Dickens at this new hotel overlooking Broadstairs' tight curve of beach. (☑ 01843-865338; www.bleakhousebroadstairs.co.uk; Fort Rd; r £155-250, apt £300; ☎)

7 LIVERPOOL INTERNATIONAL MUSIC FESTIVAL
Liverpool's old Mathew St Festival has been expanded into a showcase of local and international talent spread over two weeks in late August. (☑ 0151-239 9091; www.limfestival.org)

8 BLACK SAIL YOUTH HOSTEL
One of England's most remote youth hostels, perched high in the Lake District fells above Ennerdale, now sports double glazing and solar panel-powered lighting following a major upgrade. (☑ 0845 371 9680; www.yha.org.uk/hostel/black-sail; dm £20.50-22.50)

9 NORTHUMBERLAND NATIONAL PARK
England's least-populous national park was awarded dark-sky status by the International Dark Skies Association in late 2013 (the largest such designation in Europe), adding to the stargazing appeal of Kielder Observatory.

10 PENARTH PAVILION
One of Wales' most famous seaside landmarks, the art deco Penarth Pavilion, has been renovated, complete with a brand-new art gallery, cinema and cafe. (www.penarthpavilion.co.uk; Penarth Pier; ⊙ 10am-5pm Sun-Wed, to 8pm Thu-Sat Apr-Oct, 10am-5pm daily Nov-Mar)

Get Inspired

Books

o **Oliver Twist** (1838) Tear-jerking social commentary from Charles Dickens.

o **Pride and Prejudice** (1813) Jane Austen's quintessential English love story.

o **White Teeth** (2000) Zadie Smith's literary debut explores life in multicultural London.

o **London: The Biography** (2001) Peter Ackroyd's fascinating account of the life of Britain's capital.

o **An Utterly Impartial History of Britain** (2007) Comic jaunt through Britain's past by humourist John O'Farrell.

Films

o **Brief Encounter** (1945) David Lean's classic portrayal of typically British buttoned-up passion.

o **The Ladykillers** (1955) Classic Ealing crime caper set on the grimy streets of London.

o **Chariots of Fire** (1981) Oscar-winning story of Olympic endeavour.

o **Four Weddings and a Funeral** (1994) Classic British rom-com starring Hugh Grant.

o **The King's Speech** (2010) Story of George VI's struggle to overcome his stammer.

Music

o **Sergeant Pepper's Lonely Hearts Club Band** (The Beatles) The Fab Four's finest moment.

o **Exile on Main Street** (The Rolling Stones) Classic album from Britain's other iconic band.

o **Hounds of Love** (Kate Bush) Epic electro-pop that tackles the big issues of life and death and God.

o **London Calling** (The Clash) Seminal punk with a point.

o **Different Class** (Pulp) Brit-pop tales of English eccentricity.

Websites

o **BBC** (www.bbc.com) News and entertainment.

o **British Council** (www. britishcouncil.org) Arts and culture.

o **Traveline** (www. traveline.info) Invaluable public-transport planning.

o **Lonely Planet** (www. lonelyplanet.com) Destination information, traveller forums, hotels and more.

Short on time?

This list will give you an instant insight into the country.

Read *Notes from a Small Island,* a hilarious travelogue from US-born Anglophile Bill Bryson.

Watch *Withnail & I,* cult holiday disaster movie.

Listen *Definitely Maybe,* landmark album from Manchester bad boys Oasis.

Log on *Visit Britain* (www. visitbritain.com), Britain's official tourism website; large and comprehensive.

Stourhead (p194)

Need to Know

Currency
Pound; also called 'pound sterling' (£)

Language
English; also Scottish Gaelic and Welsh

Visas
Not required for most citizens of Europe, Australia, NZ, USA and Canada.

Money
ATMs widely available. Visa and Mastercard credit and debit cardsa generally accepted.

Mobile Phones
Phones from most other countries operate in Britain but attract roaming charges. Local SIM cards cost from £10; SIM and basic handset around £50.

Wi-Fi
Most hotels and B&Bs, and many cafes, offer wi-fi. Wi-fi hot spots are common in the cities.

Internet Access
Internet cafes are rare. Public libraries often have computers with free internet access.

Tipping
Optional, but 10% in restaurants and cafes is standard. No need to tip in bars.

When to Go

Fort William
GO May or Sep

Aberdeen
GO May–Sep

Edinburgh
GO May–Sep

Brecon
GO May–Sep

Norwich
GO May–Sep

London
GO Any time

Exeter
GO Apr–Oct

High Season (Jun–Aug)
- Weather at its best; accommodation rates at their peak.
- Roads are busy, especially in seaside areas, national parks and popular cities such as Oxford, Bath, Edinburgh and York.

Shoulder (Mar–May & Sep–Oct)
- Crowds reduce; prices drop.
- Weather often good; March to May is a mix of sunny spells and showers; September to October can feature balmy Indian summers.

Low Season (Nov–Feb)
- Wet and cold. Snow falls in mountain areas, especially up north.
- Opening hours reduced October to Easter; some places shut for winter. Big-city sights (particularly London's) operate all year.

Advance Planning

- **Two months before** Book train tickets, hotels and car hire to get the best deals. In popular areas such as London, Bath, York and Edinburgh, the earlier you book the better.

- **One month before** Reserve tables at high-profile restaurants, and book hotels and B&Bs in other areas.

- **Two weeks before** Buy tickets online for big-ticket sights such as the Tower of London and the London Eye.

- **One week before** Check the weather forecast. Then ignore it.

Daily Costs

Budget Less than £55

○ Dorm beds: £15–25

○ Cheap meals in cafes and pubs: £7–11

○ Long-distance coach: £15–40 (200 miles)

Midrange £55–120

○ Midrange hotel or B&B: £65–130 (London £100–180) per double room

○ Main course in midrange restaurant: £10–20

○ Long-distance train: £20–80 (200 miles)

○ Car hire: from £35 per day

Top End More than £120

○ Four-star hotel room: from £130 (London £180)

○ Three-course meal in a good restaurant: around £40 per person

Exchange Rates		
Australia	A$1	51p
Canada	C$1	52p
Europe	€1	74p
Japan	¥100	56p
New Zealand	NZ$1	48p
USA	US$1	66p

For current exchange rates see www.xe.com.

What to Bring

○ **Comfortable shoes** You'll be doing a lot of walking, so a pair of sturdy, comfy shoes is indispensable. If you're planning on hiking, bring a pair of proper waterproof boots.

○ **Waterproof jacket and an umbrella** The British weather is famously fickle, so come prepared.

○ **Small day pack** For carrying the waterproofs when the sun shines.

○ **Good manners** The Brits are big fans of politeness. Keep the volume down, be respectful of others' opinions and whatever you do – don't skip queues.

Arriving in Britain

○ **London Heathrow**

Train The fast Heathrow Express (www. heathrowexpress.com; £21) trains run to London Paddington every 15 minutes.

Underground The Piccadilly Line connects all terminals to central London; cheaper (£5.70) but much slower.

Taxi A taxi to central London will cost between £45 and £85.

○ **London Gatwick**

Train Gatwick Express (www.gatwickexpress. com) runs to London Victoria every 15 minutes (£20).

Getting Around

○ **Train** Britain's comprehensive rail network connects major cities and towns. Peak times are the most expensive.

○ **Car** Britain's roads are extensive and generally of a high standard. Motorways link major cities. Traffic can be a problem.

○ **Local buses** Useful for reaching smaller towns, villages and rural sights.

Sleeping

○ **Hotels** Britain has a huge and varied choice of hotels, although you'll pay a premium in London and other popular spots.

○ **B&Bs** The traditional British bed-and-breakfast offers comfort and good value. The best places can match the standards of boutique hotels.

○ **Inns** Many pubs and inns also offer accommodation, especially in rural areas.

Be Forewarned

○ **Costs** Britain can be pricey; cut costs by staying in B&Bs, prebooking train and admission tickets online, and travelling outside peak times. Many tourist offices offer discount cards covering local attractions.

○ **Driving** Petrol is expensive in Britain, and traffic jams are a fact of life during rush hour – especially in the cities.

○ **School holidays** Things are busier and prices head upwards during school holidays, especially at Christmas, Easter and in July and August.

London & Around

When it comes to must-see sights, there's simply nowhere quite like London. This sprawling, stately city has been at the centre of British history for 2000 years, and it shows no sign of slowing down just yet. With its world-class theatres, landmark museums, iconic architecture and non-stop nightlife, London is truly a city that never sleeps, and you could spend your whole trip here and never run out of things to see and do. Unfortunately, all this prestige comes at a price. London is by far the most expensive city in Britain, so it's well worth taking advantage of some of the city's free sights while you're here – many of its top museums, galleries and green spaces don't charge a penny.

London also makes an ideal base for day trips, with the lively coastal city of Brighton, the academic centre of Cambridge and the royal palaces of Hampton Court and Windsor Castle all within easy reach.

Green Park (p59), with Big Ben in the background
SCOTT E BARBOUR/GETTY IMAGES ©

London & Around

See Bloomsbury & Regent's Park Map (p79)

Gospel Oak

Kentish Town Rd

West Hampstead

Kilburn

Brondesbury

Finchley Road

Swiss Cottage

South Hampstead

Willesden La

Brondesbury Park

PRIMROSE HILL

Chalk Farm

Camden Rd

Camden Town

Primrose Hill

Mornington Cres

Kilburn High Rd

Kilburn High Rd

Abbey Rd

St John's Wood

Ave Rd

Regent's Park

Albany St

Euston

Queens Park

Kilburn Park

ST JOHN'S WOOD

Harvist Rd

Kensal Green

KILBURN

Kilburn Park

Maida Vale

Grove End Rd

Park Rd

Marylebone St

FITZROVIA

Warren St

MARYLEBONE

Harrow Rd

Shirland Rd

MAIDA VALE

Lisson Gve

Baker St

Westbourne Park

Warwick Avenue

Royal Oak

Westway

Harrow Rd

Edgware Rd

Ladbroke Grove

Westbourne Park Rd

Paddington

Marble Arch

Bond St

Oxford Circus

BBC Media Village

Latimer Road

NOTTING HILL

PADDINGTON

PADDINGTON

Wood La

White City

Wood Lane

Ladbroke Gve

BAYSWATER

Notting Hill Gate

Bayswater Rd

Lancaster Gate

MAYFAIR

Park La

Hyde Park

The Serpentine

Hyde Park Corner

Piccadilly

ST JAMES'S

Uxbridge Rd

Holland Park

KENSINGTON

Kensington Gardens

Goldhawk Rd

Shepherd's Bush

HOLLAND PARK

High St Kensington

Palace Gate

Knightsbridge

Goldhawk Rd

KNIGHTSBRIDGE

Brompton Rd

Pont St

Ravenscourt Park

Kensington (Olympia)

Warwick Gdns

Gloucester Rd

BELGRAVIA

Victoria

Hammersmith

King St

Barons Court

EARLS COURT

SOUTH KENSINGTON

South Kensington

Sloane Sq

Warwick Way

PIMLICO

West Kensington

Earl's Court

King's Rd

Wetland Centre

West Brompton

CHELSEA

Ranelagh Gardens

Grosvenor Rd

BARNES

FULHAM

Lillie Rd

WEST BROMPTON

Fulham Rd

Castelnau

Fulham Palace Rd

Dawes Rd

Fulham Broadway

Fulham Rd

King's Rd

Cremorne Rd

See Hyde Park & Kensington Map (p76)

Battersea Bridge Rd

Battersea Park

Battersea Park

WALHAM GREEN

Queenstown Rd

Parsons Green

Wandsworth Bridge Rd

BATTERSEA

Latchmore Rd

Queenstown Rd

Wandsworth Rd

Mill Hill Rd

Putney Bridge

Clapham Junction

North St

RICHMOND

Upper Richmond Rd

Thames

Putney

Clapham Common

East Putney

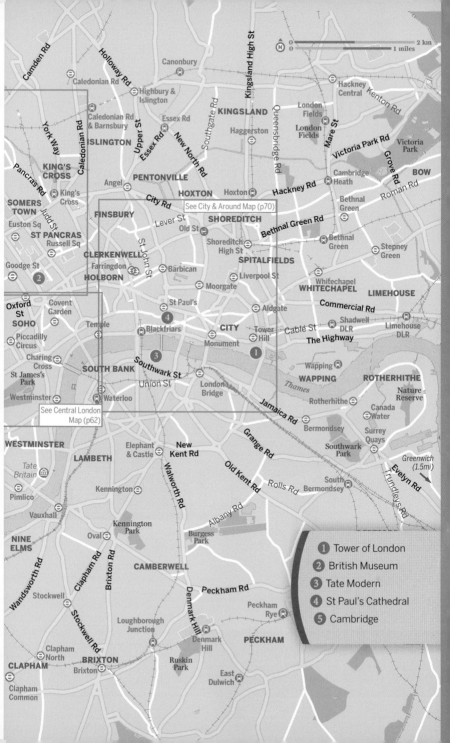

London & Around Highlights

Tower of London

London's famous Tower (p66) has variously been a castle, palace and prison over almost 1000 years of history. Equally famous are the Yeoman Warders (or 'Beefeaters') who guard the tower. To qualify, all Beefeaters must have served at least 22 years in the armed forces and earned a Good Conduct Medal.

1

2 ## Tate Modern

This abandoned power station (p71) was once an eyesore, but the inspired decision to transform it into a gallery in the late 1990s helped reinvigorate the nation's interest in modern art. Spread out over five floors, the permanent collection takes in everyone from Andy Warhol to Pablo Picasso, but it's the exhibitions in the Turbine Hall that inevitably spark the most excitement. Best of all, it's free. Tate Modern and the Millennium Bridge

British Museum

The British Museum (p78) is one of London's great wonders, with hundreds of galleries containing Egyptian, Etruscan, Greek, Roman, European and Middle Eastern artifacts. Among the must-sees are the Rosetta Stone, the controversial Parthenon Sculptures, and the Anglo-Saxon Sutton Hoo burial relics. Great Court, British Museum

St Paul's Cathedral

Towering over Ludgate Hill, in a superb position that has housed a place of worship for 1400 years, St Paul's Cathedral (p65) is one of London's most majestic structures. For Londoners, its vast dome – which still manages to dominate the skyline despite the skyscrapers crowding the Square Mile – is a symbol of resilience and pride, standing tall for more than 300 years.

Cambridge 'Backs'

The lovely university city of Cambridge is a day trip from London, and no visit is complete without taking a punt (flat-bottomed boat) along the river by the picturesque 'Backs (p120)', the green lawns that run behind the city's finest colleges. Finish your cruise with a pint in one of the city's many historic pubs. Punting on the River Cam

London's Best...

City Views

o **The Shard** Survey the scene from the capital's tallest skyscraper (p72)

o **London Eye** Ride the pods on London's giant wheel (p72)

o **Greenwich Royal Observatory** The heart of this historic maritime complex (p82)

o **Westminster Cathedral** Climb the tower for views of Old London Town (p61)

o **Tower Bridge** Get another perspective on the River Thames (p64)

Things for Free

o **British Museum** London's flagship repository (p78)

o **National Gallery** Marvel at the artistic masterpieces (p63)

o **Tate Modern** Thanks to Mr Tate, another great gallery (p71)

o **Covent Garden** The perfect spot to wander, window-shop and watch street-art performers (p63)

o **Changing of the Guard** Classic daily London event outside Buckingham Palace (p61)

Green Spaces

o **Hyde Park** London's largest green space, with paths, lawns, fountains and lakes (p76)

o **Regent's Park** Huge park, best-known as the home of London Zoo (p77)

o **Kensington Gardens** Home of Princess Diana's memorial fountain (p77)

o **Kew Gardens** Browse the rare flora of the Royal Botanical Collection (p83)

Need to Know

Traditional Pubs

○ **Princess Louise** Victorian classic, arguably London's most beautiful pub (p94)

○ **Lamb & Flag** Everyone's favourite in Covent Garden (p94)

○ **George Inn** London's last surviving galleried coaching inn (p95)

○ **Ye Olde Cheshire Cheese** An atmospheric icon of Fleet St (p94)

ADVANCE PLANNING

○ **Two months before** Reserve your hotel room and arrange theatre tickets.

○ **Two weeks before** Book a table at high-profile restaurants.

○ **One week before** Prebook online for top sights such as the London Eye, Madame Tussauds, St Paul's Cathedral and the Tower of London.

RESOURCES

○ **Visit London** (www. visitlondon.com) The official tourist website.

○ **BBC London** (www.bbc. com/london) London-centric low-down from the BBC.

○ **Evening Standard** (www. thisislondon.co.uk) Latest news from the city's daily rag.

○ **Urban Path** (www. urbanpath.com) Online guide to 'nice things' – events, restaurants, hotels, spas and shops.

GETTING AROUND

○ **Bus** Excellent network across the capital, though the famous red double-deckers are not so common these days.

○ **Underground train** London's 'tube' is the speediest way to get around town.

○ **Waterbus** Useful and scenic way to get between riverside points.

○ **Bicycle** Barclays Cycle Hire scheme allows you to hire a bike from one of 400 docking stations around London.

BE FOREWARNED

○ **Exhibitions** High-profile seasonal exhibitions at museums and galleries often charge extra and are sold out weeks ahead.

○ **Restaurants** You'll need to book for the big-name establishments.

○ **Public Transport** All-day Travelcards and Oyster cards offer the best value.

○ **Rush hour** Morning peak hour won't impact travellers much; during the evening rush, find a nice pub and wait until it's over.

Left: London Eye (p72);
Above: Covent Garden Market (p63)

London Walking Tour

This walk takes you through the West End of London, and features some of the capital's major attractions and icons.

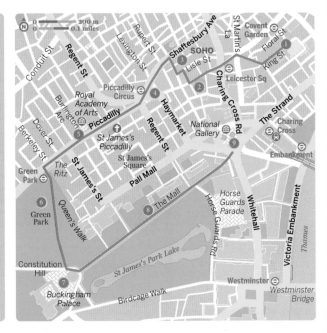

WALK FACTS
- **Start** Covent Garden
- **Finish** Trafalgar Sq
- **Distance** 2.5 miles
- **Duration** Three hours

① Covent Garden Piazza

Yes it's touristy, but this wonderful square (designed by Inigo Jones), and former market hall, is a good place to start. Grab a coffee from one of the many open-air cafes to fuel you up for the walk, and sip it while watching the never-ending stream of buskers and street performers.

② Leicester Square

A walk down King St and over Charing Cross Rd brings you to Leicester Sq. Dominated by enormous nightclubs and cinemas, this is where movies premiere and stars make handprints in the pavement. It's a London landmark, but – to be blunt – not especially scenic.

③ Chinatown & Theatreland

Head north, across Lisle St – the heart of London's Chinatown – to reach Shaftesbury Ave – the heart of London's theatreland and home to some of the West End's most prestigious theatres.

④ Piccadilly Circus

Westwards down Shaftsbury Ave brings you to Piccadilly Circus, with the famous **Eros statue** at its centre. The Circus is always hectic and traffic-choked, with the buildings cloaked in massive flashing ads, but this is an icon of London, so it's worth making the stop.

5 Piccadilly

Running west from Piccadilly Circus is the elegant street of Piccadilly. It's lined with upmarket stores, including those on highly exclusive **Burlington Arcade** (p64), thanks to the proximity of aristocratic neighbour-hoods St James's and Mayfair.

6 Green Park

Walk past the **Ritz**, one of London's fanciest hotels, and turn left into Green Park for a chance to catch your breath, or rest your legs on one of the park benches under some stunning oak trees and olde-worlde street lamps.

7 Buckingham Palace

A stroll south through Green Park leads to one of London's best-known addresses: Buckingham Palace, the Queen's residence in London. If you made an early start, you might be here for the **changing of the guard** at 11.30am.

8 The Mall

With your back to Buckingham Palace you can march down The Mall, a grand avenue alongside **St James's Park**, where royal processions often take place and the Queen's limousine or carriage is escorted by her guards.

9 Trafalgar Square

The Mall leads you under **Admiralty Arch** and pops you out at Trafalgar Sq, with its fountains and statues, dominated by **Nelson's Column**. The square is also surrounded by grand buildings, including the **National Gallery** (p63) – where a seat on the steps outside the entrance is the perfect place to end your walk.

London in...

TWO DAYS

Start with our walking tour around the **West End**. In the afternoon, tick off more icons – **Westminster Abbey** and the **Houses of Parliament**, and the instantly recognisable tower of **Big Ben**. Cross Westminster Bridge to reach the **London Eye**, then spend the late afternoon at the **British Museum**. Day two starts at **St Paul's Cathedral**, followed by crossing the Millennium Bridge to the **Tate Modern**. From here stroll along the riverside walkways to reach **Tower Bridge**, then cross to visit the **Tower of London**.

FOUR DAYS

Day three could start with a morning of browsing – in the **Tate Britain** or **National Gallery** if you're artistically inclined, or in the famous stores of **Regent Street** or **Kensington** if you're more retail minded. Then spend the afternoon enjoying the maritime splendours of **Greenwich**. Day four is for day trips: leave the capital behind for an excursion to **Hampton Court Palace**, **Windsor Castle** or **Canterbury Cathedral**.

Ritz Hotel, Park Lane

Discover London & Around

LONDON

POP 7.82 MILLION

Everyone comes to London with a preconception shaped by a multitude of books, movies, TV shows and songs. Whatever yours is, prepare to have it exploded by this endlessly fascinating, amorphous city. You could spend a lifetime exploring it and find that the slippery thing's gone and changed on you. One thing is constant: that great serpent of a river enfolding the city in its sinuous loops, linking London both to the green heart of England and the world.

⊙ Sights

The city's main geographical feature is the murky Thames, which snakes around but roughly divides the city into north and south. The old City of London (note the big 'C') is the capital's financial district, covering roughly a square mile bordered by the river and the many gates of the ancient (long-gone) city walls: Newgate, Moorgate etc. The areas to the east of the City are collectively known as the East End. The West End, on the City's other flank, is effectively the centre of London nowadays.

WESTMINSTER

Purposefully positioned outside the old City (London's fiercely independent burghers preferred to keep the monarch and parliament at arm's length), Westminster has been the centre of the nation's political power for nearly a millennium.

Westminster Abbey Church
(Map p62; ☎ 020-7222 5152; www.westminster-abbey.org; 20 Dean's Yard, SW1; adult/child £18/8, verger tours £3; ☉ 9.30am-4.30pm Mon, Tue, Thu

Westminster Abbey
DAVID TOMLINSON/GETTY IMAGES ©

& Fri, to 7pm Wed, to 2.30pm Sat; ⊖Westminster) Westminster Abbey is a mixture of architectural styles, but considered the finest example of Early English Gothic (1190–1300). It's not merely a beautiful place of worship, though. The Abbey serves up the country's history cold on slabs of stone. For centuries England's greatest have been interred here, including 17 monarchs, from Henry III (died 1272) to George II (1760).

Houses of Parliament
Historic Building

(Map p62; www.parliament.uk; Parliament Sq, SW1; ⊖Westminster) **FREE** Officially called the Palace of Westminster, the Houses of Parliament's oldest part is 11th-century Westminster Hall, which is one of only a few sections that survived a catastrophic fire in 1834. Its roof, added between 1394 and 1401, is the earliest known example of a hammerbeam roof. Most of the rest of the building is a neo-Gothic confection built by Charles Barry and Augustus Pugins (1840–1858).

Buckingham Palace
Palace

(Map p62; ☏020-7766 7300; www.royal collection.org.uk; Buckingham Palace Rd, SW1; adult/child £19.75/11.25; ⏰9.30am-7.30pm late Jul-Aug, to 6.30pm Sep; ⊖St James's Park, Victoria, Green Park) Built in 1703 for the Duke of Buckingham, Buckingham Palace replaced St James's Palace as the monarch's official London residence in 1837. When she's not giving her famous wave to far-flung parts of the Commonwealth, Queen Elizabeth II divides her time between here, Windsor and, in summer, Balmoral. To know if she's at home, check whether the yellow, red and blue standard is flying.

Westminster Cathedral
Church

(www.westminstercathedral.org.uk; Victoria St, SW1; tower adult/child £5/2.50; ⏰9.30am-5pm Mon-Fri, to 6pm Sat & Sun; ⊖Victoria) With its distinctive candy-striped red-brick and white-stone tower features, John Francis Bentley's 19th-century cathedral, the mother church of Roman Catholicism in England and Wales, is a splendid example of neo-Byzantine architecture. Although construction started here in 1896 and worshippers began attending services seven years later, the church ran out of money and the gaunt interior remains largely unfinished.

No. 10 Downing Street
Historic Building

(Map p62; www.number10.gov.uk; 10 Downing St, SW1; ⊖Westminster) The official office of British leaders since 1732, when George II presented No. 10 to Robert Walpole, this has also been the Prime Minister's London residence since refurbishment in 1902. For such a famous address, No. 10 is a small-looking building on a plain-looking street, hardly warranting comparison with the White House, for example.

Churchill War Rooms
Museum

(Map p62; www.iwm.org.uk; Clive Steps, King Charles St, SW1; adult/child £17.50/free; ⏰9.30am-6pm, last entry 5pm; ⊖Westminster) Winston Churchill coordinated the Allied resistance against Nazi Germany on a Bakelite telephone from this underground military HQ during WWII. The Cabinet War Rooms remain much as they were when the lights were flicked off in 1945, capturing the drama and dogged spirit of the time, while the multimedia Churchill Museum affords intriguing insights into the resolute, cigar-smoking wartime leader.

WEST END

A strident mix of culture and consumerism but more a concept than a fixed geographical area, the West End is synonymous with roof-raising musicals, bright lights, outstanding restaurants and indefatigable bag-laden shoppers. It casts its net around Piccadilly Circus and Trafalgar Sq to the south, Regent St to the west, Oxford St to the north, Covent Garden to the east and the Strand to the southeast.

Mayfair, west of Piccadilly Circus, hogs all of the most expensive streets from the Monopoly board. The elegant bow of **Regent Street** and frantic **Oxford Street** are the city's main shopping strips. At the heart of the West End lies **Soho**, a

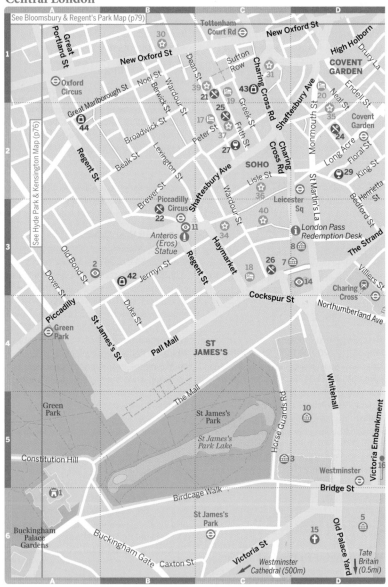

boho grid of narrow streets and squares hiding gay bars, strip clubs, cafes and advertising agencies.

Piccadilly Circus   Square

(Map p62; ⊖ Piccadilly Circus) John Nash had originally designed Regent St and Piccadilly in the 1820s to be the two most elegant streets in town but, curbed by city planners, couldn't realise his dream to the

Trafalgar Square   Square

(Map p62; ⊖Charing Cross) In many ways Trafalgar Sq is the centre of London, where rallies and marches take place, tens of thousands of revellers usher in the New Year and locals congregate for anything from communal open-air cinema and Christmas celebrations to various political protests. It is dominated by the 52m-high Nelson's Column and ringed by many splendid buildings, including the National Gallery and St Martin-in-the-Fields.

National Gallery   Gallery

(Map p62; www.nationalgallery.org.uk; Trafalgar Sq, WC2; ⊙10am-6pm Sat-Thu, to 9pm Fri; ⊖Charing Cross) FREE With some 2300 European paintings on display, this is one of the richest art galleries in the world. There are seminal paintings from every important epoch in the history of art from the mid-13th to the early 20th century, including works by Leonardo da Vinci, Michelangelo, Titian, Van Gogh and Renoir.

National Portrait Gallery   Gallery

(Map p62; www.npg.org.uk; St Martin's Pl, WC2; ⊙10am-6pm Sat-Wed, to 9pm Thu & Fri; ⊖Charing Cross, Leicester Sq) FREE The only such museum in Europe, what makes the National Portrait Gallery so compelling is its familiarity; in many cases you'll have heard of the subject (royals, scientists, politicians, celebrities) or the artist (Andy Warhol, Annie Leibovitz, Sam Taylor-Wood). Highlights include the famous 'Chandos portrait' of William Shakespeare, the first artwork the gallery acquired (in 1856) and believed to be the only likeness made during the playwright's lifetime, and a touching sketch of novelist Jane Austen by her sister.

Covent Garden Piazza   Square

(Map p62; ⊖Covent Garden) London's first planned square is now the exclusive preserve of tourists who flock here to shop in the quaint old arcades, pay through the nose for refreshments at outdoor cafes and bars and watch street performers pretend to be statues.

full. He would certainly be disappointed with what Piccadilly Circus has become: swamped with visitors, flanked by flashing advertisement panels and surrounded by shops flogging tourist tat.

Central London

Sir John Soane's Museum Museum
(Map p62; www.soane.org; 13 Lincoln's Inn Fields,
WC2; ◎10am-5pm Tue-Sat & 6-9pm 1st Tue of
month; ◉Holborn) FREE This little museum
is one of the most atmospheric and fascinating in London. The building was the
beautiful, bewitching home of architect
Sir John Soane (1753–1837), which he left
brimming with surprising personal effects
and curiosities, and the museum represents his exquisite and eccentric taste.

Burlington Arcade Shopping Arcade
(Map p62; www.burlington-arcade.co.uk; 51 Piccadilly, W1; ◎10am-9pm Mon-Fri, 9am-6.30pm Sat,
11am-5pm Sun; ◉Green Park) Flanking Burlington House, home to the Royal Academy of Arts, is this delightful arcade, built
in 1819. Today it is a shopping precinct
for the wealthy, and is most famous for
the Burlington Berties, uniformed guards
who patrol the area keeping an eye out for

such offences as running, chewing gum
or whatever else might lower the tone.

THE CITY

It's only in the last 250 years that the City
has gone from being the very essence of
London and its main population centre to
just its central business district.

Tower Bridge Bridge
(Map p70; ◉Tower Hill) London was a
thriving port in 1894 when elegant Tower
Bridge was built. Designed to be raised
to allow ships to pass, electricity has now
taken over from the original steam and
hydraulic engines. A lift leads up from
the northern tower to the **Tower Bridge
Exhibition** (Map p70; www.towerbridge.org.
uk; adult/child £8/3.40; ◎10am-6pm Apr-Sep,
9.30am-5.30pm Oct-Mar; ◉Tower Hill), where
the story of its building is recounted
within the upper walkway.

STUART BLACK/GETTY IMAGES ©

 **Don't Miss**
St Paul's Cathedral

Dominating the City of London with the world's second-largest church domes (and weighing in at around 65,000 tons), St Paul's Cathedral was designed by Christopher Wren after the Great Fire and built between 1675 and 1710. The site is ancient hallowed ground with four other cathedrals preceding Wren's English Baroque masterpiece here, the first dating from 604.

Inside, some 30m above the main paved area, is the first of three domes (actually a dome inside a cone inside a dome) supported by eight huge columns. The walkway around its base, 257 steps up a staircase on the western side of the southern transept, is called the Whispering Gallery, because if you talk close to the wall your words will carry to the opposite side 32m away. A further 119 steps brings you to the Stone Gallery, 152 iron steps above which is the Golden Gallery at the very top, with unforgettable views of London.

The Crypt has memorials to up to 300 heroes and military demigods, including Wellington, Kitchener and Nelson, whose body lies below the dome. But the most poignant memorial is to Wren himself. On a simple slab bearing his name, part of a Latin inscription translates as: 'If you seek his memorial, look about you'.

Free 1½-hour guided tours leave the tour desk six times a day (10.30am, 10.45am, 11.15am, 1pm, 1.30pm and 2pm).

NEED TO KNOW

Map p70; www.stpauls.co.uk; St Paul's Churchyard, EC4; adult/child £16.50/7.50; ⊙8.30am-4.30pm Mon-Sat; ⊖St Paul's

Don't Miss
Tower of London

The unmissable Tower of London (actually a castle of 20-odd towers) offers a window on to a gruesome and quite compelling history. This was where two kings and three queens met their death and countless others were imprisoned. Come here to see the colourful Yeoman Warders (or Beefeaters), the spectacular Crown Jewels, the soothsaying ravens and armour fit for a king.

Map p70

📞 0844 482 7777

www.hrp.org.uk/toweroflondon

Tower Hill, EC3

adult/child £22/11, audioguide £4/3

🕙 9am-5.30pm Tue-Sat, 10am-5.30pm Sun & Mon, to 4.30pm Nov-Feb

🚇 Tower Hill

Crown Jewels

To the east of the Chapel Royal and north of the White Tower is Waterloo Barracks, the home of the Crown Jewels, said to be worth up to £20 billion but, in a very real sense, priceless. Here, you file past film clips of the jewels and their role throughout history, and of Queen Elizabeth II's coronation in 1953, before you reach the vault itself. Once inside you'll be greeted by lavishly bejewelled sceptres, plates, orbs and, naturally, crowns. A travelator carries you past the dozen or so crowns and other coronation regalia.

Tower Green

On the small green in front of the Chapel Royal stood Henry VIII's scaffold, where unlucky nobles were once beheaded. Victims included Anne Boleyn and her cousin Catherine Howard (Henry's second and fifth wives), 16-year-old Lady Jane Grey (who fell foul of Henry's daughter Mary I by attempting to have herself crowned queen), and Robert Devereux, Earl of Essex, once a favourite of Elizabeth I.

Bloody Tower

Opposite Traitors' Gate (the gateway through which prisoners being brought by river entered the tower) is the huge portcullis of the Bloody Tower, taking its nickname from the 'princes in the tower' – Edward V and his younger brother, Richard – who were held here 'for their own safety' and later murdered to annul their claims to the throne. The blame is usually laid (and substantiated by Shakespeare) at the door of their uncle, Richard III, whose remains were unearthed beneath a car park in Leicester in late 2012. An exhibition inside looks at the life and times of Elizabethan adventurer Sir Walter Raleigh, who was imprisoned here three times by the capricious Elizabeth I and her successor James I.

> **Local Knowledge**

Tower of London

BY ALAN KINGSHOTT, CHIEF YEOMAN WARDER AT THE TOWER OF LONDON

1 A TOWER TOUR

To understand the Tower and its history, a guided tour with one of the Yeoman Warders is essential. Very few people appreciate that the Tower is actually our home as well; all the Warders live inside the outer walls. The Tower is rather like a miniature village – visitors are often rather surprised to see our washing hanging out beside the castle walls!

2 CROWN JEWELS

Visitors often think the Crown Jewels are the Queen's personal jewellery collection. They're not, of course; the Crown Jewels are actually the ceremonial regalia used during the Coronation. The highlights are the Sceptre and the Imperial State Crown, which contains the celebrated diamond known as the Star of Africa. People are surprised to hear that the Crown Jewels aren't insured (as they could never be replaced).

3 WHITE TOWER

The White Tower is the original royal palace of the Tower of London, but it hasn't been used as a royal residence since 1603. It's the most iconic building here. Inside you can see exhibits from the Royal Armouries, including a suit of armour belonging to Henry VIII.

4 RAVENS

A Tower legend states that if its resident ravens ever left, the monarchy would topple – a royal decree states that we must keep a minimum of six ravens at any time. We currently have nine ravens, looked after by the Ravenmaster and his two assistants.

5 CEREMONY OF THE KEYS

We hold three daily ceremonies: the 9am Official Opening, the Ceremony of the Word (when the day's password is issued), and the 10pm Ceremony of the Keys, when the gates are locked after the castle has closed. Visitors are welcome to attend the last, but must apply directly to the Tower in writing.

Tower of London

TACKLING THE TOWER

Although it's usually less busy in the late afternoon, don't leave your assault on the Tower until too late in the day. You could easily spend hours here and not see it all. Start by getting your bearings on one of the Yeoman Warder (Beefeater) tours; they are included in the cost of admission, entertaining and the easiest way to access the **Chapel Royal of St Peter ad Vincula** ❶, which is where they finish up.

When you leave the chapel, the **Tower Green Scaffold Site** ❷ is directly in front. The building immediately to your left is Waterloo Barracks, where the **Crown Jewels** ❸ are housed. These are the absolute highlight of a Tower visit, so keep an eye on the entrance and pick a time to visit when it looks relatively quiet. Once inside, take things at your own pace. Slow-moving travelators shunt you past the dozen or so crowns that are the treasury's centrepiece, but feel free to double-back for a second or even third pass – particularly if you ended up on the rear travelator the first time around. Allow plenty of time for the **White Tower** ❹, the core of the whole complex, starting with the exhibition of royal armour. As you continue onto the 1st floor, keep an eye out for **St John's Chapel** ❺. The famous **ravens** ❻ can be seen in the courtyard south of the White Tower. Head next through the towers that formed the **Medieval Palace** ❼, then take the **East Wall Walk** ❽ to get a feel for the castle's mighty battlements. Spend the rest of your time poking around the many other fascinating nooks and crannies of the Tower complex.

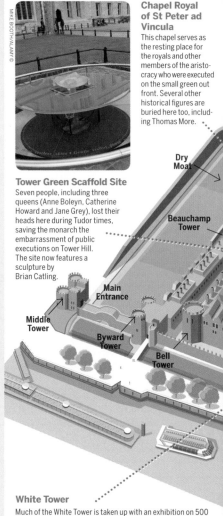

Chapel Royal of St Peter ad Vincula
This chapel serves as the resting place for the royals and other members of the aristocracy who were executed on the small green out front. Several other historical figures are buried here too, including Thomas More.

Dry Moat

Tower Green Scaffold Site
Seven people, including three queens (Anne Boleyn, Catherine Howard and Jane Grey), lost their heads here during Tudor times, saving the monarch the embarrassment of public executions on Tower Hill. The site now features a sculpture by Brian Catling.

Beauchamp Tower

Main Entrance

Middle Tower

Byward Tower

Bell Tower

White Tower
Much of the White Tower is taken up with an exhibition on 500 years of royal armour. Look for the virtually cuboid suit made to match Henry VIII's bloated body, complete with an oversized armoured codpiece to protect, ahem, the crown jewels.

St John's Chapel

Kept as plain and unadorned as it would have been in Norman times, the White Tower's 1st-floor chapel is the oldest surviving church in London, dating from 1080.

Crown Jewels

When they're not being worn for ceremonies of state, Her Majesty's bling is kept here. Among the 23,578 gems, look out for the 530-carat Cullinan I diamond at the top of the Sovereign's Sceptre with cross, the largest part of what was then the largest diamond ever found.

TOM HANLEY/ALAMY ©

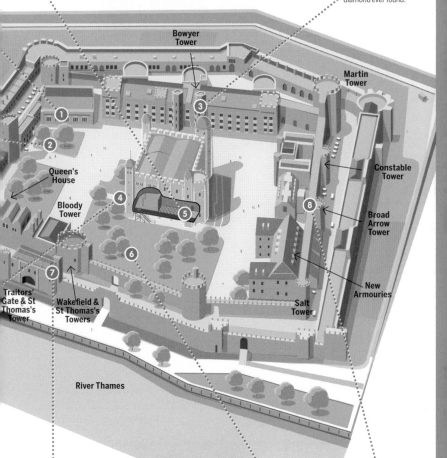

Bowyer Tower

Martin Tower

Constable Tower

Queen's House

Broad Arrow Tower

Bloody Tower

New Armouries

Traitors' Gate & St Thomas's Tower

Wakefield & St Thomas's Towers

Salt Tower

River Thames

Medieval Palace

This part of the Tower complex was begun around 1220 and was home to England's medieval monarchs. Look for the recreations of the bedchamber of Edward I (1272–1307) in St Thomas's Tower and the throne room of his father, Henry III (1216–72) in the Wakefield Tower.

DAVID GARRY/GETTY IMAGES ©

Ravens

This stretch of green is where the Tower's half-dozen ravens are kept, fed on raw meat and blood-soaked bird biscuits. According to legend, if the birds were to leave the Tower, the kingdom would fall.

East Wall Walk

Follow the inner ramparts, starting from the 13th-century Salt Tower, passing through the Broad Arrow and Constable Towers, and ending at the Martin Tower, where the Crown Jewels were stored till the mid-19th century.

LONDON & AROUND SIGHTS

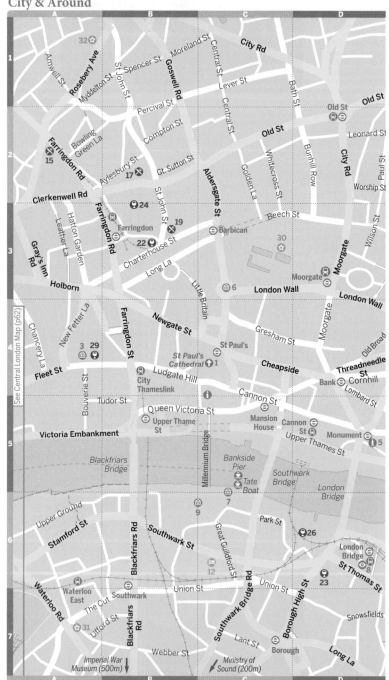

See Central London Map (p62)

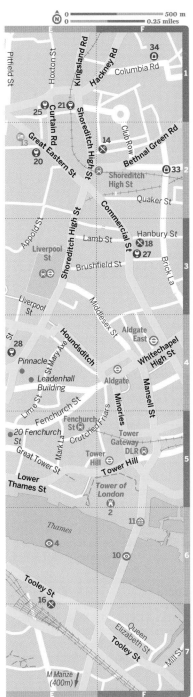

Museum of London   Museum

(Map p70; www.museumoflondon.org.uk; 150 London Wall, EC2; ⊙10am-6pm; ⊖Barbican) **FREE**
One of the capital's best museums, this is a fascinating walk through the various incarnations of the city from Anglo-Saxon village to 21st-century metropolis contained in two-dozen galleries. There are a lot of interactive displays with an emphasis on experience rather than learning.

Monument   Tower

(Map p70; www.themonument.info; Fish Street Hill, EC3; adult/child £4/2, incl Tower Bridge Exhibition £10.50/4.70; ⊙9.30am-6pm Apr-Sep, to 5.30pm Oct-Mar; ⊖Monument) Sir Christopher Wren's 1677 column, known simply as the Monument, is a memorial to the Great Fire of London of 1666, whose impact on London's history cannot be overstated. An immense Doric column made of Portland stone, the Monument is 4.5m wide and 60.6m tall – the exact distance it stands from the bakery in Pudding Lane where the fire started.

Dr Johnson's House   Museum

(Map p70; www.drjohnsonshouse.org; 17 Gough Sq, EC4; adult/child £4.50/1.50, audioguide £2; ⊙11am-5.30pm Mon-Sat May-Sep, to 5pm Oct-Apr; ⊖Chancery Lane) This wonderful house, built in 1700, is a rare surviving example of a Georgian city mansion. It has been preserved, as it was the home of the great Georgian wit Samuel Johnson, the author of the first serious dictionary of the English language and the man who proclaimed 'When a man is tired of London, he is tired of life'.

SOUTH BANK

Londoners once crossed the river to the area controlled by the licentious Bishops of Southwark for all manner of bawdy frolicking frowned upon in the City. It's a much more seemly area now, but the frisson of theatre and entertainment remains.

Tate Modern   Museum

(Map p70; www.tate.org.uk; Queen's Walk, SE1; ⊙10am-6pm Sun-Thu, to 10pm Fri & Sat; ⊖Southwark, St Paul's) **FREE** One of

City & Around

London's most popular attractions, this outstanding modern and contemporary art gallery is housed in the creatively re-vamped **Bankside Power Station** south of the Millennium Bridge. A spellbinding synthesis of funky modern art and capacious industrial brick design, Tate Modern has been extraordinarily successful in bringing challenging work to the masses. A stunning extension is aiming for a 2016 completion date. Free guided highlights tours depart at 11am, noon, 2pm and 3pm daily.

Shakespeare's Globe
Historic Building

(Map p70; www.shakespearesglobe.com; 21 New Globe Walk, SE1; adult/child £13.50/8; ☺9am-5.30pm; ⊖London Bridge) Today's London-ers may flock to Amsterdam to mis-behave but back in the bard's day they'd cross London Bridge to Southwark. Free from the city's constraints, they could settle down to a diet of whoring, bear-baiting and heckling of actors. The most famous theatre was the Globe, where a genius playwright was penning box-office hits such as *Macbeth* and *Hamlet*.

Today, admission includes the exhibition hall and a guided tour of the theatre (departing every 15 to 30 minutes). Tours shift to the nearby Rose Theatre instead when matinees are being staged.

London Eye
Viewpoint

(Map p62; ☎0871 781 3000; www.londoneye. com; adult/child £21/15; ☺10am-8pm; ⊖Wa-terloo) A ride on the London Eye, which stands at 135m in a fairly flat city, affords views 25 miles in every direction, weather permitting, and takes a gracefully slow 30 minutes. The Eye draws 3.5 million visi-tors annually; at peak times (July, August and school holidays) it may seem like they are all in the queue with you. Save money and shorten queues by buying tickets online, or cough up an extra £10 to showcase your fast-track swagger. Alter-natively, visit before 11am or after 3pm to avoid peak density.

Shard
Notable Building

(Map p70; www.the-shard.com; 32 London Bridge St, SE1; adult/child £29.95/23.95; ☺9am-10pm; ⊖London Bridge) Puncturing the skies above London, the dramatic splinter-like form of the Shard has rapidly become an icon of the city. The viewing platforms on floors 68, 69 and 72 are open to the public and the views are, as you'd expect from a 244m vantage point, sweeping, but they come at a hefty price – book online to save £5.

Imperial War Museum Museum
(www.iwm.org.uk; Lambeth Rd, SE1; ⊙10am-6pm; ⊖Lambeth North) **FREE** Fronted by a pair of intimidating 15in naval guns, this riveting museum is housed in what was once Bethlehem Royal Hospital, also known as Bedlam. Although the museum's focus is on military action involving British or Commonwealth troops during the 20th century, it also explores war in the wider sense. After extensive refurbishment, the museum reopened in summer 2014, with new state-of-the-art First World War Galleries to mark the 100th anniversary of the start of WWI.

HMS Belfast Ship
(Map p70; www.iwm.org.uk/visits/hms-belfast; Queen's Walk, SE1; adult/child £15.50/free; ⊙10am-5pm; ⊙; ⊖London Bridge) White ensign flapping on the Thames breeze, HMS *Belfast* is a magnet for naval-gazing kids of all ages. This large, light cruiser – launched in 1938 – served in WWII, helping to sink the German battleship *Scharnhorst,* shelling the Normandy coast on D Day and later participating in the Korean War. Her 6in guns could bombard a target 14 land miles distant.

PIMLICO

The origins of its name highly obscure, Pimlico is a grand part of London, bordered by the Thames but lacking a strong sense of neighbourhood. It becomes prettier the further you stray from Victoria station.

Tate Britain Gallery
(www.tate.org.uk; Millbank, SW1; ⊙10am-6pm, to 10pm 1st Fri of month; ⊖Pimlico) **FREE** You'd think that Tate Britain might have suffered since its sexy sibling, Tate Modern, took half its collection and all of the limelight across the river. On the contrary, the venerable Tate Britain, built in 1897 by Henry Tate, splendidly stretched out its definitive collection of British art from the 16th to the late 20th centuries. Join

Tate-a-Tate

Whisking art lovers between London's Tate galleries, the colourful **Tate Boat** (Map p70; www.tate.org.uk/visit/tate-boat; one-way adult/child £6.50/3.25) stops en route at the London Eye. Services from Bankside Pier run from 9.57am to 4.44pm daily at 40-minute intervals (10.20am to 4.27pm from Millbank Pier). One way tickets are £6.50 (children £3.25), with discounts available for Travelcard holders.

the free 45-minute **thematic tours** (11am, noon, 2pm & 3pm) and 15-minute **Art in Focus talks** (1.15pm Tue, Thu & Sat). Audioguides (£3.50) are also available.

CHELSEA & KENSINGTON

Known as the royal borough, Chelsea and Kensington lays claim to the highest income earners in the UK (shops and restaurants will presume you are among them).

Victoria & Albert Museum Museum
(V&A; Map p76; www.vam.ac.uk; Cromwell Rd, SW7; ⊙10am-5.45pm Sat-Thu, to 10pm Fri; ⊖South Kensington) **FREE** The Museum of Manufactures, as the V&A was known when it opened in 1852, was part of Prince Albert's legacy to the nation in the aftermath of the successful Great Exhibition of 1851, and its original aims – which still hold today – were the 'improvement of public taste in design' and 'applications of fine art to objects of utility'. It's done a fine job so far.

Natural History Museum Museum
(Map p76; www.nhm.ac.uk; Cromwell Rd, SW7; ⊙10am-5.50pm; ⊖South Kensington) **FREE** This colossal building is infused with the irrepressible Victorian spirit of collecting, cataloguing and interpreting the natural world. The main museum building is

continued on page 76

73

The River Thames

A FLOATING TOUR

London's history has always been determined by the Thames. The city was founded as a Roman port nearly 2000 years ago and over the centuries since then many of the capital's landmarks have lined the river's banks. A boat trip is a great way to experience the attractions.

There are piers dotted along both banks at regular intervals where you can hop on and hop off the regular services to visit places of interest. The best place to board is Westminster Pier, from where boats head downstream, taking you from the City of Westminster, the seat of government, to the original City of London, now the financial district and dominated by a growing band of skyscrapers. Across the river, the once shabby and neglected South Bank now bristles with as many top attractions as its northern counterpart, including the slender Shard.

In our illustration we've concentrated on the top highlights you'll enjoy from a waterborne vessel.

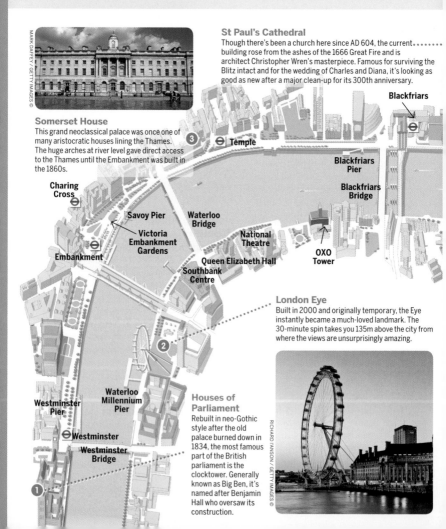

MARK DAFFEY / GETTY IMAGES ©

St Paul's Cathedral
Though there's been a church here since AD 604, the current building rose from the ashes of the 1666 Great Fire and is architect Christopher Wren's masterpiece. Famous for surviving the Blitz intact and for the wedding of Charles and Diana, it's looking as good as new after a major clean-up for its 300th anniversary.

Blackfriars

Somerset House
This grand neoclassical palace was once one of many aristocratic houses lining the Thames. The huge arches at river level gave direct access to the Thames until the Embankment was built in the 1860s.

Temple

Charing Cross

Blackfriars Pier

Blackfriars Bridge

Savoy Pier

Waterloo Bridge

Victoria Embankment Gardens

National Theatre

OXO Tower

Embankment

Queen Elizabeth Hall

Southbank Centre

London Eye
Built in 2000 and originally temporary, the Eye instantly became a much-loved landmark. The 30-minute spin takes you 135m above the city from where the views are unsurprisingly amazing.

Westminster Pier

Waterloo Millennium Pier

Westminster

Westminster Bridge

Houses of Parliament
Rebuilt in neo-Gothic style after the old palace burned down in 1834, the most famous part of the British parliament is the clocktower. Generally known as Big Ben, it's named after Benjamin Hall who oversaw its construction.

RICHARD I'ANSON / GETTY IMAGES ©

These are, from west to east, the **Houses of Parliament** ❶, the **London Eye** ❷, **Somerset House** ❸, **St Paul's Cathedral** ❹, **Tate Modern** ❺, **Shakespeare's Globe** ❻, the **Tower of London** ❼ and **Tower Bridge** ❽.

Apart from covering this central section of the river, boats can also be taken upstream as far as Kew Gardens and Hampton Court Palace, and downstream to Greenwich and the Thames Barrier.

BOAT HOPPING

Thames Clippers hop-on/hop-off services are aimed at commuters but are equally useful for visitors, operating every 15 minutes on a loop from piers at Embankment, Waterloo, Blackfriars, Bankside, London Bridge and the Tower. Other services also go from Westminster. Oyster cardholders get a discount off the boat ticket price.

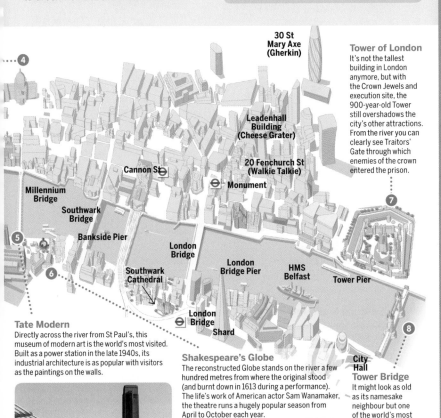

30 St Mary Axe (Gherkin)

Leadenhall Building (Cheese Grater)

Cannon St

20 Fenchurch St (Walkie Talkie)

Monument

Millennium Bridge

Southwark Bridge

Bankside Pier

London Bridge

London Bridge Pier

HMS Belfast

Tower Pier

Southwark Cathedral

London Bridge

Shard

City Hall

Tower of London
It's not the tallest building in London anymore, but with the Crown Jewels and execution site, the 900-year-old Tower still overshadows the city's other attractions. From the river you can clearly see Traitors' Gate through which enemies of the crown entered the prison.

Tate Modern
Directly across the river from St Paul's, this museum of modern art is the world's most visited. Built as a power station in the late 1940s, its industrial architecture is as popular with visitors as the paintings on the walls.

Shakespeare's Globe
The reconstructed Globe stands on the river a few hundred metres from where the original stood (and burnt down in 1613 during a performance). The life's work of American actor Sam Wanamaker, the theatre runs a hugely popular season from April to October each year.

Tower Bridge
It might look as old as its namesake neighbour but one of the world's most iconic bridges was only completed in 1894. Not to be confused with London Bridge upstream, this one's famous raising bascules allowed tall ships to dock at the old wharves to the west and are still lifted up to 1000 times a year.

DOUG MCKINLAY / GETTY IMAGES ©

DOUG MCKINLAY / GETTY IMAGES ©

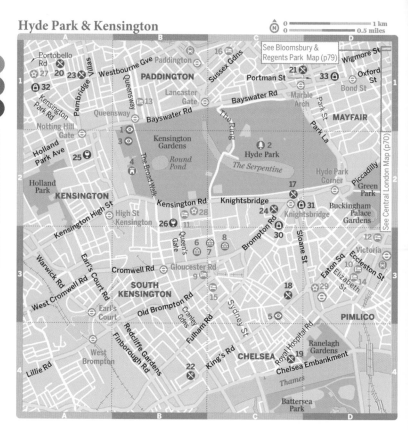

continued from page 73

as much a reason to visit as the world-famous collection within.

Science Museum
Museum

(Map p76; www.sciencemuseum.org.uk; Exhibition Rd, SW7; ☉10am-6pm; ⊖South Kensington) **FREE** With seven floors of interactive and educational exhibits, this scientifically spellbinding museum mesmerises adults and children alike. It covers everything from early technology to space travel.

Hyde Park
Park

(Map p76; ☉5.30am-midnight; ⊖Marble Arch, Hyde Park Corner, Queensway) At 145 hectares, Hyde Park is central London's largest open space. Henry VIII expropriated it from the Church in 1536, when it became a hunting ground and later a venue for duels, executions and horse racing. The 1851 Great Exhibition was held here, and during WWII the park became an enormous potato field. These days, it's an occasional concert venue (Bruce Springsteen, the Rolling Stones, Madonna) and a full-time green space for fun and frolics, including boating on the **Serpentine**.

Kensington Palace
Palace

(Map p76; www.hrp.org.uk/kensingtonpalace; Kensington Gardens, W8; adult/child £16.50/free; ☉10am-6pm Mar-Oct, to 5pm Nov-Feb; ⊖High St Kensington) Kensington Palace (1605) became the favourite royal residence under the joint reign of William and Mary and remained so until George III became king and moved across the park to Buckingham Palace. It still has private apartments where various members of

Hyde Park & Kensington

⊙ Sights
1 Diana, Princess of
   Wales Memorial
   Playground B1
   Elfin Oak .... (see 1)
2 Hyde Park C2
3 Kensington Gardens............................B2
4 Kensington Palace...............................B2
5 King's Road...C3
6 Natural History
   Museum B3
7 Science Museum C3
8 Victoria & Albert
   Museum C3

🛏 Sleeping
9 Ampersand Hotel..................................B3
10 B+B Belgravia......................................D3
11 Gore..B2
12 Goring...D3
13 La Suite West B1
14 Lime Tree Hotel D3
15 Number Sixteen...................................C3
16 Tune Hotel C1

✖ Eating
17 Dinner by Heston
   Blumenthal..C2
18 Five Fields..C3
19 Gordon Ramsay....................................C4
20 Ledbury...A1
21 Locanda Locatelli C1
22 Medlar...B4
23 Taquería..A1
24 Zuma...C2

⊙ Drinking & Nightlife
25 Churchill Arms......................................A2
26 Queen's Arms B2

⊙ Entertainment
27 Electric Cinema A1
28 Royal Albert Hall..................................B2
29 Royal Court Theatre.............................D3

⊙ Shopping
30 Harrods...C2
31 Harvey Nichols......................................C2
32 Portobello Road Market A1
33 Selfridges D1

the royal extended family live. In popular imagination it's most associated with three intriguing princesses: Victoria (who was born here in 1819 and lived here with her domineering mother until her accession to the throne), Margaret (sister of the current queen, who lived here until her 2002 death) and, of course, Diana. More than a million bouquets were left outside the gates following her death in 1997.

Kensington Gardens   Gardens
(Map p76; ⊙dawn-dusk; ⊖High St Kensington) Immediately west of Hyde Park and across the Serpentine lake, these picturesque 275-acre gardens are technically part of Kensington Palace. The Diana, Princess of Wales Memorial Playground, in the northwest corner of the gardens, has some pretty ambitious attractions for children. Next to the playground stands the delightful **Elfin Oak** (Map p76), a 900-year-old tree stump carved with elves, gnomes, witches and small creatures.

King's Road   Street
(Map p76; ⊖Sloane Sq) At the counter-cultural forefront of London fashion

during the technicolour '60s and anarchic '70s, the King's Road today is more a stamping ground for the leisure-class shopping set. The last green-haired Mohawk punks – once tourist sights in themselves – shuffled off sometime in the 1990s. Today it's all Bang & Olufsen, Kurt Geiger and a sprinkling of specialist shops; even pet canines are slim and snappily dressed.

MARYLEBONE

Not as exclusive as its southern neighbour Mayfair, hip Marylebone has one of London's most pleasant high streets and the famous, if rather disappointing, Baker St, strongly associated with Victorian-era sleuth Sherlock Holmes (there's a museum and gift shop at his fictional address, 221B).

Regent's Park   Park
(Map p79; www.royalparks.org.uk; ⊙5am-dusk; ⊖Regent's Park, Baker St) The most elaborate and ordered of London's many parks, this one was created around 1820 by John Nash, who planned to use it as an estate to build palaces for the aristocracy. Although the plan never quite came off,

Pound Savers

The **London Pass** (www.londonpass.com; 1/2/3/6 days £49/68/81/108) is a smart card that gains you fast-track entry to 55 different attractions, including pricier ones such as the Tower of London and St Paul's Cathedral. Passes can be booked online and collected from the **London Pass Redemption Desk** (Map p62; 11a Charing Cross Rd, WC2; ⏱10am-4.30pm; ⊖Leicester Square) (check online for opening hours) opposite the Garrick Theatre.

If you're a royalty buff, taking out an annual membership to the **Historic Royal Palaces** (www.hrp.org.uk; individual/joint membership £43/65) allows you to jump the queues and visit the Tower of London, Kensington Palace, Banqueting House, Kew Palace and Hampton Court Palace as often as you like.

you can get some idea of what Nash might have achieved from the buildings along the Outer Circle.

ZSL London Zoo
Zoo

(Map p79; www.londonzoo.co.uk; Outer Circle, Regent's Park, NW1; adult/child £26/18.50; ⏱10am-5.30pm Mar-Oct, to 4pm Nov-Feb; ⊖Camden Town) These famous zoological gardens have come a long way since being established in 1828, with massive investment making conservation, education and breeding the name of the game. Highlights include **Penguin Beach**, **Gorilla Kingdom**, **Animal Adventure** (the new childrens' zoo) and **Butterfly Paradise**. Feeding sessions or talks take place during the day. Arachnophobes can ask about the zoo's Friendly Spider Programme, designed to cure fears of all things eight-legged and hairy.

Madame Tussauds
Museum

(Map p79; ☎0870 400 3000; www.madame-tussauds.com/london; Marylebone Rd, NW1; adult/child £30/26; ⏱9.30am-5.30pm; ⊖Baker St) Madame Tussauds offers photo ops for days with your dream celebrity at the A-List Party (Daniel Craig, Lady Gaga, George Clooney, David and Victoria Beckham), the Bollywood gathering (Hrithik Roshan, Salman Khan) and the Royal Appointment (the Queen, Harry, William and Kate). If you're into politics, get up close and personal with Barack Obama or even London Mayor Boris Johnson.

BLOOMSBURY & ST PANCRAS

With the University of London and British Museum within its genteel environs, it's little wonder that Bloomsbury has attracted a lot of very clever, bookish people over the years.

The conversion of spectacular St Pancras station into the Eurostar terminal and a ritzy apartment complex is reviving the area's fortunes.

British Museum
Museum

(Map p79; ☎020-7323 8000; www.britishmuseum.org; Great Russell St, WC1; ⏱10am-5.30pm Sat-Thu, to 8.30pm Fri; ⊖Russell Sq, Tottenham Court Rd) **FREE** The country's largest museum and one of the oldest and finest in the world, this famous museum boasts vast Egyptian, Etruscan, Greek, Roman, European and Middle Eastern galleries, among many others. It is once again London's most visited attraction, drawing an average of five and a half million punters each year.

British Library
Library

(Map p79; www.bl.uk; 96 Euston Rd, NW1; Ritblat Gallery free, special exhibition cost varies; ⏱9.30am-6pm Mon & Wed-Fri, to 8pm Tue, to 5pm Sat, 11am-5pm Sun; ⊖King's Cross St Pancras) For visitors, the real highlight is a visit to the **Sir John Ritblat Gallery** where the most precious manuscripts, spanning almost three millennia, are held. Here you'll find the *Codex Sinaiticus* (the first complete text of the New Testament), a Gutenberg Bible (1455), the stunningly illustrated Jain sacred texts, Leonardo da Vinci's notebooks, a copy of the *Magna Carta* (1215), explorer Captain Scott's final diary, Shakespeare's First Folio (1623)

Bloomsbury & Regent's Park

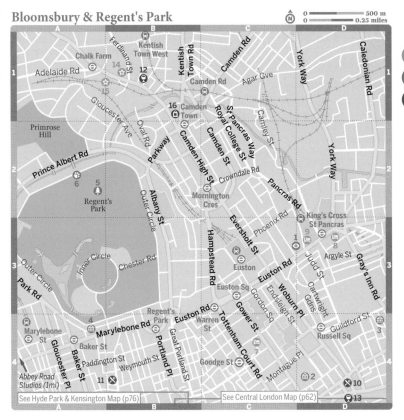

See Hyde Park & Kensington Map (p76)

See Central London Map (p62)

Bloomsbury & Regent's Park

◎ Sights
1 British Library	C3
2 British Museum	D4
3 Charles Dickens Museum	D4
4 Madame Tussauds	A4
5 Regent's Park	A2
6 ZSL London Zoo	A2

🛏 Sleeping
7 Arran House Hotel	C4
8 Rough Luxe	D3
9 St Pancras Renaissance London Hotel	D3

✖ Eating
10 Orchard	D4
11 Providores & Tapa Room	B4

🍷 Drinking & Nightlife
12 Lock Tavern	B1
13 Princess Louise	D4

✪ Entertainment
14 Barfly	B1
15 Roundhouse	B1

🛍 Shopping
16 Camden Market	B1

and the lyrics to 'A Hard Day's Night' (scribbled on the back of Julian Lennon's birthday card) plus original scores by Handel, Mozart and Beethoven.

Charles Dickens Museum Museum
(Map p79; www.dickensmuseum.com; 48 Doughty St, WC1; adult/child £8/4; ⊙10am-5pm, last admission 4pm; ⊖Chancery Lane, Russell Sq)
After a £3.5 million year-long renovation,

continued on page 82

The British Museum

A HALF-DAY TOUR

The British Museum, with almost eight million items in its permanent collection, is so vast and comprehensive that it can be daunting for the first-time visitor. To avoid a frustrating trip – and getting lost on the way to the Egyptian mummies – set out on this half-day exploration, which takes in some of the museum's most important sights. If you want to see and learn more, join a tour or hire a multimedia iPad.

A good starting point is the **Rosetta Stone ❶**, the key that cracked the code to ancient Egypt's writing system. Nearby treasures from Assyria – an ancient civilisation centred in Mesopotamia between the Tigris and Euphrates Rivers – including the colossal **Khorsabad Winged Bulls ❷**, give way to the **Parthenon Sculptures ❸**, highpoints of classical Greek art that continue to influence

Winged Bulls from Khorsabad
This awesome pair of alabaster winged bulls with human heads once guarded the entrance to the palace of Assyrian King Sargon II at Khorsabad in Mesopotamia, a cradle of civilisation in present-day Iraq.

Parthenon Sculptures
The Parthenon, a white marble temple dedicated to Athena, was part of a fortified citadel on the Acropolis in Athens. There are dozens of sculptures and friezes with models and interactive displays explaining how they all once fitted together.

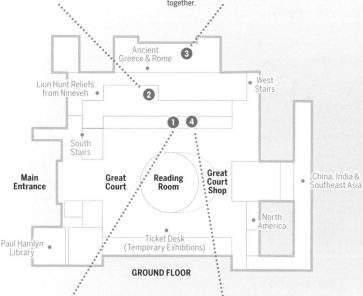

Ancient Greece & Rome ❸

West Stairs

Lion Hunt Reliefs from Nineveh ❷

South Stairs

❶ ❹

Main Entrance

Great Court

Reading Room

Great Court Shop

China, India & Southeast Asia

North America

Paul Hamlyn Library

Ticket Desk (Temporary Exhibtions)

GROUND FLOOR

Rosetta Stone
Written in hieroglyphic, demotic (cursive ancient Egyptian script used for everyday use) and Greek, the 762kg stone contains a decree exempting priests from tax on the first anniversary of young Ptolemy V's coronation.

JAMES MCCORMICK, VISITBRITAIN / GETTY IMAGES ©

Bust of Ramesses the Great
The most impressive sculpture in the Egyptian galleries, this 7.5-tonne bust portrays Ramesses II, scourge of the Israelites in the Book of Exodus, as great benefactor.

NORTH LIGHT IMAGES / GETTY IMAGES ©

us today. Be sure to see both the sculptures and the monumental frieze celebrating the birth of Athena. En route to the West Stairs is a huge bust of **Pharaoh Ramesses II** ④, just a hint of the large collection of **Egyptian mummies** ⑤ upstairs. (The earliest, affectionately called Ginger because of wispy reddish hair, was preserved simply by hot sand.) The Romans introduce visitors to the early Britain galleries via the rich **Mildenhall Treasure** ⑥. The Anglo-Saxon **Sutton Hoo Ship Burial** ⑦ and the medieval **Lewis Chessmen** ⑧ follow.

Lewis Chessmen
The much-loved 78 chess pieces portray faceless pawns, worried-looking queens, bishops with their mitres turned sideways and rooks as 'warders', gnawing away at their shields.

FEARGUS COONEY / GETTY IMAGES ©

Egyptian Mummies
Among the rich collection of mummies and funerary objects is 'Ginger', who was buried at the site of Gebelein, in Upper Egypt, more than 5000 years ago, and Katebet, a one-time chantress (ritual performer) at the Amun temple in Karnak.

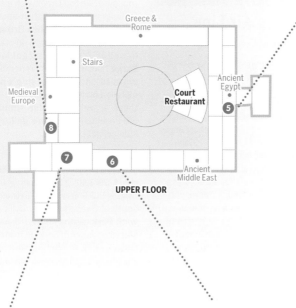

UPPER FLOOR

Sutton Hoo Ship Burial
This unique grave of an important (but unidentified) Anglo-Saxon royal has yielded drinking horns, gold buckles and a stunning helmet with face mask.

Mildenhall Treasure
Roman gods such as Neptune and Bacchus share space with early Christian symbols like the *chi-rho* (short for 'Christ') on the find's three dozen silver bowls, plates and spoons.

continued from page 79

this museum in a handsome four-storey house – the great Victorian novelist's sole surviving residence in London – is bigger and better than ever. A period kitchen in the basement and a nursery in the attic have been added, and newly acquired 49 Doughty St increases the exhibition space substantially.

GREENWICH

Greenwich (*gren*-itch) straddles the hemispheres and the ages, retaining its own sense of identity based on historic associations with the sea and science and possessing an extraordinary cluster of buildings that have earned 'Maritime Greenwich' its place on Unesco's World Heritage list.

Greenwich is easily reached on the DLR or via train from London Bridge. **Thames River Services** (www.thamesriverservices.co.uk; adult/child single £12.25/6.10, return £16/8) has boats departing from Westminster Pier (one hour, every 40 minutes), or alternatively take the cheaper Thames Clippers ferry.

Old Royal Naval College   Historic Building

(www.oldroyalnavalcollege.org; 2 Cutty Sark Gardens, SE10; ☉10am-5pm, grounds 8am-6pm; ℝDLR Cutty Sark) FREE Designed by Wren, the Old Royal Naval College is a magnificent example of monumental classical architecture. Parts are now used by the University of Greenwich and Trinity College of Music, but you can visit the **chapel** and the extraordinary **Painted Hall**, which took artist Sir James Thornhill 19 years to complete. Yeomen-led tours of the complex leave at noon daily, taking in areas not otherwise open to the public (£6, 60 minutes).

National Maritime Museum   Museum

(www.rmg.co.uk/national-maritime-museum; Romney Rd, SE10; ☉10am-5pm, Sammy Ofer Wing & ground fl galleries to 8pm Thu; ℝDLR Cutty Sark) FREE Narrating the long and eventful history of seafaring Britain, this museum is a top Greenwich attraction. Exhibits are arranged thematically, with highlights including **Miss Britain III** (the first boat to top 100mph on open water) from 1933, the 19m-long **golden state barge** built in 1732 for Frederick, Prince of Wales, and the huge **ship's propeller** installed on level one. Families will love these, as well as the **ship simulator** and the 2nd-floor **children's gallery**, where kids can let rip.

Royal Observatory   Historic Building

(www.rmg.co.uk; Greenwich Park, SE10; adult/child £7.70/3.60; ☉10am-5pm; ℝDLR Cutty Sark, ℝDLR Greenwich, ℝGreenwich) Rising south of Queen's House, idyllic **Greenwich Park** climbs up the hill, affording stunning views of London from the Royal Observatory, which Charles II had built in 1675 to help solve the riddle of longitude.

Success was confirmed in 1884 when Greenwich was designated as the prime meridian of the world, and Greenwich Mean Time (GMT) became the universal measurement of standard time.

Emirates Air Line Cable Car

Capable of ferrying 2400 people per hour across the Thames in either direction, the new **Emirates Air Line Cable Car** (www.emiratesairline.co.uk; adult/child single £4.40/2.30, return £8.80/4.60, with Oyster or Travelcard single £3.20/1.60, return £6.40/3.20; ☉7am-9pm Mon-Fri, 8am-9pm Sat, 9am-9pm Sun Apr-Sep, closes 1hr earlier Oct-Mar; ℝDLR Royal Victoria, ⊖North Greenwich) links together the Greenwich Peninsula and the Royal Docks in a five- to 10-minute journey. Oyster card and Travelcard holders get a discount for journeys. Arriving at Royal Docks, you can hop on the DLR at Royal Victoria DLR station, while in Greenwich, the underground interchange is with North Greenwich Station.

Palm House at Kew Gardens

JOHN LAMB/GETTY IMAGES ©

OUTSIDE CENTRAL LONDON

Kew Gardens   Gardens

(www.kew.org; Kew Rd; adult/child £15/free; ⏲9.30am-6.30pm Apr-Aug, earlier closing Sep-Mar; 🚢Kew Pier, 🚉Kew Bridge, ⊖Kew Gardens) In 1759 botanists began rummaging around the world for specimens to plant in the 3-hectare Royal Botanic Gardens at Kew. They never stopped collecting, and the gardens, which have bloomed to 120 hectares, provide the most comprehensive botanical collection on earth (including the world's largest collection of orchids). Recognised as a Unesco World Heritage Site, the gardens can easily swallow a day's exploration; for those pressed for time, the Kew Explorer (adult/child £4/1) hop-on/hop-off road train takes in the main sights.

Hampton Court Palace   Palace

(www.hrp.org.uk/HamptonCourtPalace; adult/child £18.20/9.10; ⏲10am-6pm Apr-Oct, to 4.30pm Nov-Mar; 🚢Hampton Court Palace, 🚉Hampton Court) Built by Cardinal Thomas Wolsey in 1514 but coaxed from him by Henry VIII just before Wolsey (as chancellor) fell from favour, Hampton Court Palace is England's largest and grandest Tudor structure. It was already one of the most sophisticated palaces in Europe when, in the 17th century, Christopher Wren designed an extension. The result is a beautiful blend of Tudor and 'restrained baroque' architecture. You could easily spend a day exploring the palace and its 60 acres of riverside gardens.

Tours

One of the best ways to orientate yourself when you first arrive in London is with a 24-hour hop-on/hop-off pass for the double-decker bus tours. The buses loop around interconnecting routes throughout the day, providing a commentary as they go, and the price includes a river cruise and three walking tours. Save a few pounds by booking online.

Original Tour   Bus Tour

(www.theoriginaltour.com; adult/child/family £29/14/86; ⏲every 20min 8.30am-5.30pm) Another hop-on-hop-off option with a river cruise thrown in as well as three themed walks: Changing of the Guard, Rock 'n' Roll and Jack the Ripper.

Big Bus Tours

Bus Tour

(www.bigbustours.com; adult/child/family £32/12/76; ⊙every 20min 8.30am-6pm Apr-Sep, to 5pm Oct & Mar, to 4.30pm Nov-Feb) Informative commentaries in eight languages. The ticket includes a free river cruise with City Cruises and three thematic walking tours (Royal London, Harry Potter film locations and Ghosts by Gaslight). Online booking discounts available.

London Walks

Walking Tour

(☏020-7624 3978; www.walks.com; adult/child £9/free) A huge choice of walks, including Jack the Ripper tours at 7.30pm daily and 3pm Saturday, Beatles tours at 11.20am Tuesday and Saturday, a Sherlock Holmes tour at 2pm Friday and a tour of Harry Potter film locations at 2pm Saturday and Sunday.

London Mystery Walks

Walking Tour

(☏07957 388280; www.tourguides.org.uk; adult/child/family £10/9/25) Tour Jack the Ripper's old haunts at 7pm on Monday, Wednesday and Friday. You must book in advance.

City Cruises

Boat Tour

(Map p62; ☏020-7740 0400; www.citycruises.com; single/return from £9.75/13, day pass £18) Ferry service between Westminster, Waterloo, Tower and Greenwich piers.

Capital Taxi Tours

Taxi Tour

(☏020-8590 3621; www.capitaltaxitours.co.uk; 2hr daytime tour per taxi £165, 2½hr evening tour per taxi £235) Takes up to five people on a variety of tours with Blue Badge, City of London and City of Westminster registered guides/drivers, cheeky Cockney Cabbie option and foreign language availability.

Sleeping

When it comes to finding a place for a good night's kip, London is one of the most expensive places in the world. 'Budget' is pretty much anything below £100 per night for a double; at the top end, how does a £18,000-per-night suite on Hyde Park Corner sound? Double rooms ranging between £100 and £180 per night are considered midrange; more expensive options fall into the top-end category.

Constitution Arch, Hyde Park Corner

WEST END

Like in Monopoly, land on a Mayfair hotel and you may have to sell your house, or at least remortgage.

Dean Street Townhouse
Boutique Hotel ££

(Map p62; 020-7434 1775; www.deanstreet-townhouse.com; 69-71 Dean St, W1; r £140-310; ✽ 🛜; ⊖Tottenham Court Rd) This 39-room gem in the heart of Soho has a wonderful boudoir atmosphere with its Georgian furniture, retro black-and-white tiled bathroom floors, beautiful lighting and girly touches (Cowshed bathroom products, hairdryer *and* straighteners in every room!). 'Medium' and 'bigger' rooms have four-poster beds and antique-style bathtubs right in the room.

Seven Dials Hotel
Hotel ££

(Map p62; 020-7240 0823; www.sevendials hotellondon.com; 7 Monmouth St, WC2; s/d/tr/q £95/105/130/150; 🛜; ⊖Covent Garden, Tottenham Court Rd) The Seven Dials is a clean and comfortable almost-budget option in a very central location. Half of the 18 rooms face onto charming Monmouth St; the ones at the back don't get much of a view but are quieter.

Haymarket Hotel
Hotel £££

(Map p62; 020-7470 4000; www.haymarket hotel.com; 1 Suffolk Pl, off Haymarket, SW1; r £325-425, ste from £505; ✽🛜🏊; ⊖Piccadilly Circus) The progeny of hoteliers and designers Tim and Kit Kemp, the Haymarket is opulently beautiful, with hand-painted Gournay wallpaper, signature fuchsia and green designs in the 50 guest rooms, a sensational 18m pool with mood lighting, an exquisite library lounge with honesty bar, and original artwork throughout. Just love the dog silhouettes on the chairs and bar stools.

Hazlitt's
Historic Hotel £££

(Map p62; 020-7434 1771; www.hazlittshotel.com; 6 Frith St, W1; s £216, d/ste from £288/660; ✽🛜; ⊖Tottenham Court Rd) Built in 1718 and comprising four original Georgian houses, this is the one-time home of essayist William Hazlitt (1778–1830). The

Booking Services

At Home in London (020-8748 1943; www.athomeinlondon.co.uk) For B&Bs.

British Hotel Reservation Centre (020-7592 3055; www.bhrconline.com) Hotels.

London Homestead Services (020-7286 5115; www.lhslondon.com) B&Bs.

LondonTown (020-7437 4370; www.londontown.com) Hotel and B&Bs.

Uptown Reservations (020-7937 2001; www.uptownres.co.uk) Upmarket B&Bs.

Visit London (0871 222 3118; www.visitlondonoffers.com) Hotels.

30 guestrooms have been furnished with original antiques from the Georgian era and boast a wealth of seductive details, including panelled walls, mahogany four-poster beds, antique desks, Victorian claw-foot tubs and sumptuous fabrics.

SOUTH BANK

Immediately south of the river is a great spot for reaching the central sights, while gauging the personality of London this side of the Thames.

Citizen M
Boutique Hotel ££

(Map p70; 020-3519 1680; www.citizenm.com/london-bankside; 20 Lavington St, SE1; r £109-189; ✽@🛜; ⊖Southwark) If Citizen M had a motto, it would be 'less fuss, more comfort'. The hotel has done away with things it considers superfluous (room service, reception, bags of space) and instead gone all out on mattresses and bedding (heavenly super king-size beds), state-of-the-art technology (everything in the room from mood lighting to TV is controlled through a tablet computer) and superb decor.

Shangri-La Hotel at the Shard
Hotel £££

(Map p70; 020-7234 8000; www.shangri-la.com/london/shangrila; 31 St Thomas St, SE1; d/ste £575/3000; ❄@🤍🏊; 🚇London Bridge, 🚊London Bridge) The Shangri-La's first UK opening gives London its first five-star hotel south of the Thames and breathtaking views from the highest hotel (above ground level) in Western Europe, occupying levels 34 to 52 of the Shard. From the 35th-floor sky lobby to the rooms, the Shangri-La concocts a stylish blend of Chinese aesthetics, Asian hospitality and sharp modernity.

PIMLICO & BELGRAVIA

Lime Tree Hotel
B&B ££

(Map p76; 020-7730 8191; www.limetreehotel.co.uk; 135-137 Ebury St, SW1; s/tr/f £110/205/225, d £165-205; @🤍; 🚊Victoria) Family run for over 40 years, this smartly renovated Georgian townhouse hotel has a pleasant back garden to catch the late afternoon rays while contemporary renovations and polite staff make it an appealing choice. No lift.

B+B Belgravia
B&B ££

(Map p76; 020-7259 8570; www.bb-belgravia.com; 64-66 Ebury St, SW1; s £89-120, d £100-140, apt £225; @🤍; 🚊Victoria) This spiffing six-floor Georgian B&B, remodelled with contemporary flair, boasts crisp common areas and a chic lounge echoing the black-and-white tiled floor. The 18 rooms (some with shower, others with bath) aren't enormous but there's a further batch of studio rooms with compact kitchens at No 82 Ebury St. A pleasant courtyard garden is out back. No lift.

Goring
Hotel £££

(Map p76; 020-7396 9000; www.thegoring.com; Beeston Pl; r £575-4350; ❄@🤍; 🚊Victoria) Kate Middleton spent her last night as a commoner in the Royal Suite here before joining the ranks of the Royal Family, propelling the Goring into an international media glare. Glistening with chandeliers, dotted with trademark fluffy sheep and overseen by highly professional staff, this family-owned hotel is a supremely grand, albeit highly relaxed slice of England and Englishness (and the garden is sumptuous).

CHELSEA & KENSINGTON

Well-turned-out Chelsea and Kensington offer easy access to the museums, natty shopping choices and some of London's best-looking streets.

Number Sixteen
Hotel £££

(Map p76; 020-7589 5232; www.firmdalehotels.com/hotels/london/number-sixteen; 16 Sumner Pl, SW7; s from £174, d £228-360; ❄@🤍; 🚊South Kensington) With uplifting splashes of colour, choice art and a sophisticated-but-fun

Number Sixteen hotel
NEIL SETCHFIELD/GETTY IMAGES ©

design ethos, ravishing Number Sixteen is four properties in one and a lovely (and rather labyrinthine) place to stay, with 41 individually designed rooms, a cosy drawing room and a fully stocked library. And wait till you see the idyllic, long back garden set around a fish pond, or have breakfast in the light-filled conservatory.

Ampersand Hotel
Boutique Hotel £££

(Map p76; ☎020-7589 5895; www.ampersand hotel.com; 10 Harrington Rd; s & d £372; ❋@☎; ⊖South Kensington) Housed in the old Norfolk Hotel building, a light, fresh and bubbly feel fills the new Ampersand, its (narrow) corridors and (stylish but smallish) rooms decorated with wallpaper designs celebrating the nearby arts and sciences of South Kensington's museums, a short stroll away. The wrapping recently off, there's a spring in its step, zest in the service and an eagerness to please.

Gore
Hotel £££

(Map p76; ☎020-7584 6601; www.gorehotel. com; 190 Queen's Gate, SW7; r from £204; ❋@☎; ⊖Gloucester Rd) With obliging staff in tails, twinkling chandeliers, walls crowded with framed portraits and prints and enough wood panelling to put paid to a sizeable chunk of woodland, this fantastic 50-room hotel wallows in old England charm. Rolling Stones fans can celebrate the Beggars Banquet launch in the bar; Judy Garland aficionados can sleep on her bed (shipped over from the US) in her namesake suite.

NOTTING HILL, BAYSWATER & PADDINGTON

Don't be fooled by Julia Roberts and Hugh Grant's shenanigans – Notting Hill and the areas immediately north of Hyde Park are as shabby as they are chic.

Scruffy Paddington has lots of cheap hotels, with a major strip of unremarkable ones along Sussex Gardens that may be worth checking if you're short on options.

Tune Hotel
Hotel £

(Map p76; ☎020-7258 3140; www.tunehotels. com; 41 Praed St, W2; r £35-80; ❋@☎; ⊖Paddington) This new 137-room Malaysian-owned budget hotel offers super-duper rates for early birds who book a long way in advance. The ethos is you get the bare bones – a twin or double room, the cheapest without window – and pay for add-ons (towel, wi-fi, TV) as you see fit, giving you the chance to just put a roof over your head, if that's all you need.

La Suite West
Boutique Hotel £££

(Map p76; ☎020-7313 8484; www.lasuite west.com; 41-51 Inverness Tce, W2; r £179-489; ❋@☎; ⊖Bayswater) The black-and-white foyer of the Anouska Hempel–designed La Suite West – bare walls, a minimalist slit of a fireplace, an iPad for guests' use on an otherwise void white marble reception desk – presages the OCD neatness of rooms hidden away down dark corridors. The straight lines, spotless surfaces and sharp angles are accentuated by impeccable bathrooms and softened by comfortable beds and warm service.

BLOOMSBURY & ST PANCRAS

One step from the West End and crammed with Georgian townhouse conversions, these are more affordable neighbourhoods.

Arran House Hotel
B&B ££

(Map p79; ☎020-7636 2186; www.arran hotel-london.com; 77-79 Gower St, WC1; s/d/ tr/q £155/175/195/225, without bathroom £95/125/155; @☎; ⊖Goodge St) This welcoming Bloomsbury B&B provides excellent value for the location. The 30 rooms range from basic singles with shared facilities to bright, well-furnished doubles with bathrooms. There is a cosy lounge at the front and gorgeous gardens at the back, perfect for a few drinks or a quiet read. Guests can use the microwave, fridge and dining room.

Rough Luxe
Boutique Hotel £££

(Map p79; ☎020-7837 5338; www.roughluxe. co.uk; 1 Birkenhead St, WC1; r £229-289; ❋☎; ⊖King's Cross St Pancras) Half rough, half

Below: Cafe menu **Right:** Shepherd Market, Mayfair

(BELOW) VISITBRITAIN/INGRID RASMUSSEN/GETTY IMAGES ©; (RIGHT) WAYNE WALTON/GETTY IMAGES ©

luxury is the strapline of this unique hotel, and the interior is true to its words: scraps of old newspaper adorn the walls along with original works of art; the bathrooms are utterly gorgeous but the vintage 1970s TV doesn't work. Rooms are tiny but service and location more than make up for it. The little patio at the back is a lovely surprise – guests are welcome to bring food and enjoy a glass of wine on balmy nights.

St Pancras Renaissance
London Hotel   Luxury Hotel £££
(Map p79; ☏ 020-7841 3540; www.marriott. co.uk; Euston Rd, NW1; d from £230; ✳ ⓩ ✖; ⊖ King's Cross St Pancras) It took the best part of a decade and £150 million to revive the former Midland Grand Hotel but, boy, was it worth it. The Gothic, red-brick building is a Victorian marvel. Disappointingly, only 38 of the 245 rooms are in the original building; the rest are in an extension at the back and rather bland.

HOXTON

Hoxton Hotel   Hotel £
(Map p70; ☏ 020-7550 1000; www. hoxtonhotels.com; 81 Great Eastern St, EC2; r from £59; ✳ @ 🛜; ⊖ Old St) This is hands down the best hotel deal in London. In the heart of Shoreditch, this sleek 208-room hotel aims to make its money by being full each night. You get an hour of free phone calls, free computer terminal access in the lobby, free printing and breakfast from Prêt à Manger. Rooms are small but stylish.

✖ Eating

Dining out in London has become so fashionable that you can hardly open a menu without banging into some celebrity chef or other. The range and quality of eating options has increased exponentially over the last few decades.

WEST END

Mayfair, Soho and Covent Garden are the gastronomic heart of London, with a blinding choice of restaurants and cuisines at budgets to suit booze hounds, theatre-goers or determined grazers.

Koya   Noodles £

(Map p62; www.koya.co.uk; 49 Frith St, W1; mains £7-15; ☺noon-3pm & 5.30-10.30pm; ⊖Tottenham Court Rd, Leicester Sq) Arrive early or late if you don't want to queue at this excellent Japanese eatery. Londoners come for their fill of authentic udon noodles (served hot or cold, in soup or with a cold sauce), the efficient service and very reasonable prices.

Orchard   Vegetarian £

(Map p79; www.orchard-kitchen.co.uk; 11 Sicilian Ave, WC1; mains £6.50-7; ☺8am-4pm Mon-Fri; 🖋; ⊖Holborn) A boon for vegetarians in central London is this delightful retro-style cafe on a quiet pedestrian street. Mains include specialities like broccoli and Yorkshire blue cheese pie, a sarnie

(that's a sandwich to Londoners) and mug of soup is just £4.95 and desserts are unusual – try the toasted oat and currant cake with Horlicks icing.

Brasserie Zédel   French ££

(Map p62; 📞020-7734 4888; www.brasserie zedel.com; 20 Sherwood St, W1; mains £8.75-30; ☺11.30am-midnight Mon-Sat, to 11pm Sun; 📞; ⊖Piccadilly Circus) This brasserie in the renovated art deco ballroom of a former Piccadilly hotel is the French-est eatery west of Calais. Choose from among the usual favourites, including *choucroute alsacienne* (sauerkraut with sausages and charcuterie, £14) and duck leg confit with Puy lentils. The set menus (£8.25/11.75 for two/three courses) and plats du jour (£12.95) offer excellent value.

Great Queen Street   British ££

(Map p62; 📞020-7242 0622; 32 Great Queen St, WC2; mains £12-16; ☺noon-2.30pm & 6-10.30pm Mon-Sat, noon-3pm Sun; ⊖Holborn) The menu at what is one of Covent Garden's best places to eat is seasonal (and changes daily), with an emphasis on quality, hearty dishes and good ingredients – there are always delicious stews, roasts and simple fish dishes. The atmosphere is lively, with a small bar downstairs. The staff are knowledgeable about the food and wine they serve and booking is essential.

National Dining Rooms   British ££

(Map p62; ☎020-7747 2525; www.peytonand byrne.co.uk; 1st fl, Sainsbury Wing, National Gallery, Trafalgar Sq, WC2; mains £15.50-20.50; ☺10am-5.30pm Sat-Thu, to 8.30pm Fri; ⊖Charing Cross) Chef Oliver Peyton's restaurant at the National Gallery styles itself as 'proudly and resolutely British', and what a great idea. The menu features an extensive and wonderful selection of British cheeses for a light lunch. For something more filling, go for the county menu, a monthly changing menu honouring regional specialities from across the British Isles.

Hawksmoor Seven Dials   Steakhouse £££

(Map p62; ☎020-7420 9390; www.thehawks moor.co.uk; 11 Langley St, WC2; steak £20-34, 2-/3-course express menu £23/26; ☺noon-3pm & 5-10.30pm Mon-Sat, noon-9.30pm Sun; ☎; ⊖Covent Garden) 🍴 Legendary among London carnivores for its mouth-watering and flavour-rich steaks from British cattle breeds, Hawksmoor's sumptuous Sunday roasts, burgers and well-executed cocktails are other show-stoppers. Book ahead.

Arbutus   Modern European £££

(Map p62; ☎020-7734 4545; www.arbutus restaurant.co.uk; 63-64 Frith St, W1; mains £18-20; ☺noon-2.30pm & 5-11pm Mon-Sat, noon-3pm & 5.30-10.30pm Sun; ☎; ⊖Tottenham Court Rd) This Michelin-starred brainchild of Anthony Demetre does great British food, focusing on seasonal produce. Try such inventive dishes as pigeon, sweet onion and beetroot tart, squid and mackerel 'burger' or *pieds et paquets* (lamb tripe parcels with pig trotters). Don't miss the bargain set 'working lunch' menu at £17.95 for two courses and £19.95 for three. Booking essential.

SOUTH BANK

Popular restaurants make the most of the iconic riverside views but scouting around turns up gems all over the place.

M Manze   British £

(www.manze.co.uk; 87 Tower Bridge Rd, SE1; mains £2.40-6.25; ☺11am-2pm Mon-Thu, 10am-2.30pm Fri & Sat; ⊖Borough) Dating to 1902, M Manze (Italian roots) started off as an ice-cream seller before moving on to selling its legendary staples: pies. It's a classic operation, from the lovely tile work to the traditional working-man's menu: pie and mash (£3.40), pie and liquor (£2.40) and you can take your eels jellied or stewed (£3.50).

Skylon   Modern European ££

(Map p62; ☎020-7654 7800; www.skylon-restaurant.co.uk; 3rd fl, Royal Festival Hall, Southbank Centre, Belvedere Rd, SE1; grill mains £12.50-30, restaurant 2-/3-course £42/48; ☺grill noon-11pm, restaurant noon-2.30pm & 5.30-10.30pm Mon-Sat, noon-4pm Sun; ☎; ⊖Waterloo) Named after the defunct 1950s tower, this excellent restaurant on top of the refurbished Royal Festival Hall is divided into grill and fine-dining sections by a large **bar** (open until 1am). The decor is cutting-edge 1950s: muted colours and period chairs (trendy then, trendier now) while floor-to-ceiling windows bathe you in magnificent views of the Thames and the City.

Magdalen   Modern British ££

(Map p70; ☎020-7403 1342; www.magdalen restaurant.co.uk; 152 Tooley St, SE1; mains £14.50-21, 2-/3-course lunch £15.50/18.50; ☺noon-2.30pm Mon-Fri, 6.30-10pm Mon-Sat; ☎; ⊖London Bridge) You can't go wrong with this formal dining room. The Modern British fare adds its own appetising spin to familiar dishes (grilled calves' kidneys, creamed onion and sage, smoked haddock *choucroute*); the desserts and English cheese selection are another delight. The welcome is warm and the service excellent.

KNIGHTSBRIDGE

Dinner by Heston Blumenthal   Modern British £££

(Map p76; ☏020-7201 3833; www.dinnerby heston.com; Mandarin Oriental Hyde Park, 66 Knightsbridge, SW1; 3-course set lunch £38, mains £28-42; ⊙noon-2.30pm & 6.30-10.30pm; 🖥; ⊖Knightsbridge) Sumptuously presented Dinner is a gastronomic tour de force, taking diners on a journey through British culinary history (with inventive modern inflections). Dishes carry historical dates to convey context, while the restaurant interior is a design triumph, from the glass-walled kitchen and its overhead clock mechanism to the large windows onto the park.

Zuma   Japanese £££

(Map p76; ☏020-7584 1010; www.zuma restaurant.com; 5 Raphael St, SW7; mains £15-75; ⊙noon-2.30pm Mon-Fri, 12.30-3.30pm Sat & Sun, 6-11pm daily; 🖥; ⊖Knightsbridge) A modern-day take on the traditional Japanese *izakaya* ('a place to stay and drink sake'), where drinking and eating harmonise, Zuma oozes style. Traditional Japanese materials – wood and stone – combine with a modern sensibility for a highly contemporary feel. The private *kotatsu* rooms are the place for large dinner groups, or dine alongside the sushi-counter, open-plan kitchen.

CHELSEA & KENSINGTON

These highbrow neighbourhoods harbour some of London's very best (and priciest) restaurants.

Five Fields   Modern British £££

(Map p76; ☏020-7838 1082; www.fivefields restaurant.com; 8-9 Blacklands Terrace, SW3; 3-course set meal £50; ⊙6.30-10pm Tue-Sat; 🖥;

⊖Sloane Square) The inventive British cuisine, consummate service and enticingly light and inviting decor of Five Fields are hard to resist, at this triumphant Chelsea restaurant, but you'll need to plan early and book way up front. It's only open five nights a week.

Medlar   Modern European £££

(Map p76; ☏020-7349 1900; www.medlar restaurant.co.uk; 438 King's Rd, SW10; 3-course lunch £27-30, dinner £35-45; ⊙noon-3pm & 6.30-10.30pm; 🖥; ⊖South Kensington, Fulham Broadway, Sloane Sq) With its uncontrived yet crisply modern green-on-grey design, immaculate and Michelin star–rated Medlar has quickly become a King's Rd sensation. With no à la carte menu and scant pretentiousness, the prix fixe modern European cuisine is delightfully assured, with kitchen magic devised by chef Joe Mercer Nairne (from Chez Bruce); prices are equally appetising and service is exemplary.

Traditional London pub, Covent Garden
MARK TURNER/GETTY IMAGES ©

Gordon Ramsay
French £££

(Map p76; ☎ 020-7352 4441; www.gordon ramsay.com; 68 Royal Hospital Rd, SW3; 3-course lunch/dinner £55/95; ⏰ noon-2.30pm & 6.30-11pm Mon-Fri; ⊖ Sloane Sq) One of Britain's finest restaurants and London's longest-running with three Michelin stars, this is hallowed turf for those who worship at the altar of the stove. It's true that it's a treat right from the taster to the truffles, but you won't get much time to savour it all. The blowout tasting Menu Prestige (£135) is seven courses of absolute perfection.

NOTTING HILL, BAYSWATER & PADDINGTON

Notting Hill teems with good places to eat, from cheap takeaways to atmospheric pubs and restaurants worthy of the fine-dining tag. Queensway has the best strip of Asian restaurants this side of Soho.

Taquería
Mexican £

(Map p76; www.taqueria.co.uk; 139-143 Westbourne Grove; tacos £5-7.50; ⏰ noon-11pm Mon-Fri, 10am-11.30pm Sat, noon-10.30pm Sun; 🛜; ⊖ Notting Hill Gate) ✐ You won't find fresher, limper (they're not supposed to be crispy!) tacos anywhere in London because these ones are made on the premises. It's a small casual place with a great vibe. Taquería is also a committed environmental establishment: the eggs, chicken and pork are free-range, the meat British, the fish MSC-certified and the milk and cream organic.

Ledbury
French £££

(Map p76; ☎ 020-7792 9090; www.theledbury. com; 127 Ledbury Rd, W11; 4-course set lunch £45, 4-course dinner £90; ⏰ noon-2pm Wed-Sun & 6.30-9.45pm daily; 🛜; ⊖ Westbourne Park, Notting Hill Gate) Two Michelin stars and swooningly elegant, Brett Graham's artful French restaurant attracts well-heeled diners in jeans with designer jackets. Dishes – such as roast sea bass with broccoli stem, crab and black quinoa, or saddle of roe deer with beetroot, pinot lees and bone crisp potato – are triumphant. London gastronomes have the Ledbury on speed-dial, so reservations are crucial.

Skylon Restaurant (p90), Southbank

MARYLEBONE

You won't go too far wrong planting yourself on a table anywhere along Marylebone's charming High St.

Locanda Locatelli
Italian ££

(Map p76; ☎020-7935 9088; www.locanda locatelli.com; 8 Seymour St, W1; mains from £13.50; ☉noon-3pm daily, 6.45-11pm Mon-Sat, to 10.15pm Sun; 🛜; ⊖Marble Arch) This dark but quietly glamorous restaurant in an otherwise unremarkable Marble Arch hotel remains one of London's hottest tables, and you're likely to see some famous faces being greeted by celebrity chef Giorgio Locatelli. The restaurant is renowned for its pasta dishes, and the mains include five fish and five meat dishes. Booking is essential.

Providores & Tapa Room
Fusion £££

(Map p79; ☎020-7935 6175; www.the providores.co.uk; 109 Marylebone High St, W1; 2-/3-/4-/5-course dinner £33/47/57/63; ☉9am-10.30pm Mon-Fri, 10am-10pm Sat & Sun; 🛜; ⊖Baker St) This place is split over two levels: tempting tapas (£2.50 to £17) on the ground floor (no bookings); and outstanding fusion cuisine in the elegant and understated dining room above. The food at Providores is truly original and tastes divine: try the Sri Lankan spiced short ribs, Cajun pork belly with Puy lentils, or beef fillet with Szechuan-pickled shiitake mushrooms.

CLERKENWELL & FARRINGDON

Clerkenwell's hidden gems are well worth digging for. Pedestrianised Exmouth Market is a good place to start.

Little Bay
European £

(Map p70; ☎020-7278 1234; www.little-bay. co.uk; 171 Farringdon Rd, EC1; mains before/after 7pm £6.45/8.45; ⊖Farringdon) The crushed-velvet ceiling, handmade twisted lamps that improve around the room (as the artist got better) and elaborately painted bar and tables showing nymphs frolicking are bonkers but fun. The hearty food is very good value.

St John
British £££

(Map p70; ☎020-7251 0848; www.stjohn restaurant.com; 26 St John St, EC1; mains £17-23; ☉noon-3pm & 6-11pm Mon-Sat, 1-3pm Sun; ⊖Farringdon) This London classic is wonderfully simple – its light bar and cafe area giving way to a surprisingly small dining room where 'nose to tail' eating is served up courtesy of celebrity chef Fergus Henderson. This was one of the places that launched Londoners on the quest to rediscover their culinary past.

Modern Pantry
Fusion £££

(Map p70; ☎020-7553 9210; www.themodern pantry.co.uk; 47-48 St John's Sq, EC1; mains £14-21.50; ☉noon-3pm Tue-Fri, 11am-4pm Sat & Sun, 6-10.30pm Tue-Sat; 🛜; ⊖Farringdon) This three-floor Georgian town house in the heart of Clerkenwell has a cracking all-day menu, which gives almost as much pleasure to read as to eat from. Ingredients are combined sublimely into unusual dishes such as tamarind miso marinated onglet steak or panko and parmesan crusted veal escalope. The breakfasts are great, too, though sadly portions can be on the small side. Reservations recommended for the evenings.

HOXTON, SHOREDITCH & SPITALFIELDS

From the hit-and-miss Bangladeshi restaurants of Brick Lane to the Vietnamese strip on Kingsland Rd, and the Jewish, Spanish, French, Italian and Greek eateries in between, the East End's cuisine is as multicultural as its residents.

Poppies
Fish & Chips ££

(Map p70; www.poppiesfishandchips.co.uk; 6-8 Hanbury St, E1; mains £7-16; ☉11am-11pm Mon-Thu, to 11.30pm Fri & Sat, to 10.30pm Sun; 🛜; ⊖Shoreditch High St, Liverpool St) Glorious recreation of a 1950s East End chippy, complete with waitresses in pinnies and hairnets, and retro memorabilia. As well as the usual fishy suspects, it also does jellied eels, homemade tartare sauce and mushy peas, and you can wash it all down with a glass of wine or beer. Also does a roaring takeaway trade.

Albion

British ££

(Map p70; ☎020-7729 1051; www.albioncaff.co.uk; 2-4 Boundary St, E2; mains £9-13; ⊗8am-11pm; ⛔; ⊖Old St) This is Sir Terence Conran's contribution to the capital's eating scene, with a combination of two eateries, a hotel and a fantastic rooftop terrace. Albion, the ground-floor 'caff', combines a bright and stylish canteen-style restaurant with a terrific deli. The menu features feel-good British food, cooked to perfection, with plenty of attention to detail.

🍷 Drinking & Nightlife

As long as there's been a city, Londoners have loved to drink. The pub is the hub of the city's social life and, despite depleting numbers, there's always one near at hand.

London's clubland is no longer confined to the West End, with megaclubs scattered throughout the city wherever there's a venue big enough, cheap enough or quirky enough to hold them.

WEST END

Gordon's Wine Bar

Bar

(Map p62; www.gordonswinebar.com; 47 Villiers St, WC2; ⊗11am-11pm Mon-Sat, noon-10pm Sun; ⊖Embankment) Gordon's is a victim of its own success; it is relentlessly busy and unless you arrive before the office crowd does (generally around 6pm), you can forget about getting a table. It's cavernous and dark, and the French and New World wines are heady and reasonably priced. You can nibble on bread, cheese and olives. Outside garden seating in summer.

French House

Bar

(Map p62; www.frenchhousesoho.com; 49 Dean St, W1; ⊗noon-11pm; ⊖Leicester Sq) French House is Soho's legendary boho boozer with a history to match: this was the meeting place of the Free French Forces during WWII, and De Gaulle is said to have drunk here often, while Dylan Thomas, Peter O'Toole and Francis Bacon all ended up on the wooden floor at least once.

Princess Louise

Pub

(Map p79; 208 High Holborn, WC1; ⊗11.30am-11pm; ⊖Holborn) This late-19th-century Victorian pub is spectacularly decorated with a riot of fine tiles, etched mirrors, plasterwork and a stunning central horseshoe bar. The old Victorian wood partitions give punters plenty of nooks and alcoves to hide in. Beers are Sam Smith's only but cost just under £3 a pint, so it's no wonder many elect to spend the whole evening here.

Lamb & Flag

Pub

(Map p62; www.lambandflagcoventgarden.co.uk; 33 Rose St, WC2; ⊗11am-11pm Mon-Sat, noon-10.30pm Sun; ⊖Covent Garden) Pocket-sized but packed with charm and history, the Lamb & Flag is still going strong after three and a half centuries (indeed, the poet John Dryden was mugged outside in 1679). Rain or shine, you'll have to elbow your way to the bar through the merry crowd drinking outside. Inside, it's all brass fittings and creaky wooden floors.

THE CITY

Vertigo 42

Bar

(Map p70; ☎020-7877 7842; www.vertigo42.co.uk; Tower 42, 25 Old Broad St, EC2; ⊗noon-3.45pm Mon-Fri & 5-11pm Mon-Sat; ⊖Liverpool St) On the 42nd floor of a 183m-high tower, this circular bar has expansive views over the city that stretch for miles on a clear day. The classic drinks list is, as you might expect, pricier than average – wine by the glass starts from £9.50 and champagne and cocktails from £14, and there's also a limited food menu. Reservations essential; minimum spend £10.

Ye Olde Cheshire Cheese

Pub

(Map p70; Wine Office Court, 145 Fleet St, EC4; ⊗11am-11pm Mon-Fri, noon-11pm Sat; ⊖Chancery Lane) The entrance to this historic pub is via a narrow alley off Fleet St. Over its long history locals have included Dr Johnson, Thackeray and Dickens. Despite (or possibly because of) this, the Cheshire feels today like a bit of a museum. Nevertheless, it's one of London's most famous pubs and it's well worth popping in for a pint.

SOUTH BANK

Rake
Pub

(Map p70; www.uttobeer.co.uk; 14 Winchester Walk, SE1; ☺noon-11pm Mon-Sat, to 8pm Sun; ⊖London Bridge) The Rake offers more than 100 beers at any one time. The selection of bitters, real ales, lagers and ciders (with one-third pint measures) changes constantly. It's a tiny place yet always busy; the bamboo-decorated decking outside is especially popular.

George Inn
Pub

(Map p70; www.nationaltrust.org.uk/george-inn; 77 Borough High St, SE1; ☺11am-11pm; ⊖London Bridge) This magnificent old boozer is London's last surviving galleried coaching inn, dating from 1676 and mentioned in Dickens' *Little Dorrit*. It is on the site of the Tabard Inn, where the pilgrims in Chaucer's *Canterbury Tales* gathered before setting out (well lubricated, we suspect) on the road to Canterbury, Kent.

CHELSEA & KENSINGTON

Queen's Arms
Pub

(Map p76; www.thequeensarmskensington.co.uk; 30 Queen's Gate Mews, SW7; ☺noon-11pm; ⊖Gloucester Rd) Just around the corner from the Royal Albert Hall, this godsend of a blue-grey painted pub in an adorable cobbled mews setting off bustling Queen's Gate beckons with a cosy interior and a right royal selection of ales and ciders on tap.

NOTTING HILL, BAYSWATER & PADDINGTON

Churchill Arms
Pub

(Map p76; www.churchillarmskensington.co.uk; 119 Kensington Church St, W8; ☺11am-11pm Mon-Wed, to midnight Thu-Sat, noon-10.30pm Sun; 🛜; ⊖Notting Hill Gate) With its cascade of geraniums and Union Jack flags swaying in the breeze, the Churchill Arms is quite a sight on Kensington Church St. Renowned for its Winston memorabilia and dozens of knick-knacks on the walls, the pub is a favourite of both locals and tourists. The attached conservatory has been serving excellent Thai food for two decades (mains £6 to £10).

CAMDEN TOWN

Lock Tavern
Pub

(Map p79; www.lock-tavern.com; 35 Chalk Farm Rd, NW1; ☺noon-midnight Mon-Thu, to 1am Fri & Sat, to 11pm Sun; ⊖Chalk Farm) An institution

'The Gherkin' and London skyline seen from Vertigo 42

MAISANT LUDOVIC/AGE FOTOSTOCK ©

in Camden, the black-clad Lock Tavern rocks for several reasons: it's cosy inside, has an ace roof terrace from where you can watch the market throngs, the food is good, the beer plentiful and it also has a roll-call of guest bands and DJs at the weekend to spice things up.

CLERKENWELL & FARRINGDON

Jerusalem Tavern   Pub
(Map p70; www.stpetersbrewery.co.uk; 55 Britton St, EC1; ⏰11am-11pm Mon-Fri; 📶; 🚇Farringdon) Starting life as one of the first London coffee houses (founded in 1703), with the 18th-century decor of occasional tile mosaics still visible, the JT is an absolute stunner, though it's both massively popular and tiny, so come early to get a seat.

8   Club
(Map p70; www.fabriclondon.com; 77a Charter-house St, EC1; admission £8-18; ⏰10pm-6am Fri, 11pm-8am Sat, 11pm-6am Sun; 🚇Farringdon) This most impressive of superclubs is still the first stop on the London scene for many international clubbers. The crowd is hip and well dressed without overkill, and the music – electro, techno, house, drum and bass and dubstep – is as superb as you would expect from London's top-rated club.

Plastic People   Club
(Map p70; www.plasticpeople.co.uk; 147-149 Curtain Rd, EC2; admission £5-10; ⏰10pm-2am Thu, to 4am Fri & Sat; 🚇Old St) This is a tiny club with just a dance floor and bar and a booming sound system that experts say easily kicks the butts of bigger clubs. Head here on Fridays and Saturdays for nights that are often given over to one long DJ set by the likes of Kieran Hebden, Kode 9 or Mr Scruff, smashing out mainly house and electronica.

Cargo   Club
(Map p70; www.cargo-london.com; 83 Rivington St, EC2; admission free-£16; ⏰noon-1am Mon-Thu, to 3am Fri & Sat, to midnight Sun; 🚇Old St) Cargo is one of London's most eclectic clubs. Under its brick railway arches you'll find a dance-floor room, bar and outside terrace. The music policy is innovative and varied, with plenty of up-and-coming bands also on the menu. Food is available throughout the day.

HOXTON, SHOREDITCH & SPITALFIELDS

Book Club   Bar
(Map p70; 📞020-7684 8618; www.wearetbc.com; 100 Leonard St, EC2A; ⏰8am-midnight Mon-Wed, to 2am Thu & Fri, 10am-2am Sat & Sun; 📶; 🚇Old St) This former Victorian warehouse has been transformed into an innovative temple to good times. Spacious and whitewashed with large windows upstairs and a basement bar below, it hosts a real variety of offbeat events,

Cargo club

such as spoken word, dance lessons and life drawing, as well as a varied program of DJ nights.

Ten Bells
Pub

(Map p70; cnr Commercial & Fournier Sts, E1; ⏱11am-11pm Mon-Sat, noon-10.30pm Sun; ⊖Liverpool St) This landmark Victorian pub, with its large windows and beautiful tiles, is perfect for a pint after a wander round Spitalfields Market. It's famous for being one of Jack the Ripper's pick-up joints, although these days it attracts a rather more salubrious and trendy clientele.

GREENWICH & SOUTH LONDON

Ministry of Sound
Club

(www.ministryofsound.com; 103 Gaunt St, SE1; admission £16-25; ⏱11pm-6.30am Fri & Sat; ⊖Elephant & Castle) This legendary club-cum-enormous-global-brand (four bars, four dance floors) lost some 'edge' in the early noughties but, after pumping in top DJs, the Ministry has firmly rejoined the top club ranks. Fridays is the Gallery trance night, while Saturday sessions offers the *crème de la crème* of house, electro and techno DJs.

Entertainment

THEATRE

London is a world capital for theatre across the spectrum from mammoth musicals to thougtful drama for the highbrow crowd.

On performance days, you can buy half-price tickets for West End productions (cash only) from the official agency **tkts** (Map p62; www.tkts.co.uk; Leicester Sq, WC2; ⏱10am-7pm Mon-Sat, noon-4pm Sun; ⊖Leicester Sq) on the south side of Leicester Sq. The booth is the one with the clock tower; beware of touts selling dodgy tickets. For a comprehensive look at what's being staged and where, visit www.officiallondontheatre.co.uk or www.theatremonkey.com.

Abbey Road

Beatles aficionados can't possibly visit London without making a pilgrimage to **Abbey Road Studios** (www.abbeyroad.com; 3 Abbey Rd, NW8) in St John's Wood. The fence outside is covered with decades of fans' graffiti. Stop-start local traffic is long accustomed to groups of tourists lining up on the zebra crossing to re-enact the cover of the fab four's 1969 masterpiece and penultimate swan song *Abbey Road*. In 2010, the crossing received the accolade of grade II listed status. To get here, take the tube to St John's Wood, cross the road, follow Grove End Rd to its end and turn right.

National Theatre
Theatre

(Map p62; ☎020-7452 3000; www.national-theatre.org.uk; South Bank, SE1; ⊖Waterloo) England's flagship theatre showcases a mix of classic and contemporary plays performed by excellent casts in three theatres (Olivier, Lyttelton and Dorfman). Outstanding artistic director Nicholas Hytner (who stepped down in March 2015) has overseen a golden decade at the theatre, with landmark productions such as *War Horse* and there are constant surprises in the program.

Royal Court Theatre
Theatre

(Map p76; ☎020-7565 5000; www.royal-courttheatre.com; Sloane Sq, SW1; ⊖Sloane Sq) Equally renowned for staging innovative new plays and old classics, the Royal Court is among London's most progressive theatres and has continued to foster major writing talent across the UK.

Tickets for concessions are £6 to £10, and £10 for everyone on Monday (four 10p standing tickets sold at the Jerwood Theatre Downstairs); tickets for under 26s are £8. Check the theatre's Facebook page for the lastest on cheap tickets.

Old Vic
Theatre

(Map p70; ☎0844 871 7628; www.oldvictheatre.
com; The Cut, SE1; ⊖Waterloo) Never has
there been a London theatre with a more
famous artistic director. American actor
Kevin Spacey took the theatrical helm in
2003, looking after this glorious theatre's
program. The theatre does both new and
classic plays, and its cast and directors
are consistently high-profile.

Donmar Warehouse
Theatre

(Map p62; ☎0844 871 7624; www.donmar
warehouse.com; 41 Earlham St, WC2; ⊖Covent
Garden) The cosy Donmar Warehouse is
London's 'thinking person's theatre'. The
new artistic director, Josie Rourke, has
staged some interesting and unusual
productions such as the Restoration
comedy *The Recruiting Officer,* by George
Farquhar, and a restaging of Conor
McPherson's *The Weir.*

ROCK, POP & JAZZ

Big-name gigs sell out quickly, so check
www.seetickets.com before you travel.

12 Bar Club
Live Music

(Map p62; www.12barclub.com; Denmark St,
WC2; admission £6-10; ⊙7pm-3am Mon-Sat, to
12.30am Sun; ⊖Tottenham Court Rd) Small,
intimate, with a rough-and-ready feel,
the 12 Bar is a favourite live-music venue,
with anything from solo acts to bands
performing nightly. The emphasis is on
songwriting and the music is very much
indie rock, with anything from folk and
jazzy influences to full-on punk and metal
sounds.

Barfly
Live Music

(Map p79; www.mamacolive.com/thebarfly; 49
Chalk Farm Rd, NW1; gigs from £8, club nights
£3-5; ⊙7pm-3am Mon-Sat, to midnight Sun;
⊖Chalk Farm) This typically grungy, indie-
rock Camden venue is well known for
hosting small-time artists looking for their
big break. The focus is on indie rock. The
venue is small, so you'll feel like the band
is just playing for you and your mates.
There are club nights most nights of the
week.

Ronnie Scott's
Jazz

(Map p62; ☎020-7439 0747; www.ronniescotts.
co.uk; 47 Frith St, W1; ⊙6.30pm-3am Mon-Sat,
to midnight Sun; ⊖Leicester Sq, Tottenham
Court Rd) Ronnie Scott originally opened
his jazz club on Gerrard St in 1959 under
a Chinese gambling den. The club moved
to its current location six years later and
became widely known as Britain's best
jazz club. Gigs are at 8.30pm (8pm Sunday) with a second one at 11.15pm Friday
and Saturday, and are followed by a late
show until 2am. Expect to pay between
£20 and £50.

100 Club
Live Music

(Map p62; ☎020-7636 0933; www.the100club.
co.uk; 100 Oxford St, W1; admission £8-20;
⊙check website for gig times; ⊖Oxford Circus,
Tottenham Court Rd) This legendary London
venue has always concentrated on jazz,
but it's also spreading its wings to swing
and rock. It once showcased Chris Barber,
BB King and the Stones, and was at the
centre of the punk revolution and the '90s
indie scene. It hosts dancing swing gigs
and local jazz musicians, as well as the
occasional big name.

Roundhouse
Live Music

(Map p79; www.roundhouse.org.uk; Chalk Farm
Rd, NW1; ⊖Chalk Farm) The Roundhouse
was once home to 1960s avant-garde
theatre, then was a rock venue, then it fell
into oblivion for a while before reopen-
ing a few years back. It holds great gigs
and brilliant performances, from circus
to stand-up comedy, poetry slam and
improvisation sessions. The round shape
of the building is unique and generally
well used in the staging.

CLASSICAL MUSIC

Royal Albert Hall
Concert Venue

(Map p76; ☎020-7589 8212, 0845 401 5045;
www.royalalberthall.com; Kensington Gore,
SW7; ⊖South Kensington) This splendid
Victorian concert hall hosts classical
music, rock and other performances, but
is most famously the venue for the BBC-
sponsored Proms. Booking is possible,
but from mid-July to mid-September
Proms punters also queue for £5 standing

(or 'promenading') tickets that go on sale one hour before curtain-up. Otherwise the box office and prepaid ticket collection counter are both through door 12 (south side of the hall).

Barbican   Performing Arts
(Map p70; ☎020-7638 8891, 0845 121 6823; www.barbican.org.uk; Silk St, EC2; ☻Barbican)
Home to the wonderful London Symphony Orchestra and its associate orchestra, the lesser-known BBC Symphony Orchestra, the arts centre hosts scores of other leading musicians each year as well, focusing in particular on jazz, folk, world and soul artists. Dance is another strong point here.

Southbank Centre   Concert Venue
(Map p62; ☎020-7960 4200; www.southbank-centre.co.uk; Belvedere Rd, SE1; ☻Waterloo)
The overhauled **Royal Festival Hall** (Map p62; ☎020-7960 4242; admission £6-60) is London's premier concert venue and seats 3000 in a now-acoustic amphitheatre. It's one of the best places for catching world and classical music artists. The sound is fantastic, the programming

impeccable and there are frequent free gigs in the wonderfully expansive foyer.

OPERA & DANCE
Royal Opera House   Opera
(Map p62; ☎020-7304 4000; www.roh.org.uk; Bow St, WC2; tickets £4-250; ☻Covent Garden)
The £210 million redevelopment for the millennium gave classic opera a fantastic setting in London, and coming here for a night is a sumptuous – if pricey – affair. Although the program has been fluffed up by modern influences, the main attractions are still the opera and classical ballet – all are wonderful productions and feature world-class performers.

Sadler's Wells   Dance
(Map p70; ☎0844 412 4300; www.sadlerswells.com; Rosebery Ave, EC1; tickets £10-49; ☻Angel)
The theatre site dates from 1683 but was completely rebuilt in 1998; today it is the most eclectic and modern dance venue in town, with experimental dance shows of all genres and from all corners of the globe. The Lilian Baylis Studio stages smaller productions.

Royal Opera House, Covent Garden

ROY RAINFORD/GETTY IMAGES ©

COMEDY

Comedy Store — Comedy

(Map p62; ☎0844 871 7699; www.thecomedy store.co.uk; 1a Oxendon St, SW1; admission £16.50-26; ⊖Piccadilly Circus) This was one of the first (and is still one of the best) comedy clubs in London. Wednesday and Sunday night's Comedy Store Players is the most famous improvisation outfit in town, with the wonderful Josie Lawrence; on Thursdays, Fridays and Saturdays Best in Stand Up features the best on London's comedy circuit.

Soho Theatre — Comedy

(Map p62; ☎020-7478 0100; www.sohotheatre. com; 21 Dean St, W1; £15-20; ⊖Tottenham Court Rd) The Soho Theatre has developed a superb reputation for showcasing new comedy-writing talent and comedians. It's also hosted some top-notch stand-up or sketch-based comedians including Alexei Sayle and Doctor Brown. Tickets cost between £10 and £20.

CINEMAS

Glitzy premieres usually take place in one of the mega multiplexes in Leicester Sq.

Electric Cinema — Cinema

(Map p76; ☎020-7908 9696; www.electric-cinema.co.uk; 191 Portobello Rd, W11; tickets £8-22.50; ⊖Ladbroke Grove) Having notched up its first centenary, the Electric is one of the UK's oldest cinemas, updated with luxurious leather armchairs, footstools, tables for food and drink in the auditorium, and the smart Electric Diner next door.

BFI Southbank — Cinema

(Map p62; ☎020-7928 3232; www.bfi.org.uk; Belvedere Rd, SE1; tickets £8-12; ⊙11am-11pm; ⊖Waterloo) Tucked almost out of sight under the arches of Waterloo Bridge is the British Film Institute, containing four cinemas that screen thousands of films each year (mostly arthouse), a gallery devoted to the moving image and the mediatheque, where you watch film and TV highlights from the BFI National Archive.

BFI IMAX Cinema — Cinema

(Map p62; www.bfi.org.uk/bfi-imax; 1 Charlie Chaplin Walk, SE1; adult/child from £9/5.75; ⊖Waterloo) The British Film Institute IMAX Cinema screens 2D and IMAX 3D documentaries about travel, space and wildlife,

Brick Lane

lasting anywhere from 40 minutes to 1½ hours, as well as recently released blockbusters à la IMAX.

Prince Charles
Cinema

(Map p62; www.princecharlescinema.com; 7 Leicester Pl, WC2; tickets £7.50-16; ⊖Leicester Sq) Ticket prices at Leicester Sq cinemas are highway robbery, so wait until the first-runs have moved to the Prince Charles, central London's cheapest cinema. This is where non-members pay only £8 to £10 for new releases. There are also mini-festivals, Q&As with film directors, old classics and, most famously, sing-along screenings of *Grease, The Sound of Music* and *Rocky Horror Picture Show*.

Shopping

From world-famous department stores to quirky backstreet retail revelations, London is a mecca for shoppers with an eye for style and a card to exercise.

WEST END

Oxford St is the place for High St fashion, while Regent St cranks it up a notch. Carnaby St is no way near the hip hub it was in the 1960s, but the lanes around it still have some interesting boutiques. Bond St has designers galore, Savile Row is all about bespoke tailoring and Jermyn St is the place for smart clobber (particularly shirts).

Selfridges
Department Store

(Map p76; www.selfridges.com; 400 Oxford St, W1; ◷9.30am-9pm Mon-Sat, 11.30am-6.15pm Sun; ⊖Bond St) Selfridges loves innovation – it's famed for its inventive window displays by international artists, gala shows and, above all, its amazing range of products. It's the trendiest of London's one-stop shops, with labels such as Boudicca, Luella Bartley, Emma Cook, Chloé and Missoni; an unparalleled food hall; and Europe's largest cosmetics department.

♥ If You Like...
Markets

1 **PORTOBELLO ROAD MARKET**
(Map p76; www.portobellomarket.org; Portobello Rd, W10; ◷8am-6.30pm Mon-Wed, Fri & Sat, to 1pm Thu; ⊖Notting Hill Gate, Ladbroke Grove) One of London's most famous street markets, in Notting Hill. New and vintage clothes are its main attraction, with antiques at its south end and food at the north.

2 **CAMDEN MARKET**
(Map p79; Camden High St, NW1; ◷10am-6pm; ⊖Camden Town, Chalk Farm) London's best-known street market, but the capital has lots more places to browse for bargains.

3 **COLUMBIA ROAD FLOWER MARKET**
(Map p70; Columbia Rd, E2; ◷8am-3pm Sun; ⊖Old St) The best place for East End barrow boy banter ('We got flowers cheap enough for ya muvver-in-law's grave'). Unmissable.

4 **BRICK LANE MARKET**
(Map p70; www.visitbricklane.org; Brick Lane, E1; ◷8am-2pm Sun; ⊖Liverpool St) An East End pearler, this is a sprawling bazaar featuring everything from fruit and veggies to paintings and bric-a-brac.

5 **GREENWICH MARKET**
(www.greenwichmarketlondon.com; College Approach, SE10; ◷10am-5.30pm; ⊠; ℝDLR Cutty Sark) Rummage through antiques, vintage clothing and collectables (Thursday and Friday), arts and crafts (Wednesday and weekends), or just chow down in the food section.

Fortnum & Mason
Department Store

(Map p62; www.fortnumandmason.com; 181 Piccadilly, W1; ◷10am-9pm Mon-Sat, noon-6pm Sun; ⊖Piccadilly Circus) London's oldest grocery store, now into its fourth century, refuses to yield to modern times. Its staff are still dressed in old-fashioned tailcoats and it keeps its glamorous food hall

supplied with hampers, cut marmalade, speciality teas and so on. Downstairs is an elegant wine bar as well as fine kitchenware, luxury gifts and perfumes.

Liberty — Department Store

(Map p62; www.liberty.co.uk; Great Marlborough St, W1; ⏰10am-8pm Mon-Sat, noon-6pm Sun; ⊖Oxford Circus) An irresistible blend of contemporary styles in an old-fashioned mock-Tudor atmosphere, Liberty has a huge cosmetics department and an accessories floor, along with a breathtaking lingerie section, all at very inflated prices. A classic London souvenir is a Liberty fabric print, especially in the form of a scarf.

Foyles — Books

(Map p62; www.foyles.co.uk; 107 Charing Cross Rd, WC2; ⏰9.30am-9pm Mon-Sat, 11.30am-6pm Sun; ⊖Tottenham Court Rd) This is London's most legendary bookshop, where you can bet on finding even the most obscure of titles. The lovely **cafe** is on the 1st floor where you'll also find **Grant & Cutler**, the UK's largest foreign-language bookseller. Ray's Jazz is up on the 5th floor.

Benjamin Pollock's Toy Shop — Toys

(Map p62; www.pollocks-coventgarden.co.uk; 1st fl, 44 Market Bldg, Covent Garden, WC2; ⏰10.30am-6pm Mon-Sat, 11am-4pm Sun; ⊖Covent Garden) Here's a traditional toyshop stuffed with the things that kids of all ages love. There are Victorian paper theatres, wooden marionettes and finger puppets, and antique teddy bears that might be too fragile to play with.

KNIGHTSBRIDGE, KENSINGTON & CHELSEA

Harrods — Department Store

(Map p76; www.harrods.com; 87 Brompton Rd, SW1; ⏰10am-8pm Mon-Sat, 11.30am-6pm Sun; ⊖Knightsbridge) Both garish and stylish at the same time, perennially crowded Harrods is an obligatory stop for London's tourists, from the cash strapped to the big, big spenders. The stock is astonishing and you'll swoon over the spectacular food hall.

Harvey Nichols
Department Store

(Map p76; www.harveynichols.com;
109-125 Knightsbridge, SW1; ⏰10am-8pm
Mon-Sat, 11.30am-6pm Sun; ⊖Knightsbridge)
At London's temple of high fashion, you'll
find Chloé and Balenciaga bags, the city's
best denim range, a massive make-up hall
with exclusive lines, great jewellery and
the fantastic restaurant, Fifth Floor.

ℹ️ Information

Dangers & Annoyances

Considering its size and wealth disparities,
London is generally safe. That said, keep your
wits about you and don't flash your cash
unnecessarily. When travelling by tube, choose a
carriage with other people in it and avoid deserted
suburban stations. Following reports of robberies
and sexual attacks, shun unlicensed or unbooked
minicabs.

Watch out for pickpockets on crowded tube
trains, night buses and streets.

When using ATMs, guard your PIN details
carefully. Don't use an ATM that looks like it's

been tampered with as there have been incidents
of card cloning.

Internet Resources

Evening Standard (www.standard.co.uk)

Londonist (www.londonist.com) London-centric
blog.

Time Out (www.timeout.com/london)

View London (www.viewlondon.co.uk)

Media

Two free newspapers bookend the working day –
Metro in the morning and the *Evening Standard* in
the evening – both available from tube stations.
Published every Wednesday, *Time Out* (also free)
is the local listing guide par excellence.

Toilets

If you're caught short around London, public
toilets can be elusive. Only a handful of tube
stations have them, but the bigger National Rail
stations usually do (often coin operated). If you

London's Oyster Diet

To get the most out of London, you need to be able to jump on and off public transport like a local, not scramble to buy a ticket at hefty rates each time. The best and cheapest way to do this is with an Oyster card, a reusable smartcard on which you can load prepaid credit or Travelcards, valid for periods from a day to a year. The card itself is £5, which is fully refundable when you leave.

London is divided into concentric transport zones, although most visitor destinations are in Zones 1 and 2. Travelcard tickets will give you unlimited transport on the tube, buses and rail services within these zones. All you need to do is touch your card to the yellow sensors on the station turnstiles or at the front of the bus.

For pay as you go, the fare will be deducted from the credit on your card at a much lower rate than if you were buying a one-off paper ticket. An oyster bus trip costs £1.45 as opposed to £2.40 for an individual fare, while a Zone 1 tube journey is £2.20 as opposed to £4.70. Even better, in any single day your fares will be capped at the equivalent of the Oyster day-pass rate for the zones you've travelled in (Zones 1-2 peak/off-peak £8.40/7).

---

can face five floors on an escalator, department stores are a good bet.

Tourist Information

City of London Information Centre (Map p70; www.visitthecity.co.uk; St Paul's Churchyard, EC4; ◷9.30am-5.30pm Mon-Sat, 10am-4pm Sun; ⊖St Paul's) Tourist information, fast-track tickets to City attractions and guided walks (adult/child £6/4).

🛈 Getting There & Away

Air

There are a number of London airports; see Getting Around for details.

Bus

Most long-distance coaches leave London from Victoria Coach Station.

Train

London's main-line terminals are all linked by the tube and each serve different destinations. Most stations have left-luggage facilities (around £4) and lockers, toilets (20p) with showers (around £3), newsstands and bookshops, and a range of eating and drinking outlets.

○ **Charing Cross** Canterbury.

○ **Euston** Manchester, Liverpool, Carlisle, Glasgow.

○ **King's Cross** Cambridge, Hull, York, Newcastle, Scotland.

○ **Liverpool Street** Stansted airport, Cambridge.

○ **London Bridge** Gatwick airport, Brighton.

○ **Marylebone** Birmingham.

○ **Paddington** Heathrow airport, Oxford, Bath, Bristol, Exeter, Plymouth, Cardiff.

○ **St Pancras** Gatwick and Luton airports, Brighton, Nottingham, Sheffield, Leicester, Leeds, Paris.

○ **Victoria** Gatwick airport, Brighton, Canterbury.

○ **Waterloo** Windsor, Winchester, Exeter, Plymouth.

🛈 Getting Around

To/From the Airports

Gatwick

Main-line trains run every 15 minutes between Gatwick's South Terminal and Victoria (from £15, 37 minutes), hourly at night, or to/from St Pancras (from £10, 56 minutes) via London Bridge, City Thameslink, Blackfriars and Farringdon.

Gatwick Express (www.gatwickexpress.com; one way/return £19.90/34.90) trains run to/from Victoria every 15 minutes from 5am to 11.45pm (first/last train 3.30am/12.32am).

The **EasyBus** (www.easybus.co.uk; one way **£10, return from £12**) minibus service between Gatwick and Earl's Court (every 30 minutes from 4.25am to 1am, about 1¼ hours) can cost as little as £2, depending on when you book. You're charged extra if you have more than one carry-on and one check-in bag.

Heathrow

The cheapest option from Heathrow is to take the underground (tube). The Piccadilly line is accessible from every terminal (£5.70, one hour to central London, departing from Heathrow every five minutes from around 5am to 11.30pm).

Faster, and much more expensive, is the Heathrow Express train to Paddington station (15 minutes, every 15 minutes 5.12am to 11.48pm). You can purchase tickets on board (£5 extra), from self-service machines (cash and credit cards accepted) at both stations, or online.

There are taxi ranks for black cabs outside every terminal; a fare to the centre of London will cost between £45 and £85.

London City

The Docklands Light Railway connects London City Airport to the tube network, taking 22 minutes to reach Bank station (£4.70). A black taxi costs around £30 to/from central London.

Stansted

The Stansted Express connects with Liverpool Street station (one way/return £23.40/33.20, 46 minutes, every 15 to 30 minutes 6am to 12.30am).

A taxi cab to/from central London costs about £100 to £110.

Bicycle

Operating 24 hours a day and already clocking in over 11 million cycle hires, the excellent **Barclays Cycle Hire Scheme** (www.tfl. gov.uk) allows you to hire a bike from one of 400 docking stations around London. The access fee is £2 for 24 hours or £10 per week; after that, the first 30 minutes is free (making the bikes perfect for short

hops), or £1/4/6/15 for one hour/90 minutes/two hours/three hours.

Car

London's streets can be congested beyond belief. If you drive into central London from 7am to 6pm on a weekday, you'll need to pay a £10 per day congestion charge (visit www.tfl.gov.uk for payment options) or face a hefty fine. If you're hiring a car to continue your trip from London, take the tube to Heathrow and pick it up from there.

Public Transport

TFL (www.tfl.gov.uk), the city's public transport provider, is the glue that binds the network together.

Boat

Passengers with daily, weekly or monthly travelcards (including an Oyster) get a third off all fares.

Thames Clippers runs regular commuter services between Embankment, Waterloo, Blackfriars, Bankside, London Bridge, Tower, Canary Wharf, Greenwich, North Greenwich and Woolwich piers (adult/child £6.80/3.40)

Harrod's (p102), Knightsbridge
TRAVELPIX LTD/GETTY IMAGES ©

from 6am to between 10pm and midnight (from 9.30am weekends).

Leisure services include the Tate Boat (p73) and Westminster–Greenwich services. There are also boats to Kew Gardens and Hampton Court Palace.

Bus

Travelling around London by double-decker bus is a great way to get a feel for the city, but it's usually slower than the tube. Heritage 'Routemaster' buses with conductors operate on route 9 (from Aldwych to Royal Albert Hall) and 15 (between Trafalgar Sq and Tower Hill); these are the only buses without wheelchair access. A new fleet of freshly designed hybrid diesel/electric hop-on/hop-off (and wheelchair-accessible) Routemasters is now running on some routes.

Buses run regularly during the day, while less frequent night buses (prefixed with the letter 'N') wheel into action when the tube stops. Single-journey bus tickets (valid for two hours) cost £2.40 (£1.40 on Oyster, capped at £4.40 per day); a weekly pass is £20.20. Buses stop on request, so clearly signal the driver with an outstretched arm.

London Underground, DLR & Overground

'The tube', as it's universally known, extends its subterranean tentacles throughout London and into the surrounding counties, with services running every few minutes from roughly 5.30am to 12.30am (from 7am to 11.30pm Sunday). The DLR links the City to Docklands, Greenwich and London City Airport.

Taxi

London's famous black cabs are available for hire when the yellow light above the windscreen is lit. Fares are metered, with flag fall of £2.40 and the additional rate dependent on time of day, distance travelled and taxi speed. A one-mile trip will cost between £5.60 and £8.80. To order a black cab by phone, try **Computer Cabs** (cash 020-7908 0207, credit card 020-7432 1432; www.comcablondon.com); they charge a £2 booking fee.

Licensed minicabs operate via agencies (most busy areas have a walk-in office with drivers waiting). They're a cheaper alternative to black cabs and quote trip fares in advance. To find a local minicab firm, visit www.tfl.gov.uk.

AROUND LONDON

Canterbury

POP 43,400

Canterbury tops the charts for English cathedral cities and is one of southern England's top attractions. Many consider the World Heritage listed cathedral that dominates its centre to be one of Europe's finest, and the town's narrow medieval alleyways, riverside gardens and ancient city walls are a joy to explore.

Stained glass window showing Thomas Becket, Canterbury Cathedral
NEIL HOLMES/GETTY IMAGES ©

Canterbury

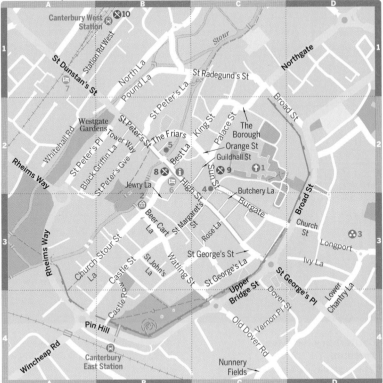

⊙ Sights

Canterbury Cathedral   Cathedral
(www.canterbury-cathedral.org; adult/concession £10.50/9.50, tour adult/concession £5/4, audio tour adult/concession £4/3; ⊗9am-5pm Mon-Sat, 12.30pm-2.30pm Sun) A rich repository of more than 1400 years of Christian history, the Church of England's mother ship is a truly extraordinary place with an absorbing history. This Gothic cathedral, the highlight of the city's World Heritage Sites, is southeast England's top tourist attraction as well as a place of worship. It's also the site of English history's most famous murder: Archbishop Thomas Becket was done in here in 1170. Allow at least two hours to do the cathedral justice.

Canterbury Heritage Museum
Museum

(www.canterbury-museums.co.uk; Stour St; adult/child £8/free; ⊙11am-5pm daily) This fine 14th-century building, once the Poor Priests' Hospital, now houses the city's captivating museum. It contains a jumble of exhibits ranging from pre-Roman times to the assassination of Thomas Becket, and from the likes of Joseph Conrad to locally born celebs. The kids' room is excellent, with a memorable glimpse of real medieval poo among other fun activities. Train fans can admire the *Invicta* locomotive, which ran on the world's third passenger railway, the 'Crab & Winkle' Canterbury–Whitstable line.

St Augustine's Abbey
Ruin

(EH; Longport; adult/child £5/3; ⊙10am-6pm Jul & Aug, to 5pm Wed-Sun Apr-Jun & Sep-Oct, 10am-4pm Sat & Sun Nov-Mar) An integral but often overlooked part of the Canterbury World Heritage Site, St Augustine's Abbey was founded in AD 597, marking the rebirth of Christianity in southern England.

Later requisitioned as a royal palace, it fell into disrepair and now only stumpy foundations remain. A small museum and a worthwhile free audio tour do their best to underline the site's importance and put flesh back onto its now-humble bones.

👉 Tours

Canterbury Historic River Tours
Boat Tour

(☎07790 534744; www.canterburyrivertours.co.uk; Kings Bridge; adult/child £8.50/5; ⊙10am-5pm Mar-Oct) Knowledgeable guides double up as energetic oars on these fascinating River Stour mini cruises, which depart from behind the Old Weaver's House.

Canterbury Guided Tours
Walking Tour

(☎01227-459779; www.canterburyguided-tours.com; adult/child/concession £7/5/6.50; ⊙11am Feb-Oct, 11am & 2pm Jul-Sep) Guided walking tours leave from opposite the

Left: Canterbury Cathedral (p107); **Below:** Cobbled street, Canterbury

(LEFT) LISA VALDER/GETTY IMAGES ©; (BELOW) VISITBRITAIN/DANIEL BOSWORTH/GETTY IMAGES ©

Canturbury Cathedral entrance. Tickets can be purchased from the tourist office.

🛏 Sleeping

House of Agnes
Hotel **££**

(☎ 01227-472185; www.houseofagnes.co.uk; 71 St Dunstan's St; r £85-130; @ 🛜) This rather wonky 13th-century beamed inn, mentioned in Dickens' *David Copperfield,* has eight themed rooms bearing names such as 'Marrakesh' (Moorish), 'Venice' (carnival masks), 'Boston' (light and airy) and 'Canterbury' (antiques and heavy fabrics). If you prefer your room to have straight lines and right angles, there are eight less exciting, but no less comfortable, rooms in an annexe in the walled garden.

ABode Canterbury
Hotel **£££**

(☎ 01227-766266; www.abodecanterbury. co.uk; 30-33 High St; r from £143; 🛜) The 72 rooms at this supercentral hotel, the only boutique hotel in town, are graded from 'comfortable' to 'fabulous', and for the most part live up to their names. They come with features such as handmade beds, cashmere throws, velour bathrobes, beautiful modern bathrooms and little tuckboxes of locally produced snacks. There's a splendid champagne bar, restaurant and tavern, too.

🍴 Eating

Boho
International **£**

(43 St Peter's St; snacks £4-14; ⏰ 9am-6pm Mon-Sat, 10am-5pm Sun) This hip eatery in a prime spot on the main drag is extraordinarily popular and you'll be lucky to get a table on busy shopping days. Cool tunes lilt through the chic retro dining space while chilled diners chow down on humungous burgers, full-monty breakfasts and imaginative, owner-cooked international mains. Boho doesn't do bookings, so be prepared to queue.

Canterbury Attractions Passport

The **Canterbury Attractions Passport** (adult/child £28/13) gives entry to the cathedral, St Augustine's Abbey, the Canterbury Tales and any one of the city's museums. It's available from the tourist office.

Deeson's
British ££

(☎ 01227-767854; 25-27 Sun St; mains £6-16; ⊙noon-3pm & 5-10pm Mon-Sat, noon-10pm Sun) Put the words 'local', 'seasonal' and 'tasty' together and you have this superb British eatery. Local fruit and veg; award-winning wines, beers and ciders; fish from Kent's coastal waters; and the odd ingredient from the proprietor's own allotment are all served in a straightforward, contemporary setting just a Kentish apple's throw from the Canterbury Cathedral gates.

Goods Shed
Market, Restaurant ££

(www.thegoodsshed.co.uk; Station Rd West; mains £12-20; ⊙market 9am-7pm Tue-Sat, 10am-4pm Sun, restaurant 8am-9.30pm Tue-Sat, 9am-3pm Sun) Farmers market, food hall and fabulous restaurant rolled into one, this converted warehouse by the Canterbury West train station is a hit with everyone from self-caterers to sit-down gourmets. The chunky wooden tables sit slightly above the market hubbub but in full view of its appetite-whetting stalls, and daily specials exploit the freshest farm goodies England has to offer.

Information

Tourist Office (☎ 01227-378100; www.canterbury.co.uk; 18 High St; ⊙9am-5pm Mon-Wed, Fri & Sat, to 7pm Thu, 10am-5pm Sun) Located in the Beaney House of Art & Knowledge. Staff can help book accommodation, excursions and theatre tickets.

Getting There & Away

There are two train stations, Canterbury East for London Victoria and Canterbury West for London's Charing Cross and St Pancras stations.

Train

Canterbury connections:

Dover Priory £8, 25 minutes, every 30 minutes

London St Pancras High-speed service, £34, 1 hour, hourly

London Victoria/Charing Cross £28.40, 1¾ hours, two to three hourly

ⓘ Getting Around

Car parks are dotted along and just inside the walls, but to avoid heavy traffic day trippers may prefer to use one of three Park & Ride sites, which cost £3 per day and connect to the centre by bus every eight minutes (7am to 7.30pm Monday to Saturday).

Leeds Castle

For many people, the immense moated **Leeds Castle** (www.leeds-castle.com; adult/child £21/13.50; ⊙10am-6pm Apr-Sep, to 5pm Oct-Mar) is the world's most romantic castle, and it's certainly one of the most-visited in Britain.

The castle was transformed over the centuries from fortress to lavish palace. Its last owner, the high-society hostess Lady Baillie, modernised some rooms for use as a princely family home and party pad, to entertain the likes of Errol Flynn, Douglas Fairbanks and JFK. Highlights include Queen Eleanor's medieval bathroom, King Henry VIII's ebony-floored banqueting hall and the boardroom where, in 1978, Israeli and Egyptian negotiators met for talks prior to the Camp David Accords. Since Lady Baillie's death in 1974, a private trust has managed the property.

The castle's vast estate offers enough attractions of its own to justify a day trip: peaceful walks, an aviary, falconry demonstrations and a restaurant. You'll also find plenty of kiddie and toddler attractions, as well as a hedge maze, overseen by a grassy bank from where fellow travellers can shout encouragement or misdirections.

Leeds Castle is just east of Maidstone. Trains run from London Victoria to Bearsted (£21, one hour) and from there you catch a special shuttle coach to the castle (£5 return) between March and October and on winter weekends.

The White Cliffs of Dover

Immortalised in song, literature and film, these resplendent cliffs are embedded in the British national consciousness, acting as a big, white 'Welcome Home' sign to generations of travellers and soldiers.

The **cliffs** rise 100m high and extend 10 miles either side of Dover, but it is the 6-mile stretch east of town – properly known as the Langdon Cliffs – that especially captivates visitors' imaginations. The chalk here is about 250m deep and the cliffs are about half a million years old, formed when the melting icecaps of northern Europe gouged a channel between France and England.

The Langdon Cliffs are managed by the National Trust, which has a **tourist office** (☏01304-202756; ⊗10am-5pm Mar-Oct, 11am-4pm Nov-Feb) and **car park** (nonmembers per park per day £3) 2 miles east of Dover along Castle Hill Rd and the A258 road to Deal, or off the A2 past the Eastern Docks.

To see the cliffs in all their full-frontal glory, **Dover White Cliffs Tours** (☏01303-271388; www.doverwhiteclifftours.com; adult/child £10/5; ⊗daily Jul & Aug, Sat & Sun Apr-Jun & Sep-Oct) runs 40-minute sightseeing trips at least three times daily from the Western Docks.

Brighton & Hove

POP 247,800

Raves on the beach, Graham Greene novels, mods and rockers in bank-holiday fisticuffs, naughty weekends for Mr and Mrs Smith, classic car runs from London, the United Kingdom's biggest gay scene and the Channel's best clubbing – this city by the sea evokes many images for the British. One thing is certain: with its bohemian, cosmopolitan, hedonistic vibe, Brighton is where England's seaside experience goes from cold to cool.

Brighton Pier (p113)

Brighton & Hove

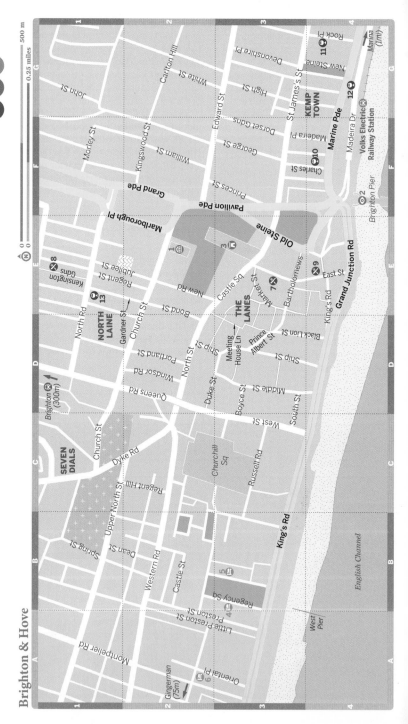

Brighton & Hove

N

0   500 m
0   0.25 miles

SEVEN DIALS

NORTH LAINE

THE LANES

KEMP TOWN

English Channel

West Pier

Brighton Pier

Marina (1ml)

Volks Electric Railway Station

Brighton (300m)

Gingerman (75m)

Brighton & Hove

Sights

Royal Pavilion
Palace

(www.royalpavilion.org.uk; Royal Pavilion Gardens; adult/child £11/6; ⏰9.30am-5.45pm Apr-Sep, 10am-5.15pm Oct-Mar) The city's must-see attraction is the Royal Pavilion, the glittering party pad and palace of Prince George, later Prince Regent and then King George IV. It's one of the most opulent buildings in England, certainly the finest example of early-19th-century chinoiserie anywhere in Europe and an apt symbol of Brighton's reputation for decadence. An unimpressed Queen Victoria called the Royal Pavilion 'a strange, odd Chinese place', but for visitors to Brighton it's an unmissable chunk of Sussex history.

Brighton Museum & Art Gallery
Museum, Gallery

(www.brighton-hove-museums.org.uk; Royal Pavilion Gardens; ⏰10am-5pm Tue-Sun) FREE Set in the Royal Pavilion's renovated stable block, this museum and art gallery has a glittering collection of 20th-century art and design, including a crimson Salvador Dalí sofa modelled on Mae West's lips. There's also an enthralling gallery of world art, an impressive collection of Egyptian artefacts, and an 'images of Brighton' multimedia exhibit containing a series of oral histories and a model of the defunct West Pier.

Brighton Pier
Landmark

(www.brightonpier.co.uk; Madeira Dr) This grand century-old pier is the place to experience Brighton's tackier side. There are plenty of stomach-churning fairground rides and dingy amusement arcades to keep you amused, and candy floss and Brighton rock to chomp on while you're doing so.

Look west and you'll see the sad remains of the **West Pier**, a skeletal iron hulk that attracts flocks of starlings at sunset. It's a sad end for this Victorian marvel, where the likes of Charlie Chaplin and Stan Laurel once performed.

Festivals & Events

There's always something fun going on in Brighton, from **Brighton Pride** (www.brighton-pride.org; ⏰early Aug) to food and drink festivals. The showpiece is May's three-week-long **Brighton Festival** (☎01273-709709; www.brightonfestival.org; ⏰May). The biggest arts festival in Britain after Edinburgh, it draws theatre, dance, music and comedy performers from around the globe.

🛏 Sleeping

Despite a glut of hotels in Brighton, prices are relatively high and you'd be wise to book well ahead for summer weekends and for the Brighton Festival in May. Expect to pay up to a third more across the board at weekends.

Hotel Pelirocco
Hotel ££

(☎01273-327055; www.hotelpelirocco.co.uk; 10 Regency Sq; s £59-75, d £109-155; 🛜) One of Brighton's sexiest and nuttiest places to stay, the Pelirocco has become the ultimate venue for a flirty rock-and-roll weekend. Flamboyant rooms, some designed by artists, include the Soviet-chic room with vodka bottles frozen into the walls, the Pin-up Parlour dedicated to Diana Dors, and the Pretty Vacant double, a shrine to the Sex Pistols.

Gay & Lesbian Brighton

Perhaps it's Brighton's longtime association with the theatre but the city has been a gay haven for more than 100 years. With upwards of 25,000 gay men and about 15,000 lesbians living here, it is the most vibrant queer community in the country outside London.

Kemptown (aka Camptown), on and off St James' St, is where it's all at. The old Brunswick Town area of Hove is a quieter alternative to the traditionally cruisy (and sometimes seedy) scene in Kemptown.

For up-to-date information on gay Brighton, check out www.gay.brighton.co.uk and www.realbrighton.com, or pick up the free monthly magazine *Gscene* (www.gscene.com) from gay venues.

Neo Hotel
Boutique Hotel **££**

(☏01273-711104; www.neohotel.com; 19 Oriental Pl; s incl breakfast £55-65, d incl breakfast £100-150; ☎) You won't be surprised to learn the owner of this gorgeous hotel is an interior stylist. The nine rooms could have dropped straight from the pages of a design magazine, each finished in rich colours and tactile fabrics, with bold floral and Asian motifs, and black-tiled bathrooms. Wonderful breakfasts include homemade smoothies and pancakes.

Snooze
Hotel **££**

(☏01273-605797; www.snoozebrighton.com; 25 St George's Tce; s/d from £55/65; ☎) The retro styling at this eccentric Kemptown pad features everything from vintage posters and bright '60s and '70s wallpaper to Bollywood film posters, floral sinks and mad clashes of colour. It's more than just a gimmick – the rooms are comfortable and spotless, and there are great meat-free breakfasts. You'll find it just off St James' St, about 500m east of New Steine.

Hotel Una
Boutique Hotel **£££**

(☏01273-820464; www.hotel-una.co.uk; 55-56 Regency Sq; s incl breakfast £55-75, d incl breakfast £115-200; ❄☎) All of the 19 generous rooms here wow guests with their bold-patterned fabrics, supersized leather sofas, in-room free-standing baths and vegan/veggie/carnivorous breakfast in bed. Some, such as the two-level suite with its own mini-cinema, and the under-pavement chambers with their own spa and Jacuzzi, are truly show-stopping and not as expensive as you might expect.

Eating

Iydea
Vegetarian **£**

(www.iydea.co.uk; 17 Kensington Gardens; mains £6-7.50; ⏰9.30am-5.30pm Mon-Sat, from 10am Sun; ☎✎) Even by Brighton's lofty standards, the food at this award-winning vegetarian cafe is a treat. The daily changing choices of curries, lasagnes, falafel, enchiladas and quiches are full of flavour and can be washed down with a selection of vegan wines, organic ales and homemade lemonades. If you're on the hop, you can get any dish to takeaway in environmentally friendly packaging.

Terre à Terre
Vegetarian **££**

(☏01273-729051; www.terreaterre.co.uk; 71 East St; mains £15; ⏰noon-10.30pm Mon-Fri, 11am-11pm Sat, to 10pm Sun; ✎) Even staunch meat-eaters will rave about this legendary vegetarian restaurant. A sublime dining experience, from the vibrant modern space to the entertaining menus and inventive dishes stuffed with excitingly zingy ingredients. There's also plenty for vegans. Desserts are on the steep side.

English's Oyster Bar
Seafood **££**

(www.englishs.co.uk; 29-31 East St; mains £9-30; ⏰noon-10.15pm Mon-Sat, 12.30-4pm Sun) An almost 70-year-old institution and celebrity haunt, this Brightonian seafood paradise dishes up everything from Essex oysters to locally caught lobster and Dover sole. It's converted from fishers' cottages, with shades of the elegant

Edwardian era inside and alfresco dining on the pedestrian square outside.

Gingerman
Modern European £££

(☎ 01273-326688; 21a Norfolk Sq; 2-/3-course menu £15/18; ⏱ 12.30-2pm & 7-10pm Tue-Sun) Hastings seafood, Sussex beef, Romney Marsh lamb, local sparkling wines and countless other seasonal, local and British treats go into the adroitly flash-fried and slow-cooked dishes served at this snug 32-cover eatery. Reservations are advised. Norfolk Sq is a short walk west along Western Rd from the Churchill Square shopping centre.

🍷 Drinking & Nightlife

Outside London, Brighton's nightlife is the best in the south, with its unique mix of seafront clubs and bars. When Britain's top DJs aren't plying their trade in London, Ibiza or Ayia Napa, chances are you'll spy them here. All of Brighton's clubs open until 2am, and many as late as 5am.

Brighton Rocks
Bar

(www.brightonrocksbar.co.uk; 6 Rock Pl; ⏱ 4-11pm Mon-Thu, to 1am Sat, from noon Sun; 🛜) Incongruously located in an alley of ga-

rages and used-car lots, this cocktail bar is firmly established on the Kemptown gay scene, but welcomes all-comers with 'Shocktails', a 'grazing' menu and theme parties.

Dorset
Pub

(www.thedorset.co.uk; 28 North Rd; ⏱ 9am-late; 🛜) In fine weather this laid-back Brighton institution throws open its doors and windows, and tables spill out onto the pavement. You'll be just as welcome for a morning coffee as for an evening pint here, and should you not leave between the two, there's a decent gastropub menu.

Concorde 2
Club

(www.concorde2.co.uk; Madeira Dr) Brighton's best-known and best-loved club is a disarmingly unpretentious den, where DJ Fatboy Slim pioneered the Big Beat Boutique and still occasionally graces the decks. Each month there's a huge variety of club nights, live bands and concerts by international names.

Audio
Club

(www.audiobrighton.com; 10 Marine Pde) Some of the city's top club nights are held at

Shopping at a gallery in Brighton

115

this ear-numbing venue. The music's top priority here, attracting a young, up-for-it crowd.

ℹ Information

Visit Brighton (☎ 01273-290337; www. visitbrighton.com) There's no tourist office but you can still call or log on for information.

ℹ Getting There & Away

Brighton is 53 miles from London and transport between the two is fast and frequent. If arriving by car, parking is plentiful but pricey, and the city-centre traffic, bus-clogged lanes and road layouts are confusing.

Train

All London-bound services pass through Gatwick Airport (£9.80, 25 to 40 minutes, up to five hourly).

London St Pancras £22.40, 1¼ hours, half-hourly

London Victoria £24, 50 minutes, three-hourly

ℹ Getting Around

Most of Brighton can be covered on foot. The city operates a pay-and-display parking scheme. In the town centre, it's usually £3.50 per hour for a maximum stay of two hours.

Cab companies include **Brighton Streamline Taxis** (☎ 01273-202020) and **City Cabs** (☎ 01273-205205), and there's a taxi rank at the junction of East St and Market St.

Windsor & Eton

POP 33,400

Dominated by the massive bulk of Windsor Castle, these twin towns have a rather surreal atmosphere, with the morning

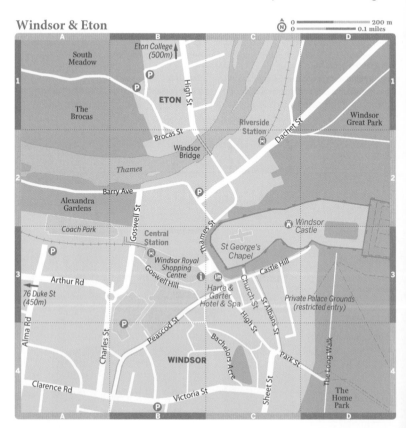

Windsor & Eton

DEREK CROUCHER/GETTY IMAGES ©

pomp and ceremony of the changing of the guards in Windsor, and the sight of school boys dressed in formal tailcoats wandering the streets of tiny Eton.

Sights

Windsor Castle   Castle, Palace
(www.royalcollection.org.uk; Castle Hill; adult/child £19/11; ⊗9.45am-5.15pm) The largest and oldest occupied fortress in the world, Windsor Castle is a majestic vision of battlements and towers. It's used for state occasions and is one of the Queen's principal residences; if she's at home, you'll see the Royal Standard flying from the Round Tower. Join a free guided tour (every half-hour) or take a multilingual audio tour of the lavish state rooms and beautiful chapels. Note, some sections may be off-limits on any given day if they're in use.

Eton College   Notable Building
(www.etoncollege.com) Eton is the largest and most famous public (meaning very private) school in England, and arguably the most enduring and illustrious symbol of England's class system. At the time

of writing, it wasn't possible to visit the school due to building work, but check the visitors tab on the website to see whether tours have resumed.

Sleeping

Windsor and Eton are easily doable as a day trip from London. If you wish to remain after the hordes of visitors have gone home, there's a good selection of quality hotels and B&Bs, but few budget options.

**Harte & Garter
Hotel & Spa**   Hotel ££
(☏01753-863426; www.foliohotels.com/harteandgarter; High St; d from £99; 🛜)
Right opposite the castle, this Victorian hotel blends period style with modern furnishings. High ceilings, giant fireplaces, decorative cornices and dark woods seamlessly combine with contemporary fabrics, plasma-screen TVs and tradi-tional, cast-iron baths. Some rooms enjoy wonderful views over the castle and all guests can enjoy the luxurious spa in the converted stable block.

117

76 Duke Street
B&B ££

(☎01753-620636; www.76dukestreet.co.uk; 76 Duke St; s/d £85/100; ☎) Presided over by a welcoming hostess, this centrally located B&B offers two immaculate double rooms. The second bedroom is only available if booked along with the first, so it's ideal for a family or two couples.

❶ Information

Royal Windsor Information Centre (www.windsor.gov.uk; Old Booking Hall, Windsor Royal Shopping Arcade; ☉9.30am-5pm) Pick up a heritage walk brochure (50p).

❶ Getting There & Away

Trains from Windsor Central station go to Slough, with regular connections to **London Paddington** (30 to 45 minutes). Trains from Windsor Riverside station go to **London Waterloo** (one hour). Services run half-hourly from both and tickets cost £8.50.

Cambridge

POP 123,900

Abounding with exquisite architecture, steeped in history and tradition and renowned for its quirky rituals, Cambridge is a university town extraordinaire. The tightly packed core of ancient colleges, the picturesque 'Backs' (college gardens) leading on to the river and the leafy green meadows that seem to surround the city give it a far more tranquil appeal than its historic rival Oxford.

The first Cambridge college, Peterhouse (never Peterhouse College), was founded in 1284, and in 1318 the papal bull by Pope John XXII declared Cambridge to be an official university.

◉ Sights

Most colleges close to visitors for the Easter term and all are closed for exams from mid-May to mid-June. Also, opening hours vary from day to day, so if you have your heart set on visiting a particular college, contact it for information in advance to avoid disappointment.

CAMBRIDGE UNIVERSITY

King's College Chapel
Chapel

(☎01223-331212; www.kings.cam.ac.uk/chapel; King's Pde; adult/child £7.50/free; ☉non-term 9.45am-4.30pm, term 9.45am-3.15pm Mon-Sat, 1.15-2.30pm Sun) In a city crammed with show-stopping buildings, this is the scene-stealer. Grandiose, 16th-century King's College Chapel is one of England's most extraordinary examples of Gothic architecture. Its inspirational, intricate 80m-long, fan-vaulted ceiling is the world's largest and soars upwards before exploding into a series of stone fireworks. This hugely atmospheric space is a fitting stage for the chapel's world-famous choir; hear it in full voice during the magnificent, free, evensong (in term time only – 5.30pm Monday to Saturday, 10.30am and 3.30pm Sunday).

Cambridge

Trinity College

College

(www.trin.cam.ac.uk; Trinity St; adult/child £2/1;
⏰10am-4.30pm, closed early-Apr-mid-Jun) The
largest of Cambridge's colleges, Trinity
offers an extraordinary Tudor gateway, an
air of supreme elegance and a sweeping
Great Court – the largest of its kind in the
world. It also boasts the renowned and
suitably musty **Wren Library** (⏰noon-
2pm Mon-Fri), containing 55,000 books
dated before 1820 and more than 2500
manuscripts. Works include those by

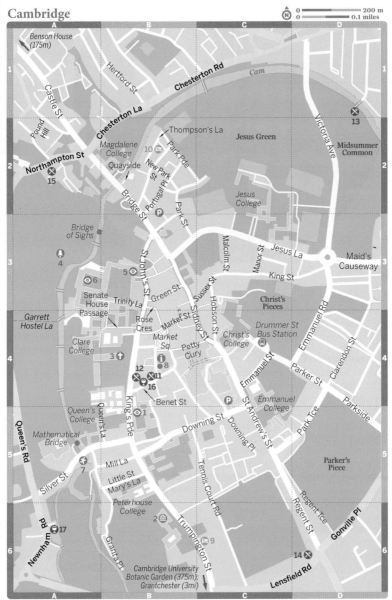

Cambridge

0 ————— 200 m
0 ————— 0.1 miles

Benson House
(175m)

Hertford St

Chesterton Rd

Cam

Castle St

Pound Hill

Chesterton La

Thompson's La

Jesus Green

Victoria Ave

13

Magdalene
College

10

Park Pde

Northampton St

15

Quayside

New Park St

Portugal Pl

Midsummer
Common

Bridge St

Park St

Jesus
College

Bridge
of Sighs

4

Senate
House
Passage

6

St John's St

Green St

Malcolm St

Manor St

Jesus La

King St

Maid's
Causeway

5

Trinity La

Garrett
Hostel La

Clare
College

3

Rose
Cres

Market St

Sidney St

Sussex St

Hobson St

Christ's
Pieces

Drummer St
Bus Station

Emmanuel Rd

Clarendon St

Market
Sq

Petty
Cury

Christ's
College

Emmanuel St

Parker St

Parkside

8

12
16

11

Benet St

Queen's
College

Mathematical
Bridge

Queen's Rd

7

Silver St

King's Pde

1

Downing St

Downing Pl

St Andrew's St

Emmanuel
College

Park Tce

Mill La

Little St
Mary's La

Tennis Court Rd

Parker's
Piece

Peterhouse
College

2

Trumpington St

9

Regent Tce

Regent St

Gonville Pl

Newnham Rd

17

Grantа Pl

Cambridge University
Botanic Garden (375m);
Grantchester (3mi)

14

Lensfield Rd

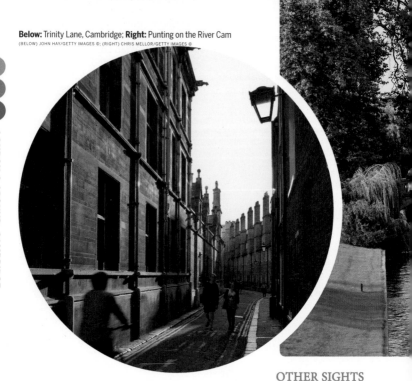

Below: Trinity Lane, Cambridge; **Right:** Punting on the River Cam
(BELOW) JOHN HAY/GETTY IMAGES ©; (RIGHT) CHRIS MELLOR/GETTY IMAGES ©

Shakespeare, St Jerome, Newton and Swift – and AA Milne's original *Winnie the Pooh;* both Milne and his son, Christopher Robin, were graduates

Corpus Christi College   College

(www.corpus.cam.ac.uk; King's Pde; admission £2.50; ⊙10.30am-4.30pm mid-Jun–Sep, 2-4pm Oct–early-Apr) One of Cambridge's ancient colleges, Corpus Christi was founded in 1352, a heritage reflected in its exquisite buildings – a monastic atmosphere still radiates from the medieval **Old Court**. Look out for the fascinating sundial and plaque to playwright and past student Christopher Marlowe (1564–93), author of *Doctor Faustus* and *Tamburlaine*. New Court (a mere 200 years old) leads to the **Parker Library**, which holds the world's finest collection of Anglo-Saxon manuscripts (open Thursday afternoons to tourist office–run tours).

OTHER SIGHTS

The Backs   Park

Behind the Cambridge colleges' grandiose facades and stately courts, a series of gardens and parks line up beside the river. Collectively known as the Backs, the tranquil green spaces and shimmering waters offer unparalleled views of the colleges and are often the most enduring image of Cambridge for visitors. The picture-postcard snapshots of college life and graceful bridges can be seen from the riverside pathways and pedestrian bridges – or the comfort of a chauffeur-driven punt.

Fitzwilliam Museum   Museum

(www.fitzmuseum.cam.ac.uk; Trumpington St; donation requested; ⊙10am-5pm Tue-Sat, noon-5pm Sun) FREE Fondly dubbed 'the Fitz' by locals, this colossal neoclassical pile was one of the first public art museums in Britain, built to house the fabulous treasures that the seventh Viscount Fitzwilliam bequeathed to his old university. Expect Roman and Egyptian grave goods, art-

works by many of the great masters and some more quirky collections: banknotes, literary autographs, watches and armour.

Activities

Punt hire costs £14 to £16 per hour, chauffeured trips of the Backs cost £10 to £12, and a return trip to Grantchester will set you back £20 to £30. All companies offer discounts if you pre-book tickets online.

Cambridge Chauffer Punts
Punting

(www.punting-in-cambridge.co.uk; Silver St Bridge) One of the biggest punting companies in Cambridge, with regular chauffeured punting tours.

Granta Canoe & Punt Hire Company
Punting

(www.puntingincambridge.com; Newnham Rd) Handily sited punt-rental company if you're heading towards Grantchester. Runs reduced services in the winter.

Tours

Walking Tours
Walking Tour

(☎ 01223-457574; www.visitcambridge.org; Peas Hill) The tourist office runs guided two-hour tours (adult/child £17.50/15.50) of central Cambridge, which take in two of the most memorable colleges; depending on opening hours they might include King's College Chapel, Queens', Pembroke or St John's. The price includes admission to the colleges. Year-round, tours run at 11am Monday to Friday, at 11am, noon and 2pm Saturday, and at 1pm Sunday. In July and August there are extra daily tours at noon and 2pm. They're popular: book.

Sleeping

Benson House
B&B ££

(☎ 01223-311594; www.bensonhouse.co.uk; 24 Huntingdon Rd; s £70, d £90-115; P ☎) Lots of little things lift Benson a cut above, meaning you can sleep among feather pillows and cotton linen, before breakfasting off

Royal Doulton bone china, tucking into kippers, croissants and fresh fruit.

Varsity
Boutique Hotel £££

(☎01223-306030; www.thevarsityhotel.co.uk; Thompson's Lane; d £180-345; 📶) In the 48 individually styled rooms of riverside Varsity, wondrous furnishings and witty features (union-jack footstools, giant postage stamps) sit beside floor-to-ceiling glass windows, monsoon showers and iPod docks. The views from the roof terrace are frankly gorgeous.

Hotel du Vin
Hotel £££

(☎01223-227330; www.hotelduvin.com; Trumpington St; d £200-230, ste £250-340; @📶) Arguably the country's swishest, coolest chain delivers again here. Achingly beautiful rooms sport roll-top baths and Egyptian cotton sheets, the cosy cellar bar is vaulted, the bistro (mains £18) is chic and the modern mural in reception depicts a suitably wine-soaked May Ball.

 Eating

Aromi
Italian £

(www.aromi.co.uk; 1 Benet St; mains £4.50; ⊙9am-8pm Fri-Sun, to 5pm Mon-Thu; 🖋) Sometimes you should yield to temptation. So be drawn in by a window full of stunning Sicilian piazza and feast on light, crisp bases piled high with fresh spinach and Parma ham. Then succumb to the indecently thick hot chocolate; may as well make it a large.

Kingston Arms
Pub ££

(www.kingston-arms.co.uk; 33 Kingston St; mains £5-16; ⊙noon-2pm & 6-10pm Mon-Fri, noon-10pm Sat & Sun; 📶) Great gastropub grub – from roasts to white-onion soup and recession-busting mains (held at £4.99), keeps stomachs satisfied at the award-winning Kingston. Meanwhile 12 real ales, stacked board games and a students-meet-locals clientele deliver a contemporary Cambridge vibe. It's 1 mile southeast of the centre, along Parkside then down student-central Mill Rd.

Oak
Bistro ££

(☎01223-323361; www.theoakbistro.co.uk; 6 Lensfield Rd; mains £12-20, set lunch 2/3 courses £13/16; ⊙noon-2.30pm & 6-9.30pm Mon-Sat) Truffles (white and black), olive pesto and rosemary jus are the kind of flavour intensifiers you'll find at this friendly but classy neighbourhood eatery where locally sourced duck, fish and beef come cooked just so. The set lunch is a bargain.

Chop House
British ££

(www.cambscuisine.com/cambridge-chop-house; 1 King's Pde; mains £14-20; ⊙noon-10.30pm Mon-Sat, to 9.30pm Sun) The window seats here deliver some of the best views in town – onto King's College's hallowed walls. The food is pure English establishment too: hearty steaks and chops and chips, plus a scattering of fish dishes and suet puds. Sister restaurant **St John's Chop House** (21-24 Northampton St) sits near the rear entrance to St John's College.

Midsummer House
Fine Dining £££

(☎01223-369299; www.midsummerhouse.co.uk; Midsummer Common; 5/7/10 courses £45/75/95; ⊙noon-1.30pm Wed-Sat, 7-9pm Tue-Sat) At the region's top tables Chef Daniel Clifford's double Michelin-starred creations are distinguished by depth of flavour and immense technical skill. Sample braised oxtail, coal-baked celeriac and scallops with truffle before dollops of dark chocolate, blood orange and marmalade ice cream. Wine flights start at £55.

 Drinking

Eagle
Pub

(www.gkpubs.co.uk; Benet St; ⊙9am-11pm Mon-Sat, to 10.30pm Sun) Cambridge's most famous pub has loosened the tongues and pickled the grey cells of many an illustrious academic; among them Nobel Prize–winning scientists Crick and Watson, who discussed their research into DNA here (note the blue plaque by the door). Fifteenth-century, wood-panelled and rambling, its cosy rooms include one with WWII airmens' signatures on the ceiling. The food, served all day, is good too.

SIMON GREENWOOD/GETTY IMAGES ©

Granta Pub

(www.gkpubs.co.uk; Newnham Rd; ⊙11am-11pm, to 10.30pm Sun) If the exterior of this picturesque waterside pub, overhanging a pretty mill pond, looks strangely familiar, it could be because it is the darling of many a TV director. No wonder, with its snug deck, riverside terrace and punts (p121) moored up alongside, it's a highly atmospheric spot to sup and watch the world drift by.

🛈 Information

Tourist Office (📞0871 226 8006; www.visitcambridge.org; Peas Hill; ⊙10am-5pm Mon-Sat, plus 11am-3pm Sun Apr-Oct)

🛈 Getting There & Away

Train

The train station is off Station Rd, which is off Hills Rd. Destinations:

- **Birmingham New Street** (£32, four hours, hourly)
- **London King's Cross** (£18, one hour, two to four per hour)
- **Stansted** (£15, 30 minutes, two per hour)

Car

Cambridge's centre is largely pedestrianised. Use one of the five free Park & Ride car parks on major routes into town, from where buses (tickets £2.90) serve the city centre every 10 minutes between 7am and 7pm daily, then every 20 minutes until 10pm.

🛈 Getting Around

Bicycle

Cambridge is very bike-friendly, and two wheels provide a great way of getting about town.

Station Cycles (www.stationcycles.co.uk; Station Rd; per half-day/day/week £7/10/25; ⊙8am-6pm Mon-Fri, 9am-5pm Sat, 10am-4pm Sun) At the train station.

City Cycle Hire (www.citycyclehire.com; 61 Newnham Rd; per half-day/day/week £7/10/25; ⊙9am-5.30pm Mon-Fri, plus 9am-5pm Sat Apr-Oct) A mile southwest of the city centre.

Bus

Bus routes run around town from the main bus station in Drummer St. Many operate until around 11.30pm. C1, C3 and C7 stop at the train station. A Dayrider ticket (£3.90) provides 24 hours, unlimited, city-wide bus travel.

Oxford & Central England

Celebrated as the home of English academia, Oxford also sits slap bang at the very centre of England. With its dreaming spires and dazzling architecture, it opens a fascinating window on the nation's history, but it also provides an ideal gateway for exploring further afield. Just beyond this studious city rise the tranquil hills and implausibly pretty villages of the Cotswolds, quintessential olde-worlde English villages, filled with flower-clad cottages, stone churches, frilly tea-rooms and antique shops. Nearby is Shakespeare's birthplace in Stratford-upon-Avon, now a point of pilgrimage for fans of the Bard. Further north the gentle landscape gives way to countryside with a slightly harder edge, with the rugged moors of the Peak District and Ironbridge Gorge, birthplace of the Industrial Revolution. And then, of course, there are two of the nation's most impressive stately homes to discover, Blenheim Palace and Chatsworth House – both of which are a simply essential part of any English itinerary.

The River Derwent at Chatsworth House (p161)
CHRIS MELLOR/GETTY IMAGES ©

Oxford & Central England

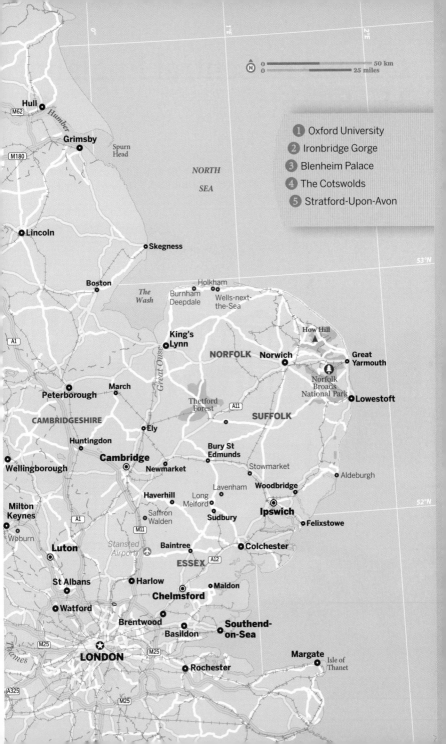

1	Oxford University
2	Ironbridge Gorge
3	Blenheim Palace
4	The Cotswolds
5	Stratford-Upon-Avon

0 — 50 km
0 — 25 miles

Hull
M62
Grimsby
M180
Spurn
Head

NORTH

SEA

Lincoln

Skegness

53°N

Boston
Holkham
The
Wash
Burnham
Deepdale
Wells-next-
the-Sea

A1

How Hill

King's
Lynn
NORFOLK   **Norwich**
Great
Yarmouth
Great Ouse
Norfolk
Broads
National Park
Lowestoft

March

Peterborough
Thetford
Forest
A11
SUFFOLK

CAMBRIDGESHIRE

Ely

Huntingdon
Bury St
Edmunds

Cambridge
Stowmarket
Aldeburgh

Wellingborough
Newmarket
Lavenham
Woodbridge

Haverhill
Long
Melford
Ipswich

Milton
Keynes
Saffron
Walden
Sudbury

A1
Felixstowe

M11

Woburn
Stansted
Airport
Baintree
Colchester

Luton
ESSEX
A12

St Albans
Harlow
Maldon

Watford
Chelmsford

Brentwood
Southend-
on-Sea

Basildon

Thames
M25
LONDON
M25
Margate
Isle of
Thanet

Rochester

A325

M25

52°N

0°

1°E

2°E

Oxford & Central England Highlights

Oxford University's Colleges

Don't expect a neat, orderly campus here. Oxford University consists of 39 separate colleges scattered around the city, rubbing shoulders with other historic buildings and sometimes more workaday modern streets. Each college is a historic and architectural gem in its own right, so it's worth visiting as many as you can. Magdalen College (p135)

2 Ironbridge Gorge

During the 18th and 19th centuries, the Midlands was the heart of the Industrial Revolution, and its towns and villages echoed to the sound of spinning looms and clattering mills. This river gorge (p155) – now a World Heritage Site – was the first place in Britain to perfect the art of smelting iron ore, and its period buildings have been turned into museums exploring the area's industrial past.

Blenheim Palace

This vast pile in the Oxfordshire countryside is the family seat of the Dukes of Marlborough, but it's perhaps best-known as the birthplace of Winston Churchill. Designed by Sir John Vanbrugh, the house is spectacular enough, but for many people it's the lavish grounds (partly designed by Capability Brown) that steal the show.

Exploring the Cotswolds

For a picture-perfect vision of rural England, there are few places finer than the quiet villages and winding lanes of the Cotswolds. Filled with honey-stoned cottages, village greens and country pubs, they're the ideal place for leisurely exploration, either by bike, bus or car. Even in summer, it's usually possible to dodge the crowds and discover your own patch of olde-worlde England. Castle Combe, Cotswolds

Shakespeare at Stratford-upon-Avon

What could be more English than taking in one of Shakespeare's play in the birthplace of the nation's best-known playwright? After visiting William's birthplace and his grave – and all the houses he's connected with in between – make sure you leave time to see the Royal Shakespeare Company in action. Royal Shakespeare Company Theatre (p154)

Oxford & Central England's Best...

Historic Churches

o **Christ Church Cathedral, Oxford** England's smallest cathedral in one of Oxford University's grandest colleges (p134)

o **Holy Trinity Church, Stratford-upon-Avon** William Shakespeare's final resting place with famous epitaph (p152)

o **Ely Cathedral** Marvel at the audacious architecture of the famous 'Ship of the Fens' (p164)

o **Lincoln Cathedral** Relive the climax of *The Da Vinci Code* at this wonderful cathedral (p158)

Architecture

o **Haddon Hall** The perfect medieval manor (p146)

o **Iron Bridge** Arched bridge showcasing the new technology of cast iron (p157)

o **Burghley House** This magnificent house was state-of-the-art in Elizabethan times (p146)

o **Warwick Castle** Classic medieval stronghold, which still hosts jousting tournaments (p149)

o **Radcliffe Camera** A Palladian dome with an unparalleled Oxford panorama (p135)

Natural Wonders

o **Peak District** England's oldest national park, with moors, valleys and lakes – but no peaks

o **Sherwood Forest** Famous as Robin Hood's hideout, this nature reserve is now a popular picnic spot (p154)

o **Peak Cavern** See stalagtites and stalagmites galore in this subterranean cavern, known locally as the Devil's Arse (p162)

o **River Avon** Cruise along this historic waterway from Shakespeare's home town (p153)

Country Towns

- **Stratford-upon-Avon** A delightful Midlands market town and birthplace of the Bard

- **Bakewell** Deep in the Peak District, famous for its eponymous pudding

- **Buxton** Former spa town, still with trappings of Regency elegance

- **Stow-on-the-Wold** A Cotswolds classic, famous for its large market square, surrounded by antique shops

- **Chipping Campden** Of all the pretty Cotswolds towns, this is the gem

Need to Know

ADVANCE PLANNING

- **Two months before** Book hotels in Oxford and the Cotswolds; reserve seats for the Royal Shakespeare Company in Stratford-upon-Avon.

- **One month before** Check opening times for Oxford colleges and the main Shakespeare attractions.

- **Two weeks before** Book tickets online for sights including Chatsworth House, Blenheim Palace and Warwick Castle.

RESOURCES

- **Oxford** (www.visitoxford.org)

- **The Cotswolds** (www.visitcotswolds.co.uk)

- **Heart of England** (www.visitheartofengland.com)

- **Peak District** (www.visitpeakdistrict.com)

- **Warwick, Stratford-upon-Avon, Coventry** (www.shakespeare-country.co.uk)

GETTING AROUND

- **Bus** Long-distance buses between main centres are good. Various companies offer services to the Cotswolds and Peak District villages.

- **Train** Connections between the major towns are fast and frequent, but to reach rural areas you'll have to take the bus.

- **Car** Easiest way of getting around the region, but cities and main motorways can get heavy with traffic. Oxford and other big cities have useful Park & Ride systems: park your car on the outskirts, take a shuttle bus into the centre.

BE FOREWARNED

- **Oxford** Many colleges are closed for the Easter term and summer exams. Check www.ox.ac.uk/colleges for full details of opening days and hours.

- **Major Sights** Popular areas including Stratford-upon-Avon, Warwick, Oxford and the Peak District get busy in summer.

- **Royal Shakespeare Company** Tickets for major productions are often sold out months in advance, so book early.

ft: Burghley House (p146); **Above:** Fallow deer
") DAVE PORTER/GETTY IMAGES ©; (ABOVE) JAY BEE/GETTY IMAGES ©

Oxford & Central England Itineraries

Follow the three-day itinerary to explore the best of the Cotswolds. The five-day trip leads further north, through the Midlands and into the Peak District. Combine them for a longer tour of the whole region.

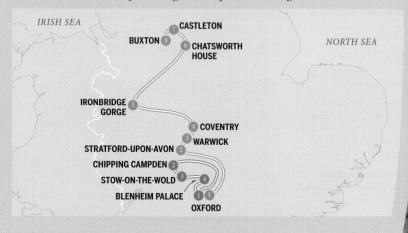

IRISH SEA

CASTLETON ⑦

BUXTON ⑧ CHATSWORTH ⑥ HOUSE

NORTH SEA

IRONBRIDGE GORGE ⑤

COVENTRY ④

WARWICK ③

STRATFORD-UPON-AVON ②

CHIPPING CAMPDEN ②

STOW-ON-THE-WOLD ③ ④

BLENHEIM PALACE ④ ①

OXFORD

3 DAYS

OXFORD TO OXFORD

A COTSWOLDS LOOP

Start your tour in the graceful city of ❶ **Oxford**. It's easy to spend a day here, sauntering round the elegant colleges and other university buildings. Top sights include Christ Church, as well as architectural landmarks such as the Radcliffe Camera and Bodleian Library.

On your second day, head west into the rural landscape of the Cotswolds. This is an area famous for pretty towns and villages, but finest of them all is ❷ **Chipping Campden**, with its graceful curving main street flanked by a wonderful array of stone cottages, quaint shops and historic inns. There's also a good selection

of places to stay. Take a look at St James Church and the historic Market Hall, then enjoy an afternoon stroll in the surrounding countryside. Alternatively, visit ❸ **Stow-on-the-Wold**, another classic Cotswolds town, its large market square featuring several antique shops.

Day three, and it's time to head back towards Oxford, stopping on the way at ❹ **Blenheim Palace**, one of the region's greatest stately homes. Finish your tour with a good dinner at one of Oxford's excellent eateries.

5 DAYS A MIDLANDS MEANDER

Start your tour in **1 Oxford**, then head north to world-famous **2 Stratford-upon-Avon**, birthplace of William Shakespeare. It's then a short hop to **3 Warwick Castle**, for historical insights and family fun, possibly diverting to **4 Coventry** for a moment of reflection at the famous cathedral. While fans of medieval monuments are never far from a highlight, if you're interested in more recent eras don't miss **5 Ironbridge Gorge**, the crucible of the Industrial Revolution, now a World Heritage Site with several fascinating museums.

Then it's back to classic British history, and one of the country's finest stately homes, **6 Chatsworth House**. Leave time to admire the stunning interiors and stroll in the ornamental gardens, famous for fountains and cascades, as well as exhibitions of contemporary sculpture. If time allows, take a longer stroll in the wilder landscape of the surrounding Peak District near **7 Castleton**.

This tour ends in **8 Buxton**, a picturesque sprawl of Georgian terraces, Victorian amusements and pretty parks.

Broadway, the Cotswolds (p145)
STUART BLACK/GETTY IMAGES ©

Discover Oxford & Central England

At a Glance

○ **Oxford** (p134) Academia and architecture combine in this most picturesque of cities.

○ **The Cotswolds** (p142) A vision of the English countryside, full of timeless villages and cobbled streets.

○ **The Midlands** (p149) The cradle of the Industrial Revolution, packed with history and heritage.

○ **Peak District** (p159) Wild moors, tranquil valleys and stately spa towns in England's oldest national park.

Divinity School, Bodleian Library, Oxford
JON BOWER AT APEXPHOTOS/GETTY IMAGES ©

OXFORD

POP 171,000

Oxford is a privileged place, one of the world's most famous university towns. The elegant honey-coloured buildings of the 39 colleges that make up the university wrap around tranquil courtyards along narrow cobbled lanes, and inside their grounds, a studious calm reigns.

◉ Sights

If you have your heart set on visiting Oxford's iconic buildings, remember that not all are open to the public. For the colleges that are, visiting hours change with the term and exam schedule; check www.ox.ac.uk/colleges for full details of visiting hours and admission.

UNIVERSITY BUILDINGS & COLLEGES

Christ Church   College
(www.chch.ox.ac.uk; St Aldate's; adult/child £8/6.50; ☉10am-4.30pm Mon-Sat, 2-4.30pm Sun) The largest of all of Oxford's colleges (containing England's smallest cathedral) and the one with the grandest quad, Christ Church is also its most popular. Its magnificent buildings, illustrious history and latter-day fame as a location for the *Harry Potter* films have tourists coming in droves. The college was founded in 1524 by Cardinal Thomas Wolsey, who suppressed the monastery existing on the site to acquire the funds for his lavish building project.

Bodleian Library   Library
(☎01865-287400; www.bodley.ox.ac.uk; Catte St; tours £5-13; ☉9am-5pm Mon-Sat, 11am-5pm Sun) Oxford's Bodleian Library is one of the old-

est public libraries in the world and quite possibly the most impressive one you'll ever see. Casual visitors are welcome to wander around the central quad and visit the exhibition space in the foyer. For £1 you can also access the Divinity School, but the rest of the complex can only be visited on guided tours (check online or at the information desk for times; it pays to book ahead).

Magdalen College　College
(www.magd.ox.ac.uk; High St; adult/child £5/4; ⊙1-6pm) Set amid 40 hectares of lawns, woodlands, river walks and deer park, Magdalen (*mawd*-lin), founded in 1458, is one of the wealthiest and most beautiful of Oxford's colleges. It has a reputation as an artistic college, and some of its famous students have included writers Julian Barnes, Alan Hollinghurst, CS Lewis, John Betjeman, Seamus Heaney and Oscar Wilde, not to mention Edward VIII, TE Lawrence 'of Arabia' and Dudley Moore.

Radcliffe Camera　Library
(Radcliffe Sq) The Radcliffe Camera is the quintessential Oxford landmark and one of the city's most photographed buildings. The spectacular circular library/reading room, filled with natural light, was built between 1737 and 1749 in grand Palladian style, and has Britain's third-largest dome. The only way to see the interior is to join one of the extended tours (£13; 90 minutes) of the Bodleian Library (p134).

New College　College
(www.new.ox.ac.uk; Holywell St; adult/child £3/2 Mar-Sep, free Oct-Feb; ⊙11am-5pm Mar-Sep, 2-4pm Oct-Feb) This 14th-century college was the first in Oxford for undergraduates and is a fine example of the glorious Perpendicular Gothic style. The chapel here is full of treasures, including superb stained glass, much of it original, and Sir Jacob Epstein's disturbing statue of Lazarus. During term time, visitors can attend the beautiful Evensong, a choral church service held nightly at 6pm.

Merton College　College
(www.merton.ox.ac.uk; Merton St; admission £3; ⊙2-5pm Mon-Fri, 10am-5pm Sat & Sun)

Founded in 1264, Merton is the oldest of the three original colleges and the first to adopt collegiate planning, bringing scholars and tutors together into a formal community and providing a planned residence for them. Its distinguishing architectural features include large gargoyles whose expressions suggest that they're about to throw up, and the charming 14th-century **Mob Quad** – the first of the college quads.

All Souls College　College
(www.all-souls.ox.ac.uk; High St; ⊙2-4pm Mon-Fri) FREE One of the wealthiest Oxford colleges, All Souls was founded in 1438 as a centre of prayer and learning. It's one of several graduate colleges, though it doesn't accept just any old Oxford graduate. Each year, the university's top finalists sit a fellowship exam, with an average of only two making the grade. Today fellowship of the college is one of the highest academic honours in the country.

Trinity College　College
(www.trinity.ox.ac.uk; Broad St; adult/child £2/1; ⊙10am-noon Mon-Fri, 2-4pm daily) Founded in 1555, this small college is worth a visit to see the lovely garden quad, designed by Christopher Wren. Its exquisitely carved chapel is one of the most beautiful in the city and a masterpiece of English baroque. Famous students have included William Pitt the Elder and Cardinal Newman.

OTHER SIGHTS

Ashmolean Museum　Museum
(www.ashmolean.org; Beaumont St; ⊙10am-5pm Tue-Sun; ♿) FREE Britain's oldest public museum, second in repute only to London's British Museum, was established in 1683 when Elias Ashmole presented the university with the collection of curiosities amassed by the well-travelled John Tradescant, gardener to Charles I. A 2009 makeover has left the museum with new interactive features, a giant atrium, glass walls revealing galleries on different levels and a beautiful rooftop restaurant.

Oxford

0   500 m
0   0.25 miles

Oxford

Pitt Rivers Museum · Museum

(www.prm.ox.ac.uk; Parks Rd; ⏰noon-4.30pm Mon, 10am-4.30pm Tue-Sun;) FREE Hidden away through a door at the back of the main exhibition hall of the Oxford University Museum of Natural History, this wonderfully creepy anthropological museum houses a treasure trove of objects from around the world – more than enough to satisfy any armchair adventurer. One of the reasons this museum is so brilliant is because there are no computers here or shiny modern gimmicks. The dim light lends an air of mystery to the glass cases stuffed with the prized booty of Victorian explorers.

Tours

Oxford Official Guided Walking Tours · Walking Tour

(☎01865-252200; www.visitoxfordandox-fordshire.com; 15-16 Broad St; adult/child from £9/8) Book at the tourist office for tours of Oxford city and colleges (10.45am and 1pm year-round, plus 11am and 2pm at busy times) or a bewildering array of themed tours, including *Inspector Morse*, *Alice in Wonderland* and *Harry Potter*, and family walking tours in the school holidays. Check the website for details.

Bill Spectre's Ghost Trails · Walking Tour

(☎07941 041811; www.ghosttrail.org; adult/child £8/6; ⏰6.30pm Fri & Sat) For a highly entertaining and informative look at Oxford's dark underbelly, join Victorian undertaker Bill Spectre on a 1¾-hour tour of the city's most haunted sites. It departs from **Oxford Castle Unlocked** (www.oxfordcastleunlocked.co.uk; 44-46 Oxford Castle; adult/child £10/7; ⏰tours 10am-4.20pm); audience participation likely.

Sleeping

Oxford Coach & Horses · B&B ££

(☎01865-200017; www.oxfordcoachand horses.co.uk; 62 St Clements St; s/d from £115/130; P🛜) Once a coaching inn, this 18th-century building has been painted powder blue and given a fresh, modern makeover. Rooms are spacious and light-filled, and the ground floor has been converted into a large, attractive breakfast room.

Burlington House · B&B ££

(☎01865-513513; www.burlington-house. co.uk; 374 Banbury Rd, Summertown; s/d from £70/97; P🛜) Twelve big, bright and elegant rooms with patterned wallpaper and splashes of colour are available at this Victorian merchant's house. The fittings are luxurious and the bathrooms immaculate; the service is attentive; and breakfast comes complete with organic eggs and granola. It has good public transport links to town.

Messing About on the River

An unmissable Oxford experience, punting is all about sitting back and quaffing Pimms (the quintessential English summer drink) as you watch the city's glorious architecture float by. Which, of course, requires someone else to do the hard work – punting is far more difficult than it appears. If you decide to go it alone, a deposit is usually charged. Most punts hold five people including the punter. Hire them from **Magdalen Bridge Boathouse** (☏01865-202643; www.oxfordpunting.co.uk; High St; chauffered per 30min £25, self-punt per hour £20; ☾9.30am-dusk Feb-Nov) or **Cherwell Boat House** (☏01865-515978; www.cherwellboathouse.co.uk; 50 Bardwell Rd; per hour £15-18; ☾10am-dusk mid-Mar–mid-Oct).

Old Bank Hotel   Hotel £££

(☏01865-799599; www.oldbank-hotel.co.uk; 92 High St; r from £250; ▣⛁) Slap bang in the centre of Oxford, this grand hotel's front rooms look over St Mary's Church and into the very heart of Oxford University. The elegant, pale-hued bedrooms are sleek and spacious, and the whole place is strewn with interesting contemporary art. Downstairs there's a buzzing restaurant.

Eating

Edamame   Japanese £

(www.edamame.co.uk; 15 Holywell St; mains £6-8; ☾11.30am-2.30pm Wed-Sun, 5-8.30pm Thu-Sat) The queue out the door speaks volumes about the quality of the food here. This tiny joint, all light wood and friendly bustle, is the best place in town for authentic Japanese cuisine. Arrive early and be prepared to wait.

Missing Bean   Cafe £

(www.themissingbean.co.uk; 14 Turl St; mains £3-4; ☾8am-6.30pm Mon-Sat, 10am-5.30pm Sun) Oxford's best coffee can be found here, as well as loose-leaf teas and smoothies for those less caffeine inclined. The fresh muffins, cakes and ciabatta sandwiches make this a great lunchtime stop.

Rickety Press   Modern British ££

(☏01865-424581; www.thericketypress.com; 67 Cranham St; mains £13-17; ☾noon-2.30pm & 6-9.30pm) Hidden in the back streets of Jericho, this old corner pub serves up beautifully presented, tasty food in casual surrounds. Call in for lunch or before 7pm for a great-value express menu (two/three courses £13/15).

Café Coco   Mediterranean ££

(☏01865-200232; www.cafecoco.co.uk; 23 Cowley Rd; breakfast £4-10, lunch £7-12; ☾10am-midnight Thu-Sat, 10am-5pm Sun) This Cowley Rd institution is a popular brunching destination for the hip and hungry. The menu ranges from cooked breakfasts and waffles to pizza, salads, Mediterranean mains and pecan pie.

Le Manoir aux Quat'Saisons   Modern French £££

(☏01844-278881; www.manoir.com; Church Rd, Great Milton; mains £48-54, 5-course lunch/dinner £79/134; ☾7.30-10am, 11.45am-2.15pm & 6.45-9.30pm; ▨) Chef Raymond Blanc has been working his magic at this impressive stone manor house for more than 30 years, presenting imaginative, complex and exquisitely presented dishes. You could consider staying overnight in one of the luxurious rooms. Book well ahead and dress smartly.

Drinking

Bear Inn   Pub

(www.bearoxford.co.uk; 6 Alfred St; ☾11am-11pm; ⛁) Arguably Oxford's oldest pub (there's been a pub on this site since 1242), this atmospherically creaky place requires all but the most vertically challenged to duck their heads. There's a curious tie collection on the walls and ceiling (though you can no longer exchange yours for a pint).

Eagle & Child
Pub

(www.nicholsonspubs.co.uk/theeagleandchild
oxford; 49 St Giles; ⊙11am-11pm; 🖥) Affectionately known as the 'Bird & Baby', this
atmospheric place, dating from 1650, was
once the favourite haunt of authors JRR
Tolkien and CS Lewis. Its wood-panelled
rooms and selection of real ales still attract
a mellow crowd.

Turf Tavern
Pub

(www.theturftavern.co.uk; 4 Bath Pl; ⊙11am-
11pm) Hidden down a narrow alleyway, this
tiny medieval pub (dating from at least
1381) is one of the town's best loved; it's
where US president Bill Clinton famously
'did not inhale'. Home to 11 real ales, it's
always packed with a mix of students,
professionals and lucky tourists who
manage to find it.

White Horse
Pub

(www.whitehorseoxford.co.uk; 52 Broad St;
⊙11am-11pm) This tiny 16th-century pub
was a favourite retreat for TV detective
Inspector Morse, and it can get pretty
crowded in the evenings. It's a great
place for a quiet afternoon pint of whatever the guest ale happens to be.

🛈 Getting There & Away

Car

Driving and parking in Oxford is a nightmare.
Use the five Park & Ride car parks on major
routes leading into town. Parking costs £2 to
£4 a day and buses (10 to 15 minutes, every 15
minutes) cost £2.70.

Train

There are half-hourly services to London
Paddington (£25, 1¼ hours), Winchester (£17, 1¼
hours), Birmingham (£27, 1¼ hours), Manchester
(£60, three hours) and Newcastle (£106, 4¾
hours).

🛈 Information

Tourist Office (☎01865-252200; www.
visitoxfordandoxfordshire.com; 15-16 Broad St;
⊙9.30am-5pm Mon-Sat, 10am-3.30pm Sun)

| Local Knowledge |

Oxford University

RECOMMENDATIONS FROM
PETER BERRY, WALKING-TOUR
GUIDE, BLACKWELL BOOKSHOP

1 CHRIST CHURCH
Christ Church (along with Magdalen College)
is the most popular sight, partly thanks to its links
with Lewis Carroll. These spots can be crowded, but
going with a guide helps you jump the queues and
make the most of your time here.

2 EXETER COLLEGE
To escape the crowds see slightly less-well-
known places such as Exeter College, which has
the most beautiful chapel of all the Oxford colleges,
with an exquisite tapestry by Pre-Raphaelite artists
William Morris and Edward Burne-Jones. Another
favourite is **New College**, also with a beautiful
chapel and a large section of the ancient City Walls.

3 BRIDGE OF SIGHS
Hertford College has academic buildings on
each side of New College Lane joined by the ornate
Bridge of Sighs, named after the famous bridge in
Venice (although as that bridge led to a prison it had
small windows – ours are much larger). Alumni here
include authors Jonathan Swift and Evelyn Waugh.

4 BODLEIAN LIBRARY
The 17th-century Bodleian Library is one of the
oldest libraries in the world. Priceless items stored
here include the original manuscripts of Tolkien's
The Hobbit. On the other side of Broad St is the
20th-century part of the library; an underground
conveyor belt carries books between the two.

5 UNIVERSITY CHURCH OF ST MARY THE VIRGIN
Originally just for the university, the services
are now open to 'town and gown' (locals and
students). Climb the tower's 127 steps for
spectacular views of the 'dreaming spires' of
Oxford and out to the Cotswold Hills beyond.

Don't Miss
Blenheim Palace

One of the country's greatest stately homes, Blenheim Palace (pronounced blen-num) is a baroque fantasy designed by Sir John Vanbrugh and Nicholas Hawksmoor, and was built between 1705 and 1722. The land and funds to build the house were granted to John Churchill, Duke of Marlborough, by a grateful Queen Anne after his decisive victory at the 1704 Battle of Blenheim

www.blenheimpalace.com

adult/child £22/12, park & gardens only £13/6.50

🕙 10.30am-5.30pm daily, closed Mon & Tue Nov–mid-Feb

The Palace

Now a Unesco World Heritage Site, Blenheim Palace is home to the 11th duke and duchess of Marlborough. Inside, the house is stuffed with statues, tapestries, ostentatious furniture, priceless china and giant oil paintings in elaborate gilt frames. Visits start in the **Great Hall**, a vast space topped by 20m-high ceilings adorned with images of the first duke. Next up is the **Churchill Exhibition**, which is dedicated to the life, work and writings of Sir Winston Churchill, who was born at Blenheim in 1874. The British prime minister was a descendant of the Dukes of Marlborough, as was the late Princess Diana.

From here you can choose to wander through the various grand state rooms at your own pace or wait to join one of the free **guided tours**, which depart regularly throughout the day (except Sundays). Highlights include the famous **Blenheim Tapestries**, a set of 10 large wall hangings commemorating the first duke's achievements; the **State Dining Room**, with its painted walls and ceilings; and the magnificent **Long Library**. Afterwards, head upstairs to the 'Untold Story' exhibition, where a ghostly chamber maid leads you through a series of tableaux recreating important scenes from the palace's history.

The Grounds

If the crowds in the house become too oppressive, retire to the lavish gardens and vast parklands, parts of which were landscaped by Lancelot 'Capability' Brown. A minitrain takes visitors to the Pleasure Gardens, which feature a yew maze, adventure playground and butterfly house. For quieter and longer strolls, there are glorious walks leading to an arboretum, cascade and temple.

`Local Knowledge`

Blenheim Palace

RECOMMENDATIONS FROM
JOHN FORSTER, ARCHIVIST
TO HIS GRACE THE DUKE OF MARLBOROUGH

1 THE GREAT HALL

The Great Hall is the first room visitors see, and its size, proportions and drama really establish the monumental purpose of the palace. Look out for the Victory Arch, the stone friezes by Grinling Gibbons, and the ceiling painting by Thornhill, which shows the kneeling Duke presenting the battle plan of his victory at Blenheim to Britannia.

2 THE LONG LIBRARY

Though Sir John Vanbrugh was Blenheim's chief architect, he left his assistant Nicholas Hawksmoor to complete the Long Library. At 56m long, it's the second-longest private library in the country. The ceiling is particularly lovely, with its intricate stucco work and two false domes.

3 THE SALOON

In general the palace emphasises the Duke's military achievements, but this room shows the virtues of peace. The wall and ceiling paintings depict the peaceful people of the four continents, while the Duke's uplifted sword as he rides to victory is stayed by the hand of the figure of Peace.

4 THE BLENHEIM TAPESTRY IN THE GREEN WRITING ROOM

This is the most important of the 10 'Victory Tapestries' commissioned by the 1st Duke to commemorate his exploits in the War of the Spanish Succession (1702–11). It's on a huge scale (7.62m x 4.42m), and even though it's over 300 years old, the details of the battle and its key protagonists (including the Duke himself) remain perfectly clear.

5 THE TEMPLE OF DIANA

It's a five-minute walk from the palace to this 18th-century lakeside temple, where Winston Churchill proposed to his wife Clementine. Even today, it's a popular place for marriage proposals – very romantic!

THE COTSWOLDS

Glorious villages riddled with beautiful old mansions of honey-coloured stone, thatched cottages, atmospheric churches and rickety almshouses draw crowds of visitors to the Cotswolds. The booming medieval wool trade brought the area its wealth and left it with such a proliferation of beautiful buildings that its place in history is secured for evermore.

Minster Lovell
POP 1340

Set on a gentle slope leading down to the meandering River Windrush, Minster Lovell is a gorgeous village with a cluster of stone cottages nestled beside an ancient pub and riverside mill. One of William Morris' favourite spots, the village has changed little since medieval times. It's divided into two halves: Old Minster, recorded in the Domesday Book (1086) and the rather newer Minster Lovell, across the river. The main sight in Old

Minster is **Minster Lovell Hall**, the 15th-century manor house that was home to Viscount Francis Lovell.

The revamped, luxurious **Old Swan & Minster Mill** (☎01993-774441; www.oldswanandminstermill.com; Old Minster; d/ste from £165/285, mains £14-22; ⊙Old Swan noon-3pm & 6-9pm; P 🛜 🛗 🐾) has charming period-style rooms in the 17th-century Old Swan or sleek, contemporary design in the 19th-century converted mill, covered with creepers.

Burford
POP 1190

Slithering down a steep hill to a medieval crossing point on the River Windrush, the remarkable village of Burford is little changed since its glory days at the height of the wool trade.

◉ Sights & Activities

Burford's main attraction lies in its incredible collection of buildings, including the

Left: Lower Slaughter (p147), Cotswolds;
Below: Children at Woburn Safari Park (p145)

(LEFT) JOE DANIEL PRICE/GETTY IMAGES ©: (BELOW) VISITBRITAIN/ROD EDWARDS/GETTY IMAGES ©

16th-century **Tolsey House (cnr High & Sheep Sts)**, where the wealthy wool merchants held their meetings. This quaint building perches on sturdy pillars and now houses a small museum on Burford's history. Just off the main street, you will find the town's 14th-century **almshouses** and the **Church of St John the Baptist** (www.burfordchurch.org; Church Lane).

Sleeping & Eating

Star Cottage
B&B ££

(01993-822032; www.burfordbedandbreakfast.co.uk; Meadow Lane, Fulbrook; s/d from £70/80;) In the village of Fulbrook, a 15-minute walk from Burford, this wonderful old Cotswold cottage has two comfortable and character-filled en suite rooms, the smaller of which has a grand canopied bed. The cooked breakfasts are excellent.

Bull
Hotel ££

(01993-822220; www.bullatburford.co.uk; 105 High St; s/d from £65/80; P) You'll be following in the footsteps of guests as illustrious as Charles II and Horatio Nelson if you stay at this 15th-century hotel. The plusher rooms feature four-poster beds and antique furniture, and the restaurant is pure gourmet, with beautifully executed dishes making the most of local ingredients.

Angel
Pub ££

(01993-822714; www.theangelatburford.co.uk; 14 Witney St; mains £14-17; noon-11.30pm;) Set in a lovely 16th-century coaching inn, this atmospheric pub serves up a tasty menu of modern British food. Dine by roaring fires in winter, or eat alfresco in the lovely walled garden in warmer weather. There are three traditionally decorated rooms upstairs (£90 to £120) if you wish to linger.

143

Huffkins
Bakery, Cafe ££

(www.huffkins.com; 98 High St; mains £7-12; ⏰8am-5pm Mon-Sat, 10am-5pm Sun) Since 1890 Huffkins has been baking and serving delicious scones, cakes and pies. More substantial fare includes cooked breakfasts, macaroni cheese, Welsh rarebit and burgers.

Chipping Campden
POP 2206

An unspoiled gem in an area full of pretty villages, Chipping Campden is a glorious reminder of life in the Cotswolds in medieval times. The graceful curving main street is flanked by a picturesque array of wayward stone cottages, fine terraced houses, ancient inns and historic homes, many made of that honey-coloured stone that the Cotswolds is so famous for.

◎ Sights & Activities

Standing out from the splendour of other historic buildings along the High St is the highly photogenic 17th-century **Market Hall**, with multiple gables and an elaborate timber roof; this is where dairy produce used to be sold. Chipping Campden made its fortune during the wool boom, so it's little wonder that one of the most prominent buildings in town is the 14th-century **Grevel House**, former home of successful wool merchant William Grevel. Nearby on Church St is a remarkable row of **almshouses** dating from the 17th century, and the Jacobean lodges and gateways of the now-ruined **Campden House**, a large and lavish 15th-century house, the remains of which you can see clearly from the Shipston Rd. At the western end of the High St is the 15th-century **St James' Church** (www.stjameschurchcampden.co.uk; Church St; ⏰10am-5pm Mon-Sat, 2-5.45pm Sun Apr-Oct, 11am-3pm Mon-Sat, 2-4pm Sun Nov-Mar); built in the Perpendicular style, it has a magnificent tower and some graceful 17th-century monuments.

The surviving **Court Barn Museum** (☎01386-841951; www.courtbarn.org.uk; Church St; adult/child £4/free; ⏰10am-4pm Tue-Sun) is now a craft and design museum featuring work from the Arts and Crafts Movement, such as silverwork, pottery and hand-dyed cloth.

Market Hall, Chipping Campden

LAURIE NOBLE/GETTY IMAGES ©

Detour:
Woburn Abbey & Safari Park

Once a Cistercian abbey but dissolved by Henry VIII and awarded to the earl of Bedford, **Woburn Abbey** (www.woburn.co.uk; Park St, Woburn; adult/child £15/7.25; ⊘house 11am-5pm Easter-Oct) is a wonderful country pile set within a 1200-hectare deer park. The opulent house displays paintings by Gainsborough, van Dyck and Canaletto.

On an equally grand scale is **Woburn Safari Park** (www.woburnsafari.co.uk; adult/child £21/16; ⊘10am-5pm), the country's largest drive-through animal reserve. Rhinos, tigers, lions, zebras, bison, monkeys, elephants and giraffes roam the grounds, while in the 'foot safari' area, you can see sea lions, penguins and lemurs.

For both attractions, buy a **Woburn Passport** (adult/child £27/20), which can be used on two separate days within any 12-month period.

The abbey and safari park are easily accessible by car off the M1 motorway.

About 4 miles northeast, **Hidcote Manor Garden** (NT; www.nationaltrust.org.uk; Hidcote Bartrim; adult/child £10/5; ⊘10am-6pm) is one of the finest examples of Arts and Crafts landscaping in Britain, with outdoor 'rooms' filled with flowers and rare plants for the arboreally inclined.

Sleeping & Eating

Eight Bells Inn   Pub ££
(☏01386-840371; www.eightbellsinn.co.uk; Church St; s/d from £80/115, mains £13-19) This 14th-century inn is an atmospheric place to stay, featuring bright, modern rooms with iron bedsteads, soothing neutral decor and warm accents. The pub downstairs wins points for its flagstone floors and good modern British country cooking.

Cotswold House & Spa   Hotel £££
(☏01386-840330; www.cotswoldhouse.com; The Square; r from £162; ⊘restaurant 6.30-9.30pm Tue-Sat, noon-2.30pm Sun; P🛜🍽) This chic Regency townhouse-turned-boutique hotel has ultracomfortable king-sized beds, lush furnishings and, in the top rooms, private gardens and hot tubs. Indulge in a spa treatment and then dine in style in the Dining Room (three-course set dinner £45).

❶ Information

Tourist Office (☏01386-841206; www.campdenonline.org; High St; ⊘9.30am-5pm daily Apr-Oct, 9.30am-1pm Mon-Thu, to 4pm Fri-Sun Nov-Mar) Pick up a town guide (£1.50) for a self-guided walk around the most significant buildings. Enquire about the guided tours run by the Cotswold Voluntary Wardens (from May to September; suggested donation £3).

Broadway

POP 2540

This pretty village, a quintessentially English place with a smattering of antique shops, tearooms and art galleries, has inspired writers, artists and composers in times past with its graceful, golden-hued cottages set at the foot of a steep escarpment. Take the time to wander down to the lovely 12th-century **Church of St Eadburgha**, a signposted 1-mile walk from town. Near here, a path leads uphill for 2 miles to **Broadway Tower** (www.broadwaytower.co.uk; Middle Hill; adult/child £4.80/3; ⊘10am-5pm), a crenulated, 18th-century Gothic folly on the crest of the escarpment with all-encompassing views from the top.

For modern comfort within a 300-year-old exterior, try the wonderfully friendly **Crown & Trumpet** (☏01386-853202;

145

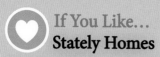

If You Like…
Stately Homes

As well as showstoppers including Blenheim Palace (140) and Chatsworth (p161), central England is home to a number of other lavish stately homes.

1 HARDWICK HALL
(NT; www.nationaltrust.org.uk; house & garden adult/child £12/6, garden only £6/3; house noon-4.30pm Wed-Sun, garden 9am-6pm daily) One of the most complete Elizabethan mansions in the country, Hardwick Hall featured all the latest mod-cons including fully glazed windows – a massive luxury in the 16th century. The hall is 10 miles southeast of Chesterfield, just off the M1.

2 HADDON HALL
(www.haddonhall.co.uk; adult/child £10/5.50; noon-5pm daily May-Sep, noon-5pm Sat-Mon Mar-Apr, Oct) Glorious Haddon Hall looks exactly like a medieval manor house should – all stone turrets, time-worn timbers and walled gardens. The house is 2 miles south of Bakewell on the A6.

3 BURGHLEY HOUSE
(www.burghley.co.uk; adult/child incl sculpture garden £13/6.50, garden only £7.50/6.50; 11am-5pm Sat-Thu mid-Mar–late Oct) Lying just a mile south of Stamford in Essex, flamboyant Burghley House (pronounced 'bur-lee') was built by Queen Elizabeth's chief adviser William Cecil, whose descendants have lived here ever since.

4 SANDRINGHAM
(www.sandringhamestate.co.uk; Sandringham; adult/child £13/6.50; 11am-4.30pm Easter-Oct; P) The Queen's country estate is set in 25 hectares of landscaped gardens and lakes, and open to the hoi polloi when the court is not at home. It's 6 miles northeast of King's Lynn off the B1440.

www.cotswoldholidays.co.uk; 14 Church St; r £60; P) the Broadway 'local' with five ensuite rooms (complete with sloped floors, exposed beams and low ceilings) above the lively pub.

Winchcombe
POP 4540

Winchcombe is very much a working, living place, with butchers, bakers and small independent shops lining the main street. It was the capital of the Saxon kingdom of Mercia and one of the most important towns in the Cotswolds until the Middle Ages.

Sights & Activities

Sudeley Castle   Castle
(www.sudeleycastle.co.uk; adult/child £14/5; 10am-5pm mid-Mar–Oct) Winchcombe's main attraction, this magnificent castle has welcomed many a monarch over its thousand-year history, including Richard III, Henry VIII and Charles I. It is most famous as the home of Catherine Parr (Henry VIII's widow) and her second husband, Thomas Seymour. Princess Elizabeth (before she became Elizabeth I) was part of the household for a time until Seymour's inappropriate displays of affection towards her prompted Catherine to banish her from the premises.

Hailes Abbey   Ruin
(EH; www.english-heritage.org.uk; Hailes; adult/child £4.50/2.70; 10am-5pm Apr-Nov) Two miles northeast of Winchcombe are the meagre ruins of this Cistercian abbey, once one of the country's main pilgrimage centres, due to a long-running medieval scam. The abbey was said to possess a vial of Christ's blood, which turned out to be merely coloured water. Before the deception came to light, thousands of pilgrims contributed to the abbey's wealth.

Sleeping & Eating

White Hart Inn   Hotel ££
(01242-602359; www.whitehartwinchombe.co.uk; High St; s/d from £60/70, without bathroom £40/50;) Appealingly old-fashioned, this central inn caters well to walkers. Choose one of the three cheaper 'rambler' rooms, with shared bathrooms

and iron bedsteads, or go for greater luxury in a superior room.

5 North St
Modern European £££

(☏01242-604566; www.5northstreetrestaurant.co.uk; 5 North St; 2-/3-course lunch £24/28, 3–7-course dinner £44-70; ☺7-9.30pm Tue-Sat) This Michelin-starred restaurant is a treat from start to finish, from its splendid 400-year-old timbered exterior to what you eventually find on your plate. Marcus Ashenford's cooking is rooted in traditional ingredients, but the odd playful experiment (such as Guinness ice cream) adds that extra magic.

Stow-on-the-Wold
POP 2050

The highest town in the Cotswolds (244m), Stow is anchored by a large market square surrounded by handsome buildings and steep-walled alleyways, originally used to funnel the sheep into the fair. Today, it's famous for its twice-yearly Stow Horse Fair (May and October) and attracting a disproportionate number of people from passing coach tours.

 ## Sleeping & Eating

Number 9
B&B ££

(☏01451-870333; www.number-nine.info; 9 Park St; s/d from £45/65; ☎) Centrally located and wonderfully atmospheric, this friendly B&B is all sloping floors, low ceilings and exposed beams. The three rooms are cosy but spacious and each has its own bathroom.

Bell at Stow
Pub ££

(☏01451-870916; www.thebellatstow.com; Park St; mains £13-16; ☺11am-11pm) Stow has plenty of cool old pubs but the Bell is the best. Lurking on the eastern edge of town, it serves a lively and varied menu stretching from Wiener schnitzel to jerk chicken to jambalaya. A selection of fresh fish dishes is chalked up on the blackboard daily.

The Slaughters
POP 400

The picture-postcard villages of Upper and Lower Slaughter manage to maintain their unhurried medieval charm in spite of receiving a multitude of visitors. The

Sudeley Castle

village names have nothing to do with abattoirs; they are derived from the Old English 'sloughtre', meaning slough or muddy place. Today the River Eye is contained within limestone banks and meanders peacefully through the village past the 17th-century Lower Slaughter Manor to the **Old Mill** (www.oldmill-lowerslaughter. com; adult/child £2.50/1; ⏰10am-6pm), which houses a small museum, cafe and ice-cream parlour, famous for its fantastic organic ice cream.

Upper Slaughter is less visited than Lower Slaughter, and it's a pleasant stroll between the two villages. For eating or sleeping, you can do no better than **Lords of the Manor** (☎01451-820243; www.lordsofthemanor.com; Upper Slaughter; d £199-495, 3-course meal £69; ⏰restaurant noon-3pm Sun, 6-9pm daily; P🛜). The Michelin-starred restaurant is one of the best around, with imaginative, beautifully presented dishes.

Bibury

POP 627

Once described by William Morris as 'the most beautiful village in England', Bibury is a Cotswold gem with a cluster of gorgeous riverside cottages and tangle of narrow streets flanked by wayward stone buildings. The main attraction is **Arlington Row**, a stunning sweep of cottages, now thought to be the most photographed street in Britain. Also worth a look is the 17th-century **Arlington Mill**, just a short stroll away across Rack Isle, a wildlife refuge once used as a cloth-drying area.

Few visitors make it past these two sights, but for a glimpse of the real Bibury, venture into the village proper behind Arlington Row, where you'll find the Saxon **Church of St Mary**.

Kelmscott

Three miles east of Lechlade along the A417 lies the gorgeous Tudor pile that is **Kelmscott Manor** (☎01367-252486; www. kelmscottmanor.org.uk; Kelmscott; adult/child £9/4.50; ⏰11am-5pm Wed & Sat Apr-Oct), once the summer home of William Morris, the poet, artist and founder of the Arts and Crafts Movement. The interior is true to his philosophy that one should not own anything that is neither beautiful nor useful, and the house contains many of Morris' personal effects, as well as fabrics and furniture designed by him and his associates.

Painswick

POP 1770

One of the most beautiful and unspoilt towns in the Cotswolds, hilltop Painswick is an absolute gem. Despite its obvious charms, Painswick

Painswick
ANDREA PUCCI/GETTY IMAGES ©

sees only a trickle of visitors, so you can wander the narrow winding streets and admire the picture-perfect cottages, handsome stone townhouses and medieval inns in your own good time.

 Sights & Activities

Running downhill beside and behind the church is a series of gorgeous streetscapes. Look out for **Bisley Street**, the original main drag, which was superseded by the now ancient-looking **New Street** in medieval times. Just south of the church, rare **iron stocks** stand in the street.

St Mary's Church   Church
(www.stmaryspainswick.org.uk; New St; ⊙9.30am-6pm Apr-Sep, to 4pm Oct-Mar) The village centres on this fine 14th-century, Perpendicular Gothic wool church, surrounded by tabletop tombs and clipped yew trees that resemble giant lollipops. Legend had it that only 99 trees could ever grow here, as the devil would appear and shrivel the 100th tree where it ever planted. They planted it anyway, to celebrate the millennium and – lo and behold! – one of the trees toppled several years later. We're assured it's now making a good recovery.

Painswick Rococo Garden Gardens
(www.rococogarden.org.uk; adult/child £6.50/3; ⊙11am-5pm mid-Jan–Oct) A mile north of town, this is the only garden of its type in England, designed by Benjamin Hyett in the 1740s and now restored to its former glory. Winding paths soften the otherwise strict geometrical precision, bringing visitors around the central vegetable garden to the many Gothic follies dotted in the grounds. There's also a children's nature trail and maze.

Sleeping

Cardynham House   Hotel **££**
(☏ 01452-814006; www.cardynham.co.uk; Tibbiwell St; s/d from £70/90, lunch £12-14, dinner £14-17; ⊙bistro noon-3pm Tue-Sun, 6.30-9.30pm Tue-Sat; ☏⌨) Each of the differently themed rooms at 15th-century

Cardynham House has four-poster beds and heavy patterned fabrics. For a private pool and garden, book the Pool Room. Downstairs, the bistro (mains £10 to £20) serves hearty British fare.

Cotswolds88   Hotel **£££**
(☏ 01452-813688; www.cotswolds88.com; Kemps Lane; r/ste from £110/250, 2-/3-course lunch £15/20, dinner £43/50; ⊙restaurant noon-2.30pm & 7-9.30pm Wed-Sun; Ⓟ ⌨) This is a happy marriage of 18th-century architecture and over-the-top decor – from the wallpaper to the psychedelic lighting. Spacious, individually decorated rooms come with every creature comfort, and the suites have four-poster beds and spa baths. The restaurant is also excellent, featuring sophisticated yet playful fare.

THE MIDLANDS

Warwick

POP 31,345

Regularly name-checked by Shakespeare, Warwick was the ancestral seat of the Earls of Warwick, who played a pivotal role in the Wars of the Roses. Despite a devastating fire in 1694, Warwick remains a treasure-house of medieval architecture with rich veins of history and charming streets, dominated by the soaring turrets of magnificent Warwick Castle.

◉ Sights

Warwick Castle   Castle
(☏ 0871 265 2000; www.warwick-castle.com; castle adult/child £22.80/16.80, castle & dungeon £28.80/24, Kingdom Ticket incl castle, dungeon & exhibition £30.60/27; ⊙10am-6pm Apr-Sep, to 5pm Oct-Mar; Ⓟ) Founded in 1068 by William the Conqueror, stunningly preserved Warwick Castle is the biggest show in town. The ancestral home of the Earls of Warwick remains impressively intact, and the Tussauds Group has filled the interior with attractions that bring the castle's rich history to life in a flamboyant but undeniably family-friendly way. As

well as waxworks populating the private apartments there are jousting tournaments, daily trebuchet firings, themed evenings and a dungeon. Discounted online tickets provide fast-track entry. Parking costs £6.

Sleeping

Tilted Wig   Pub **££**
(☎01926-400110; www.tiltedwigwarwick.co.uk; 11 Market Pl; d £65-90, mains £8.50-14; P ⊚) Bang on the epicentral Market Pl, this brilliantly named 17th-century Georgian inn has four freshly refurbished, snug but comfortable rooms and some of the better pub grub in town, such as roast duck breast in port wine reduction. Guests can get a three-course meal for just £10 per person.

Park Cottage Guest House   B&B **££**
(☎01926-410319; www.parkcottagewarwick.co.uk; 113 West St; s £55-70, d £75-90; P ⊚) Southwest of the centre, this stand-alone 16th-century wattle-and-daub building once served as the dairy for Warwick Castle. There are seven pretty rooms, each with a teddy bear, original floors and a courtyard garden.

Eating

Merchants   Brasserie **££**
(☎01926-403833; www.merchantswarwick.co.uk; Swan St; mains £10.50-19.90; ⊙noon-9pm Mon-Thu, to 9.30pm Fri & Sat) With stylish leather furniture and chalkboard menus, this black-fronted restaurant and wine bar specialises in steaks.

Tailors   Modern British **£££**
(☎01926-410590; www.tailorsrestaurant.co.uk; 22 Market Pl; 2-/3-course lunch menu £15/19, 2-/3-course dinner menu £28/32.50; ⊙noon-1.45pm & 6.30-9pm Tue-Sat) Set in a former gentlemen's tailor shop, this elegant eatery serves prime ingredients – guinea fowl, pork belly and lamb from named farms – delicately presented in neat little towers.

ℹ Information

Tourist Office (☎01926-492212; www.visitwarwick.co.uk; Court House, Jury St; ⊙9.30am-4.30pm Mon-Fri, 10am-4pm Sat) Within the flagstone-floored Court House (1725). Sells the informative *Warwick Town Trail* leaflet (50p).

ℹ Getting There & Away

Trains run to Birmingham (£7.50, 40 minutes, half-hourly), Stratford-upon-Avon (£5.40, 30 minutes, hourly) and London (£28.80, 1½ hours, every 20 minutes), from the station, northeast of the centre.

··

Stratford-upon-Avon

POP 22,187

The author of some of the most quoted lines ever written in the English language, William Shakespeare was born in Stratford in 1564 and died here in 1616, and the five houses linked to his life form the centrepiece of the tourist attractions. Experiences in this unmistakably Tudor town range from the touristy (medieval re-creations and Bard-themed tearooms) to the humbling (Shakespeare's modest grave in Holy Trinity Church) and the sublime (taking in a play by the world-famous Royal Shakespeare Company).

◎ Sights & Activities

Shakespeare's Birthplace   Historic Building
(☎01789-204016; www.shakespeare.org.uk; Henley St; incl Nash's House & New Place & Halls Croft adult/child £15.90/9.50; ⊙9am-5.30pm Jul-Sep, to 5pm Oct-Jun) Start your Shakespeare quest at the house where the world's most popular playwright supposedly spent his childhood days. In fact, the jury is still out on whether this really was Shakespeare's birthplace, but devotees of the Bard have been dropping in since at least the 19th century, leaving their signatures scratched onto the windows. Set behind a modern facade, the house has restored Tudor rooms, live presentations from famous Shakespearean characters, and an engaging exhibition on Stratford's favourite son.

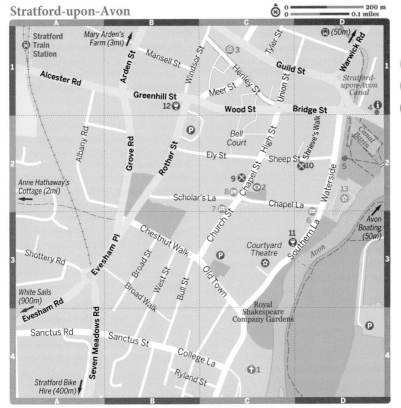

Stratford-upon-Avon

Nash's House & New Place
Historic Site

(☎01789-204016; www.shakespeare.org.uk; cnr Chapel St & Chapel Lane; incl Shakespeare's Birthplace & Halls Croft adult/child £15.90/9.50; ⏰10am-5pm mid-Mar–Oct) When Shakespeare retired, he swapped the bright lights of London for a comfortable town house at New Pl, where he died of unknown causes in April 1616. The house was demolished in 1759, but an attractive Elizabethan knot garden occupies part of the grounds. Archaeologists recently dug beneath the plot in search of Shakespearean treasures; their finds are displayed in the adjacent Nash's House, where Shakespeare's granddaughter Elizabeth lived. Displays describe the town's history and there's a collection of 17th-century furniture and tapestries.

Stratford-upon-Avon

Holy Trinity Church
Church

(☎01789-266316; www.stratford-upon-avon. org; Old Town; Shakespeare's grave adult/child £2/1; ⏰8.30am-6pm Mon-Sat, 12.30-5pm Sun Apr-Sep, reduced hours Oct-Mar) The final resting place of the Bard is said to be the most visited parish church in all of England. Inside are handsome 16th- and 17th-century tombs (particularly in the Clopton Chapel), some fabulous carvings on the choir stalls and, of course, the grave of William Shakespeare, with its ominous epitaph: 'cvrst be he yt moves my bones'.

Anne Hathaway's Cottage
Historic Building

(☎01789-204016; www.shakespeare.org.uk; Cottage Lane, Shottery; adult/child £9.50/5.50; ⏰9am-5pm mid-Mar–Oct) Before tying the knot with Shakespeare, Anne Hathaway lived in Shottery, a mile west of the centre of Stratford, in this delightful thatched farmhouse. As well as period furniture, it has gorgeous gardens and an orchard and arboretum, with examples of all the trees mentioned in Shakespeare's plays. A footpath (no bikes allowed) leads to Shottery from Evesham Pl.

Mary Arden's Farm
Historic Site, Farm

(☎01789-204016; www.shakespeare.org.uk; Station Rd, Wilmcote; adult/child £12.50/8; ⏰10am-5pm mid-Mar–Oct) Shakespeare genealogists can trace the family tree to the childhood home of the Bard's mother at Wilmcote, 3 miles west of Stratford. Aimed squarely at families, the working farm traces country life over the centuries, with nature trails, falconry displays and a collection of rare-breed farm animals. You can get here on the **City Sightseeing** (☎01789-412680; www. city-sightseeing.com; adult/child £12.50/6.50; ⏰every 30min Apr-Sep, less frequently Oct-Mar) bus, or cycle via Anne Hathaway's Cottage, following the Stratford-upon-Avon Canal towpath.

 Tours

Options include the popular and informative two-hour **guided town walks** (☎07855-760377; www.stratfordtownwalk. co.uk; adult/child £5/2; ⏰11am Mon-Thu, 2pm Fri, 11am & 2pm Sat & Sun) that depart from Waterside, opposite Sheep St, which is also the starting point for the spooky

Mary Arden's Farm

Stratford Town Ghost Walk (☏07855-760377; www.stratfordtownwalk.co.uk; adult/child £6/4; ⊙7.30pm Mon & Thu-Sat).

Avon Boating   Boat Tour
(☏01789-267073; www.avon-boating.co.uk; The Boathouse, Swan's Nest Lane; river cruises adult/child £5.50/3.50; ⊙9am-dusk Apr-Oct) Runs 40-minute river cruises that depart every 20 minutes from either side of the main bridge.

 Sleeping

Legacy Falcon   Hotel ££
(☏08444 119 005; www.legacy-hotels.co.uk; Chapel St; d/f from £83/113; P ⊕ ⊛) Definitely request a room in the original 15th-century building, not the soulless modern annex or dingy 17th-century garden house of this epicentral hotel. This way you'll get the full Tudor experience – creaky floorboards, wonky timbered walls and all. Open fires blaze in the wi-fi'd public areas; rooms have wired broadband but the best asset is the unheard-of-for-Stratford free car park.

White Sails   Guesthouse ££
(☏01789-550469; www.white-sails.co.uk; 85 Evesham Rd; d from £100; ❄) Plush fabrics, framed prints, brass bedsteads and shabby-chic tables and lamps set the scene at this gorgeous and intimate guesthouse on the edge of the countryside. The four individually furnished rooms come with flatscreen TVs, climate control and glamorous bathrooms.

**Church Street
Townhouse**   Boutique Hotel £££
(☏01789-262222; www.churchstreettownhouse. com; 16 Church St; d £110-200; ⊕) Some of the dozen rooms at this exquisite hotel have free-standing clawfoot bathtubs, and all have iPod docks, flatscreen TVs and luxurious furnishings. Light sleepers should avoid room 1, nearest the bar. The building itself is a centrally located 400-year-old gem with a first-rate restaurant and bar. Minimum two-night stay on weekends.

Shakespeare Historic Houses

Five of the most important buildings associated with Shakespeare contain museums that form the core of the visitor experience at Stratford. All are run by the Shakespeare Birthplace Trust.

Tickets for the three houses in town, Shakespeare's Birthplace, Nash's House & New Place and Halls Croft, cost £15.90/9.50 per adult/child. If you also visit Anne Hathaway's Cottage and Mary Arden's Farm, buy a combination ticket covering all five properties (£23.90/14).

Arden Hotel   Hotel £££
(☏01789-298682; www.theardenhotelstratford. com; Waterside; d incl breakfast from £129; P @) Facing the Swan Theatre, this elegant property has a sleek brasserie and champagne bar. Rooms feature designer fabrics and bathrooms are full of polished stone.

 Eating

**Church Street
Townhouse**   Bistro ££
(☏01789-262222; www.churchstreettown-house.com; 16 Church St; mains £12.25-17; ⊙8am-11pm; ⊕) This lovely restaurant is a fantastic place for immersing yourself in Stratford's historic charms. The food is delightful and well presented, and the ambience impeccably congenial.Music students from Shakespeare's old grammar school across the way tinkle the piano ivories daily at 5.30pm, though it can be hard to hear over the bar noise.

Lambs   Modern European ££
(☏01789-292554; www.lambsrestaurant.co.uk; 12 Sheep St; mains £11.75-18.75; ⊙5-9.30pm Mon & Tue, noon-2pm & 5-9.30pm Wed-Sat, noon-2.30pm & 6-9pm Sun) Lambs swaps

Detour:
Sherwood Forest National Nature Reserve

If Robin Hood wanted to hide out in Sherwood Forest today, he'd have to disguise himself and the Merry Men as daytrippers on mountain bikes. Now covering just 182 hectares of old growth forest, it's nevertheless a major destination for Nottingham city dwellers.

Until a proposed new visitor centre opens, the **Sherwood Forest visitor centre** (www.nottinghamshire.gov.uk; Swinecote Rd, Edwinstowe; parking £3; ⏰10am-5pm Easter-Oct, to 4.30pm Nov-Mar), on the B6034, is an uninspiring collection of faded late-20th-century buildings housing cafes, gift shops and 'Robyn Hode's Sherwode', with wooden cut-outs, murals and mannequins telling the tale of the famous woodsman. It's the departure point for walking trails passing such Sherwood Forest landmarks as the **Major Oak** (1 mile return), a broad-boughed oak tree (propped up by supporting rods) alleged to have sheltered Robin of Locksley. For informative guided walks try **Ezekial Bone Tours** (📞07941 210986; www.bonecorporation.co.uk; Robin Hood Town Tours adult/child £12/7, Guts & Gore tours £7; ⏰Sat May-Sep). The week-long **Robin Hood Festival** (www.nottinghamcity.gov.uk) is a massive medieval re-enactment that takes place here every August.

Shakespeare chintz in favour of Venetian blinds and modern elegance but throws in authentic 16th-century ceiling beams for good measure. The menu embraces Gressingham duck, deep-fried goats cheese and slow-roasted lamb shank, backed up by a strong wine list.

Edward Moon's Modern British **££**
(📞01789-267069; www.edwardmoon.com; 9 Chapel St; mains £10-18; ⏰12.30-3pm & 5-10pm Mon-Fri, noon-10pm Sat & Sun) Named after a famous travelling chef who cooked up the flavours of home for the British colonial service, this snug eatery serves delicious, hearty English dishes, many livened up with herbs and spices from the East.

 Drinking

Old Thatch Tavern Pub
(http://oldthatchtavernstratford.co.uk; Greenhill St; ⏰11.30am-11pm Mon-Sat, noon-6pm Sun; 📶) To truly appreciate Stratford's olde-worlde atmosphere, join the locals for a pint at the town's oldest pub. Built in 1470, this thatched-roofed, low-ceilinged treasure has great real ales and a gorgeous summertime courtyard.

Dirty Duck Pub
(Black Swan; Waterside; ⏰11am-11pm Mon-Sat, to 10.30pm Sun) Also called the 'Black Swan', this enchanting riverside alehouse is the only pub in England to be licensed under two names. It's a favourite thespian watering hole, with a roll-call of former regulars (Olivier, Attenborough et al) that reads like a who's who of actors.

 Entertainment

Royal Shakespeare Company Theatre
(RSC; 📞0844 800 1110; www.rsc.org.uk; Waterside; tickets £10-62.50) Coming to Stratford without seeing a Shakespeare production would be like visiting Beijing and bypassing the Great Wall. The three theatre spaces run by the world-renowned Royal Shakespeare Company have witnessed performances by such legends as Lawrence Olivier, Richard Burton, Judi Dench, Helen Mirren, Ian McKellan and Patrick Stewart.

 Information

Tourist Office (📞01789-264293; www.shakespeare-country.co.uk; Bridge Foot; ⏰9am-

5.30pm Mon-Sat, 10am-4pm Sun) Just west of Clopton Bridge on the corner with Bridgeway.

ⓘ Getting There & Away

If you drive to Stratford, be warned that town car parks charge high fees, 24 hours a day.

Train

From Stratford train station, London Midland runs to Birmingham (£7.30, 50 minutes, half-hourly), and Chiltern Railways runs to London Marylebone (£9, 2 hours, up to two per hour).

The nostalgic **Shakespeare Express** (☏0121-708 4960; www.shakespeareexpress.com; adult/child £15/10) steam train chugs twice every Sunday in July and August between Stratford and Birmingham Snow Hill; journey time is one hour.

ⓘ Getting Around

A bicycle is handy for getting out to the outlying Shakespeare properties. **Stratford Bike Hire** (☏07711-776340; www.stratfordbikehire.com; 7 Seven Meadows Rd; per half-day/day from £10/15) will deliver to your accommodation.

Punts, canoes and rowing boats are available for hire from Avon Boating (p153) near Clopton Bridge.

III to astound the world with the first-ever iron bridge, constructed in 1779. The bridge remains the focal point of this World Heritage Site, and 10 very different museums tell the story of the Industrial Revolution in the very buildings where it took place.

◉ Sights

The Ironbridge museums are administered by the **Ironbridge Gorge Museum Trust** (☏01952-433424; www.ironbridge.org. uk). You can buy tickets as you go, but the good-value **passport ticket** (adult/child £27.50/16.50) allows year-round entry to all of the sites.

Museum of the Gorge   Museum
(☏01952-433424; www.ironbridge.org.uk; The Wharfage; adult/child £4.15/3.25; ☺10am-5pm Mar-early Nov, to 4pm early Nov-Feb) Kick off your visit here for an overview of the World Heritage Site using film, photos and 3-D models. Housed in a Gothic warehouse by the river, it's filled with entertaining, hands-on exhibits.

Ironbridge Gorge

Strolling or cycling through the woods, hills and villages of this peaceful river gorge, it's hard to believe such a sleepy enclave could really have been the birthplace of the Industrial Revolution. Nevertheless, it was here that Abraham Darby perfected the art of smelting iron ore with coke in 1709, making it possible to mass-produce cast iron for the first time.

Abraham Darby's son, Abraham Darby II, invented a new forging process for producing single beams of iron, allowing Abraham Darby

Museum of the Gorge
MCPHOTO/AGE FOTOSTOCK ©

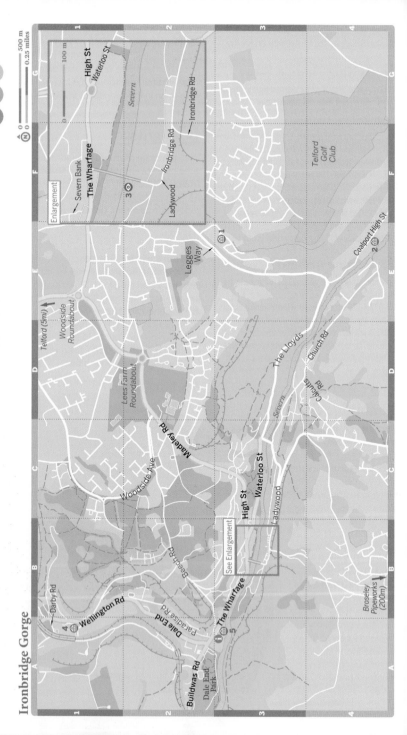

Ironbridge Gorge

Iron Bridge   Bridge

(www.ironbridge.org.uk; ⏰toll house 10am-5pm Sat & Sun Mar-early Nov, to 4pm Sat & Sun early Nov-Feb, daily during school holidays) **FREE** The flamboyant, arching and gravel-strewn Iron Bridge, which gives the area its name, was built to flaunt the new technology invented by the pioneering Darby family. At the time of its construction in 1779, nobody could believe that anything so large – it weighs 384 tonnes – could be built from cast iron without collapsing under its own weight. There's a small exhibition on the bridge's history at the former **toll house**.

Blists Hill Victorian Town Museum

(☎01952-433424; www.ironbridge.org.uk; Legges Way; adult/child £16.50/11; ⏰10am-5pm Mar-early Nov, to 4pm early Nov-Feb) Set at the top of the Hay Inclined Plane (a cable lift that once transported coal barges uphill from the Shropshire Canal), Blists Hill is a lovingly restored Victorian village repopulated with townsfolk in period costume, busy with day-to-day chores. There's even a bank, where you can exchange your modern pounds for shillings to use at the village shops. In summer, a Victorian fair is an added attraction for young ones.

Museum of Iron   Museum

(www.ironbridge.org.uk; Wellington Rd; adult/child £8.50/5.75, incl Darby Houses £9.25/6.75; ⏰10am-5pm Mar-early Nov, to 4pm early Nov-Feb) Set in the brooding buildings of Abraham Darby's original iron foundry, the Museum of Iron contains some excellent interactive exhibits. As well as producing the girders for the Iron Bridge, the factory became famous for heavy machinery and extravagant ornamental castings, including the gates for London's Hyde Park.

Coalport China Museum & Tar Tunnel   Museum

(www.ironbridge.org.uk; museum adult/child £8.50/5.75, Tar Tunnel £3.25/2.50; ⏰10.30am-4pm Mar-early Nov) As ironmaking fell into decline, Ironbridge diversified into manufacturing china pots, using the fine clay mined around Blists Hill. Dominated by a pair of towering bottle kilns, the atmospheric old china works now contains an absorbing **museum** tracing the history of the industry, with demonstrations of traditional pottery techniques.

A short stroll along the canal brings you to the 200-year-old **Tar Tunnel**, an artificial watercourse that was abandoned when natural bitumen started trickling from its walls.

ℹ Information

Tourist Office (☎01952-433424; www.ironbridge.co.uk; The Wharfage; ⏰10am-5pm) Located at the Museum of the Gorge.

ℹ Getting Around

At weekends and on bank holidays from Easter to October, the Gorge Connect bus (free to Museum Passport holders) runs from Telford bus station to all of the museums on the north bank of the Severn. A Day Rover pass costs £2.20/1.55 per adult/child.

Lincoln

POP 100,160

A bustling metropolis by Lincolnshire standards, but a sleepy backwater compared with almost anywhere else, Lincolnshire's county town is a tangle of cobbled medieval streets surrounding its colossal 12th-century cathedral. Ringed by historic city gates – including the Newport Arch on Bailgate, a relic from the original Roman settlement – this is one of the Midlands' most beautiful cities: the lanes that topple over the edge of Lincoln Cliff are lined with Tudor town houses, ancient pubs and quirky independent stores.

Detour:
Sulgrave Manor

The impressively preserved Tudor mansion **Sulgrave Manor** (www.sulgravemanor.org.uk; adult/child £7.90/3.60, garden only £3.60/free; ⊙11am-4pm Sat & Sun Apr-Jul, Sep & Oct, 11am-4pm Tue-Sun Aug) was built by Lawrence Washington in 1539 and the Washington family lived here for almost 120 years before Colonel John Washington, the great-grandfather of America's first president George Washington, sailed to Virginia in 1656.

Sulgrave Manor is southwest of Northampton, just off the B4525 near Banbury.

◎ Sights

Lincoln Cathedral   Cathedral
(☏01522-561600; http://lincolncathedral.com; Minster Yard; adult/child £8/1 Mon-Sat, by donation Sun; ⊙7.15am-8pm Mon-Fri, to 6pm Sat & Sun, evensong 5.30pm Mon-Sat, 3.45pm Sun) Towering over Lincoln like a medieval skyscraper, Lincoln's magnificent cathedral is a breathtaking representation of divine power on earth. The great tower rising above the crossing is the third-highest in England at 83m, but in medieval times, a lead-encased wooden spire added a further 79m, topping even the great pyramids of Giza.

One-hour **guided tours** take place at least twice daily; there are less-frequent tours of the roof and the tower. All are included in admission; booking is essential.

Lincoln Castle   Castle
(www.lincolnshire.gov.uk/lincolncastle; adult/child £2/1.20; ⊙10am-6pm May-Aug, to 5pm Apr & Sep, to 4pm Oct-Mar) One of the first castles erected by the victorious William the Conqueror to keep his new kingdom in line, Lincoln Castle offers awesome views over the city and miles of surrounding countryside. Highlights include the chance to view one of the four surviving copies of the **Magna Carta** (dated 1215) and the grim **Victorian prison chapel**, from when this was the county jailhouse and execution ground.

Free 75-minute **guided tours** run once or twice daily (on weekends only in December and January).

Bishops' Palace   Historic Site
(EH; ☏01522-527468; www.english-heritage.org.uk; adult/child £4.70/2.80; ⊙10am-6pm Wed-Sun Apr-Sep, to 5pm Wed-Sun Oct, to 4pm Sat & Sun Nov-Mar) Beside Lincoln Cathedral lie the time-ravaged but still imposing ruins of the 12th-century Bishops' Palace, gutted by parliamentary forces during the Civil War. From here, the local bishops once controlled a diocese stretching from the Humber to the Thames. Entertaining audioguides are included in admission.

🛏 Sleeping

Castle Hotel   Boutique Hotel ££
(☏01522-538801; www.castlehotel.net; Westgate; s £90, d £110-140, incl breakfast; Ⓟ🛜) Each of the 18 rooms at this boutique hotel have been exquisitely refurbished in olive, truffle and oyster tones. Built on the site of Lincoln's Roman forum in 1852, the red-brick building's incarnations variously include a school and WWII lookout station. Take advantage of the great-value dinner, bed and breakfast deals linked to its award-winning restaurant Reform (p159).

Bail House   B&B ££
(☏01522-541000; http://bailhouse.jpchotelsandleisure.co.uk; 34 Bailgate; d from £79; Ⓟ@🛜♨🚼) Stone walls, worn flagstones, secluded gardens and one room with an extraordinary timber-vaulted ceiling are just some of the charms of this lovingly restored Georgian town house in central Lincoln. There's limited on-site parking, a garden and children's playground, and even a seasonal heated outdoor swimming pool.

🍴 Eating

La Bottega Delitalia
Cafe, Deli £

(9 West Pde; dishes £2.15-7.45; ⊙9am-4pm Mon-Wed, to 9pm Thu & Fri, 8.30am-3pm Sat) Authentic Italian fare such as lobster ravioli in creamy tomato and basil sauce is made from scratch at this inexpensive cafe-deli. Cash only.

Reform
Modern British ££

(☎01522-538801; www.castlehotel.net; The Castle Hotel, Westgate; mains £13.50-23.95; ⊙noon-2.30pm & 7-9pm Mon-Sat, noon-3pm & 7-9pm Sun) Inspired by local, seasonal produce, the Castle Hotel's sophisticated restaurant serves starters such as feta beignets with pomegranate and mint-and-coriander Israeli couscous, followed by mains such as pork confit with artichoke risotto and sage onion rings. The real showstoppers, however, are desserts such as warm plum-and-raspberry crumble tart with white-chocolate ice cream and quince purée.

Bronze Pig
Modern British ££

(☎01522-524817; http://thebronzepig.co.uk; 6 West Pde; mains £15-24; ⊙dinner by reservation Wed-Sat) BBC Masterchef 2012 finalist, Irishman Eamonn Hunt, and Sicilian chef Pompeo Siracusa have taken Lincoln's dining scene by storm since opening the Bronze Pig. Their exceptional Modern British cooking has an Italian accent and food is locally sourced. Reserve well ahead and prepare to be wowed.

ℹ️ Information

Tourist Office
(☎01522-545458; www.visitlincoln.com; 9 Castle Hill; ⊙10am-5pm Mon-Sat, 10.30am-4pm Sun) Friendly office in a handsome 16th-century building.

ℹ️ Getting There & Away

Train
Getting to and from Lincoln by rail usually involves changing trains.

Sheffield £14.10, 80 minutes, hourly

York £36.30, two hours, two per hour

PEAK DISTRICT

Rolling across the southernmost hills of the Pennines, the Peak District is one of the most beautiful parts of the country. Founded in 1951, the Peak District National Park was England's first national park and is Europe's busiest. But escaping the crowds is easy if you avoid summer weekends. Even at the busiest times, there are 555 sq miles of open English countryside in which to find your own viewpoint to soak up the glorious scenery.

Locals divide the Peak District into the Dark Peak – dominated by exposed moorland and gritstone 'edges' – and the

Stanage Edge, the Peak District National Park
ALAN COPSON/GETTY IMAGES ©

White Peak, made up of the limestone dales to the south.

The Peak's most famous walking trail is the **Pennine Way**, which runs north from Edale for more than 250 miles, finishing in the Scottish Borders.

Information

The Peak District National Park Authority website (www.peakdistrict.gov.uk) is a goldmine of information on transport, activities and local events.

Buxton

POP 22,115

At the heart of the Peak District National Park (albeit outside the park boundary) Buxton is a picturesque sprawl of Georgian terraces, Victorian amusements and parks in the rolling hills of the Derbyshire dales. The town built its fortunes on its natural warm-water springs, which attracted health tourists in Buxton's heyday.

◎ Sights

Buxton's historic centre is a riot of Victorian pavilions, concert halls and glasshouse domes. Its most famous building is the flamboyant, turreted **Opera House** (☎0845 127 2190; www.buxtonoperahouse.org.uk; Water St; tours £2.50; ⊘tours 11am Sat), which hosts an impressive variety of stage shows.

The Opera House adjoins the equally flamboyant **Pavilion Gardens** (www.paviliongardens.co.uk; ⊘9.30am-5pm) FREE, dotted with domed pavilions.

Another glorious piece of Victoriana, the **Devonshire Dome**, forms part of the University of Derby campus and is also home to **Devonshire Spa** (☎01298-338408; www.devonshiredome.co.uk; 1 Devonshire Rd; 2hr body spa £20, ocean or frangipani wrap £50, day package from £95), which offers a full range of pampering treatments.

In Victorian times, spa activities centred on the extravagant **Buxton Baths** complex, built in grand Regency style in 1854.

At the base of the Slopes is the **Pump Room**, which dispensed Buxton's spring water for nearly a century. Modern-day health-tourists queue up to fill plastic bottles from a small spout known as **St Ann's Well**.

🛏 Sleeping

Old Hall Hotel   Historic Hotel ££
(☎01298-22841; www.oldhallhotelbuxton.co.uk; The Square; s/d incl breakfast from £69/79; @⎚) There's a tale to go with every creak of the floorboards at this history-soaked establishment, supposedly the oldest hotel in England. Among other esteemed residents, Mary, Queen of Scots, stayed here from 1576 to 1578, albeit against her will. The rooms are still the grandest in town, and there are several bars, lounges and dining options.

Roseleigh Hotel   B&B ££
(☎01298-24904; www.roseleighhotel.co.uk; 19 Broad Walk; s/d from £41/80; P@⎚) This gorgeous family-run B&B in a roomy old Victorian house has lovingly decorated rooms, many with fine views out over the Pavilion Gardens. The owners are a welcoming couple, both seasoned travellers, with plenty of interesting stories.

Victorian Guest House   B&B ££
(☎01298-78759; www.buxtonvictorian.co.uk; 3a Broad Walk; d from £95; P⎚) Overlooking the Pavilion Gardens, this elegant house has eight individually decorated bedrooms furnished with Victorian and Edwardian antiques. The home-cooked breakfasts are renowned.

Eating

Number 13   Modern British ££
(☎01298-25397; www.number13.co.uk; cnr Market St & South Ave; mains £11-16; ⊘noon-10.30pm Mon-Thu, to midnight Fri & Sat, noon-7pm Sun) 🍴 Don't be fooled by the low prices – this is serious cooking that just happens to be affordable too. Dishes such as coq au vin in garlic and red wine or sausage and root mash with smoked onion marmalade are expertly prepared and

GLENN BEANLAND/GETTY IMAGES ©

⭐ Don't Miss
Chatsworth House

Known as the 'Palace of the Peak', **Chatsworth House** (📞01246-565300; www.chatsworth.org; house & gardens adult/child £18/10, gardens only £12/7, playground £6, park admission free; ⏱11am-4.30pm mid-Mar–late Dec, garden 11am-6pm mid-Mar–late Dec) has been occupied by the earls and dukes of Devonshire for centuries.

While the core of the house dates from the 16th century, Chatsworth was altered and enlarged over the centuries. The current building has a Georgian feel, dating back to the last overhaul in 1820. Inside, the lavish apartments and mural-painted staterooms are packed with priceless paintings and period furniture. Look out for the portraits of the current generation of Devonshires by Lucian Freud.

The house sits in 25 sq miles of grounds and ornamental gardens, some landscaped by Lancelot 'Capability' Brown.

Chatsworth is 3 miles northeast of Bakewell.

exquisitely presented. Live jazz swings in the bar on Sunday afternoons.

Columbine Restaurant
Modern British ££

(📞01298-78752; www.columbinerestaurant.co.uk; 7 Hall Bank; mains £13.50-17.50; ⏱7-10pm Mon-Sat May-Oct & Dec, 7-10pm Wed-Sat Jan-Apr & Nov) 🥢 On the lane leading down beside the Town Hall, this understated restaurant is the top choice among in-the-know Buxtonites. The chef conjures up imaginative dishes primarily made from local produce. Bookings recommended.

ℹ Information

Tourist Office (📞01298-25106; www.visitpeakdistrict.com; Pavilion Gardens; ⏱9.30am-5pm; 📶) Helpful, well-organised office with useful leaflets on walks in the area. Hour-long Roman Buxton town walks, by donation, depart at 11am and 2pm Saturdays.

Castleton

POP 735

Guarding the entrance to the forbidding Winnats Pass gorge, charming Castleton is a magnet on summer weekends for East Midlands visitors – try coming midweek to enjoy the sights in relative peace and quiet.

Sights

Peveril Castle   Castle

(EH; www.english-heritage.org.uk; adult/child £4.70/2.80; ⊙10am-6pm Apr-Sep, 10am-5pm Oct, 10am-4pm Sat & Sun Nov-Mar) Topping the ridge to the south of Castleton, this evocative castle has been so ravaged by the centuries that it almost looks like a crag itself. Constructed by William Peveril, son of William the Conqueror, the castle was used as a hunting lodge by Henry II, King John and Henry III, and the crumbling ruins offer swooping views over the Hope Valley.

Castleton Museum   Museum

(☎01629-816572; Buxton Rd; ⊙10am-5.30pm Apr–mid-Sep, 10am-5pm mid-Sep–Oct, reduced hours Nov-Mar) FREE Attached to the tourist office, the cute town museum has displays on everything from mining and geology to rock climbing, hang-gliding and the curious Garland Festival.

Peak Cavern   Cave

(☎01433-620285; http://devilsarse.com; adult/child £9.25/7.25, incl Speedwell Cavern £15.50/11.75; ⊙10am-5pm Apr-Oct, 10am-5pm Sat & Sun Nov-Mar) Castleton's most convenient cave is easily reached by a pretty streamside walk from the village centre. It has the largest natural cave entrance in England, known (not so prettily) as the Devil's Arse. Dramatic limestone formations are lit with fibre-optic cables.

Speedwell Cavern   Cave

(☎01433-620512; www.speedwellcavern.co.uk; adult/child £10/8, incl Peak Cavern £15.50/11.75; ⊙9.30am-4pm) About half a mile west of Castleton at the mouth of Winnats Pass,

Left: The grounds of Peveril Castle; **Below:** A typical pub lunch

(LEFT) VISITBRITAIN/TONY PLEAVIN/GETTY IMAGES ©; (BELOW) VISITBRITAIN/DANIEL BOSWORTH/GETTY IMAGES ©

this claustrophobe's nightmare is reached via an eerie boat ride through flooded tunnels, emerging by a huge subterranean lake called the Bottomless Pit. New chambers are discovered here all the time by potholing expeditions.

Sleeping

Ye Olde Nag's Head Hotel   Pub £
(☏01433-620248; www.yeoldenagshead.co.uk; Cross St; d from £50; 🛜) The cosiest of the 'residential' pubs along the main road, offering 10 comfortable, well-appointed rooms (some with four-poster beds and spas), ale-tasting trays and a popular restaurant, plus regular live music.

Causeway House   B&B ££
(☏01433-623921; www.causewayhouse.co.uk; Back St; s/d from £35/70) The floors within this ancient character-soaked stone cottage are worn and warped with age, but the quaint bedrooms are bright and welcoming. Doubles have en suites but the two single rooms (one of which can be used as a twin) share a bathroom.

Eating & Drinking

1530   Italian ££
(☏01433-621870; www.1530therestaurant. co.uk; Cross St; mains £9.50-17; ⏰noon-2pm & 6-8.30pm Wed & Thu, noon-2pm & 6-9.30pm Fri & Sat, noon-2pm & 6-8pm Sun & Mon; 🖍) Crispy thin-crust pizzas and fresh pastas such as king prawn, crab, crayfish and calamari linguine are the speciality of Castleton's swish Italian flag-bearer.

Samuel Fox   Modern British £££
(☏01433-621562; www.samuelfox.co.uk; Stretfield Rd, Bradwell; lunch mains £6-18.50, dinner mains £13.50-22.50; ⏰kitchen 6-9pm Tue, noon-2pm & 6-9pm Tue-Sat, noon-3.30pm Sun) In the Hope Valley village of Bradwell, 2.5 miles southeast of Castleton, this enchanting inn owned by pedigreed chef James Duckett serves exceptional food such

163

If You Like...
Cathedrals

If you've been inspired by the majestic proportions of Lincoln Cathedral (p158), here are a few more English ecclesiastical wonders.

1 ELY CATHEDRAL
(www.elycathedral.org; The Gallery; adult/child £8/free, entry & tower tour £14.50/free; ⊙7am-6.30pm, evensong 5.30pm Mon-Sat, 4pm Sun, choral service 10.30am Sun) The stunning silhouette of Ely Cathedral is locally dubbed the 'Ship of the Fens' as it is visible across the flat fenland for vast distances.

2 COVENTRY CATHEDRAL
(☏024-7652 1200; www.coventrycathedral.org.uk; Priory Row; adult/child £8/5.75; ⊙10am-4pm) Coventry's original cathedral was destroyed by Nazi bombing during WWII, but was replaced by this modernist masterpiece designed by Sir Basil Spence.

3 HEREFORD CATHEDRAL
(☏01432-374200; www.herefordcathedral.org; 5 College Cloisters; cathedral entry by £5 donation, Mappa Mundi £6; ⊙9.15am to evensong, Mappa Mundi 10am-5pm Mon-Sat May-Sep, to 4pm Mon-Sat Oct-Apr, evensong 5.30pm Mon-Sat, 3.30pm Sun) Highlights of Hereford's cathedral are the 'chained library' and the magnificent Mappa Mundi, depicting the globe circa 1290.

4 LICHFIELD CATHEDRAL
(☏01543-306100; www.lichfield-cathedral.org; admission by donation; ⊙7.30am-6.15pm Sun-Fri, 8am-6.15pm Sat) Crowned by three dramatic towers, Lichfield Cathedral is a stunning Gothic fantasy, constructed in stages from 1200 to 1350.

5 WORCESTER CATHEDRAL
(☏01905-732900; www.worcestercathedral.co.uk; admission by £5 donation, tower adult/child £4/2, tours £4/free; ⊙7.30am-6pm, tower 11am-5pm Sat Apr-Oct, tours 11am & 2.30pm Mon-Sat Mar-Nov, 11am & 2.30pm Sat Dec-Feb; 🚻) Rising above the River Severn, Worcester's majestic cathedral is best known as the final resting place of Magna Carta signatory King John.

as rare roasted venison with pickled red cabbage and roast pheasant with braised sprouts, bacon and parsnips. Rates for the gorgeous pastel-shaded guest rooms upstairs (single/double £95/130) include a sumptuous breakfast as well as sherry, grapes and chocolates.

ℹ Information

Tourist Office (☏01433-620679; www.peakdistrict.gov.uk; Buxton Rd; ⊙10am-5.30pm Apr–mid-Sep, 10am-5pm mid-Sep–Oct, reduced hours Nov-Mar) In the Castleton Museum.

Bakewell

POP 3949

The second-largest town in the Peak District, pretty Bakewell is a great base for exploring the White Peak. The town is ringed by famous walking trails and stately homes, but it's probably best known for its famous pudding (of which the Bakewell Tart is just a poor imitation).

◎ Sights

Up on the hill above Rutland Sq, **All Saints Church** (www.bakewellchurch.co.uk; ⊙9am-4pm Mon-Sat, to 6pm Sun Apr-Oct, 10am-3.45pm daily Nov-Mar) is packed with ancient features, including a 14th-century font, a pair of Norman arches, some fine heraldic tombs and a collection of crude stone gravestones and crosses dating back to the 12th century.

Set in a time-worn stone house near the church, the **Old House Museum** (www.oldhousemuseum.org.uk; Cunningham Pl; adult/child £3.50/2, incl Spirit of the 1940s £5/2; ⊙11am-4pm Apr-early Nov) explores local history. Check out the Tudor loo and the displays on wattle and daub, a traditional technique for building walls using woven twigs and cow dung. Nearby, its recently opened collection **Spirit of the 1940s** (www.oldhousemuseum.org.uk; Tanners Yard; adult/child £2/50p, incl Old House Museum £5/2; ⊙10.30am-4pm Fri-Mon Apr-

early Nov) incorporates an evocative '40s street scene, letters and photographs, and wartime memorabilia.

Sleeping

Melbourne House & Easthorpe
B&B ££

(☎01629-815357; www.bakewell-accommodation.co.uk; Buxton Rd; d from £70; P) In a picturesque, creeper-covered building dating back more than three centuries and a new annexe, this inviting B&B is handily situated on the main road leading to Buxton.

Rutland Arms Hotel
Hotel £££

(☎01629-812812; www.rutlandarmsbakewell.co.uk; The Square; s £82-95, d £139-195; P 🛜) Jane Austen is said to have stayed in room 2 of this aristocratic, recently refurbished stone coaching inn while working on *Pride and Prejudice*. The more expensive of its 33 rooms have lots of Victorian flourishes.

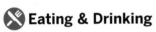 Eating & Drinking

Piedaniel's
French ££

(☎01629-812687; www.piedaniels-restaurant.com; Bath St; mains £17, 2-/3-course lunch £16/18 Tue-Fri; ⊙noon-2pm & 7-9pm Tue-Sat)

Chefs Eric and Christiana Piedaniel's Modern French cuisine is the toast of in-town restaurants. A whitewashed dining room is the exquisite setting for the likes of lobster bisque with *quenelles* (feather-light flour, egg and cream dumplings) followed by monkfish in salmon mousse. Weekday lunch menus are exceptional value.

Castle Inn
Pub

(☎01629-812103; www.oldenglishinns.co.uk; Bridge St; 🛜 👬) The ivy-draped Castle Inn is one of the better pubs in Bakewell, with four centuries of practice in rejuvenating hamstrung hikers. Gourmet burgers are a menu highlight (mains £8 to £17).

 Information

Tourist Office (☎01629-813227; www.visitpeakdistrict.com; Bridge St; ⊙9.30am-5pm Apr-Oct, 10.30am-4.30pm Nov-Mar) In the old Market Hall; the helpful staff can book accommodation.

Bath & Southwest England

If it's scenic splendour you're after, the southwest serves it up in spades. From the grand cityscapes of Bristol, Bath and Exeter to Dartmoor's wild heaths and Cornwall's epic coastline, this is a region that never fails to inspire.

Fringed by craggy cliffs and golden beaches, swathed by great plains and stony moors, it offers a wealth of opportunity for hiking, biking and other fresh air pursuits. It's also awash with architecture: cathedrals and abbeys, stately homes and castles – as well as the mysterious stone circles of Avebury and Stonehenge.

But the southwest also has an eye to the future, with a growing number of cutting-edge restaurants and cultural sights, including the gigantic greenhouses of the Eden Project, Bath's futuristic bath complex and Bristol's new M Shed Museum. In fact, there's so much to see and do, you'll be hard pressed to fit it all into one visit.

Bath (p176)

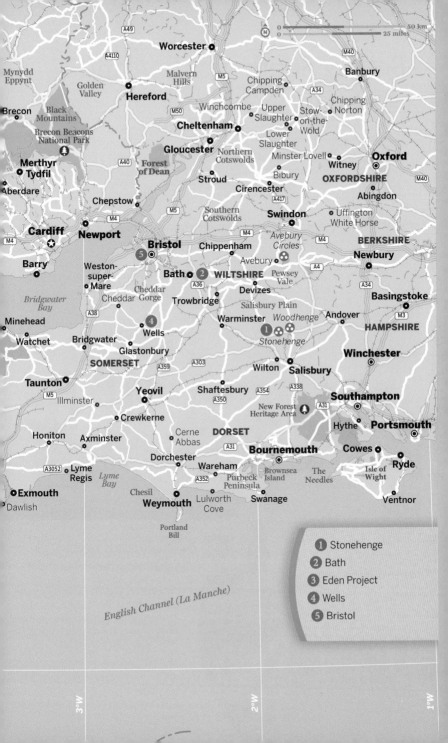

Bath & Southwest England Highlights

Stonehenge

The imposing trilithons of Stonehenge (p192) – a 5000-year-old circle of vast standing stones topped with horizontal lintels – are immediately recognisable all around the world, a visual shorthand for the enigma of prehistoric culture. Despite being one of the most studied sites on earth, we still don't know the real meaning of this mysterious ancient monument.

Bath's Roman Baths

Ever since the Romans arrived in Bath (p176), life has revolved around the three hot springs that bubble up near the abbey. For almost 2000 years the baths have attracted tourists from all over Europe, and now form one of the best-preserved ancient Roman spas in the world.

Eden Project

Record producer turned eco-champion Tim Smit has transformed an old clay pit near St Austell in Cornwall into the space-age Eden Project (p207), where the massive greenhouses (or 'biomes') – the largest in the world – re-create a range of natural habitats, from tropical rainforest to dry desert. The rest of the site explores all the hot-topic issues surrounding climate change, sustainability and environmental protection.

Bristol

During the 18th and 19th centuries, Bristol (p185) was one of Britain's most important ports, and its streets are lined with spectacular architecture, best seen around the genteel suburb of Clifton and its famous suspension bridge. The city's also known for its culture and museums – don't miss a visit to the SS *Great Britain*, a ground-breaking trans-Atlantic liner that's been restored to its former glory.

Wells

The pretty little market town of Wells (p182) qualifies as England's smallest city thanks to the magnificent monument of Wells Cathedral, which sits in the centre beside the grand Bishop's Palace – still the ecclesiastical seat of the Bishop of Bath and Wells. Ancient buildings and cobbled streets radiate out from the cathedral green to a marketplace that has been the bustling heart of Wells for some nine centuries. Wells Cathedral (p183)

171

Bath & Southwest England's Best...

Cathedrals & Abbeys

o **Salisbury Cathedral** Climb the tallest spire of any English cathedral (p190)

o **Winchester Cathedral** Plain on the outside, but the interior is awe-inspiring (p188)

o **Wells Cathedral** A medieval gem in this miniature city (p183)

o **Bath Abbey** The last great medieval church raised in England (p176)

o **Glastonbury Abbey** Evocative ruins and legendary burial place of King Arthur (p185)

Iconic Landmarks

o **St Michael's Mount** Cornwall's island-topped abbey, star of a thousand postcards (p208)

o **Eden Project** The world's largest greenhouses in a former Cornish claypit (p207)

o **Royal Crescent** The epitome of Georgian architecture in beautiful Bath (p176)

o **Clifton Suspension Bridge** Brunel's 19th-century masterpiece over the Avon Gorge (p186)

Artistic Links

o **Tate St Ives** Home to Barbara Hepworth's studio and an offshoot of the Tate Gallery (p205)

o **Minack Theatre** Catch a play at this amazing clifftop theatre (p208)

o **Greenway** Visit Agatha Christie's summer hideaway (p201)

o **Bristol** Guerrilla graffiti artist Banksy's home town (p185)

o **Jane Austen Centre** Enjoy afternoon tea at this literary museum in Bath (p179)

Need to Know

Views

o **Dartmoor** An otherworldly landscape of moors and tors (p202)

o **Cheddar Gorge** Wander the clifftops of England's deepest gorge (p184)

o **Glastonbury Tor** Legends swirl around this mystical hill in the heart of Somerset (p185)

o **Land's End** Stirring coastal scenery at the very edge of England (p208)

ADVANCE PLANNING

o **Two months before** Book hotels in popular spots such as Bath; reserve a Special Access Visit at Stonehenge.

o **One month before** Arrange car hire and book train tickets.

o **Two weeks before** Buy tickets online for major sights such as the Roman Baths, SS *Great Britain* and the Eden Project.

RESOURCES

o **Southwest England** (www.visitsouthwest.co.uk)

o **Bath** (www.visitbath.co.uk)

o **Somerset** (www.visitsomerset.co.uk)

o **Wiltshire** (www.visitwiltshire.co.uk)

o **Devon** (www.visitdevon.co.uk)

o **Cornwall** (www.visitcornwall.com)

GETTING AROUND

o **Bus** Long-distance buses between main towns and cities are good. Local buses are infrequent in some rural areas.

o **Train** Connections between the major towns are fast and frequent, and there are several scenic branch lines.

o **Car** The easiest way to get around, but beware of traffic jams, especially in summer. Bigger cities have Park & Ride systems, where you can park your car safely and catch a bus to the centre.

BE FOREWARNED

o **High season** The southwest counties (especially Devon and Cornwall) are packed in July and August, when thousands of families head for the beach.

o **Bath** Crowds are a fact of life in Bath, and can be oppressive in summer. Spring and autumn are less hectic.

o **Minor roads** Many of the southwest's minor roads are narrow, winding and tricky to navigate. GPS can be more of a hindrance than a help.

Bath & Southwest England Itineraries

Our suggested three-day loop from Bath takes in two spectacular medieval cathedral towns and the prehistoric icon of Stonehenge. The five-day trip saunters through the southwest, via the key highlights.

BATH TO BATH
3 DAYS HISTORICAL HIGHLIGHTS

Start your tour in the beautiful city of
❶ **Bath**. A day here should include a visit to the Roman Baths, which give the city its name – go early or late in the day to avoid the crowds. Other sights include Bath Abbey and the fabulous Georgian architecture around the centre, especially the Royal Crescent and the nearby Circus.

Then it's off for a day trip to nearby
❷ **Bristol**, a historic harbour city with a wealth of fascinating sights. Factor in the SS *Great Britain*, a wander around Clifton and the Suspension Bridge, and a visit to the new M Shed Museum – and leave plenty of

time for lunch at one of the city's excellent eateries.

Head onwards into Wiltshire for a stop to see the mighty cathedral spire in
❸ **Salisbury** en route to one of England's most unmistakable landmarks, the trilithons of ❹ **Stonehenge**. True fans of ancient Britain might like to divert via the southwest's other great stone circle at ❺ **Avebury** – it's even bigger than Stonehenge, and has a pub in the middle. From here it's a short loop back to Bath.

5 DAYS

BATH TO ST IVES

THE WAY OUT WEST

Start your tour with a couple of days in
①Bath, admiring the elegant architecture
and historic sites, then head south to
the little city of **②Wells**, where the star
of the show is the medieval gem of Wells
Cathedral.

It's then a short hop to visit the nearby
caves of **③Cheddar Gorge** and the grassy
hump of **④Glastonbury Tor**, the supposed
burial site of King Arthur, and the focal
point for a whole host of other myths and
legends.

Detour west for a spectacular drive
across the wild moors and lonely tors of
⑤Dartmoor, the southwest's largest and
wildest national park.

Soon after you'll cross the border into
Cornwall, once an independent Celtic
kingdom, now known for its beautiful
beaches and pretty seaside towns. Key
sights include the crumbling castle of
⑥Tintagel, the eco-domes of the **⑦Eden
Project** and the iconic abbey of **⑧St
Michael's Mount**. The artistic harbour of
⑨St Ives makes an ideal base.

St Ives (p205)
JOHN HARPER/GETTY IMAGES ©

Discover Bath & Southwest England

At a Glance

○ **Hampshire & Wiltshire** (p188) Prehistoric remains and historic cities litter these ancient counties.

○ **Bristol** (p185) The southwest's biggest city, with culture and nightlife to match.

○ **Bath** (p176) Home to Britain's grandest Georgian architecture.

○ **Devon & Cornwall** (p196; p201) The far west of England, with miles of unspoilt coast and countryside.

Bath Abbey
SURAARK/GETTY IMAGES ©

BATH

POP 90,144

Britain is littered with beautiful cities, but precious few can hold a candle to Bath. Founded on top of a network of natural hot springs, Bath's heyday really began during the 18th century, when local entrepreneur Ralph Allen and his team of father-and-son architects, John Wood the Elder and Younger, turned this sleepy backwater into the toast of Georgian society, and constructed fabulous landmarks such as the Circus and Royal Crescent.

◎ Sights

Bath Abbey   Church

(☏01225-422462; www.bathabbey.org; requested donation £2.50; ☾9am-6pm Mon-Sat, 1-2.30pm & 4.30-5.30pm Sun) Looming above the city centre, Bath's huge abbey church was built between 1499 and 1616, making it the last great medieval church raised in England. Its most striking feature is the west facade, where angels climb up and down stone ladders, commemorating a dream of the founder, Bishop Oliver King.

Tower tours (towertours@bathabbey.org; adult/child £6/3; ☾11am-5pm Apr-Aug, to 4pm Sep-Oct, to 3pm Dec-Mar) leave on the hour from Monday to Friday, or every half-hour on Saturdays, but don't run on Sundays.

Royal Crescent   Historic Site

Bath is justifiably celebrated for its glorious Georgian architecture, and it doesn't get any grander than on Royal Crescent, a semicircular terrace of majestic townhouses overlooking the green sweep of Royal Victoria Park. Designed by John Wood

DAVID WILLIAMS/GETTY IMAGES ©

⭐ Don't Miss
Roman Baths

In typically ostentatious style, the Romans constructed a complex of bathhouses above Bath's three natural hot springs, which emerge at a steady 46°C (115°F). Situated alongside a temple dedicated to the healing goddess Sulis Minerva, the baths now form one of the best-preserved ancient Roman spas in the world, encircled by 18th and 19th century buildings. As Bath's premier attraction, the Roman Baths can get very, very busy. Avoid the worst crowds by buying tickets online, visiting early on a midweek morning, and avoiding July and August.

NEED TO KNOW

📞 01225-477785; www.romanbaths.co.uk; Abbey Churchyard; adult/child/family £13.50/8.80/38; ⏰ 9am-6pm, to 9pm Jul & Aug

the Younger (1728–82) and built between 1767 and 1775, the houses appear perfectly symmetrical from the outside, but the owners were allowed to tweak the interiors to their own specifications; consequently no two houses on the Crescent are quite the same.

Bath Assembly Rooms 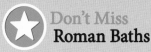 Historic Building

(www.nationaltrust.org.uk/main/w-bathassembly rooms; 19 Bennett St; adult/child £2.50/free; ⏰ 10.30am-6pm) Opened in 1771, the city's

glorious Assembly Rooms were where fashionable Bath socialites once gathered to waltz, play cards and listen to the latest chamber music. Rooms open to the public include the card room, tearoom and ballroom, all lit by their original 18th-century chandeliers. It's free if you already have a ticket to the Fashion Museum.

Holburne Museum Gallery

(📞 01225-388569; www.holburne.org; Great Pulteney St; ⏰ 10am-5pm) FREE Sir William Holburne, the 18th-century aristocrat and

177

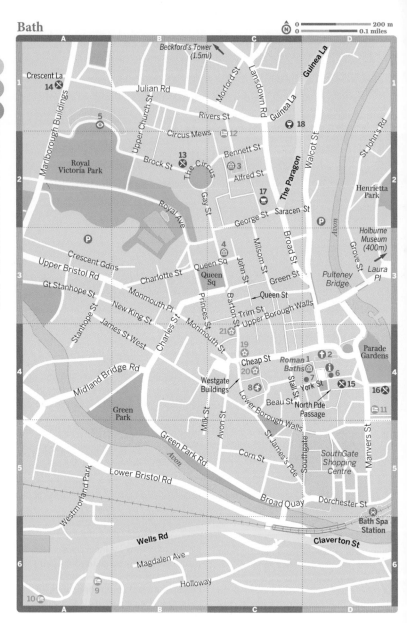

0   200 m
0   0.1 miles

art fanatic, amassed a huge collection which now forms the core of the Holburne Museum, in a lavish mansion at the end of Great Pulteney St. Fresh from a three-year refit, the museum houses a roll-call of works by artists including Turner, Stubbs, William Hoare and Thomas Gainsborough, as well as 18th-century majollica and porcelain. Admission to temporary exhibitions incurs a fee.

Bath

Jane Austen Centre   Museum

(☏01225-443000; www.janeausten.co.uk; 40 Gay St; adult/child £8/4.50; ◷9.45am-5.30pm) Bath is known to many as a location in Jane Austen's novels, including *Persuasion* and *Northanger Abbey*. Though Austen only lived in Bath for five years from 1801 to 1806, she remained a regular visitor, and a keen student of the city's social scene. This museum houses memorabilia of her life in Bath, and there's a Regency tearoom which serves crumpets and cream teas in suitably frilly surroundings.

Fashion Museum   Museum

(☏01225-477282; www.fashionmuseum.co.uk; Assembly Rooms, Bennett St; adult/child £8/6; ◷10.30am-5pm) In the basement of the Assembly Rooms, this museum contains costumes worn from the 16th to late-20th centuries.

American Museum in Britain   Museum

(☏01225-460503; www.americanmuseum.org; Claverton Manor; adult/child £9/5; ◷noon-5pm) Britain's largest collection of American folk art, including Native American textiles, patchwork quilts and historic maps, is housed in a fine mansion a couple of miles from the city centre. Several rooms have been decorated to resemble a 17th-century Puritan house, an 18th-century tavern and a New Orleans boudoir c 1860. Catch bus 18/418/U18 from the bus station.

Tours

Mayor's Guide Tours   Walking Tour

(☏01225-477411; www.bathguides.org.uk; ◷10.30am & 2pm Sun-Fri, 10.30am Sat) FREE Excellent historical tours, provided free by the Mayor's Corp of Honorary guides, leave from outside the Pump Room. There are extra tours at 7pm on Tuesdays and Thursdays May to September. They cover about 2 miles and are wheelchair accessible.

Jane Austen's Bath   Walking Tour

(☏01225-443000; www.janeausten.co.uk/jane-austen-centre-walking-tours; adult/child £12/10; ◷11am Sat & Sun) A guided tour of the Georgian city, organised by the Jane Austen Centre. 1½-hr tours leave from the Abbey churchyard.

Sleeping

Bath gets incredibly busy, especially in the height of summer and at weekends, when prices are at a premium. Very few hotels have parking, although some offer discounted rates at municipal car parks.

139 Bath   B&B ££

(☏01225-314769; www.139bath.co.uk; 139 Wells Rd; r £125-195; Ⓟ🛜) It's a bit out of the centre, but this swish B&B has been thoughtfully designed, with supremely comfy beds, plus spoils such as cafetière

Thermae Bath Spa

Taking a dip in the Roman Baths might be off the agenda, but you can still sample the city's curative waters at **Thermae Bath Spa** (☎0844-888 0844; www.thermaebathspa.com; Bath St; ⊙9am-10pm, last entry 7.30pm). Here the old **Cross Bath**, incorporated into an ultramodern shell of local stone and plate glass, is now the setting for a variety of spa packages. The New Royal Bath ticket includes steam rooms, waterfall shower and a choice of bathing venues – including the jaw-dropping open-air rooftop pool, where you can swim in the thermal waters in front of a backdrop of Bath's stunning cityscape.

coffee and spa baths in some rooms. Posh, but perhaps pricey for what you get.

Grays Boutique B&B B&B £££
(☎01225-403020; www.graysbath.co.uk; Upper Oldfield Park; d £120-195; 🛜) An elegant B&B straight out of an interiors magazine. All the rooms are individual: some with feminine flowers or polkadot prints, others with maritime stripes, but all simple and stylish (we particularly liked room two, with its French bed and bay window). Breakfast is served in the conservatory, with eggs, milk and bacon from local farms. The owners run a smaller but equally smart B&B on the east side of town, **Brindleys** (☎01225-310444; www.brindleysbath.co.uk; 14 Pulteney Gardens; d £110-185).

Halcyon Hotel £££
(☎01225-444100; www.thehalcyon.com; 2/3 South Pde; d £125-145; 🛜) Just what Bath needed: a smart city-centre hotel that doesn't break the bank. Situated on a terrace of townhouses off Manvers St, the Halcyon offers style: uncluttered rooms, contemporary bed linen and Philippe Starck bath fittings.

Queensberry Hotel Hotel £££
(☎01225-447928; www.thequeensberry.co.uk; 4 Russell St; d £115-225; [P] 🛜) The quirky Queensberry is Bath's best boutique spoil. Four Georgian town houses have been combined into one seamlessly stylish whole. Some rooms are cosy in gingham checks and country creams, others feature bright upholstery, original fireplaces and freestanding tubs. The Olive Tree Restaurant is excellent, too. Rates exclude breakfast.

Eating

Sally Lunn's Tearoom £
(4 North Pde Passage; mains £5-15; ⊙10am-9pm) Eating a bun at Sally Lunn's is just one of those things you have to do in Bath. It's all about proper English tea here, brewed in bone-china teapots, with finger sandwiches and dainty cakes served by waitresses in frilly aprons.

Circus Modern British ££
(☎01225-466020; www.thecircuscafeand restaurant.co.uk; 34 Brock St; mains lunch £8.30-13.50, dinner £16.50-18.50; ⊙10am-10pm Mon-Sat) Chef Ali Golden has turned this bistro into one of Bath's destination addresses. Her taste is for British dishes with a continental twist, à la Elizabeth David: rabbit, guinea-fowl, roast chicken, spring lamb, infused with herby flavours and rich sauces. It occupies the ground floor and basement of a town house near the Circus. Reservations recommended.

Marlborough Tavern Gastropub ££
(☎01225-423731; www.marlborough-tavern. com; 35 Marlborough Bldgs; lunch £9-13, dinner mains £13.50-21.50; ⊙noon-11pm) The queen of Bath's gastropubs, with food that's closer to a fine-dining restaurant – think duo of venison and pork tenderloin rather than standard meat-and-two-veg. Chunky wooden tables and racks of wine behind the bar give it an exclusive, classy feel.

Sotto Sotto Italian ££
(☎01225-330236; www.sottosotto.co.uk; 10a North Pde; pasta £9, mains £13-17; ⊙noon-2.30pm & 5-10.30pm) Bath's best Italian, hidden away in a vaulted cellar. Ingredients

are shipped in from Italy and everything's just like mamma made, from the classic house lasagne to more unusual options such as veal, grilled swordfish and sea bass in parma ham.

Menu Gordon Jones   Modern British £££

(☎01225-480871; www.menugordonjones. co.uk; 2 Wellsway; 5-course lunch £40, 6-course dinner £50; ☺12.30-2pm & 7-9pm Tue-Sat) If you enjoy dining with an element of surprise, then Gordon Jones' restaurant will be right up your culinary boulevard. Menus are dreamt up daily by the chef, and showcase his taste for experimental ingredients (candied citrus, cod tongues, biodynamic wines) and madcap presentation (test-tubes, edible cups, slate plates). It's superb value given the skill on show.

🍷 Drinking

Star Inn   Pub

(www.star-inn-bath.co.uk; 23 The Vineyards, off The Paragon; ☺noon-11pm) Not many pubs are registered relics, but the Star is – it still has many of its 19th-century bar fittings. It's the brewery tap for Bath-based Abbey Ales; some ales are served in traditional jugs, and you can even ask for a pinch of snuff in the 'smaller bar'.

Same Same But Different   Cafe

(7a Prince's Bldgs, Bartlett St; ☺8am-6pm Mon-Wed, to 11pm Thu-Sat, 10am-5pm Sun) Boho hang-out for the town's trendies, tucked down an alley off George St. Savour wine by the glass, snack on tapas or sip a cappuccino with the Sunday papers.

⭐ Entertainment

Theatre Royal   Theatre

(www.theatreroyal.org.uk; Sawclose) Bath's historic theatre dates back 200 years. Major touring productions go in the main auditorium, while smaller shows appear in the Ustinov Studio.

Komedia   Cabaret, Comedy

(www.komedia.co.uk; 22-23 Westgate St) Live comedy and cabaret at this Bath offshoot of the Brighton-based original.

Bath's Architecture

RECOMMENDATIONS FROM DR AMY FROST, BATH PRESERVATION TRUST

1 THE ROYAL CRESCENT

The elegant proportions of the Royal Crescent display all the qualities that British architects sought to perfect in the 18th century. Go around the back however, and it's another story. The uniform facades conceal a mix-and-match of features – each house is different inside because they were built by different craftsman for different clients.

2 THE CIRCUS

The Circus is much more decorative than the Royal Crescent, from the Masonic symbols above the doorways to the acorns that run along the rooflines. Its design was inspired by Rome's Colosseum, but its architect, John Wood the Elder, was also fascinated by stone circles – so it's really ancient Rome meets Stonehenge.

3 THE ASSEMBLY ROOMS

Life in Georgian Bath was all about being part of the social elite, and the Assembly Rooms were the place to be seen. The grandest of the interiors is the ballroom, with a balcony for musicians and a fabulous set of 18th-century English chandeliers. In the tea rooms some of the stone is slightly pink, showing the damage caused by fire when the Rooms were bombed in 1942.

4 UPPER BOROUGH WALLS

Most of Bath's medieval wall was lost during the building boom of the 18th century. But on Upper Borough Walls you will find a rare surviving fragment. You're actually walking alongside the battlements, almost two storeys above the original ground level of the medieval city. The Georgians literally built on top of it.

Little Theatre Cinema   Cinema

(St Michael's Pl) Bath's excellent art-house cinema screens fringe films and foreign-language flicks.

ⓘ Information

Bath Visitor Centre (☏0906 711 2000, accommodation bookings 0844 847 5256; www.visitbath.co.uk; Abbey Churchyard; ⌚9.30am-5pm Mon-Sat, 10am-4pm Sun) Sells the **Bath Visitor Card** (http://visitbath.co.uk/special-offers/bath-visitor-card; £3). The general enquiries line is charged at 50p per minute.

ⓘ Getting There & Away

Bath Spa station is at the end of Manvers St. Many services connect through Bristol (£9.90, 20 minutes, two or three per hour), especially to the north of England.

London Paddington or **London Waterloo** (£42, 1½ hours, half-hourly)

Cardiff Central (£19.40, one hour, hourly)

Exeter (£32, 1¼ hours, hourly)

Salisbury (£16.90, one hour, hourly)

ⓘ Getting Around

Bath has serious traffic problems (especially at rush hour). **Park & Ride services** (☏01225-464446; return Mon-Fri £3, Sat £2.50; ⌚6.15am-7.30pm Mon-Sat) operate from Lansdown to the north, Newbridge to the west and Odd Down to the south. It takes about 10 minutes to the centre; buses leave every 10 to 15 minutes. If you brave the city, the best value car-park is underneath the new SouthGate shopping centre (two/eight hours £3.30/10, after 6.30pm £2).

WELLS

POP 10,406

In Wells, small is beautiful. This tiny, picturesque metropolis is England's smallest city, and only qualifies for the 'city' title thanks to a magnificent medieval cathedral, which sits in the centre beside the grand Bishop's Palace.

Left: Wells Cathedral; **Below:** Cloisters, Wells Cathedral
(LEFT) IAN WOOLCOCK/SHUTTERSTOCK ©; (BELOW) JULIAN ELLIOTT PHOTOGRAPHY/GETTY IMAGES ©

◎ Sights

Wells Cathedral   Cathedral

(Cathedral Church of St Andrew; www.wells
cathedral.org.uk; Cathedral Green; requested
donation adult/child £6/3; ⊘7am-7pm) Wells'
gargantuan Gothic cathedral sits plum in
the centre of the city, surrounded by one
of the largest cathedral closes anywhere
in England. It was built in stages between
1180 and 1508, and consequently showcases several Gothic styles. Among its
notable features are the West Front, decorated with more than 300 carved figures,
and the famous scissor arches – an ingenious architectural solution to counter
the subsidence of the central tower.

Cathedral Close   Historic Site

Wells Cathedral forms the centrepiece of
a cluster of ecclesiastical buildings dating
back to the Middle Ages. Facing the west
front, on the left are the 15th-century
Old Deanery and the **Wells & Mendip
Museum** (www.wellsmuseum.org.uk;

8 Cathedral Green; adult/child £3/1; ⊘10am-
5.30pm Easter-Oct, 11am-4pm Wed-Mon Nov-
Easter), with exhibits on local life, cathedral
architecture and the infamous Witch of
Wookey Hole.

Further along, **Vicars' Close** is a
stunning 14th-century cobbled street,
with a chapel at the end; members of the
cathedral choir still live here. It is thought
to be the oldest complete medieval street
in Europe. **Penniless Porch**, a corner
gate leading onto Market Sq, is so-called
because beggars asked for alms here.

Bishop's Palace   Historic Building

(www.bishopspalacewells.co.uk; adult/child
£7/3; ⊘10am-6pm Apr-Oct, to 4pm Nov-Mar)
Built for the bishop in the 13th century,
this moat-ringed palace is purportedly
the oldest inhabited building in England.
Inside, the palace's state rooms and
ruined great hall are worth a look, but it's
the shady gardens that are the real draw.

183

The natural springs after which Wells is named bubble up in the palace's grounds.

Famously, the palace's population of mute swans have been trained to ring a bell when they want to be fed.

Sleeping

Beryl
B&B ££

(📞01749-678738; www.beryl-wells.co.uk; Hawkers Lane; d £100-150; P⚡) This grand gabled mansion offers a taste of English eccentricity. Every inch of the house is crammed with antique atmosphere, and the rooms boast grandfather clocks, chaises longues and four-posters galore. It's about a mile from Wells.

Ancient Gate House Hotel
Hotel ££

(📞01749-672029; www.ancientgatehouse.co.uk; Browne's Gate; s £90-100, d £110-130; 🛜) This old hostelry is partly built right into the cathedral's west gate. Rooms are decorated in regal reds and duck-egg blues; the best have four-poster beds and knockout cathedral views through latticed windows. They're £15 extra, but worth it.

Eating

Old Spot
British ££

(📞01749-689099; www.theoldspot.co.uk; 12 Sadler St; lunch £18.50, dinner mains £14-21.50; ⏰12.30-2.30pm Wed-Sun, 7-9.30pm Tue-Sat) Run by husband-and-wife team Ian and Clare Bates, this restaurant focuses on British classics with a streak of Italian spice – rump of lamb with polenta and peperonata, or guinea-fowl with risotto.

Goodfellows
Bistro, Cafe £££

(📞01749-673866; www.goodfellows.co.uk; 5 Sadler St) There's a choice of settings at Goodfellows: a continental-style **cafe** (lunch £10-17, dinner £20-25; ⏰8.30am-4pm Mon & Tue, 8.30am-5pm & 6-10pm Wed-Sat) for quick lunches, cakes and pastries, or a full-blown **seafood bistro** (3-/6-course menu £42/55; ⏰noon-2pm Tue-Sat, 6.30-9.30pm Wed-Sat) for sit-down dining. The quality at both is excellent.

 Information

Tourist office (📞01749-672552; www.wellstourism.com; Market Pl; ⏰9.30am-5.30pm Apr-Oct, 10am-4pm Nov-Mar) Stocks the *Wells City Trail* leaflet (30p) and sells discount tickets to Wookey Hole and Cheddar Gorge.

CHEDDAR GORGE

Carved out by glacial meltwater during the last Ice Age, the limestone cliffs of **Cheddar Gorge** (www.cheddargorge.co.uk; Explorer Ticket adult/child £18.50/12; ⏰10am-5.30pm) form England's deepest natural canyon, in places towering 138m above the twisting B3135 road.

The gorge is famous for its bewildering network of subterranean caves, a few of which are open to the public. **Cox's Cave** and **Gough's Cave**, both lined with stalactites and stalagmites, are subtly illuminated to bring out the spectrum of colours in the rock. To explore the more remote caverns, you'll need to organise a caving trip with **X-Treme** (📞01934-742343; www.cheddargorge.co.uk/x-treme; 1½-hr trip adult/child £21/19); be prepared to get cold, wet and very muddy. Rock-climbing sessions are also available.

Cheddar gets extremely busy during summer and school holidays, when the gorge road turns into one long traffic jam. You can normally escape the worst crowds by climbing the 274-step staircase known as **Jacob's Ladder**, which leads to a spectacular viewpoint and a 3-mile cliff trail. There's a 15% discount for online booking.

GLASTONBURY

POP 8429

Ley lines converge, white witches convene and every shop is filled with the aroma of smouldering joss-sticks in good old Glastonbury, the southwest's undisputed capital of alternative culture.

The famous **Glastonbury Festival** (www.glastonburyfestivals.co.uk), a majestic (and frequently mud-soaked) extravaganza of music, theatre, dance, cabaret, carnival, spirituality and general all-round weirdness has been held on and off on a farm in Pilton, just outside Glastonbury, for the last 40-something years.

Sights

Glastonbury Tor   Landmark
(NT; www.nationaltrust.org.uk/glastonbury-tor) Topped by the ruined medieval **Chapel of St Michael**, the iconic hump of Glastonbury Tor is visible for miles around, and provides Somerset with one of its most unmistakable landmarks. It takes half an hour to walk up from the start of the trail on Well House Lane; the steepest sections are stepped. You can walk to the trailhead from the town centre in about 20 minutes, or catch the regular Tor Bus, which shuttles from Dunstan's car park near the Abbey to the trailhead on Well House Lane.

Glastonbury Abbey   Ruins
(✆ 01458-832267; www.glastonburyabbey.com; Magdalene St; adult/child £6/4; ⏰ 9am-8pm) The scattered ruins of Glastonbury Abbey give little hint that this was once one of England's great seats of ecclesiastical power. It was torn down following Henry VIII's dissolution of the monasteries in 1539, and the last abbot, Richard Whiting, was hung, drawn and quartered on the tor. Precious little remains save for a few nave walls, the ruined **St Mary's chapel**, and the crossing arches, which may have been scissor-shaped like those in Wells Cathedral.

ℹ Information

Glastonbury Tourist Office (✆ 01458-832954; www.glastonburytic.co.uk; The Tribunal, 9 High St; ⏰ 10am-5pm)

BRISTOL
POP 393,300

Bristol might just be Britain's most overlooked city. While most visitors speed past en route to Bath without giving the southwest's biggest metropolis so much as a second glance, they're missing out on one of Britain's quirkiest and coolest cities.

◎ Sights

Brunel's SS Great Britain   Historic Site
(✆ 0117-926 0680; www.ssgreatbritain.org; Great Western Dock, Gas Ferry Rd; adult/child/family £13.75/7/36.50; ⏰ 10am-5.30pm Apr-Oct, to 4.30pm Nov-Mar) Bristol's pride and joy is the mighty steamship SS *Great Britain*, designed by the genius engineer Isambard Kingdom Brunel in 1843. Driven by a revolutionary screw propeller, this massive vessel was one of the largest and most technologically advanced steamships ever built, measuring 322ft (98m) from stern to tip. Originally built as a

Clifton Wood, Bristol Harbourside
KENNETH COX/GETTY IMAGES ©

luxury transatlantic liner, she later fell into disrepair but has since been painstakingly restored to her full glory.

M Shed   Museum

(☎ 0117-352 6600; www.bristolmuseums.org. uk/m-shed; Princes Wharf; ⏱ 10am-5pm Tue-Fri, to 6pm Sat & Sun; ♿) **FREE** Opened in 2011 alongside the iconic cranes of Bristol's dockside, this impressive museum is a treasure trove of memorabilia rummaging through the city's past. The exhibits are divided into three sections (People, Place and Life), and provide a panoramic overview of Bristol's history – from slaves' possessions and vintage buses to Wallace and Gromit figurines and a set of decks once used by Massive Attack. It's all highly interactive, child-friendly – and, best of all, free.

Clifton Suspension Bridge   Bridge

(www.cliftonbridge.org.uk) Clifton's most famous (and photographed) landmark is a Brunel masterpiece, the 76m-high Clifton Suspension Bridge, which spans the Avon Gorge. Construction began in 1836, but Brunel died before its completion in 1864. Designed to carry light horse-drawn traffic and foot passengers, these days the

bridge carries around 12,000 cars every day – testament to the vision of Brunel's design. It's free to walk or cycle across; car drivers pay a £1 toll.

Sleeping

Brooks Guest House   B&B ££

(☎ 0117-930 0066; www.brooksguesthouse-bristol.com; Exchange Ave; d £85-120; 🛜) If you want to be in the heart of things, this brilliantly central B&B is a fine bet. It's in a modern building opposite St Nick's Market. Rooms are boxy, but pleasantly finished with flock wallpaper, John Lewis bed linen and Hansgröhe power showers. Discounted parking is available for £14 a day at the nearby Queen Charlotte St car park.

Number 38   B&B £££

(☎ 0117-946 6905; www.number38clifton. com; 38 Upper Belgrave Rd, Clifton; d £135-210; 🅿 🛜) Perched on the edge of the Downs, this upmarket B&B is the choice for the style-conscious. The rooms are huge and contemporary – sombre greys and smooth blues dictate the palette, luxury is provided by waffle bathrobes and REN

Powderham Castle

bath goodies, and city views unfold from the roof terrace. The two suites have old-fashioned tin baths.

Eating

Canteen
Cafe £

(☎0117-923 2017; www.canteenbristol.co.uk; 80 Stokes Croft; mains £4-10; ☺10am-10pm)
🍽 Occupying the ground floor of an old office block in gritty Stokes Croft, this community-run cafe sums up Bristol's alternative character: it's all about slow food, local suppliers and fair prices, whether you pop in for a bacon butty, veggie chilli or sit-down supper. There's regular live music, and artists' studios to explore.

Riverstation
British ££

(☎0117-914 4434; www.riverstation.co.uk; The Grove; 2-/3-course lunch £12.75/15.50, dinner mains £15.50-19.50; ☺noon-2.30pm & 6-10pm) One of Bristol's original dining destinations, and still leading the pack. The riverside location is hard to beat, with a view over the Floating Harbour, but it's the food that keeps the punters coming back: classic in style with a strong European flavour, from French fish soup to steak *à la béarnaise*. The **bar+kitchen** downstairs is open all day for coffee and cakes.

Fishers
Seafood ££

(☎0117-974 7044; www.fishers-restaurant. com; 35 Princess Victoria St; mains £11.95-15.50; ☺noon-2.30pm & 6.30-10pm) Top choice for a fish supper, from baked bream to megrim sole; the hot shellfish platter (£43 for two people) is made for sharing. The simple setting, with its whitewashed walls, ships' lanterns and nautical knick-knacks, contributes to the maritime vibe.

ℹ Information

Bristol Tourist Information Centre (☎0906 711 2191; www.visitbristol.co.uk; E-Shed, 1 Canons Rd; ☺10am-4pm Mon-Sat, 11am-4pm Sun) Calling the phone number costs the premium rate of 50p per minute.

♥ If You Like…
Castles

The southwest is home to an impressive array of historic castles and fortresses. Here are a few that are particularly worth seeking out.

1 CORFE CASTLE
(NT; ☎01929-481294; www.nationaltrust. org.uk; The Square; adult/child £8/4; ☺10am-6pm Apr-Sep, to 4pm Oct-Mar) One of Dorset's most iconic landmarks, Corfe Castle was all but blown to bits during the English Civil War, and its fractured defences feel wonderfully atmospheric. It's 20 miles east of Dorchester.

2 POWDERHAM CASTLE
(☎01626-890243; www.powderham.co.uk; adult/child £11/10; ☺11am-4.30pm Sun-Fri Apr-Oct; P) Powderham was built in 1391 and heavily remodelled in the Victorian era. It's still the home of the Earl of Devon

3 PENDENNIS CASTLE
(EH; ☎01326-316594; adult/child £7/4.20; ☺10am-6pm Jul & Aug, to 5pm Apr-Jun & Sep, to 4pm Oct-Mar) This Tudor castle sits on Pendennis Point, just outside the Cornish seaport of Falmouth. Highlights include the atmospheric Tudor gun deck, a WWI guard house and the WWII-era Half-Moon Battery.

4 TINTAGEL CASTLE
(EH; ☎01840-770328; adult/child £6.10/3.70; ☺10am-6pm Apr-Sep, to 5pm Oct, to 4pm Nov-Mar) This dramatic clifftop castle on the north Cornish coast is said to be King Arthur's legendary birthplace, but the ruins mostly date from the 13th century. It's about 22 miles northeast of Padstow.

ℹ Getting There & Away

Bristol is an important rail hub, with regular services to London provided by **First Great Western** (www.firstgreatwestern.co.uk) and services to northern England and Scotland mainly covered by **Cross Country** (www. crosscountrytrains.co.uk).

Exeter (£27, one hour, hourly)

Glasgow (£148, 6½ hours, hourly)

London (£42, 1¾ hours, hourly)

Penzance (£45, 5½ hours, hourly)

Truro (£45, five hours, hourly)

EXMOOR NATIONAL PARK

Barely 21 miles across and 12 miles north to south, Exmoor might be the little sister of England's national parks, but what she lacks in scale she more than makes up for in scenery. Part wilderness expanse, part rolling fields, dotted with bottle-green meadows, wooded combes and crumbling cliffs, Exmoor seems to sum up everything that's green and pleasant about the English landscape.

It's a haven for ramblers, mountain-bikers and horse-riders, and it's also home to lots of rare wildlife, including some of England's largest herds of wild red deer; best spotted on a dawn safari.

Several companies offer 4WD 'safari' trips across the moor: the best season to visit is autumn, especially from October onwards, when the annual autumn 'rutting' season begins, and stags can be seen bellowing, charging and clashing horns in an attempt to impress their prospective mates. Standard 2½-hour safari trips cost around £30, although longer expeditions can usually be arranged with plenty of advance notice.

Barle Valley Safaris (☏01643-841326; www.exmoorwildlifesafaris.co.uk; adult/child £30/25)

Red Stag Safari (☏01643-841831; www.redstagsafari.co.uk; safari £25-38)

ⓘ Information

Exmoor National Park Authority (ENPA; www.exmoor-nationalpark.gov.uk) There are national park tourist offices in :

Dulverton (☏01398-323841; www.exmoor-nationalpark.gov.uk; 7-9 Fore St, Dulverton; ☉10am-5pm),

Dunster (☏01643-821835; www.exmoor-nationalpark.gov.uk; Dunster Steep, Dunster; ☉10am-5pm) and

Lynmouth (☏01598-752509; www.exmoor-nationalpark.gov.uk; The Esplanade, Lynmouth; ☉10am-5pm).

HAMPSHIRE & WILTSHIRE

Winchester

POP 116,600

Calm, collegiate Winchester is a mellow must-see for all visitors. The past still echoes strongly around the flint-flecked walls of this ancient cathedral city.

◎ Sights

Winchester Cathedral Cathedral
(☏01962-857225; www.winchester-cathedral.org.uk; The Close; adult/child incl cathedral body & crypt tours £7.50/free; ☉9.30am-5pm Sat, 12.30-3pm Sun) One of southern England's most awe-inspiring buildings, 11th-century Winchester Cathedral boasts a fine Gothic facade, one of the longest medieval naves in Europe (164m), and a fascinating jumble of features from all eras. Other highlights include the intricately carved medieval choir stalls, which sport everything from mythical beasts to a mischievous green man, and one of the UK's finest illuminated manuscripts. The cathedral's three separate, excellent **tours** of the ground floor, crypt and tower can get busy – book ahead.

Winchester College Historic Building
(☏01962-621100; www.winchestercollege.org; College St; adult/child £6/5; ☉10.45am & noon Mon-Sat, plus 2.15pm & 3.30pm Mon, Wed, Fri-Sun) Winchester College delivers a rare chance to nosey around a prestigious English private school. It was set up by William Wykeham, Bishop of Winchester in 1393, 14 years after he founded

Oxford's New College. Hour-long guided tours take in the 14th-century Gothic chapel, complete with wooden vaulted roof, the dining room (called College Hall), and a vast 17th-century open classroom (called School), where exams are still held. A revealing insight into how the other half learns.

Wolvesey Castle
Castle

(EH; ☎ 02392-378291; www.english-heritage.org.uk; College St; ⊙ 10am-5pm Apr-Oct) **FREE** The fantastical, crumbling remains of early-12th-century Wolvesey Castle huddle within the the city's walls. Completed by Henry de Blois, it served as the Bishop of Winchester's residence throughout the medieval era, with Queen Mary I and Philip II of Spain celebrating their wedding feast here in 1554. According to legend, its name comes from a Saxon king's demand for an annual payment of 300 wolves' heads. Today the bishop lives in the (private) **Wolvesey Palace** next door.

Round Table & Great Hall
Historic Building

(☎ 01962-846476; www.hants.gov.uk/greathall; Castle Ave; suggested donation £2; ⊙ 10am-5pm) **FREE** Winchester's cavernous Great

Hall is the only part of 11th-century Winchester Castle that Oliver Cromwell spared from destruction. Crowning the wall like a giant-sized dartboard of green and cream spokes is what centuries of mythology has dubbed King Arthur's Round Table. It's actually a 700-year-old copy, but is fascinating nonetheless. It's thought to have been constructed in the late 13th century and then painted in the reign of Henry VIII (King Arthur's image is unsurprisingly reminiscent of Henry's youthful face).

Sleeping

St John's Croft
Boutique B&B ££

(☎ 01962-859976; www.st-johns-croft.co.uk; St John's St; s/d £45/85; P 🛜) You may well fall in love with this oh-so-casually stylish, rambling Queen Anne town house, where rattan carpets are teamed with bulging bookcases, and Indian art with shabby-chic antiques. The rooms are vast, the garden is tranquil and breakfast is served beside the Aga in the country-house kitchen.

Great Hall, Winchester Castle

Wykeham Arms
Inn £££

(☎01962-853834; www.wykehamarmswinchester.co.uk; 75 Kingsgate St; s/d/ste £65/150/180; P ⬤) At 250-odd years old, the Wykeham bursts with history – it used to be a brothel and also put Nelson up for a night (some say the events coincided). Creaking stairs lead to plush bedrooms that manage to be both deeply established but also on-trend; brass bedsteads meet jazzy throws, oak dressers sport stylish lights. Simply smashing.

Eating

Chesil Rectory
British ££

(☎01962-851555; www.chesilrectory.co.uk; 1 Chesil St; mains £14-20; ⊙noon-2.20pm & 6-9.30pm) It's almost as if they created a checklist for a great date: hushed tones, flickering candles, dark beams. They get the food right too, from lighter offerings such as white onion risotto, to flavourful braised ox cheek, or roasted guinea fowl with red wine.

Black Rat
Fine Dining £££

(☎01962-844465; www.theblackrat.co.uk; 88 Chesil St; mains £23, 2-/3-course lunch £23/26; ⊙7-9pm daily, noon-2.15pm Sat & Sun) The aromas are irresistible, the food frankly fabulous, the cooking highly technical and the ingredients dare to surprise – expect cuttlefish, rabbit saddle, black garlic, sea-weed salt, loveage and blowtorched back fat. That'll be why the Black Rat deserves its Michelin star.

ⓘ Information

Tourist Office (☎01962-840500; www.visitwinchester.co.uk; High St; ⊙10am-5pm Mon-Sat, plus 11am-4pm Sun May-Sep)

ⓘ Getting There & Away

Trains leave half-hourly to hourly for London Waterloo (£33, 1¼ hours) and hourly for Portsmouth (£11, 11/4 hours). There are also fast links to the Midlands.

Salisbury

POP 40,300

Centred on a majestic cathedral that's topped by the tallest spire in England, the gracious city of Salisbury makes a charming base from which to discover the rest of Wiltshire.

◉ Sights

Salisbury Cathedral
Cathedral

(☎01722-555120; www.salisburycathedral.org.uk; Cathedral Close; requested donation adult/child £6.50/3; ⊙9am-5pm Mon-Sat, noon-4pm Sun) England is endowed with countless stunning churches, but few can hold a candle to the grandeur and sheer spectacle of 13th-century Salisbury Cathedral. This early

Salisbury Museum
BARRY WINIKER/GETTY IMAGES ©

Salisbury

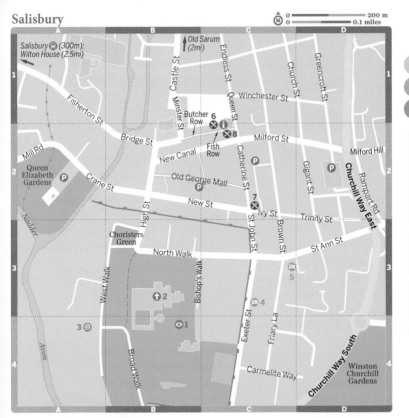

English Gothic–style structure has an elaborate exterior decorated with pointed arches and flying buttresses, and a sombre, austere interior designed to keep its congregation suitably pious. Its statuary and tombs are outstanding; don't miss the daily tower tours and the Cathedral's original, 13th-century copy of the Magna Carta. It's best experienced on a **Tower Tour** (adult/child £10/8; ⏱1-5 daily).

Cathedral Close   Historic Site

Salisbury's medieval cathedral close, a hushed enclave surrounded by beautiful houses, has an other-worldly feel. Many of the buildings date from the 13th century, although the area was heavily restored during an 18th-century clean-up by James Wyatt. The close is encircled by a sturdy outer wall, constructed in 1333;

Salisbury

◎ Sights
1 Cathedral Close	B4
2 Salisbury Cathedral	B3
3 Salisbury Museum	A4

⊟ Sleeping
4 Spire House	C3
5 St Ann's House	C3

⊗ Eating
6 Charter 1227	C2
7 Cloisters	C2
8 Fish Row	C2

the stout gates leading into the complex are still locked every night.

Salisbury Museum   Museum

(☎ 01722-332151; www.salisburymuseum.org.uk; 65 Cathedral Close; adult/child £5/2; ⏱10am-5pm Mon-Sat, plus noon-5pm Sun Jun-Sep) The hugely important archaeological finds

continued on page 194

191

Don't Miss
Stonehenge

Welcome to Britain's most iconic archaeological site. This compelling ring of monolithic stones has been attracting a steady stream of pilgrims, poets and philosophers for the last 5000 years and is still a mystical, ethereal place – a haunting echo from Britain's forgotten past, and a reminder of those who once walked the ceremonial avenues across Salisbury Plain.

EH

☏ 0870 333 1181

www.english-heritage.org.uk

adult/child incl visitor centre £14/8.30

 9am-8pm Jun-Aug, 9.30am-7pm Apr, May & Sep, 9.30am-5pm Oct-Mar

P

The Stone Circle

The first phase of building started around 3000 BC, when the outer circular bank and ditch were erected. A thousand years later, an inner circle of granite stones, known as bluestones, was added. It's thought that these mammoth 4-tonne blocks were hauled from the Preseli Mountains in South Wales, some 250 miles away – an almost inexplicable feat for Stone Age builders equipped with only the simplest of tools. Although no one is entirely sure how the builders transported the stones so far, it's thought they probably used a system of ropes, sledges and rollers fashioned from tree trunks – Salisbury Plain was still covered by forest during Stonehenge's construction.

Visitor Centre

Stonehenge's swish new visitor centre sees you standing in the middle of an atmospheric 360 degree projection of the stone circle through the ages and seasons – complete with mid-summer sunrise and swirling star-scape. Engaging audio-visual displays detail the transportation of the stones and the building stages, while 300 finds from the wider site include flint chippings, bone pins and arrowheads. There's also a striking re-creation of the face of a Neolithic man whose body was found nearby. The visitor centre is 1½ miles from the stones. A fleet of trolley buses makes the 10-minute trip, though it's more atmospheric to walk.

Tours

Stone Circle Access Visits are an unforgettable experience. Visitors normally have to stay outside the stone circle itself, but on these self-guided walks, you get to wander around the core of the site, getting up-close views of the iconic bluestones and trilithons. They take place in the evening or early morning so the quieter atmosphere and the slanting sunlight add to the effect. Each visit only takes 26 people; to secure a place book at least two months in advance.

Local Knowledge

Stonehenge

RECOMMENDATIONS
FROM PAT SHELLEY, GUIDE,
SALISBURY & STONEHENGE
GUIDED TOURS

1 **THE MAIN CIRCLE**
Stonehenge covers a large area but the focal point is, of course, the main circle of stones, including the distinctive trilithons – 'gateways' of two vertical stones with a lintel across the top. For me, nowhere sums up the magic and mystery of ancient Britain better than Stonehenge.

2 **INSIDE THE CIRCLE**
The main stones are fenced off, and you can't get very close – the only way to actually see inside the circle is on a special access tour, which you need to reserve in advance. The site also has a brand new visitor centre which provides background on the monument's history.

3 **THE SLAUGHTER STONE**
Look out for the Slaughter Stone, once thought to be a Neolithic altar for human sacrifice. In reality it's a toppled monolith; over the centuries iron ore has mixed with rain in holes in the stone to give the appearance of blood.

4 **THE CURSUS & THE AVENUE**
This is the route to Stonehenge that Neolithic people would have used. Walk northeast along the bridleway from the car park to reach the Cursus, a long ditchlike earthwork that runs in an east–west line. Turn right to meet the Avenue, an ancient path leading back towards Stonehenge. Watching the giant stones looming up ahead is an unforgettable experience.

5 **WOODHENGE & THE BARROWS**
About 2 miles northeast of the stone circle, Woodhenge is an even older site where archaeologists are still discovering new evidence. There's not much to see, but it was featured on a TV show in the US called *Secrets of Stonehenge*, so many people want to visit. In the area surrounding Woodhenge and Stonehenge, the many hillocks or 'barrows' are ancient burial mounds.

DAVID C TOMLINSON/GETTY IMAGES ©

Don't Miss
Stourhead

Overflowing with vistas, temples and follies, **Stourhead** (NT; ☎01747-841152; www.nationaltrust.org.uk; Mere; house or garden adult/child £8/4, house & garden £13/7; ⊙house 11am-4.30pm mid-Mar–Oct, 11am-3pm Sat & Sun Nov to mid-Mar; P) is landscape gardening at its finest. The Palladian house has some fine Chippendale furniture and paintings by Claude and Gaspard Poussin, but it's a sideshow to the magnificent 18th-century gardens, which spread out across the valley. A picturesque 2-mile circuit takes you past the most ornate follies, around the lake and to the Temple of Apollo; a 3½-mile side trip can be made from near the Pantheon to **King Alfred's Tower** (adult/child £3/2; ⊙noon-4pm Sat & Sun Mar-Oct), a 50m-high folly with wonderful views.

Stourhead is off the B3092, 8 miles south of Frome (in Somerset).

here include the Stonehenge Archer; the bones of a man found in the ditch surrounding the stone circle – one of the arrows found alongside probably killed him. With gold coins dating from 100 BC and a Bronze Age gold necklace, it's a powerful introduction to Wiltshire's prehistory.

Sleeping

St Ann's House　Boutique B&B ££
(☎01722-335657; www.stannshouse.co.uk; 32 St Ann St; s £59-64, d £89-110; 🛜) The aromas wafting from breakfast may well

spur you from your room: great coffee; baked peaches with raspberry, honey and almonds; poached eggs and Parma ham. Utter elegance reigns upstairs, where well-chosen antiques, warm colours and Turkish linen ensure a supremely comfortable stay.

Spire House　B&B ££
(☎01722-339213; www.salisbury-bedandbreakfast.com; 84 Exeter St; s/d/f £60/75/90; P🛜) In this B&B of beautifully kept, sweet rooms the easygoing vibe extends to breakfast (add £5): chalk up your choice

on a blackboard the night before, options include slow-cooked, blueberry-studded porridge, croissants and pastries, or local bacon and eggs.

Eating

Fish Row
Deli, Cafe £

(www.fishrowdelicafe.co.uk; 3 Fish Row; snacks from £5; ⏰8.30am-5.30pm Mon-Sat, 9.30am-4.30pm Sun.) Local produce is piled high at this heavily beamed deli-cafe – the New Forest Blue, Old Sarum and Nanny Williams cheeses come from just a few miles away. Grab some potato salad and a wedge of quiche to go, or duck upstairs to eat alongside weathered wood, stained glass and old church pews.

Cloisters
Pub ££

(www.cloisterspubsalisbury.co.uk; 83 Catherine St; mains £9-13; ⏰11am-9pm Sat & Sun, 11am-3pm & 6-9pm Mon-Fri) The building dates from 1350, it's been a pub since the 1600s and today improbably warped beams reinforce an age-old vibe. It's a convivial spot for tasty beef-and-ale pie, sausage and mash or fancier foods such as an impressive lamb shank slow-braised in red wine.

Charter 1227
British £££

(☎01722-333118; www.charter1227.co.uk; 6 Ox Row, Market Pl; mains £15-26; ⏰noon-2.30pm & 6-9.30pm Tue-Sat, noon-2.30pm Sun) Ingredients that speak of ancient England have a firm foothold here – feast on suckling pig, Wiltshire ham hock or roast John Dory. Canny locals eat between 6pm and 8pm Tuesday to Thursday (two/three courses for £20/25) or at lunchtime, when dishes are £5.50 each.

ⓘ Information

Tourist Office (☎01722-342860; www.visitwiltshire.co.uk; Fish Row; ⏰9am-5pm Mon-Fri, 10am-4pm Sat, 10am-2pm Sun)

ⓘ Getting There & Away

Trains run half-hourly from the following stations:

London Waterloo (£38, 1¾ hours).

Bath (£10, one hour)

Bristol (£11, 1¼ hours)

Exeter (£25, two hours)

Spire of Salisbury Cathedral (p190)

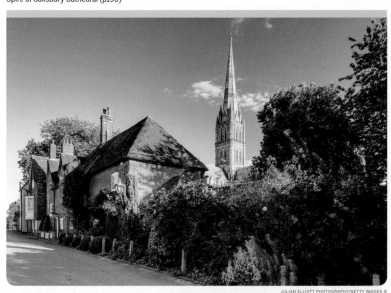

JULIAN ELLIOTT PHOTOGRAPHY/GETTY IMAGES ©

Avebury

While the tour buses head straight for Stonehenge, prehistoric purists make for the massive stone circle at Avebury. It's bigger, older and a great deal quieter, and a large section of the village is actually inside the stones – footpaths wind around them, allowing you to really soak up the extraordinary atmosphere.

With a diameter of about 348m, Avebury is the largest stone circle in the world. It's also one of the oldest, dating from around 2500 to 2200 BC, between the first and second phase of construction at Stonehenge. The site originally consisted of an outer circle of 98 standing stones of up to 6m in length, many weighing 20 tons, which had been carefully selected for their shape and size. The stones were surrounded by another circle delineated by a 5m-high earth bank and ditch up to 9m deep. Inside were smaller stone circles to the north (27 stones) and south (29 stones).

In the Middle Ages, when Britain's pagan past was an embarrassment to the church, many of the stones were buried, removed or broken up. In 1934, wealthy businessman and archaeologist Alexander Keiller supervised the re-erection of the stones, and planted markers to indicate those that had disappeared; he later bought the site for posterity using funds from his family's marmalade fortune.

The site is 6 miles west of Marlborough on the A4361.

DEVON

Exeter

POP 117,800

Well heeled and comfortable, Exeter exudes evidence of its centuries-old role as the spiritual and administrative heart of Devon. The city's Gothic cathedral presides over pockets of cobbled streets, while medieval and Georgian buildings, and fragments of the Roman city stretch out all around.

◉ Sights

Exeter Cathedral   Cathedral
(Cathedral Church of St Peter; ☎01392 285983; www.exeter-cathedral.org. uk; The Close; adult/child £6/ free; ⊙9.30am-4.45pm Mon-Sat, 11.30am-3.30pm Sun)
Magnificent in warm, honey-coloured stone, Exeter's cathedral is one of Devon's most prestigious sights. Dating largely from the 12th and 13th centuries, one end of the exterior is framed by extraordinary medieval statuary, while inside the ceiling is mesmerising – the

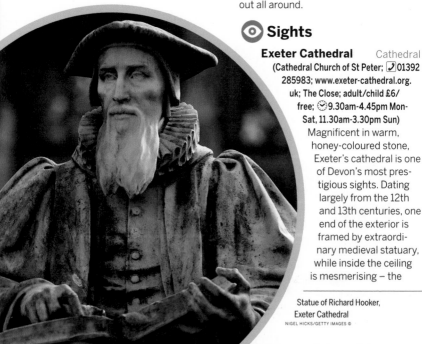

Statue of Richard Hooker,
Exeter Cathedral
NIGEL HICKS/GETTY IMAGES ©

longest unbroken Gothic vaulting in the world, it sweeps up to meet ornate ceiling bosses in gilt and vibrant colours. Other highlights include elegant wood carvings and striking sculptures.

Underground Passages
Underground

(☎01392-665887; www.exeter.gov.uk/passages; Paris St; adult/child £6/4; ⏰9.30am-5.30pm Mon-Sat, 10am-4pm Sun Jun-Sep, 11.30am-4pm Tue-Sun Oct-May) Prepare to crouch down, don a hard hat and possibly get spooked in what is the only publicly accessible system of its kind in England. These medieval vaulted passages were built to house pipes bringing fresh water to the city. Guides lead you on a scramble through the network telling tales of ghosts, escape routes and cholera. The last tour is an hour before closing; they're popular – book ahead.

Sleeping

ABode Exeter
Hotel ££

(☎01392-319955; www.abodehotels.co.uk/exeter; Cathedral Yard; r £90-300; 🛜) At ABode, Georgian grandeur meets minimalist chic. Wonky floors and stained glass combine with recessed lighting, pared-down furniture and neutral tones. The rooms range from 'comfortable' and 'enviable' to 'fabulous', where slanted ceilings frame grandstand cathedral views. Prices depend on availability; book ahead to bag bargains.

Raffles
B&B ££

(☎01392-270200; www.raffles-exeter.co.uk; 11 Blackall Rd; s/d/f £55/78/88; 🅿🛜) The antique dealer owner has peppered each room of this late-Victorian town house with heritage features – look out for Bakelite radios, wooden plant stands and polished trunks. Largely organic breakfasts and a walled garden add to the appeal.

Magdalen Chapter
Boutique Hotel £££

(☎01392-281 000; www.themagdalenchapter.com; Magdalen St; d £160-250; @🛜♨) Undoubtedly Exeter's coolest hotel (staff wear converse trainers and low-slung

Cathedral Roof Tours

For a sensational view of Exeter Cathedral book one of these high-rise **guided walks** (☎01392-285983; www.exeter-cathedral.org.uk; adult/child £10/5; ⏰2pm Tue-Thu, 11am Sat Apr-Sep). Climb 251 steps up a spiral staircase, head out onto the sweeping roof to stroll its length, then gaze down on the city from the top of the North Tower. They're popular so book two weeks ahead.

slacks) the Magdalen is replete with funky flourishes. Lush purple corridors lead to dove-grey bedrooms, each with iPad, coffee machine, complementary mini bar and mood-lighting. There's even a tiny, heated outdoor pool that leads into an indoor enclave made toasty by a log burner.

Eating

Rusty Bike
Modern British ££

(☎01392-214440; www.rustybike-exeter.co.uk; 67 Howell Rd; mains £15-19; ⏰6-10pm daily, noon-3pm Sat & Sun) A vintage football table and bashed-about chairs set the scene for some seriously stylish rustic cuisine. Menus change daily depending on deliveries from local suppliers. So expect rarities like confit goose and pistachio; beef chuck and carrots; or truffle-laced pheasant breast – delivered, of course, by the local gamekeeper.

Michael Caines
Fine Dining £££

(☎01392-319 955; www.michaelcaines.com; Cathedral Yard; mains £24; ⏰noon-2.30pm & 6-9pm Mon-Sat) Run by the eponymous, double Michelin-starred chef, the food here is a complex blend of prime Westcountry ingredients and full-bodied French flavours. Gastronomes linger over the seven-course tasting menu (£65), but the set lunches (two/three courses £13/18) are some of the best deals in town.

Below: Cycling on the Camel Trail (p202), near Padstow; **Right:** Sutton Harbour, Plymouth

(BELOW) WILL GRAY/GETTY IMAGES ©; (RIGHT) LEE PENGELLY/GETTY IMAGES ©

@Angela's   Modern British **£££**
(☎ 01392-499038; www.angelasrestaurant.
co.uk; 38 New Bridge St; mains £20; ⏰ 6-9.30pm
Mon-Sat) Dedication to sourcing local
ingredients sometimes sees the chef here
rising before dawn to bag the best fish
at Brixham Market. The garlic-infused
roasted monkfish is worth the trip alone,
while the Devon duck is made memorable
by a rich caramelised orange sauce. Also
open for reservations only at lunch Friday
and Saturday.

ℹ Information

Main Tourist Office (☎ 01392-665700; www.
heartofdevon.com; Dix's Field; ⏰ 9.30am-
4.30pm)

ℹ Getting There & Away

Air

Exeter International (www.exeter-airport.
co.uk) Flights connect with Europe and the UK,
including Amsterdam, Glasgow,
the Isles of Scilly, Manchester,
Newcastle and Paris, plus the Channel
Islands.

Train

Main-line and branch-line trains run from Exeter
St David's and Exeter Central stations:

London Paddington (£46, 2½ hours, half-
hourly)

Penzance (£15, three hours, hourly)

Plymouth (£9, one hour, half-hourly)

Plymouth

POP POP 258,000

If parts of Devon seem like nature documentaries or costume dramas, Plymouth
is a healthy dose of reality. Its location, on
the edge of a stunning natural harbour
and just behind Dartmoor, brings endless possibilities for boat trips, sailing or
hiking. Add a rich maritime history, one
of the country's best aquariums and a

playful 1930s lido, and you have a place to reconnect with the real before another foray into Devon's chocolate-box-pretty moors and shores.

◎ Sights

Plymouth Hoe　　　　Headland
Francis Drake supposedly spied the Spanish fleet from this grassy headland overlooking Plymouth Sound (the city's wide bay); the bowling green on which he finished his game was probably where his **statue** now stands. The wide villa-backed promenade features scores of war memorials, including the immense **Plymouth Naval Memorial**, which commemorates Commonwealth WWI and WWII sailors who have no grave but the sea.

Barbican　　　　Neighbourhood
(www.plymouthbarbican.com) In the historic Barbican district, part-cobbled streets are lined with Tudor and Jacobean buildings, galleries, restaurants and funky bars. The Pilgrim Fathers' *Mayflower* set sail to found America from here in 1620. The **Mayflower Steps** mark the approximate embarcation point; track down the passenger list on the side of **Island House** nearby. Other famous departures are also commemorated at the steps, including Captain James Cook's 1768 voyage of discovery, and the first emigrant ships to Australia and New Zealand.

Plymouth Gin Distillery　　Distillery
(☏01752-665292; www.plymouthdistillery. com; 60 Southside St; tours £7; ◷6 tours daily) They've been concocting gin at this heavily beamed distillery since 1793, making it the oldest producer of the spirit in the world. The Royal Navy ferried it round the world in countless officers' messes and the brand was specified in the first recorded recipe for a dry martini in the 1930s. Tours thread past the stills and take in a tutored tasting before retiring to the medieval bar for a complementary G&T. Book ahead.

199

Plymouth

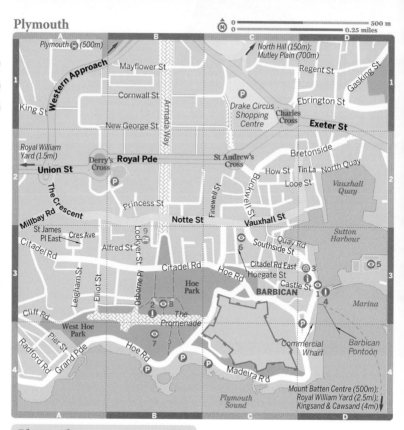

Plymouth

National Marine Aquarium
Aquarium

(☏0844 893 7938; www.national-aquarium.
co.uk; Rope Walk; adult/child £14/10; ⏱10am-
5pm, to 6pm Apr-Sep) The sharks here swim
in coral seas that teem with moray eels
and vividly coloured fish – there's even a
loggerhead turtle called Snorkel who was
rescued from a Cornish beach. Walk-
through glass arches ensure huge rays
glide over your head, while the gigantic
Atlantic reef tank reveals just what's lurking a few miles offshore.

🛏 Sleeping

St Elizabeth's House
Boutique Hotel ££

(☏01752-344840; www.stelizabeths.co.uk;
Longbrook St, Plympton St Maurice; d £99-119,
ste £150; P🛜) Prepare to be pampered.
In this 17th-century manor house turned
boutique bolthole, freestanding slipper
baths, oak furniture and Egyptian cotton
grace the rooms; the suites feature palatial bathrooms and private terraces. It's
set in the suburb-cum-village of Plympton
St Maurice, 5 miles east of Plymouth.

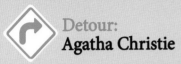

Detour:
Agatha Christie

High on Devon's must-see list, **Greenway** (NT; ☏01803-842382; www.nationaltrust.org. uk; Greenway Rd, Galmpton; adult/child £9.40/5.20; ⏱10.30am-5pm Wed-Sun Mar-Oct, plus Tue late-Jul–late-Aug) is the captivating summer home of crime writer Agatha Christie sits beside the placid River Dart. Part-guided tours allow you to wander between rooms where the furnishings and knick-knacks are much as she left them. The bewitching waterside gardens include features that pop up in her mysteries, so you get to spot locations made notorious by fictional murders. Car parking places have to be prebooked; the best way to arrive is by ferry or on foot.

Imperial   Hotel ££
(☏01752-227311; www.imperialplymouth.co.uk; Lockyer St; s £60, d £62-86, f £92-100; P ☏) In the 1840s an admiral used to slumber in this elegant townhouse. Now you sleep amid heritage features, swish modern furnishings and all the mod-cons, before breakfasting on top-notch local produce (the homemade kedgeree is quite a treat). It's very high quality for the price.

 Eating

Rock Salt   Modern British ££
(☏01752-225522; www.rocksaltcafe.co.uk; 31 Stonehouse St; mains £7-20; ⏱10am-9.30pm, from 8am Wed-Sat; ☏) First-class ingredients and creative flavours – no wonder Rock Salt keeps bagging awards. Their range is remarkable: from stylish all-day breakfasts and afternoon cupcakes to confit Dartmoor lamb. And all in a friendly setting that feels like a funky neighbourhood brasserie.

River Cottage
Canteen   Modern British ££
(☏01752-252702; www.rivercottage.net; Royal William Yard; mains £10-17; ⏱11am-10.30pm Mon-Sat, to 4pm Sun; ☏) Hugh Fearnley-Whittingstall's gaff focuses firmly on local, sustainable, seasonal, organic goodies. Expect meats to be roasted beside an open fire, fish to be simply grilled and familiar veg to be given a revelatory makeover.

It's in the Royal William Yard, 2 miles west of the city centre; catch bus 34.

ℹ Information
Tourist Office (☏01752-306330; www. visitplymouth.co.uk; 3 The Barbican; ⏱9am-5pm Mon-Sat, 10am-4pm Sun Apr-Oct, 10am-4pm Mon-Sat Nov-Mar)

ℹ Getting There & Away
Plymouth is on the intercity London Paddington–Penzance line; regular services include those to London (£40, 3½ to four hours, every 30 minutes), Bristol (£20, two hours, two or three per hour) and Exeter (£9, one hour, two or three per hour).

CORNWALL

Padstow
POP 3162

If anywhere symbolises Cornwall's changing character, it's Padstow. This once-sleepy fishing port has been transformed into one of the county's most cosmopolitan corners thanks to celebrity chef Rick Stein, whose property portfolio encompasses several restaurants, shops and hotels around town, as well as a seafood school and fish-and-chip bar.

Padstow is surrounded by fine beaches, including the so-called **Seven Bays**: Trevone, Harlyn, Mother Ivey's, Booby's, Constantine, Treyarnon and

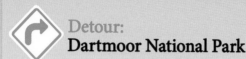

Detour:
Dartmoor National Park

Dartmoor is an ancient, compelling landscape, so different from the rest of Devon that a visit feels like falling straight into Tolkien's *Return of the King*. Exposed granite hills (called tors) crest on the horizon, linked by swathes of honey-tinged moors. The centre of this 368-sq-mile wilderness is the higher moor; an elemental, treeless expanse. Moody and utterly empty, you'll either find its remote beauty exhilarating or chilling, or quite possibly a bit of both.

Steven Spielberg chose to film part of his WWI epic *War Horse* in this landscape; a century earlier it inspired Sir Arthur Conan Doyle to write *The Hound of the Baskervilles*.

Dartmoor is also a natural breakout zone with a checklist of charms: superb walking, cycling, riding, climbing and white-water kayaking; rustic pubs and fancy restaurants; wild camping nooks and country-house hotels – perfect boltholes when the fog rolls in.

Dartmoor National Park Authority (DNPA; www.dartmoor.gov.uk) runs the **Higher Moorland Tourist Office** (DNPA; ☎01822-890414; ⊙10am-5pm Apr-Sep, to 4pm Mar & Oct, 10.30am-3.30pm Thu-Sun Nov-Feb) in Princetown. Other DNPA centres include those at **Haytor Vale** (☎01364-661520; ⊙10am-5pm Apr-Sep, to 4pm Mar & Oct, 10.30am-3.30pm Thu-Sun Nov-Feb) and **Postbridge** (☎01822-880272; ⊙10am-5pm Apr-Sep, to 4pm Mar & Oct, 10.30am-3.30pm Thu-Sun Nov-Feb). Dartmoor's **official visitor website** is www.dartmoor.co.uk.

Porthcothan. Bus 556 runs close to most of them.

Between Easter and October, cruise boats including the **Jubilee Queen** (☎07836-798457; www.padstowboattrips.co.uk; adult/child £11/6) and **Padstow Sealife Safaris** (☎01841-521613; www.padstowsealifesafaris.co.uk; 2hr cruise adult/child £39/£25) run trips to local seal and seabird colonies.

Activities

Camel Trail   Cycling

The old Padstow–Bodmin railway was closed in the 1950s, and has now been turned into Cornwall's most popular bike trail. The main section starts in Padstow and runs east through Wadebridge (5.75 miles), but the trail runs on all the way to Poley Bridge on Bodmin Moor (18.3 miles).

Bikes can be hired from **Padstow Cycle Hire** (☎01841-533533; www.padstowcyclehire.com; South Quay; adult/child per day £14/6; ⊙9am-5pm, to 9pm summer) or **Trail Bike Hire** (☎01841-532594; www.trailbikehire.co.uk; Unit 6, South Quay; adult £12, child £5-8; ⊙9am-6pm) at the Padstow end, or from **Bridge Bike Hire** (☎01208-813050; www.bridgebikehire.co.uk; adult £12-15, child £6-9; ⊙10am-5pm) at the Wadebridge end. Pumps and helmets are usually included, but tandems and kids' trailers cost extra.

Sleeping

Althea Library   B&B ££
(☎01841-532579; www.altheahouse-padstow.co.uk; 64 Church St, Padstow; d £98-124; P ⊙) If you want to be in the heart of Padstow, this charming ivy-clad house is hard to better. Both rooms are suites with sofas, Nespresso coffee machines, in-room fridges and roll-top baths. Rafters is accessed via a private staircase, while Driftwood has a pine four-poster bed, and there's a cottage for longer stays.

Treann House   B&B ££
(☎01841-553855; www.treannhousepadstow.co.uk; 24 Dennis Rd, Padstow; d £100-130; ⊙)

This stylish number makes a fancy place to stay. The three rooms are finished with stripped floors, crisp sheets and antique beds, and the Estuary Room has its own dinky balcony with a panorama over Padstow's rooftops.

 Eating

Margot's Bistro
British ££

(☎01840-533441; www.margotsbistro.co.uk; 11 Duke St, Padstow; mains £14.50-17.50; ⏰noon-2pm Wed-Sat, 7-10pm Tue-Sat) While the food snobs head for Stein's, Margot's is where you'll be sent by the locals. Run by madcap chef Adrian Oliver, known for his chaotic style and homely, seasonal food, it's a fantastically convivial place – but the tables are packed in sardine-tight.

Rick Stein's Cafe
European ££

(☎01841-532700; Middle St, Padstow; mains £10-18; ⏰8am-9.30pm) Stein's backstreet bistro takes its inspiration from the chef's globetrotting travels, with dishes ranging all the way from the Far East to the Mediterranean: classic mussels with saffron, or Thai-spiced seafood broth. It's a lot more relaxed than its sister restaurant, but you'd still be wise to book.

Paul Ainsworth at No 6
British £££

(☎01840-532093; www.number6inpadstow. co.uk; 6 Middle St, Padstow; 2-/3-course lunch £19/25, dinner mains £26-30; ⏰noon-2.30pm & 6.30-9pm) Paul Ainsworth is Padstow's hottest chef, and thanks to a shiny Michelin star, his restaurant has become the town's most desirable table. Known for his modern take on surf-and-turf, Ainsworth's cooking combines local seafood, meat and game into fresh, surprising concoctions. His signature dessert, 'A Trip to the Fairground' was created for BBC2's *Great British Menu* in 2011.

Restaurant Nathan Outlaw
Seafood £££

(☎01208-862737; www.nathan-outlaw.com; Rock Rd, Rock; tasting menu £99; ⏰7-9pm Tue-Sat) A former Rick Stein trainee, Nathan Outlaw has now established his own stellar seafood reputation with two Michelin stars – the only chef in Cornwall to do so. There's a choice of Outlaw venues, both in Rock. Foodies plump for the flagship

Saddle Tor, Dartmoor National Park

ADAM BURTON/GETTY IMAGES ©

restaurant, which serves a superb £99 tasting menu. Expensive, but very much a never-to-be-forgotten experience.

Information

Padstow Tourist Office (☎01841-533449; www.padstowlive.com; North Quay, Padstow; ⏱10am-5pm Mon-Sat)

Newquay

POP POP 19,423

Bright, breezy and brash: that's Newquay, Cornwall's premier party town and the spiritual home of British surfing.

Sights & Activities

Newquay has a truly stunning location amongst some of North Cornwall's finest beaches. The best-known is **Fistral**, England's most famous surfing beach. It's nestled on the west side of Towan Head, a 10-minute walk from the town centre.

To the east of Towan Head are Newquay's other main beaches. Just below town are **Towan**, **Great Western** and **Tolcarne**, followed by nearby **Lusty Glaze**. All offer good swimming and lifeguard supervision throughout the summer.

You'll need transport to reach Newquay's other beaches. North of Lusty Glaze is **Porth**, a long, narrow beach that's popular with families, followed a couple of miles later by the massive curve of **Watergate Bay**, home to Jamie Oliver's much-vaunted restaurant, Fifteen Cornwall. Two miles north brings you to **Mawgan Porth**, a horseshoe-shaped bay which often stays quieter than its neighbours.

You'll find even more beaches to the southwest of Newquay, including the large, sandy, family-friendly beaches of **Crantock** (about 3 miles from town) and **Holywell Bay** (6 miles from town).

Sleeping

Scarlet Hotel £££
(☎01637-861600; www.scarlethotel.co.uk; r winter/summer from £155/285; P 🛜 ♨) For out-and-out luxury, Cornwall's fabulously chic, adults-only eco-hotel takes the crown. In a regal location above Mawgan Porth, 5 miles from Newquay, it screams designer style, from the huge seaview rooms with their funky furniture and minimalist decor to the luxurious spa, complete with meditation lounge, outdoor hot tubs and wild swimming pool. The restaurant's a beauty, too.

Bedruthan Hotel Hotel £££
(☎01637-860555; www.bedruthan.com; Mawgan Porth; d from £130; P 🛜 ♨ 👪) Run by the same team as the Scarlet, the Bedruthan is a family-friendly version but with the same attention to style and detail. It offers contemporary rooms in bright primary colours, artworks and bold pattern prints, plus villas and apartments for longer stays. Activities aplenty will keep the small ones occupied.

Eating

Beach Hut Bistro ££
(☎01637-860877; Watergate Bay; mains £10-18; ⏱9am-9pm) Lodged beneath Jamie Oliver's Fifteen Cornwall, this beachside bistro is a great bet for simple surf 'n' turf: sticky pork ribs, 'extreme' burgers and a different fish every day.

Fifteen Cornwall Italian £££
(☎01637-861000; www.fifteencornwall.com; Watergate Bay; lunch/dinner menu £28/60; ⏱8.30am-10am, noon-2.30pm & 6.15-9.15pm) Owned by celeb chef and self-marketing mogul Jamie Oliver, this restaurant on Watergate Bay serves Jamie's trademark Italian food while simultaneously training young apprentices. The vibe is relaxed and the beach view is stunning, but the prices are on the high side.

ℹ Information

Newquay Tourist Office (📞01637-854020; www.visitnewquay.com; Marcus Hill; ⊙9.30am-5.30pm Mon-Sat, to 12.30pm Sun)

ℹ Getting There & Away

There are trains every couple of hours on the branch line between Newquay and Par (£4.50, 45 minutes) on the main London–Penzance line.

....

St Ives

POP 9870

Once a busy pilchard harbour, St Ives later became the centre of Cornwall's arts scene in the 1920s and '30s, and the town's cobbled streets are crammed with quirky galleries and crafts shops – although the outsider edge has been somewhat dulled by the steady dribble of chain stores and generic restaurants.

◉ Sights & Activities

Tate St Ives   Gallery
(📞01736-796226; www.tate.org.uk/stives; Porthmeor Beach; adult/child £7/4.50, with Barbara Hepworth Museum £10/6; ⊙10am-5pm

Mar-Oct, to 4pm Nov-Feb) Hovering like a concrete curl above Porthmeor Beach, St Ives' celebrated art museum focuses on the key artists of the 'St Ives School', including luminary names such as Terry Frost, Patrick Heron, Naum Gabo, Ben Nicholson and Barbara Hepworth, displayed alongside more contemporary artists. Of particular local interest are the naive works of fisherman-turned-artist Alfred Wallis, who didn't start painting until the ripe old age of 67.

Barbara Hepworth Museum   Museum
(📞01736-796226; Barnoon Hill; adult/child £6/4, with Tate St Ives £10/6; ⊙10am-5pm Mar-Oct, to 4pm Nov-Feb) Barbara Hepworth (1903–75) was one of the leading abstract sculptors of the 20th century and a key figure in the St Ives art scene. Her studio on Barnoon Hill has remained almost untouched since her death and the adjoining garden contains several of her most notable sculptures. Hepworth's work is scattered throughout St Ives; look for works outside the Guildhall and inside the 15th-century parish church of St Ia.

Surfers, Newquay

NICK DOLDING/GETTY IMAGES ©

🛏 Sleeping

No 1 St Ives
B&B ££

(☎01736-799047; www.no1stives.co.uk; 1 Fern Glen; d £95-139; P 🛜) Despite its pretentious 'bouchique' tag, this 19th-century granite cottage is still one of the nicest B&Bs in St Ives. Rooms vary in size, but all sport the same palette of cool greys and off-whites, and have extra spoils such as filtered water, goose-down duvets, iPod docks and White Company bath-stuffs. It's five minutes' walk from town, but there's only space for four cars.

Little Leaf Guest House
B&B ££

(☎01736-795427; www.littleleafguesthouse. co.uk; Park Ave; r £65-120; 🛜) A friendly and cosy five-roomer, on a terrace overlooking the town's rooftops. Rooms are sweet and simple, finished in creamy colours and pine furniture. Ask for rooms 2 or 5 if you're after a sea view.

Tide House
Hotel £££

(☎01736-791803; www.thetidehouse.co.uk; Skidden Hill; d £140-240) Even in increasingly chi-chi St Ives, this beautiful hotel feels unusually special. It has everything going for it: 16th-century building, harbourside location, gorgeous design and seriously luxurious rooms (all named after Cornish lighthouses), ranging from a romantic penthouse to a split-level mezzanine. Definitely the place to push the boat out.

🍴 Eating

Blas Burgerworks
Cafe £

(☎01736-797272; The Warren; burgers £5-10; ☺noon-9.30pm) 🌱 A fantastic burger joint, with an eco-friendly manifesto and an imaginative menu. Go for a 6oz Classic Blasburger, or branch out with a guacamole and corn salsa-topped Rancheros, or a Smokey with beetroot, aged cheddar and homemade piccalilli (plenty of veggie options, too). The owners also run the excellent **Halsetown Inn** (☎01736-795583; www.halsetowninn.co.uk), just outside St Ives.

Porthminster Beach Café
Bistro ££

(☎01736-795352; www.porthminstercafe.co.uk; Porthminster Beach; mains £10.50-16.50, dinner £10-22; ☺9am-10pm) This is no ordinary beach cafe: it's a full-blown bistro with a gorgeous suntrap terrace and a superb Mediterranean-influenced menu, specialising in seafood. Tuck into rich bouillabaisse, seafood curry or Provençal fish soup, and settle back to enjoy the breezy beach vistas.

Alba
Modern British ££

(☎01736-797222; www. thealbarestaurant.com; Old Lifeboat House; 2-/3-course dinner menu £16.95/19.95; ☺noon-2pm & 6-10pm) In a converted boathouse near the lifeboat station, this longstanding restaurant has been consistently turning out some of the town's top food for many years. With

St Ives (p205)
DAVE PORTER/GETTY IMAGES ©

DOUG MCKINLAY/GETTY IMAGES ©

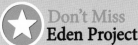

Don't Miss
Eden Project

Lodged at the bottom of a disused clay-pit, the giant biomes of the Eden Project – the largest greenhouses in the world – have become Cornwall's most celebrated landmark and a definite must-see. Looking like a Bond villain's lair, Eden's bubble-shaped biomes maintain miniature ecosystems that enable all kinds of weird and wonderful plants to flourish – from stinking rafflesia flowers and banana trees in the rainforest biome to cacti and soaring palms in the Mediterranean biome.

Exhibits around the complex explore ecological and conservation themes, covering everything from global warming to rubber production and chocolate-making. Landscaped gardens wind their way between the biomes, but the highlight is the gravity-defying treetop walkway that winds its way through the canopy of the Rainforest Biome.

In summer, the biomes provide a backdrop for live concerts during the Eden Sessions, and in winter host a full-size ice-rink.

The Eden site is at Bodelva, about five miles' drive from St Austell. There are discounts for buying tickets online and arriving by public transport. Bus 101 runs regularly from St Austell train station; bus 527 travels from Newquay.

NEED TO KNOW

📞 01726-811911; www.edenproject.com; adult/child/family £23.50/13.50/68; 🕙 10am-6pm Apr-Oct, to 4.30pm Nov-Mar

its banquette seats and sharp decor, it feels classy, especially if you get one of the prime tables next to the panoramic window. The menu is a mix of British and European flavours.

Seagrass
Modern British ££

(☎01736-793763; www.seagrass-stives.com; Fish St; 2-/3-course menu £16.95/19.95; ☻6-9pm) A popular, small bistro just off the wharf, focusing mainly on local seafood – there's a special Oyster and Shells menu, featuring langoustines, whole crab, lobster and oysters.

ℹ Information

St Ives Tourist Office (☎01736-796297; www.stivestic.co.uk; Street-an-Pol; ☻9am-5.30pm Mon-Fri, 9am-5pm Sat, 10am-4pm Sun) Inside the Guildhall.

ℹ Getting There & Away

The branch line from St Ives is worth taking just for the coastal views: trains terminate at St Erth (£3, 14 minutes, half-hourly), where you can catch connections along the Penzance–London Paddington main line.

Sennen & Land's End

In the far west, the coastline peaks and plunges all the way to the sandy scoop of **Sennen**, which overlooks one of Penwith's most stunning stretches of sand on **Whitesand Bay** (pronounced Whitsand).

From here, there's a wonderful stretch of coast path that leads for about a mile-and-a-half along the clifftops all the way to **Land's End**, the westernmost point of mainland England, where the coal-black cliffs plunge dramatically down into the pounding surf, and the views stretch all the way to the Isles of Scilly on a clear day. Unfortunately, the decision to build the **Legendary Land's End** (www.landsend-landmark.co.uk; adult/child £10/7; ☻10am-5pm Mar-Oct; ♿) theme park just behind the headland in the 1980s hasn't done much to enhance the view.

Land's End is 9 miles from Penzance.

Minack Theatre

In terms of theatrical settings, the **Minack** (☎01736-810181; www.minack.com) takes top billing. Carved directly into the crags overlooking Porthcurno Bay and the azure-blue Atlantic, this amazing clifftop amphitheatre was the lifelong passion of local lady Rowena Cade, who dreamt up the idea in the 1930s and oversaw the theatre until her death in 1983. It's now a hugely popular place for alfresco theatre, with a 17-week season running from mid-May to mid-September: regulars bring wine, picnic supplies, wet-weather gear and – most importantly of all, considering the seats are carved out of granite – a comfy cushion.

The Minack is 3 miles from Land's End and 9 miles from Penzance.

St Michael's Mount

Looming from the waters of Mount's Bay and connected to the mainland via a cobbled causeway, this abbey-crowned island is an unforgettable sight. There's been a monastery here since at least the 5th century, but the present **abbey** (NT; ☎01736-710507; www.stmichaelsmount.co.uk; adult/child £8.75/4.25; ☻house 10.30am-5.30pm Sun-Fri late Mar-Oct, gardens Mon-Fri Apr-Jun, Thu & Fri Jul-Sep) was mostly built by Benedictine monks during the 12th century. Highlights include the rococo drawing room, the armoury, the 14th-century church and the amazing clifftop gardens. Though owned by the St Aubyn family, the abbey is run by the National Trust.

Recent excavations including a Bronze Age axe head, dagger and metal clasp have proved the island has been inhabited since ancient times.

You can catch the ferry (adult/child £2/1) from nearby Marazion at high tide, but it's worth timing your arrival for low tide so you can walk across the causeway, just as the monks and pilgrims did centuries ago.

The 13/13A bus shuttles between Marazion and Penzance (£2) three times a day.

Lost Gardens of Heligan

This is Cornwall's real-life secret **garden** (☎01726-845100; www.heligan.com; adult/child £12/6; ⏰10am-6pm Mar-Oct, to 5pm Nov-Feb). Formerly the family estate of the Tremaynes, Heligan's magnificent 19th-century gardens fell into disrepair following WWI, and have since been restored to their former splendour by the brains behind the Eden Project, Tim Smit, and a huge army of gardeners, horticulturalists and volunteers.

It's a horticultural wonderland: wandering round the grounds you'll discover formal lawns, working kitchen gardens, fruit-filled greenhouses, a secret grotto and an 82ft-high rhododendron (claimed to be the world's largest). For many people, though, it's the jungle valley which really steals the show – a Lost World landscape of gigantic ferns, towering palms and tropical blooms.

Heligan is 7 miles from St Austell. Bus 526 links Heligan with Mevagissey and St Austell train station.

York &
Northern
England

The old North–South divide may not be quite as pronounced as it once was, but there's definitely something different about England's **northern half.** Dominated by the twin cities of Manchester and Liverpool, this was once the epicentre of industrial England, and the landscape is littered with reminders of its historic past – not to mention its musical heritage, cultural prowess and world-famous football teams. Meanwhile, much older cities like York and Chester conceal medieval cathedrals and cobbled streets, still circled by their original city walls.

Beyond the cities the landscape takes on a noticeably wilder character around the national parks of the Yorkshire Dales and the Lake District, which have inspired generations of hikers, poets and artists alike.

Even further north stretches the amazing Roman rampart of Hadrian's Wall, one of Britain's most impressive relics from the classical age.

Whitby, North Yorkshire

Grasmere (p247), the Lake District

York & Northern England

0 — 50 km
0 — 25 miles

1 York
2 Hill Top
3 Hadrian's Wall
4 Castle Howard
5 Liverpool

A9
Kinross
FIFE
Crail
Kirkcaldy
56°N
Falkirk
M9
2°W
NORTH SEA
EDINBURGH
A1
A68
NORTH SEA
Moorfoot
Hills
A702
Crookham
Bamburgh
M74
Wooler
Hawick
A697
Alnwick
Moffat
NORTHUMBERLAND
Rothbury
A74(M)
Border
Forest Park
Simonside
Hills
Morpeth
Dumfries
Northumberland
National Park
Housesteads
Roman Fort
& Museum
Newcastle-
upon-Tyne
55°N
Brampton
Hexham
Segedunum
Solway
Firth
Carlisle
Vindolanda
Roman Fort
& Museum
3
Hadrian's
Wall
Sunderland
Seaham
CUMBRIA
Durham
Peterlee
Penrith
The Pennines
Hartlepool
Workington
Kirkby
Stephen
Langdon
Beck
Stockton-
on-Tees
Middlesbrough
Keswick
A66
Whitby
Lake District
National Park
2
Keld
Darlington
Grosmont
Robin
Hood's Bay
Windermere
Leyburn
Thirsk
North York
Moors NP
Helmsley
Scarborough
Kendal
Yorkshire Dales
National Park
Kilburn
Malton
Norton
4
Bridlington
Barrow-in-
Furness
IRISH
SEA
Ingleton
Morecambe
Fountains Abbey &
Studley Royal
Cleveland
Hills
A1
Castle
Howard
54°N
Great
Driffield
Barrow
Island
Settle
Harrogate
1
54°N
Lancaster
Skipton
York
YORKSHIRE
M6
Ilkley
Keighley
Beverley
Blackpool
Preston
Haworth
Leeds
Selby
Hull
Liverpool
Bay
Blackburn
Bumley
Halifax
Goole
Humber
Southport
Bolton
Wakefield
Scunthorpe
Wigan
Huddersfield
M180
5
Manchester
Doncaster
Grimsby
Liverpool
Warrington
Rotherham
Gainsborough
A16
Colwyn
Bay
Birkenhead
Castleton
Sheffield
Rhyl
Liverpool
Airport
Buxton
Lincoln
Burgh le
Marsh
Vale of
Conwy
Clwydian
Ranges
Manchester
Airport
Chester
Peak District
National Park
Chesterfield
Sherwood
Forest
Newark-
on-Trent
The
Wash
Vale of
Llangollen
Wrexham
Dovedale
Newark-
Coed-
y-Brenin
Forest
Berwyn
Mountains
A49
Stoke-
on-Trent
Nottingham
Grantham
A458
Shrewsbury
Telford
Gailey
Packington
A38
Melton
Mowbray
A10
Llanidloes
Birmingham
M1
Coventry
A1
Isle of Man
Point of Avre
Bride
IRISH
SEA
ISLE OF
MAN
Dalby
Douglas
54°N
20 km
0 — 10 miles
Isle of Man
(see inset)
IRISH
SEA
A595
1°W
5°W
0° (Greenwich)

York & Northern England Highlights

York

The ancient city of York (p220) is a medieval masterpiece, with narrow streets and twisting alleyways encircled by sturdy city walls, all crowned by the glorious architecture of the Minster. With even older Roman and Viking heritage too, it's not surprising that York is bidding for Unesco World Heritage status.

1

2 Hill Top

The delightful cottage of Hill Top (p244) was Beatrix Potter's first house in the Lake District, and it features in lots of her books and illustrations, making it an absolute must for Potter fans. Admission includes an informative guided tour with one of the house's guides, but half the fun is spotting all the tiny Potteresque details for yourself.

Hadrian's Wall

3

The awesome engineering project of Hadrian's Wall (p250) stretches for 117km across the north of England. Along the wall, several of the original garrison forts are still standing, including wonderful examples at Vindolanda and Housesteads, offering a unique insight into the day-to-day world of the soldiers and legionnaires who lived along this monument to Roman Britain.

4

Castle Howard

The finest stately home in the north of England, and one of the best in the whole of Britain, the palatial edifice of Castle Howard (p227) was designed by the architect Sir John Vanbrugh for the third earl of Carlisle in the early 18th century, and it set the baroque benchmark for everyone else to follow. Surrounded by gardens and parkland, this is perhaps the quintessential English country estate.

5

Liverpool

Forever famous as the birthplace of The Beatles, and still with a healthy Fab Four heritage industry, the city of Liverpool (p237) is only now rediscovering and celebrating its (sometimes glorious, sometimes harsh) maritime past, spearheaded by a major renaissance on the Albert Dock, home to several fine museums, hotels and restaurants, and a clutch of classic buildings. Albert Dock (p239)

215

York & Northern England's Best…

Wild Spots

o **Lake District** The UK's favourite national park, famous for its natural scenery (p243)

o **Yorkshire Dales** A bucolic landscape of hills, dales and rolling fields (p226)

o **Hadrian's Wall** Look out across England's stormy northern frontier (250)

Museums

o **Imperial War Museum North** A Manchester must-see, and one of Britain's great modern museums (p233)

o **Jorvik Viking Centre** Travel back in time to Viking York – sights, smells and all (p221)

o **International Slavery Museum** This moving museum explores Liverpool's participation in the slave trade (p239)

o **Chesters Roman Fort & Museum** This Roman cavalry fort has many fascinating architectural artefacts in its museum (p250)

Old-World Architecture

o **York City Walls** Medieval battlements circling the city, with great views (p221)

o **The Rows, Chester** Quirky two-tier shopping streets dating from Tudor times (p236)

o **Fountains Abbey** Magnificent ruins of one of the north's great medieval abbeys (p228)

o **Durham Cathedral** This truly mighty cathedral dates from the early Middle Ages (p249)

Timeless Towns & Villages

o **Chester** A hotch-potch of medieval buildings and cobbled lanes (p236)

o **Haworth** Wander the streets of the Brontës' home town (p232)

o **Durham** This ancient university town has history aplenty (p248)

o **Grasmere** Visit the former homes of William Wordsworth at this Lakeland village (p247)

ADVANCE PLANNING

o **Two months before** Book hotels, especially in popular areas such as the Lake District, York and the Yorkshire Dales.

o **One month before** Consider booking in advance for major sights such as Castle Howard, Hill Top and Jorvik. Book long-distance train tickets for the best deals.

o **One week before** Check the weather forecast if you plan to visit the Lake District or Yorkshire Dales, but remember conditions are always variable.

RESOURCES

o **Manchester** (www.visitmanchester.com)

o **Liverpool** (www.visitliverpool.com)

o **Northwest England** (www.visitnorthwest.com)

o **Lake District National Park** (www.lakedistrict.gov.uk)

o **Lake District** (www.golakes.co.uk)

o **Yorkshire** (www.yorkshire.com)

o **Yorkshire Dales National Park** (www.yorkshiredales.org.uk)

o **Hadrian's Wall** (www.visithadrianswall.co.uk)

GETTING AROUND

o **Bus** Good long-distance bus networks cover most of the north, but it's slower than train or car.

o **Train** Lots of regular links between the big cities, plus several scenic branch-lines.

o **Car** You'll regret taking a car into the cities – use Park & Ride schemes or other public transport instead.

BE FOREWARNED

o **Crowds** Be prepared for summer crowds and traffic jams, especially in the Yorkshire Dales and the Lake District.

o **Weather** Statistically speaking, the north is colder and wetter than most of the rest of England – come prepared.

o **Football** The beautiful game (also known as soccer) is practically a religion in Liverpool and Manchester; the cities can get rowdy on match days.

ft: Durham Cathedral (p249); **Above:** Derwent Water, the Lake District (p243)

York & Northern England Itineraries

The three-day loop takes in the verdant Yorkshire Dales and the stately Castle Howard. The five-day trip mixes modern cities with countryside and rich history.

HADRIAN'S WALL

LAKE DISTRICT NATIONAL PARK

YORKSHIRE DALES NATIONAL PARK

NORTH SEA

CASTLE HOWARD

FOUNTAINS ABBEY

YORK

IRISH SEA

LIVERPOOL

MANCHESTER

YORK TO YORK

SPIRIT OF YORKSHIRE

In the historic city of ❶ **York**, start with a walk around the city walls, via the ancient 'bars' (gateways). Then head for York Minster, the finest medieval cathedral in northern England, and some say in all of Europe. Other highlights include rickety looking buildings in the cobbled lanes around the Shambles.

On day two, take a trip to ❷ **Castle Howard,** a stately home of theatrical grandeur and architectural audacity a few miles outside York, recognisable from its starring role in the TV series and film of *Brideshead Revisited*. Return to York in time for a late afternoon river cruise, or have fun on an evening ghost tour.

On day three, head into the ❸ **Yorkshire Dales National Park**, for picturesque hills and a classic rural landscape. The wild valley of Ribblesdale is particularly scenic. If time allows, stop off at the classic ruins of ❹ **Fountains Abbey** on the way back.

5 DAYS

YORK TO HADRIAN'S WALL
NORTHERN HIGHLIGHTS

Start your tour with a day in ❶ **York**, admiring the elegant architecture and historic sites, then head southwest, across the Pennine Hills to ❷ **Manchester**. Art and architecture fans will love the galleries, especially the imposing structure of the Imperial War Museum North. Fans of another kind will want to visit Old Trafford, home of Manchester United.

Then another great northern city: ❸ **Liverpool** famous as the birthplace of The Beatles. It's now rediscovering its maritime past, focused on the Albert Dock, with fine museums, restaurants, and some classic old buildings.

After the cities, it's time for a breath of fresh air – a short journey northwards takes you to the ❹ **Lake District.** This is where you will find England's highest mountains and the region's most beautiful lakes, including Windermere and Grasmere.

From here it's easy to head north towards ❺ **Hadrian's Wall**, the country's most impressive remains from the Roman era.

Imperial War Museum North (p233), Manchester
CHRIS CONWAY/GETTY IMAGES ©

Discover York & Northern England

Swaledale, Yorkshire Dales National Park (p226)
DAVID HENDERSON/GETTY IMAGES ©

YORK

POP 152,850

Nowhere in northern England says 'medieval' quite like York, a city of extraordinary cultural and historical wealth that has lost little of its pre-industrial lustre. A magnificent circuit of 13th-century walls enclose its medieval spider's web of narrow streets. At the heart of the city lies the immense, awe-inspiring minster, one of the most beautiful Gothic cathedrals in the world. York's long history and rich heritage is woven into virtually every brick and beam, and the modern, tourist-oriented city – with its myriad museums, restaurants, cafes and traditional pubs – is a carefully maintained heir to that heritage.

◎ Sights

If you plan on visiting a number of sights, you can save yourself some money by using a **York Pass** (www.yorkpass.com; 1/2/3 days adult £36/48/58, child £20/24/28). It gives you free access to more than 30 pay-to-visit sights in and around York, including York Minster, Jorvik and Castle Howard. You can buy it at the York Tourist Office (p226) or online.

National Railway Museum   Museum

(www.nrm.org.uk; Leeman Rd; ⊙10am-6pm; P ♿) **FREE** While many railway museums are the sole preserve of lone men in anoraks comparing dog-eared notebooks and getting high on the smell of machine oil, coal smoke and nostalgia, this place is different. York's National Railway Museum – the biggest in the world, with more than 100 locomotives – is so well presented and crammed with fascinating stuff that it's interesting even to folk whose eyes don't mist over at the thought of a 4-6-2 A1 Pacific class thundering into a tunnel.

Jorvik Viking Centre — Museum

(www.jorvik-viking-centre.co.uk; Coppergate; adult/child £9.95/6.95; ⊙10am-5pm Apr-Oct, to 4pm Nov-Mar) Interactive multimedia exhibits aimed at bringing history to life often achieve exactly the opposite, but the much-hyped Jorvik manages to pull it off with aplomb. It's a smells-and-all reconstruction of the Viking settlement unearthed here during excavations in the late 1970s, brought to you courtesy of a 'time-car' monorail that transports you through 9th-century Jorvik. You can reduce time waiting in the queue by booking your tickets online and choosing the time you want to visit (£1 extra).

City Walls — Archaeological Site

(⊙8am-dusk) **FREE** If the weather's good, don't miss the chance to walk the City Walls, which follow the line of the original Roman walls and give a whole new perspective on the city. Allow 1½ to two hours for the full circuit of 4.5 miles or, if you're pushed for time, the short stretch from **Bootham Bar** to **Monk Bar** is worth doing for the views of the minster.

Yorkshire Museum — Museum

(www.yorkshiremuseum.org.uk; Museum St; adult/child £7.50/free; ⊙10am-5pm) Most of York's Roman archaeology is hidden beneath the medieval city, so the recently revamped displays in the Yorkshire Museum are invaluable if you want to get an idea of what Eboracum was like. There are maps and models of Roman York, funerary monuments, mosaic floors and wall paintings, and a 4th-century bust of Emperor Constantine.

Shambles — Street

The Shambles takes its name from the Saxon word *shamel,* meaning 'slaughterhouse' – in 1862 there were 26 butcher shops on this street. Today the butchers are long gone, but this narrow cobbled lane, lined with 15th-century Tudor buildings that overhang so much they seem to meet above your head, is the most picturesque in Britain, and one of the most visited in Europe, often crammed with visitors intent on buying a tacky souvenir before rushing back to the tour bus.

York Castle Museum — Museum

(www.yorkcastlemuseum.org.uk; Tower St; adult/child £8.50/free; ⊙9.30am-5pm) This excellent museum has displays of everyday life through the centuries, with reconstructed domestic interiors, a Victorian street and a prison cell where you can try out a condemned man's bed – in this case, that of highwayman Dick Turpin (imprisoned here before being hanged in 1739). There's a bewildering array of evocative objects from the past 400 years, gathered together by a certain Dr Kirk from the 1920s onwards for fear the items would become obsolete and disappear completely.

 ## Tours

Ghost Hunt of York — Walking Tour

(www.ghosthunt.co.uk; adult/child £5/3; ⊙tours 7.30pm) The kids will just love this award-winning and highly entertaining 75-minute tour laced with authentic ghost stories. It begins at the Shambles, whatever the weather (it's never cancelled) and there's no need to book, just turn up and wait till you hear the handbell ringing...

Yorkwalk — Walking Tour

(www.yorkwalk.co.uk; adult/child £6/5; ⊙tours 10.30am & 2.15pm Feb-Nov) Offers a series of two-hour walks on a range of themes, from the classics – Roman York, the snickelways (narrow alleys) and City Walls – to walks focused on chocolates and sweets, women in York, and the inevitable graveyard, coffin and plague tour. Walks depart from Museum Gardens Gate on Museum St; there's no need to book.

YorkBoat — Boat Tour

(www.yorkboat.co.uk; King's Staith; adult/child from £7.50/3.50; ⊙tours 10.30am, noon, 1.30pm & 3pm Feb-Nov) Hour-long cruises on the River Ouse, departing from King's Staith and, 10 minutes later, Lendal Bridge. Special lunch, dinner and evening cruises are also offered.

York

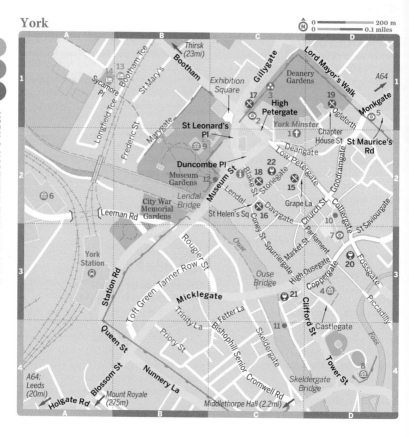

York

Sleeping

Beds are hard to find in midsummer, even with the inflated prices of the high season. It's also worth looking at serviced apartments if you're planning to stay two or three nights. **In York Holidays** (☏01904-632660; www.inyorkholidays.co.uk) offers a good selection of places from about £110 a night for a two-person apartment.

Abbeyfields
B&B ££

(☏01904-636471; www.abbeyfields.co.uk; 19 Bootham Tce; s/d from £55/84; 🛜) 🌱
Expect a warm welcome and thoughtfully arranged bedrooms here, with chairs and bedside lamps for comfortable reading. Breakfasts are among the best in town, with sausage and bacon from the local butcher, freshly laid eggs from a nearby farm and the aroma of newly baked bread.

Elliotts B&B
B&B ££

(☏01904-623333; www.elliottshotel.co.uk; 2 Sycamore Pl; s/d from £55/75; P@🛜)
A beautifully converted 'gentleman's residence', Elliotts leans towards the boutique end of the guesthouse market, with stylish and elegant rooms and some designer touches such as contemporary art and colourful textiles. An excellent location, both quiet and central.

Middlethorpe Hall
Hotel £££

(☏01904-641241; www.middlethorpe. com; Bishopthorpe Rd; s/d from £139/199; P🛜) This breathtaking 17th-century country house is set in eight hectares of parkland, once the home of diarist Lady Mary Wortley Montagu. The rooms are divided between the main house, restored courtyard buildings and three cottage suites. All the rooms are beautifully decorated with original antiques and oil paintings that have been carefully selected to reflect the period.

1 YORK MINSTER
The Minster is the best-known sight in York, and rightly so. I highly recommend going to the top of the Lantern Tower for spectacular views over the medieval streets surrounding the Minster, with the modern city beyond and the North York Moors visible 30 miles away. It's a stiff climb up 275 steps, but well worth the effort.

2 BOOTHAM BAR
In York, a 'bar' is a medieval gateway in the city walls and Bootham Bar is the oldest. To enjoy a great view of the city and a great sense of surrounding history, stop at the cafe in the square in front of York Art Gallery, opposite Bootham Bar. Beyond the city walls, you can see the massive towers of the Minster, while just to the right is the old King's Manor dating from the 15th century.

3 STROLLING THE STREETS
A great pleasure is just walking the old streets. My favourite strolls meander through the narrow 'gates' (streets) and 'snickleways' (alleys) from Stonegate – an old Roman road and one of the most beautiful streets in the city – to the best-known of York's medieval thoroughfares, the Shambles.

4 DRINKING IN HISTORY
Many of York's old pubs have historic links and many are haunted too. My favourites include the Blue Bell on Fossgate and the Ye Olde Starre on Stonegate. The King's Arms tends to flood in winter, but its riverside tables are a great meeting spot in the summer.

5 ST MARY'S ABBEY
St Mary's Abbey is beautiful little bit of medieval York, now sitting in the Museum Gardens. The abbey dates from the 13th century and was mostly destroyed by Henry VIII in the Dissolution of the Monasteries in 1539.

PAUL HARRIS/GETTY IMAGES ©

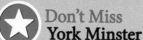

Don't Miss
York Minster

The remarkable York Minster is the largest medieval cathedral in all of Northern Europe, and one of the world's most beautiful Gothic buildings. Seat of the archbishop of York, primate of England, it is second in importance only to Canterbury, seat of the primate of *all* England – the separate titles were created to settle a debate over the true centre of the English church. If this is the only cathedral you visit in England, you'll still walk away satisfied.

The first church on this site was a wooden chapel built for the baptism of King Edwin of Northumbria on Easter Day 627, whose location is marked in the crypt. It was replaced with a stone church built on the site of a Roman basilica, parts of which can be seen in the foundations. The first Norman minster was built in the 11th century and again, you can see surviving fragments in the foundations and crypt.

The present minster, built mainly between 1220 and 1480, manages to encompass all the major stages of Gothic architectural development. The transepts (1220–55) were built in Early English style; the octagonal chapter house (1260–90) and nave (1291–1340) in the Decorated style; and the west towers, west front and central (or lantern) tower (1470–72) in Perpendicular style.

NEED TO KNOW

www.yorkminster.org; Deangate; adult/child £10/free, combined ticket incl tower £15/5; ⏱9am-5.30pm Mon-Sat, 12.45-5.30pm Sun, last admission 5pm

Mount Royale
Hotel £££

(☎01904-628856; www.mountroyale.co.uk; The Mount; s/d/ste from £95/125/225; P 🛜 🛝) A grand, early-19th-century heritage-listed building converted into a superb luxury hotel, complete with a solarium, beauty spa and outdoor heated tub and swimming pool. The rooms in the main house are gorgeous, but best of all are the open-plan garden suites, reached via an arcade of tropical fruit trees and bougainvillea.

Eating

Mannion's
Cafe, Bistro £

(☎01904-631030; www.mannionandco.co.uk; 1 Blake St; mains £5-9; 🕑9am-5.30pm Mon-Sat, 10am-5pm Sun) Expect to queue for a table at this busy bistro (no reservations), with its maze of cosy, wood-panelled rooms and selection of daily specials. Regulars on the menu are eggs Benedict for breakfast, a chunky Yorkshire rarebit made with home-baked bread, and lunch platters of cheese and charcuterie from the attached deli. Oh, and pavlova for pudding.

Cafe No 8
Cafe, Bistro ££

(☎01904-653074; www.cafeno8.co.uk; 8 Gillygate; 2-/3-course meal £18/22, Fri & Sat £22/27; 🕑10am-10pm; 🛜🚻) 🅿 A cool little place with modern artwork mimicking the Edwardian stained glass at the front, No 8 offers a day-long menu of classic bistro dishes using fresh local produce, including duck breast with blood orange and juniper, and Yorkshire pork belly with star anise, fennel and garlic. It also does breakfast daily (mains £5) and Sunday lunch (three courses £25). Booking recommended.

Parlour at Grays Court
Cafe ££

(www.grayscourtyork.com; Chapter House St; mains £8-14; 🕑10am-5pm; 🛜) An unexpected find in the heart of York, this 16th-century house (now a hotel) has more of a country atmosphere. Enjoy gourmet coffee and cake in the sunny garden, or indulge in a light lunch in the historic setting of the oak-panelled Jacobean gallery. The menu runs from Yorkshire rarebit to confit duck, and includes traditional afternoon tea (£18.50).

Bettys
Teahouse ££

(www.bettys.co.uk; St Helen's Sq; mains £6-14, afternoon tea £18.50; 🕑9am-9pm; 🚻) Old-school afternoon tea, with white-aproned waiters, linen tablecloths and a teapot collection ranged along the walls. The house speciality is the Yorkshire Fat Rascal, a huge fruit scone smothered in melted butter, but the smoked haddock with poached egg and hollandaise sauce (seasonal) is our favourite lunch dish. No bookings – queue for a table at busy times.

1331
Steak ££

(☎01904-661130; www.1331-york.co.uk; 13 Grape Lane; mains £9-17; 🕑6-10pm Mon-Thu, 11am-1am Fri & Sat, 11am-10pm Sun; 🛜🗝🚻) This courtyard complex houses a bar, cocktail lounge and even a private cinema, along with this appealing first-floor restaurant serving a menu of crowd-pleasing classics ranging from sausage and mash with onion gravy or slow-braised lamb shank, to good old steak and chips. Vegetarians are catered for, too, with a good selection of dishes such as chickpea and coriander burgers.

Drinking

Blue Bell
Pub

(53 Fossgate; 🕑11am-11pm Mon-Sat, noon-10.30pm Sun) This is what a real English pub looks like – a tiny, 200-year-old wood-panelled room with a smouldering fireplace, decor untouched since 1903, a pile of ancient board games in the corner, friendly and efficient bar staff, and Timothy Taylor and Black Sheep ales on tap. Bliss, with froth on top – if you can get in (it's often full).

Ye Olde Starre
Pub

(www.taylor-walker.co.uk; 40 Stonegate; 🕑11am-11pm Sun-Wed, to midnight Thu-Sat) Licensed since 1644, this is York's oldest pub – a warren of small rooms and a small beer garden, with a half-dozen real ales on tap. It was used as a morgue by the Roundheads (supporters of parliament) during the Civil War, but the atmosphere has improved a lot since then.

King's Arms

Pub

(King's Staith; ⏰11am-11pm Sun-Thu, to 1am Fri & Sat) York's best-known pub enjoys a fabulous riverside location, with tables spilling out onto the quayside. It's the perfect spot on a summer evening, but be prepared to share it with a few hundred other people.

❶ Information

York Tourist Office (☎01904-550099; www. visityork.org; 1 Museum St; ⏰9am-6pm Mon-Sat, 10am-5pm Sun Apr-Sep, shorter hours Oct-Mar) Visitor and transport info for all of Yorkshire, plus accommodation bookings, ticket sales and internet access.

❶ Getting There & Away

Car

A car is more hindrance than help in the city centre, so use one of the Park & Ride car parks at the edge of the city.

Train

York is a major railway hub, with frequent direct services to Edinburgh (£80, 2½ hours, every half hour), Newcastle (£16, one hour, every half hour), London King's Cross (£80, two hours, every half hour) and Manchester (£17, 1½ hours, every 15 minutes). There are also trains to Cambridge (£65, three hours, hourly), changing at Peterborough.

YORKSHIRE DALES NATIONAL PARK

The Yorkshire Dales – named from the old Norse word *dalr,* meaning 'valleys' – is the central jewel in the necklace of three national parks strung across northern England, with the dramatic fells of the Lake District to the west and the brooding heaths of the North York Moors to the east.

From well-known names such as Wensleydale and Ribblesdale to the obscure and evocative Langstrothdale and Arkengarthdale, the park's glacial valleys are characterised by a distinctive landscape of high heather moorland, stepped skylines and flat-topped hills. The Dales have been protected as a national park since the 1950s, assuring their status as a walkers' and cyclists' paradise. But there's plenty for nonwalkers as well, from exploring the legacy of literary vet James Herriot of *All*

Swaledale, Yorkshire Dales National Park

DEREK CROUCHER/GETTY IMAGES ©

JOE CORNISH/GETTY IMAGES ©

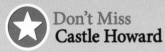

Don't Miss
Castle Howard

Stately homes may be two-a-penny in England, but you'll have to try pretty damn hard to find one as breathtakingly stately as Castle Howard, a work of theatrical grandeur and audacity set in the rolling Howardian Hills. This is one of the world's most beautiful buildings, instantly recognisable from its starring role in the 1980s TV series *Brideshead Revisited* and in the 2008 film of the same name (both based on Evelyn Waugh's 1945 novel of nostalgia for the English aristocracy).

When the Earl of Carlisle hired his pal Sir John Vanbrugh to design his new home in 1699, he was hiring a bloke who had no formal training and was best known as a playwright. Luckily, Vanbrugh hired Nicholas Hawksmoor who had worked as Christopher Wren's clerk of works – not only would Hawksmoor have a big part to play in the house's design, but he and Vanbrugh would later work wonders with Blenheim Palace. Today the house is still home to the Hon Simon Howard and his family and he can often be seen around the place.

As you wander about the peacock-haunted grounds, views open up over the hills, Vanbrugh's playful Temple of the Four Winds and Hawksmoor's stately mausoleum, but the great baroque house with its magnificent central cupola is an irresistible visual magnet. Inside, the house is full of treasures – the breathtaking Great Hall with its soaring Corinthian pilasters, Pre-Raphaelite stained glass in the chapel, and corridors lined with classical antiquities.

Castle Howard is 15 miles northeast of York, off the A64. There are several organised tours from York – check with the tourist office for up-to-date schedules.

NEED TO KNOW

www.castlehoward.co.uk; adult/child house & grounds £14/7.50, grounds only £9.50/6; ◷ house 11am-4.30pm Apr-Oct, grounds 10am-5pm Mar-Oct & Dec, to 4pm Nov, Jan & Feb; Ⓟ

WOJTEK BUSS/GETTY IMAGES ©

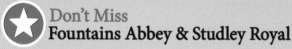

Don't Miss
Fountains Abbey & Studley Royal

The alluring and strangely obsessive water gardens of the Studley Royal estate were built in the 18th century to enhance the picturesque ruins of 12th-century Fountains Abbey. Together, they present a breathtaking picture of pastoral elegance and tranquillity that have made them a Unesco World Heritage site and the most visited of all the National Trust's pay-to-enter properties.

After falling out with the Benedictines of York in 1132, a band of rebel monks came here to establish their own monastery. Struggling to make it alone, they were formally adopted by the Cistercians in 1135. By the middle of the 13th century, the new abbey had become the most successful Cistercian venture in the country. After the Dissolution, when Henry VIII confiscated church property, the abbey's estate was sold into private hands, and between 1598 and 1611 **Fountains Hall** was built using stone from the abbey ruins. The hall and ruins were united with the Studley Royal estate in 1768.

The remains of the abbey are impressively grandiose, gathered around the sunny Romanesque **cloister**, with a huge vaulted **cellarium** leading off the west end of the church. Here, the abbey's 200 lay brothers lived, and food and wool from the abbey's farms were stored. At the east end is the soaring **Chapel of Nine Altars** and on the outside of its northeast window is a Green Man carving (a pre-Christian fertility symbol).

Fountains Abbey is 4 miles west of Ripon off the B6265. Bus 139 travels from Ripon to Fountains Abbey visitor centre year-round (£2.60 return, 15 minutes, four times daily Monday to Saturday, seven on Sundays in summer).

NEED TO KNOW
NT; www.fountainsabbey.org.uk; adult/child £10.50/5.25; ☺10am-6pm Apr-Sep, to 5pm Sat-Thu Oct-Mar

Creatures Great and Small fame to sampling the favourite teatime snack of the British TV characters Wallace and Gromit at the Wensleydale Creamery.

The *Visitor* newspaper, available from tourist offices, lists local events and walks guided by park rangers, as well as many places to stay and eat. The official park website (www.yorkshiredales.org.uk) is also useful.

❶ Getting There & Around

About 90% of visitors to the park arrive by car, and the narrow roads can become extremely crowded in summer.

By train, the best and most interesting access to the Dales is via the famous **Settle–Carlisle Line** (SCL; www.settle-carlisle.co.uk). Trains run between Leeds and Carlisle, stopping at Skipton, Settle, and numerous small villages, offering unrivalled access to the hills straight from the station platform.

Devonshire Fell Hotel £££

(📞 01756-718111; www.devonshirefell.co.uk; Burnsall; r from £140; P @ 🛜 🚻) A sister property to Bolton Abbey's Devonshire Arms Country House Hotel, this former gentleman's club for mill owners has a much more contemporary feel, with beautiful modern furnishings crafted by local experts. The conservatory (used as a lounge and breakfast room) has a stunning view over the valley. It's 3 miles southeast of Grassington on the B6160.

Whimsical Cottage Cafe £

(📞 01756-752414; 1 Garr's Lane; mains £4-9; ⏰ 10am-4pm; 🚻) This cute little white cottage, just uphill from the village square, serves good coffee and unusual homemade cakes (parsnip and apple sponge is unexpectedly delicious), as well as hot pies for lunch – chicken, ham and leek, or steak and Guinness. Breakfast served till 11.30am.

Grassington

The perfect base for jaunts around the south Dales, Grassington's handsome Georgian centre teems with walkers and visitors throughout the summer months, soaking up an atmosphere that – despite the odd touch of faux rusticity – is as attractive and traditional as you'll find in these parts.

🛏 Sleeping & Eating

Ashfield House B&B ££

(📞 01756-752584; www.ashfieldhouse.co.uk; Summers Fold; r from £100; P @ 🛜) A secluded 17th-century country house behind a walled garden, with exposed stone walls, open fireplaces and an all-round cosy feel. It's just off the main square.

Grassington
CHRISTINA BOLLEN/ALAMY ©

Ribblesdale & The Three Peaks

Scenic Ribblesdale cuts through the southwestern corner of the Yorkshire Dales National Park, where the skyline is dominated by a trio of distinctive hills known as the **Three Peaks** – Whernside (735m), Ingleborough (724m) and Pen-y-ghent (694m). Easily accessible via the Settle–Carlisle railway line, this is one of England's most popular areas for outdoor activities, attracting thousands of hikers, cyclists and cavers each weekend. The village of Horton-in-Ribblesdale makes the best base for exploring.

Hawes

Hawes is the beating heart of Wensleydale, a thriving and picturesque market town (market day is Tuesday) that has the added attraction of its own waterfall in the village centre.

The main sights are the beautifully presented **Dales Countryside Museum** (☎01969-666210; Station Yard; adult/child £4/free; ☉10am-5pm, closed Jan; P), and the fascinating **Wensleydale Creamery** (www.wensleydale.co.uk; adult/child £2.50/1.50; ☉10am-4pm; ♿), which produces the animated TV characters Wallace and Gromit's favourite crumbly white cheese.

Richmond

POP 8415

The handsome market town of Richmond is one of England's best-kept secrets, perched on a rocky outcrop overlooking the River Swale and guarded by the ruins of a massive castle. A maze of cobbled streets radiates from the broad, sloping market square (market day is Saturday), lined with elegant Georgian buildings and photogenic stone cottages, with glimpses of the surrounding hills and dales peeking through the gaps.

Left: River Ure, near Hawes, Wensleydale; **Below:** Richmond Castle, Richmond

(LEFT) KEITH WOOD/GETTY IMAGES ©; (BELOW) JAMES EMMERSON/GETTY IMAGES ©

👁 Sights

Top of the pile is the impressive heap of **Richmond Castle** (www.english-heritage.org.uk; Market Pl; adult/child £4.90/2.90; ⏰10am-6pm Apr-Sep, to 5pm Oct, to 4pm Sat & Sun only Nov-Mar), founded in 1070 and one of the first castles in England since Roman times to be built of stone. The best part is the view from the top of the well-preserved 30m-high keep, which towers over the River Swale. Walkers can follow paths along the River Swale from the town.

🛏 Sleeping

Frenchgate Hotel   Hotel **££**
(📞01748-822087; www.thefrenchgate.co.uk; 59-61 Frenchgate; s/d from £88/118; P) Nine elegant bedrooms occupy the upper floors of this converted Georgian town house, now a boutique hotel decorated with local art. The rooms have cool designer fittings that set off a period fireplace here, a Victorian roll-top bath

there. Downstairs there's an excellent restaurant (three-course dinner £39) and a hospitable lounge with oak beams and an open fire.

Millgate House   B&B **£££**
(📞01748-823571; www.millgatehouse.com; Market Pl; r £110-145; P@🐾) 🍃 Behind an unassuming grey door lies the unexpected pleasure of one of the most attractive guesthouses in England. While the house itself is a Georgian gem crammed with period details, it is overshadowed by the multi-award-winning garden at the back, which offers superb views over the River Swale and the Cleveland Hills. If possible, book the Garden Suite.

🍴 Eating & Drinking

Cross View Tearooms   Tearoom **£**
(www.crossviewtearooms.co.uk; 38 Market Pl; mains £5-8; ⏰9am-5.30pm; 🚼) 🍃 So popular with locals that you might have

231

to queue for a table at lunchtime, the Cross View is the place to go for a hearty breakfast, homemade cakes, a hot lunch, or just a nice cup of tea.

Rustique
French ££

(☎ 01748-821565; www.rustiqueyork.co.uk; Chantry Wynd, Finkle St; mains £10-21; ☺ noon-9pm) Tucked away in an arcade, this cosy bistro has consistently impressed with its mastery of French country cooking, from *confit de canard* (duck slow roasted in its own fat) to *paupiette de poulet* (chicken breast stuffed with brie and sun-dried tomatoes). Booking is recommended.

HAWORTH

POP 6380

It seems that only Shakespeare himself is held in higher esteem than the beloved Brontë sisters – Emily, Anne and Charlotte – judging by the 8 million visitors a year who trudge up the hill from the train station to pay their respects at the handsome parsonage where the literary classics *Jane Eyre* and *Wuthering Heights* were penned.

◉ Sights

Haworth Parish Church
Church

(Church St; ☺ 9am-5.30pm) Your first stop in Haworth should be the parish church, a lovely old place of worship built in the late 19th century on the site of the older church that the Brontë sisters knew, which was demolished in 1879. In the surrounding churchyard, gravestones are covered in moss or pushed to one side by gnarled tree roots, giving the place a tremendous feeling of age.

Brontë Parsonage Museum
Museum

(www.bronte.info; Church St; adult/child £7.50/3.75; ☺ 10am-5.30pm) Set in a pretty garden overlooking the church and graveyard, the house where the Brontë family lived from 1820 to 1861 is now a museum. The rooms are meticulously furnished and decorated exactly as they were in the Brontë era, including Charlotte's bedroom, her clothes and her writing paraphernalia. There's also an informative exhibition, which includes the fascinating miniature books the Brontës wrote as children.

ℹ Information

Haworth Tourist Office (☎ 01535-642329; www.haworth-village.org.uk; 2-4 West Lane; ☺ 9am-5.30pm) The tourist office has an excellent supply of information on the village, the surrounding area and, of course, the Brontës.

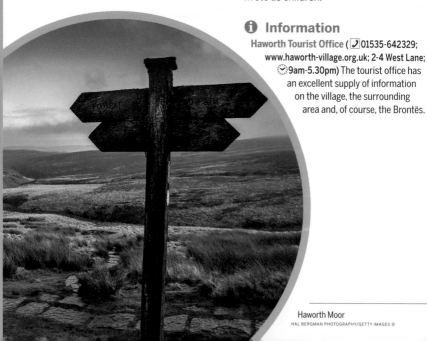

Haworth Moor
HAL BERGMAN PHOTOGRAPHY/GETTY IMAGES ©

MANCHESTER

POP 394,270

Raised on lofty ambition and not afraid to declare its considerable bona fides, Manchester is – by dint of geography and history – England's second city (apologies to Birmingham), although if you were to ask a Mancunian what it's like to be second they might reply: 'Don't know; ask a Londoner.'

Even accounting for northern bluster, the uncrowned capital of the north is well deserving of the title. It has a rich history and culture, easily explored in its myriad museums and galleries. And while history and heritage make the city interesting, its distractions of pure pleasure make Manchester fun: you can dine, drink and dance yourself into happy oblivion in the swirl of hedonism that is one of Manchester's most cherished characteristics.

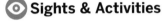 Sights & Activities

CITY CENTRE

Museum of Science & Industry
Museum

(MOSI; ☎ 0161-832 2244; www.msim.org.uk; Liverpool Rd; charges vary for special exhibitions; ⏰ 10am-5pm) **FREE** If there's anything you want to know about the Industrial (and post-Industrial) Revolution and Manchester's key role in it, you'll find the answers here among this collection of steam engines and locomotives, factory machinery from the mills, and the excellent exhibition telling the story of Manchester from the sewers up.

People's History Museum
Museum

(☎ 0161-838 9190; www.phm.org.uk; Left Bank, Bridge St; ⏰ 10am-5pm) **FREE** The story of Britain's 200-year march to democracy is told in all its pain and pathos at this superb museum, housed in a refurbished Edwardian pumping station. You clock in on the 1st floor (literally: punch your card in an old mill clock, which managers would infamously fiddle with so as to make employees work longer) and plunge into the heart of Britain's struggle for basic democratic rights, labour reform and fair pay.

National Football Museum
Museum

(☎ 0161-605 8200; www.nationalfootballmuseum.com; Corporation St, Urbis, Cathedral Gardens; ⏰ 10am-5pm Mon-Sat, 11am-5pm Sun) **FREE** Britain is the birthplace of football and Manchester the home of both the most popular and richest clubs in the world. Fittingly, this blockbuster museum charts the evolution of British football from its earliest days to the multi-billion pound phenomenon it is today. One of the highlights is **Football Plus**, a series of interactive stations that allow you to test your skills in simulated conditions; buy a credit (£2.50, four for £9) and try your luck – it's recommended for kids over seven.

SALFORD QUAYS

Just west of the city centre, and easily reached via Metrolink (£2), is Salford Quays, home to the city's big-ticket attractions and new hub of the BBC's northern HQ. Check out www.thequays.co.uk for more info.

Imperial War Museum North
Museum

(☎ 0161-836 4000; www.iwm.org.uk/north; Trafford Wharf Rd; ⏰ 10am-5pm; 🚇 Harbour City, MediaCityUK) **FREE** War museums generally appeal to those with a fascination for military hardware and battle strategy (toy soldiers optional), but Daniel Libeskind's visually stunning Imperial War Museum North takes a radically different approach. War is hell, it tells us, but it's a hell we revisit with tragic regularity.

Old Trafford (Manchester United Museum & Tour)
Stadium

(☎ 0161-868 8000; www.manutd.com; Sir Matt Busby Way; tours adult/child £18/12; ⏰ museum 9.30am-5pm, tours every 10min except match days 9.40am-4.30pm; 🚇 Old Trafford) You don't have to be a fan of the world's most famous football club to enjoy a visit to their impressive 75,000-plus capacity stadium, but it helps. The museum tour includes a walk down the tunnel onto the

Manchester

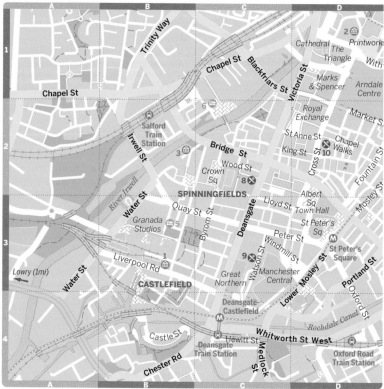

Manchester

◎ Sights

🛏 Sleeping

✕ Eating

edge of the playing surface of the 'Theatre of Dreams', where Manchester United's superstar footballers exercised their

Premier League supremacy for 20 years, guided by the peerless Sir Alex Ferguson.

Lowry   Arts Centre

(📞0161-876 2020; www.thelowry.com; Pier 8, Salford Quays; ⏱11am-6pm Sun-Fri, 10am-8pm Sat; 🚃Harbour City, MediaCity UK) Looking more like a shiny steel ship than an arts centre, the Lowry is the quays' most notable success. With multiple performance spaces, bars, restaurants and shops, it attracts more than a million visitors a year to its myriad functions, which include everthing from big-name theatrical productions to comedy, kids' theatre and even weddings. The centre is also home to 300 beautifully humanistic depictions of urban landscapes by LS Lowry (1887–1976), who was born in nearby Stretford, and after whom the complex is named.

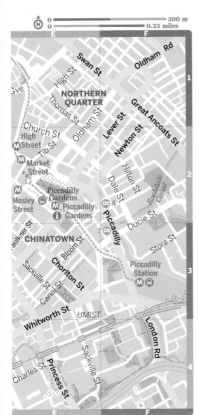

free-standing baths and lots of high-tech electronics)? Present. This former schoolhouse (ah, now you get it) is small but sumptuous – beyond the art-deco lobby are the fabulous bedrooms, each an example of style and luxury. If only school left such comfortable memories.

Lowry   Hotel £££

(📞0161-827 4000; www.roccofortecollection. com; 50 Dearman's Pl; r £120-950; P@🤝) Visiting rock stars and luxury hunters tend to favour this modern, five-star hotel (not to be confused with the arts centre in Salford Quays), where the fabulous bedrooms have enormous beds and ergonomically designed furniture...for maximum comfort, of course. There's an excellent restaurant on the premises, and a health spa where you can soothe your-self with a skin-brightening treatment or an aromatherapy head-massage.

Malmaison   Hotel £££

(📞0161-278 1000; www.malmaison.com; Pic-cadilly St; r from £119; 🚇Piccadilly) Drop-dead trendy and full of crushed-red velvet, deep purples, art-deco ironwork and signature black-and-white tiles: Mal-maison Manchester follows the chain's quirky design style and passion for cool, although rarely at the expense of comfort; the rooms are terrific. The **Smoak Grill** (📞0161-278 1000; www.smoak-grill.com; mains £13-25) downstairs is hugely popular.

🍴 Eating

Australasia   Modern Australian £££

(📞0161-831 0288; www.australasia.uk.com; 1 The Avenue, Spinningfields; mains £13-26; ⏰noon-midnight; 🍴) One of Manchester's most successful building conversions has been that of the basement archive of the *Manchester Evening News* into this sur-prisingly bright and beautiful restaurant, which serves contemporary Australian cuisine with flavours of southeast Asia – the lunchtime selection of fresh sushi is particularly good, as are the specials. A late licence sees it turn into a very cool bar.

Sleeping

ABode   Hotel ££

(📞0161-247 7744; www.abodehotels.co.uk; 107 Piccadilly St; r from £100; @🤝) The original fittings at this converted textile factory have been combined successfully with 61 bedrooms divided into four categories of ever-increasing luxury: Comfortable, Desirable, Enviable and Fabulous, the lat-ter being five seriously swanky top-floor suites.

Great John Street
Hotel   Hotel £££

(📞0161-831 3211; www.greatjohnstreet.co.uk; Great John St; r £160-320; @🤝) Elegant designer luxury? Present. Fabulous rooms with all the usual delights (Egyp-tian cotton sheets, fabulous toiletries,

Sam's Chop House
British ££

(📞0161-834 3210; www.samschophouse.co.uk; Back Pool Fold, Chapel Walks, off Cross St; mains £12.50-20; ⏱noon-3pm & 5-9.30pm Mon-Fri, 12.30-10pm Sat, noon-8pm Sun) Arguably the city's top gastropub, Sam's is a Victorian classic that serves dishes straight out of a Dickens novel. The highlight is the crispy corned beef hash cake starter, which is salt-cured for 10 days on the premises. The gravy-loving Mrs Todgers from *Martin Chuzzlewit* would certainly approve.

James Martin Manchester
Modern British ££

(📞0161-828 0345; www.jamesmartinmanchester.co.uk; Manchester235, Great Northern, Watson St; mains £16-18; ⏱5-11pm) Inside the opulent Manchester 235 casino, itself a converted linen warehouse, this elegant restaurant is all wooden floors, exposed brick walls and wonderfully comfortable seating. It's the perfect ambience to enjoy celebrity chef James Martin's terrific menu, a tasty exploration of modern British dishes like slow roast belly of Redhill pork or West Coast plaice, served with herb dumplings.

Lime Tree
Modern British £££

(📞0161-445 1217; www.thelimetreerestaurant.co.uk; 8 Lapwing Lane; mains £16-26; ⏱noon-2.30pm Tue-Fri, 5.30-10pm Mon-Sat, noon-8pm Sun; 🚇West Didsbury) The ambience is refined without being stuffy, the service is relaxed but spot on, and the food is divine – Mancunians book in advance and travel from far afield just to enjoy the superb menu. The 21-day dry-aged fillet steak in peppercorn sauce (£21) is to die for.

🛈 Information

Tourist Office (www.visitmanchester.com; Piccadilly Plaza, Portland St; guided tours daily adult/child £7/6; ⏱10am-5.15pm Mon-Sat, to 4.30pm Sun) This is mostly a self-service tourist office, with brochures and interactive maps to help guide visitors.

🛈 Getting There & Away

Air

Manchester Airport (📞0161-489 3000; www.manchesterairport.co.uk), south of the city, is the largest airport outside London and is served by 13 locations throughout Britain as well as more than 50 international destinations.

Train

Manchester Piccadilly is the main station for intercity services.

Liverpool Lime St £11.90, 45 minutes, half-hourly

London Euston £80, three hours, seven daily

🛈 Getting Around

To/From the Airport

The airport is 12 miles south of the city. A train to or from Victoria station costs £4.10, and a coach is £3.50. A taxi is nearly four times as much in light traffic.

Public Transport

For enquiries about local transport, including night buses, contact **Travelshop** (📞0161-228 7811; www.tfgm.com; 9 Portland St, Piccadilly Gardens; ⏱8am-8pm).

Centreline bus 4 provides a free service around the heart of Manchester every 10 minutes.

There are frequent **Metrolink** (www.metrolink.co.uk) trams between Victoria and Piccadilly train stations and G-Mex (for Castlefield), as well as further afield to Salford Quays.

CHESTER

POP 80,130

Chester is one of English history's greatest gifts to the contemporary visitor. Its red-sandstone wall, which today gift-wraps a tidy collection of Tudor and Victorian buildings, was built during Roman times.

◉ Sights

City Walls
Landmark

A good way to get a sense of Chester's unique character is to walk the 2-mile circuit along the walls that surround the historic centre. Originally built by the Romans around AD 70, the walls were altered substantially over the following centuries but have retained their current position since around 1200. The tourist office's *Walk Around Chester Walls* leaflet is an excellent guide.

Rows   Architecture

Besides the City Walls, Chester's other great draw is the Rows, a series of two-level galleried arcades along the four streets that fan out in each direction from the **Central Cross**. The architecture is a handsome mix of Victorian and Tudor (original and mock) buildings that house a fantastic collection of individually owned shops.

Chester Cathedral   Cathedral

(☎ 01244-324756; www.chestercathedral.com; 12 Abbey Sq; admission £3; ⊙ 9am-5pm Mon-Sat, 1-4pm Sun) Originally a Benedictine abbey built on the remains of an earlier Saxon church dedicated to St Werburgh (the city's patron saint), Chester Cathedral was shut down in 1540 as part of Henry VIII's dissolution frenzy, but reconsecrated as a cathedral the following year. Although the cathedral itself was given a substantial Victorian facelift, the 12th-century cloister and its surrounding build-

ings are essentially unaltered and retain much of the structure from the early monastic years.

ℹ Getting There & Away

The train station is about a mile from the city centre via Foregate St and City Rd, or Brook St. City-Rail Link buses are free for people with rail tickets, and operate between the station and **Bus Stop A** (Frodsham St). Destinations:

Liverpool £6.65, 45 minutes, hourly

London Euston £65.20, 2½ hours, hourly

Manchester £12.60, one hour, hourly

LIVERPOOL

POP 469,020

Few English cities are as shackled by reputation as Liverpool, and none has worked so hard to outgrow the cliches that have been used to define it.

A hardscrabble town with a reputation for wit and an obsessive love of football, Liverpool also has an impressive cultural heritage: it has more listed buildings than any other outside London, has recently undergone an impressive program of

Watergate Street, Chester

Liverpool

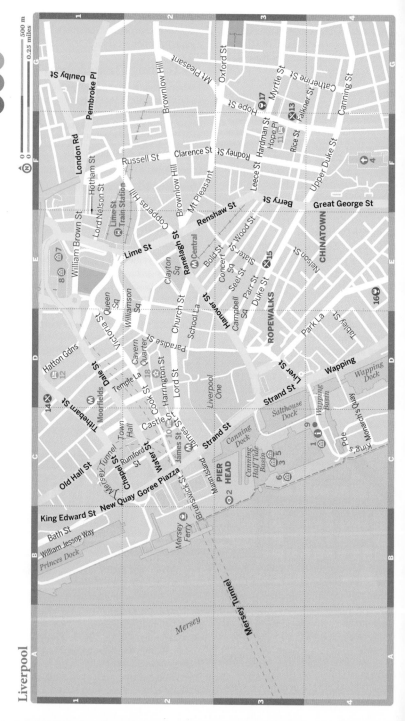

Liverpool

urban regeneration, and its collection of museums and galleries is easily among the best in the country. And then there's the Beatles.

The main attractions are Albert Dock (west of the city centre), and the trendy Ropewalks area (south of Hanover St and west of the two cathedrals). Lime St station, the bus station and the Cavern Quarter – a mecca for Beatles fans – lie just to the north.

⊙ Sights

CITY CENTRE

World Museum   Museum
(0151-478 4399; www.liverpoolmuseums.org.uk/wml; William Brown St; ⊙10am-5pm) FREE Natural history, science and technology are the themes of the oldest museum in town, which opened in 1853 and whose exhibits range from live bugs to human anthropology. This vastly entertaining and educational museum is spread across five themed floors, from the live

fish aquarium on the first floor to the planetarium on the fifth, where you'll also find exhibits dedicated to space (moon rocks, telescopes etc) and time (clocks and timepieces from the 1500s to 1960). Highly recommended.

Liverpool Cathedral   Church
(0151-709 6271; www.liverpoolcathedral.org.uk; Upper Duke St; visitor centre & tower admission £5; ⊙8am-6pm) Liverpool's Anglican cathedral is a building of superlatives. Not only is it Britain's largest church, it's also the world's largest Anglican cathedral. It is the work of Sir Gilbert Scott, who also gave us the red telephone box and the Southwark Power Station in London, now the Tate Modern. The central bell is the world's third largest (with the world's highest and heaviest peal), while the organ, with its 9765 pipes, is likely the world's largest operational model.

Walker Art Gallery   Art Museum
(0151-478 4199; www.liverpoolmuseums.org.uk/walker; William Brown St; ⊙10am-5pm) FREE The city's foremost art gallery is the national gallery for northern England, housing an outstanding collection of art from the 14th to the 21st centuries. Its strong suits are pre-Raphaelite art, modern British art and sculpture – not to mention the rotating exhibits of contemporary expression. It's a family-friendly place, too: the ground-floor Big Art for Little People gallery is designed for under-eights and features interactive exhibits and games that will (hopefully) result in a lifelong love affair with art.

ALBERT DOCK

International Slavery
Museum   Museum
(0151-478 4499; www.liverpoolmuseums.org.uk/ism; Albert Dock; ⊙10am-5pm) FREE Museums are, by their very nature, like a still of the past, but the extraordinary International Slavery Museum resonates very much in the present. It reveals slavery's unimaginable horrors – including Liverpool's own role in the triangular slave trade – in a clear and uncompromising manner. It does this through a remarkable

series of multi-media and other displays, and it doesn't baulk at confronting racism, slavery's shadowy ideological justification for this inhumane practice.

Beatles Story   Museum
(0151-709 1963; www.beatlesstory.com; Albert Dock; adult/child £14.95/9, incl Elvis & Us £15.95/7; 9am-7pm, last admission 5pm) Liverpool's most popular museum won't illuminate any dark, juicy corners in the turbulent history of the world's most famous foursome – there's ne'er a mention of internal discord, drugs or Yoko Ono – but there's plenty of genuine memorabilia to keep a Beatles fan happy. You can also get a combo ticket for the **Elvis & Us** (0151-709 1963; www.elvisandus.com; Mersey Ferries Terminal, Pier Head; admission £6; 9am-7pm Apr-Sep, 10am-6pm Oct-Mar) exhibit at the Beatles Story extension on Pier Head.

Merseyside Maritime
Museum   Museum
(0151-478 4499; www.liverpoolmuseums.org.uk/maritime; Albert Dock; 10am-5pm) FREE

The story of one of the world's great ports is the theme of this excellent museum and, believe us, it's a graphic and compelling pageturner. One of the many great exhibits is Emigration to a New World, which tells the story of nine million emigrants and their efforts to get to North America and Australia; the walk-through model of a typical ship shows just how tough conditions on board really were.

Tate Liverpool   Gallery
(0151-702 7400; www.tate.org.uk/liverpool; Albert Dock; special exhibitions adult/child from £5/4; 10am-5.50pm Jun-Aug, closed Mon Sep-May) FREE Touted as the home of modern art in the north, this gallery features a substantial checklist of 20th-century artists across its four floors, as well as touring exhibitions from the mother ship on London's Bankside. But it's all a little sparse, with none of the energy we'd expect from the world-famous Tate.

Tours

Beatles Fab Four
Taxi Tour   Taxi Tour
(0151-601 2111; www.thebeatlesfabfourtaxitour.co.uk; 2/3hr tour £45/55) Themed tours of the city's mop-top landmarks – there's the three-hour original Lennon tour or the two-hour Epstein express tour. Pick-ups arranged when booking. Up to five people per tour.

Liverpool Beatles
Tour   Guided Tour
(0151-281 7738; www.beatlestours.co.uk; tours from £65) Your own personalised tour of every bit of Beatles minutiae, from cradle to grave. Tours range from the three-hour Helter Skelter excursion to the Fantastic All-Day Tour, by the end of which, presumably, you'll be convinced you

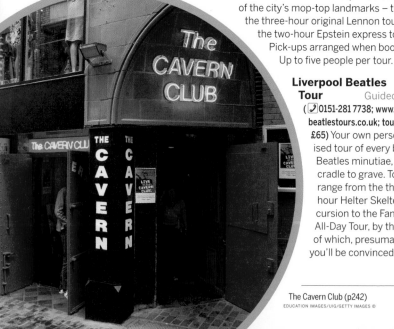

The Cavern Club (p242)

(Never) Let it Be

They broke up more than 40 years ago and two of their members are dead, but the Beatles are bigger business than ever in Liverpool.

Most of it centres around tiny Mathew St, site of the original Cavern Club, which is now the main thoroughfare of the 'Cavern Quarter'. Here you can shuck oysters in the Rubber Soul Oyster Bar, buy a George pillowcase in the From Me to You shop and put it on the pillows of the Hard Day's Night Hotel.

Wandering around Mathew St is plenty of fun – and the Beatles Shop is best for memorabilia – but if you really want a bit of Beatles lore, you'll have to visit the National Trust–owned **Mendips**, the home where John lived with his Aunt Mimi from 1945 to 1963 (which is also the time period covered by Sam Taylor-Wood's superb 2009 biopic of the young Lennon, *Nowhere Boy*) and **20 Forthlin Road**, the plain terraced home where Paul grew up; you can only do so by prebooked **tour** (☎0151-427 7231; www.nationaltrust.org.uk; Jury's Inn, 31 Keel Wharf, Wapping Dock; adult/child £22/7; ☉10am, 11am & 2.15pm Wed-Sun Mar-Nov). Tours also leave from **Speke Hall** (NT; www.nationaltrust.org.uk; house & gardens adult/child £10/5, gardens only adult/child £6.10/3.15; ☉11am-5pm Wed-Sun).

were actually in the band. Pick-ups are arranged upon booking.

Magical Mystery Tour Guided Tour

(☎0151-709 3285; www.cavernclub.org; per person £16.95; ☉tours 10.30am, 11.30am, 1pm & 2pm) Two-hour tour that takes in all Beatles-related landmarks – their birthplaces, childhood homes, schools and places such as Penny Lane and Strawberry Field – before finishing up in the Cavern Club (which isn't the original). Departs from opposite the tourist office on Albert Dock.

Sleeping

Richmond Hotel Hotel ££

(www.richmondliverpool.com; 24 Hatton Garden; d from £80, 2-bedroom apt from £199) Centrally located and fully renovated, the Richmond offers a convenient choice of accommodation, from classic doubles and suites to fully equipped, self-catering one-, two- and three-bedroom apartments. All of the rooms have high-spec decor, including 50in flatscreen TVs and fancy toiletries. Guests also have access to the hotel spa.

62 Castle St Boutique Hotel ££

(☎0151-702 7898; www.62castlest.com; 62 Castle St; r from £80; P@☎) This elegant property successfully blends the traditional Victorian features of the neoclassical building with a sleek, contemporary style. The 20 fabulously different suites come with high-definition plasma-screen TVs, drench showers and luxe toiletries as standard.

Hope Street Hotel Boutique Hotel £££

(☎0151-709 3000; www.hopestreethotel. co.uk; 40 Hope St; r/ste from £130/190; @☎) Luxurious Liverpool's pre-eminent flag-waver is this stunning boutique hotel on the city's most elegant street. King-sized beds draped in Egyptian cotton, oak floors with underfloor heating, LCD TVs and sleek modern bathrooms (with REN bath and beauty products) are but the most obvious touches of class at this supremely cool address. Breakfast, taken in the marvellous London Carriage Works, is not included.

🍴 Eating

Monro
Gastropub ££

(☎ 0151-707 9933; www.themonro.com; 92 Duke St; 2-course lunch £11.95, dinner mains £14-20; ⏰ 11am-11pm) The Monro has fast become one of the city's favourite spots for lunch, dinner and, especially, weekend brunch. The constantly changing menu of classic British dishes made with ingredients sourced as locally as possible has transformed this handsome old pub into a superb dining experience. It's tough to find pub grub this good elsewhere, unless you go to its sister pub, the **James Monro** (☎ 0151-236 9700; www.thejamesmonro.com; 69 Tithebarn St; ⏰ 11am-11pm).

HoST
Asian, Fusion ££

(www.ho-st.co.uk; 31 Hope St; mains £9.50-13; ⏰ 11am-11pm; ⛾ ♿) A bright, airy room with the look of a chic, contemporary New York brasserie serves up excellent pan-Asian dishes like Indonesian braised lamb with fried rice and red duck coconut curry with lychees. The starter nibbles are pretty delicious, too.

London Carriage Works
Modern British £££

(☎ 0151-705 2222; www.thelondoncarriage-works.co.uk; 40 Hope St; 2-/3-course meal £17.50/22.50, mains £16-30; ⏰ 7-10am & noon-10pm Mon-Fri, 8-11am & noon-10pm Sat, to 9pm Sun) Liverpool's dining revolution is being led by Paul Askew's award-winning restaurant, which successfully blends ethnic influences from around the globe with staunch British favourites and serves up the result in a beautiful dining room – actually more of a bright glass box divided only by a series of sculpted glass shards. Reservations are recommended.

🍷 Drinking & Nightlife

Philharmonic
Pub

(36 Hope St; ⏰ 10am-11.30pm) This extraordinary bar, designed by the shipwrights who built the *Lusitania,* is one of the most beautiful bars in all of England. The interior is resplendent with etched and stained glass, wrought iron, mosaics and ceramic tiling – and if you think that's good, just wait until you see inside the marble men's toilets, the only heritage-listed lav in the country.

24 Kitchen Street
Club

(www.facebook.com/24kitchenstreet; 24 Kitchen St; tickets £8-12; ⏰ 9pm-4am Fri & Sat) A multi-purpose venue that splits its focus between the arts and electronic music. The converted Victorian building is one of the best places in town to dance in.

⭐ Entertainment

Cavern Club
Live Music

(☎ 0151-236 1965; www.cavernclub.org; 8-10 Mathew St; admission before/after 2pm free/£4; ⏰ 10am-midnight Mon-Wed & Sun, to 1.30am Thu, to 2am Fri & Sat) It's a reconstruction, and not even on the same spot, but the 'world's most famous club' is still a great spot to see local bands.

ℹ Information

There is a small **tourist office** (☎ 0151-707 0729; www.visitliverpool.com; Anchor Courtyard; ⏰ 10am-6pm) in Albert Dock, and a separate **accommodation hotline** (☎ 0845-601 1125; ⏰ 9am-5.30pm Mon-Fri, 10am-4pm Sat).

ℹ Getting There & Away

Air

Liverpool John Lennon Airport (☎ 0870-750 8484; www.liverpoolairport.com; Speke Hall Ave) serves a variety of international destinations as well as destinations in the UK (Belfast, London and the Isle of Man).

Train

Liverpool's main station is Lime St. It has hourly services to almost everywhere, including the following:

Chester £6.65, 45 minutes

London Euston £79, 3¼ hours

Manchester £11.90, 45 minutes

ℹ Getting Around

To/From the Airport

The airport is 8 miles south of the centre. **Arriva Airlink** (www.arriva.co.uk; adult £2; ⏰ 6am-11pm) buses 80A and 180 depart from Paradise St Interchange, and **Airportxpress 500** (www.arriva.co.uk) buses leave from outside Lime St station. Buses from both stations take half an hour and run every 20 minutes. A taxi to the city centre should cost no more than £18.

Boat

The famous **Mersey ferry** (www.merseyferries.co.uk; one way/return £2.30/2.80) crossing for Woodside and Seacombe departs from Pier Head Ferry Terminal, next to the Royal Liver Building (to the north of Albert Dock).

Public Transport

Local public transport is coordinated by **Merseytravel** (www.merseytravel.gov.uk). Highly recommended is the Saveaway ticket (adult/child £5/2.50) which allows for one day's off-peak (after 9.30am) travel on all bus, train and ferry services throughout Merseyside. Tickets are available at shops and post offices throughout the city.

Merseyrail (www.merseyrail.org) is an extensive suburban rail service linking Liverpool with the Greater Merseyside area. There are four stops in the city centre: Lime St, Central (handy for Ropewalks), James St (close to Albert Dock) and Moorfields (for the Liverpool War Museum).

THE LAKE DISTRICT

If you're a lover of the great outdoors, the Lake District is one corner of England where you'll want to linger. This sweeping panorama of slate-capped fells, craggy hilltops, misty mountain tarns and glittering lakes has been pulling in the crowds ever since the Romantics pitched up in the early 19th century, and it remains one of the country's most popular beauty spots.

Windermere & Bowness-on-Windermere

POP 5423

Of all England's lakes, none carries the cachet of Windermere. Stretching for 10.5 silvery miles from Ambleside to Newby Bridge, it's one of the classic Lake District vistas, and has been a centre for tourism since the first steam trains chugged into town in 1847.

The town itself is split between Windermere, 1.5 miles uphill from the lake, and bustling Bowness-on-Windermere (usually shortened to Bowness), with its touristy collection of teashops, ice-cream stalls and cruise boats.

 Activities

Windermere Lake Cruises   Boating
(015395-31188; www.windermere-lakecruises.co.uk; tickets from £2.70) Since the launch of the first passenger ferry in 1845, cruising has been an essential part of every Windermere itinerary. Some of the vessels are modern, but there are a couple of period beauties dating back to the 1930s. All cruises allow you to disembark as you please and catch a later ferry back.

 Sleeping

The Boundary   B&B ££
(015394-48978; www.theboundaryonline.co.uk; Lake Rd, Windermere Town; d £100-191; P 🛜) Not the cheapest sleep in Windermere, but definitely one of the swishest. Owners Steve and Helen have given this Victorian house a sleek, boutique makeover: chic decor, monochrome colours, retro furniture and all. Steve's a cricket obsessive, so all the rooms are named after famous batsmen.

Rum Doodle   B&B ££
(015394-45967; www.rumdoodlewindermere.com; Sunny Bank Rd, Windermere Town; d £85-119; P 🛜) Forget boutique B&B: this little place is all about quirky English style. Each of the nine rooms is named after an explorer with corresponding decorative twist: Jungle has old suitcases and giant map, Wish has a four-poster and faux-bookcase wallpaper, while Summit and Burley hunker under attic eaves. There's a two-night minimum in summer.

Don't Miss
Hill Top

In the tiny village of Near Sawrey, 2 miles south of Hawkshead, the idyllic farmhouse of Hill Top is a must-see for Beatrix Potter buffs: it was the first house she lived in after moving to the Lake District, and also where she wrote and illustrated many of her famous tales.

NT

☏ 015394-36269

www.nationaltrust.org.uk/hill-top

adult/child £9/4.50

⊙ 10.30am-4.30pm Sat-Thu mid-Feb–Oct, longer hours Jul & Aug

The House

Beatrix Potter purchased the house in 1905, largely on the proceeds of her first bestseller, *The Tale of Peter Rabbit*. It still contains much of Potter's own furniture and belongings, including her writing desk, kitchen dresser and doll collection, and nearly every room has decorative details that fans will recognise from the author's illustrations.

There's no electric light inside the house, so it can be dark on dull days; note also that photography is only permitted in the gardens, not inside the house itself. Thanks to its worldwide fame (helped by the 2006 biopic *Miss Potter*, starring Renée Zellweger), Hill Top is one of the Lakes' most popular spots, so queues are inevitable in season. Entry is by timed ticket to avoid overcrowding; try visiting later in the day to avoid the worst of the crowds.

The Stories

The house itself featured extensively in stories such as *Samuel Whiskers, Tom Kitten, Jemima Puddle-Duck* and *Pigling Bland,* and you might recognise the cast-iron kitchen range from many of Potter's illustrations of her characters' under-ground burrows. The cottage garden outside is a dead ringer for the one explored by Peter Rabbit.

The Gallery

As well as being a children's author, Beatrix Potter was also a talented botanical painter and amateur naturalist. This small **gallery** (NT; www.nationaltrust.org.uk/beatrix-potter-gallery; Red Lion Sq; adult/child £5/2.50; ⏰10.30am-5pm Sat-Thu mid-Mar–Oct), housed in the offices of Potter's husband, solicitor William Heelis, contains a collection of her watercolours depicting local flora and fauna. She was particularly fascinated by mushrooms. There's discounted admission if you show your ticket from Hill Top.

Local Knowledge

Hill Top
RECOMMENDATIONS FROM JOANNE HUDSON, VISITOR SERVICES MANAGER AT HILL TOP

1 THE KITCHEN
Hill Top was Beatrix Potter's first house in the Lake District, and it features in lots of her books and illustrations. The kitchen is particularly interesting: here you can see the dresser from *Samuel Whiskers*, the grandfather clock from the *Tailor of Gloucester* and the kitchen range from *Tom Kitten*.

2 THE RAT HOLE FROM SAMUEL WHISKERS
One of my favourite details at Hill Top is the rat hole which features in *Samuel Whiskers*. Rats were a perennial problem at Hill Top – Beatrix caught 96 in her first year here alone!

3 THE GARDEN & VEGETABLE PATCH
Although it's probably not quite the same as it was in Beatrix's day, Hill Top's garden and vegetable patch are one of the highlights for many visitors. A version of it appeared as Mr McGregor's garden in *Peter Rabbit* and *Benjamin Bunny*. It looks particularly lovely in summer when the fruit trees are blossoming – and look out for the rhubarb patch where Jemima Puddle-Duck laid her eggs!

4 THE TOWER BANK ARMS
Just up the road from Hill Top is this lovely old inn, which has barely changed since the days when Beatrix lived here. The outside is almost exactly as it appears in *Jemima Puddle-Duck*. It serves really good food and feels lovely and cosy, especially if you can manage to get a spot by the fire!

5 THE BEATRIX POTTER GALLERY
In nearby Hawkshead, this gallery is housed inside the offices of the solicitor William Heelis, Beatrix's husband. It has an amazing collection of her illustrations, including many original watercolours from the books. The exhibition changes every year to focus on a different book, so there's always something new to see.

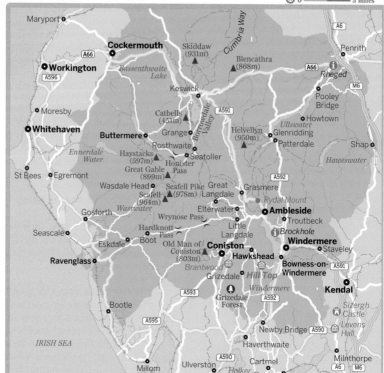

Eating

Hooked   Seafood ££

(☏015394-48443; www.hookedwindermere.
co.uk; Ellerthwaite Sq, Windermere Town; mains
£16.95-19.95; ⏰5.30-10.30pm Tue-Sun) This
seafood restaurant in Windermere Town
has a loyal following. Fish arrives daily
from the Fleetwood docks, and chef Paul
White dabbles in everything from fish
classics to fusion concoctions: moules
marinières to start, perhaps, then a whole
Thai-spiced sea bass or king scallops with
pea purée and black pudding. The only
drawback is the limited space: bookings
essential.

Brown Horse Inn   Pub ££

(☏015394-43443; www.thebrownhorseinn.
co.uk; Winster; mains £11.95-17.95; ⏰lunch

noon-2pm, dinner 6-9pm) Three miles from
Windermere in Winster, the Brown Horse
is one of Windermere's top dining pubs.
Produce is sourced from the Brown Horse
Estate, furnishing the chefs with meat
and game such as venison, spring lamb
and roast pigeon. Beams and fireplaces
conjure a rustic atmosphere, and there
are two home-brewed ales on tap (Old
School and Best Bitter). Worth the drive.

ℹ Information

Brockhole National Park Visitor Centre

(☏015394-46601; www.lake-district.gov.uk;
⏰10am-5pm Easter-Oct, to 4pm Nov-Easter)
In a 19th-century mansion 3 miles north of
Windermere on the A591, this is the Lake
District's flagship visitor centre, and also has a
teashop, an adventure playground and gardens.

Bowness Tourist Office (☎015394-42895; bownesstic@lake-district.gov.uk; Glebe Rd, Bowness-on-Windermere; ◷9.30am-5.30pm Easter-Oct, 10am-4pm Fri-Sun Nov-Easter) Beside the lake jetties.

Windermere Tourist Office (☎015394-46499; windermeretic@southlakeland.gov.uk; Victoria St, Windermere Town; ◷9am-5.30pm Mon-Sat, 9.30am-5.30pm Sun Apr-Oct, shorter hours winter) Opposite Natwest bank.

Grasmere

POP 1458

Even without its Romantic connections, gorgeous Grasmere would still be one of the Lakes' biggest draws. It's one of the prettiest of the Lakeland hamlets, huddled at the base of a sweeping valley dotted with woods, pastures and slate-coloured hills, but most of the thousands of trippers come in search of its famous former residents: opium-eating Thomas de Quincey, unruly Coleridge and grand old man William Wordsworth.

◉ Sights

Dove Cottage
Historic Building

(☎015394-35544; www.wordsworth.org.uk; adult/child £7.50/4.50; ◷9.30am-5.30pm) On the edge of Grasmere, this tiny, creeper-clad cottage (formerly a pub called the Dove & Olive Bough) was famously inhabited by William Wordsworth between 1799 and 1808. The cottage's cramped rooms are full of artefacts: try to spot the poet's passport, a pair of his spectacles and a portrait of his favourite dog Pepper, given to him by Sir Walter Scott. Entry is by timed ticket to avoid overcrowding, and includes an informative guided tour.

St Oswald's Church
Church

(Church Stile) In the churchyard of this tiny chapel in the centre of Grasmere are the Wordsworth family graves: look out for tombstones belonging to William, Mary, Dorothy and all three children. Samuel Taylor Coleridge's son, Hartley, is also buried here.

Grasmere

Detour:
Rydal Mount

The poet William Wordsworth's most famous residence in the Lake District is Dove Cottage, but he actually spent much more time at **Rydal Mount** (www.rydalmount.co.uk; adult/child £7/3; ⏱9.30am-5pm Mar-Oct, 11am-4pm Wed-Mon Nov, Dec & Feb), a much grander house halfway between Ambleside and Grasmere. This was the Wordsworth family's home from 1813 until the poet's death in 1850, and the house contains a treasure trove of Wordsworth memorabilia.

Downstairs you can wander around the library, dining room and drawing room (look out in the cabinets for William's pen, inkstand and picnic box, and a famous portrait of the poet by the American painter Henry Inman hanging above the fireplace). Upstairs are the family bedrooms and Wordsworth's attic study, containing his encyclopedia and a sword belonging to his brother John, who was lost in a shipwreck in 1805. Below the house is Dora's Field, which Wordsworth planted with daffodils in memory of his eldest daughter, who died from tuberculosis in 1847.

The house is 1.5 miles northwest of Ambleside, off the A591.

Sleeping

How Foot Lodge
B&B ££

(☎015394-35366; www.howfoot.co.uk; Town End; d £75-80; P) Just a stroll from Dove Cottage, this stone house has six rooms finished in fawns and beiges; the nicest are the Deluxe Doubles, one with sun terrace and the other with private sitting room. Rates are an absolute bargain considering the location.

Moss Grove Organic
Hotel £££

(☎015394-35251; www.mossgrove.com; r Sun-Thu £114-209, Fri & Sat £129-259; P🛈) ◢ This eco-chic hotel champions its green credentials: sheep-wool insulation, organic paints, reclaimed timber beds, but for once, eco also equals elegance. Rooms are enormous, and bathrooms sparkle with sexy showers and underfloor heating. Breakfast is served buffet-style in the kitchen-diner downstairs.

Eating & Drinking

Sarah Nelson's Gingerbread Shop
Bakery £

(www.grasmeregingerbread.co.uk; Church Cottage; ⏱9.15am-5.30pm Mon-Sat, 12.30-5pm Sun) In business since 1854, this famous sweetshop next to the village church makes Grasmere's essential souvenir: traditional gingerbread with a half-biscuit, half-cakey texture, cooked according to the same top-secret recipe (12 pieces for £4.95). Friendly service by ladies dressed in frilly pinafores and starched bonnets is an added bonus.

Jumble Room
Modern British ££

(☎015394-35188; www.thejumbleroom.co.uk; Langdale Rd; dinner mains £14.50-21; ⏱5.30-10pm Wed-Mon) Husband-and-wife team Andy and Crissy Hill have turned this village bistro into a much-loved dining landmark. It's a fun and friendly place to dine. Spotty crockery, cow murals and primary colours set the boho tone, matched by a magpie menu taking in everything from Dithose chicken to a 9oz 'flatiron' steak.

DURHAM

POP 47,785

England's most beautiful Romanesque cathedral, a huge castle and, surrounding them both, a cobweb of hilly, cobbled streets usually full of upper-crust students attending England's third university of choice (after Oxford and Cambridge) make Durham an ideal day trip from Newcastle or overnight stop.

Sights

Durham Cathedral   Cathedral

(www.durhamcathedral.co.uk; by donation, tower £5, guided tours adult/child £5/free; ⊗7.30am-6pm Mon-Sat, to 5.30pm Sun) This monumental cathedral is the definitive structure of the Anglo-Norman Romanesque style, a resplendent monument to the country's ecclesiastical history and, since 1986, a Unesco World Heritage site. Beyond the main door – and the famous **Sanctuary Knocker**, which medieval felons would strike to gain 37 days asylum within the cathedral before standing trial or leaving the country – the interior is spectacular. Climbing the tower's 325 steps rewards you with show-stopping vistas.

Durham Castle   Castle

(☎0191-334 2932; www.dur.ac.uk/durham.castle; admission by guided tour only, adult/child £5/3.50; ⊗by reservation) Built as a standard motte-and-bailey fort in 1072, Durham Castle was the prince bishops' home until 1837, when it became the University of Durham's first college. It remains a university hall, and it's possible to stay here (contact the castle for information and availability). Highlights of the 45-minute tour include the groaning 17th-century **Black Staircase** and the beautifully preserved **Norman chapel** dating from 1080.

Sleeping

Honest Lawyer   Inn ££

(☎0191-378 3780; www.honestlawyerhotel.com; Croxdale; d £68-88; P🔊) An easy 3-mile drive south of Durham on the A167, this handy spot has mostly motel-style rooms with countrified chequered fabrics and parking outside the door. The main building has a timber bar and restaurant serving good pub grub in generous portions.

Gadds Town-house   Boutique Hotel £££

(☎0191-384 1037; www.gaddstownhouse.com; 34 Old Elvet; d £110-250; 🔊) Each of Gadds' 11 opulent-and-then-some rooms has a theme, with Le Jardin featuring a shed and garden furniture, a huge projection screen and popcorn machine in Premiere,

Cloisters, Durham Cathedral

If You Like...
Roman Ruins

The impressive fort at Housesteads (p251) is undoubtedly the wall's best-preserved site, but several more intriguing Roman ruins are within easy reach.

1 CHESTERS ROMAN FORT & MUSEUM
(EH; ☏01434-681379; www.english-heritage. org.uk; adult/child £5.60/3.40; ⊙10am-6pm Apr-Sep, to 5pm Oct, 10am-4pm Sat & Sun Nov-Mar) The best-preserved remains of a Roman cavalry fort in England are at Chesters, set among idyllic green woods and meadows near the village of Chollerford. It's 5.5 miles from Hexham.

2 VINDOLANDA ROMAN FORT & MUSEUM
(www.vindolanda.com; adult/child £6.50/4, with Roman Army Museum £10/5.50; ⊙10am-6pm Apr-Sep,to 5pm Oct, to 4pm Nov & Dec) The extensive site of Vindolanda offers a fascinating glimpse into the daily life of a Roman garrison town. The time-capsule museum contains many fascinating Roman artefacts, while the rest of the site includes the fort, town, reconstructed turrets and temple. It's 1.5 miles north of Bardon Mill between the A69 and B6318.

3 BIRDOSWALD ROMAN FORT
(EH; ☏016977-47602; www.english-heritage. org.uk; adult/child £5.60/3.40; ⊙10am-6pm Apr-Sep, to 5pm Oct, 10am-4pm Sat & Sun Nov-Mar) The remains of this once-formidable fort are on a minor road off the B6318, about 3 miles west of Greenhead; a fine stretch of wall extends from here to Harrow's Scar Milecastle.

and the Edwardian Express recreating a night in a yesteryear sleeper compartment. The most 'normal' room is the Garden Lodge, complete with outdoor tub and underfloor heating. The restaurant is superb.

Eating

Cellar Door
Durham   Modern British ££
(☏0191-383 1856; www.thecellardoordurham.co.uk; 41 Saddler St; mains £14-17.50;

⊙11.30am-10.30pm) Accessed from an inconspicuous door on Saddler St, this 12th-century building has glorious river views, including from the alfresco terrace. The Mediterranean-meets-Britain menu features starters such as twice-baked goats cheese soufflé, mains such as seared venison with chestnut dressing, and desserts including brioche bread-and-butter pudding. Service is spot on.

Oldfields   British ££
(☏0191-370 9696; www.oldfieldsrealfood. co.uk; 18 Claypath; 2-/3-course lunch £10/13, dinner mains £12-17.50; ⊙noon-10pm; 🛜) Serving strictly seasonal menus that use only local or organic ingredients sourced within a 60-mile radius of Durham – such as North Sea fish casserole, pan haggerty and wild boar pie – this award-winning restaurant in the 1881 boardroom of the former HQ of the Durham Gas Company is passionate about great British food.

ℹ Information

Tourist Office (World Heritage Site Visitor Centre; ☏0191-334 3805; www.thisisdurham. com; 7 Owengate; ⊙9.30am-6pm Jul & Aug, to 5pm late Mar-Jun & Sep, to 4.30pm Oct-late Mar) Small but helpful, with all the usual tourist information.

ℹ Getting There & Away

Trains run to:

Edinburgh £56.20, two hours, hourly

London King's Cross £121, three hours, hourly

York £21.90, one hour, four hourly

HADRIAN'S WALL

Named in honour of the emperor who ordered it built, Hadrian's Wall was one of Rome's greatest engineering projects, a spectacular 73-mile testament to ambition and the practical Roman mind. Even today, almost 2000 years after the first stone was laid, the awe-inspiring sections that remain are proof that when the Romans wanted something done, they just knuckled down and did it. When completed, the mammoth structure ran across the narrow neck of the island, from the Solway Firth in the west almost to the mouth of the Tyne in the east.

A series of forts was developed along the length of the wall, including **Housesteads** (EH; www.english-heritage.org.uk; adult/child £6.40/3.80; ☺10am-6pm Apr-Sep, to 5pm Oct, to 4pm Nov-Mar), the wall's most dramatic site, and the best-preserved Roman fort in the whole country. Remains here include an impressive hospital, granaries, barrack blocks, and even communal flushable latrines.

Carlisle, in the west, and Newcastle in the east are logical start/end points; Haltwhistle, Hexham and Corbridge make good bases. The B6318 follows the course of the wall from the outskirts of Newcastle to Birdoswald. The main A69 road and the railway line follow 3 or 4 miles to the south.

ⓘ Information

Hadrian's Wall Country (www.visithadrianswall.co.uk) The official portal for the whole of Hadrian's Wall Country.

Detour:
Angel of the North

Nicknamed the Gateshead Flasher, this extraordinary 200-tonne, rust-coloured human frame with wings, more soberly known as the **Angel of the North**, has been looming over A1(M) about 5 miles south of Newcastle since 1998. At 20m high and with a wingspan wider than a Boeing 767, Antony Gormley's most successful work is the UK's largest sculpture and the most viewed piece of public art in the country.

Northumberland National Park Visitor Centre (☎01434-344396; www.northumberlandnationalpark.org.uk; Bardon Mill, Once Brewed; ☺9.30am-5.30pm Apr-Oct, 10am-3pm Sat & Sun Nov-Mar) On Military Rd (B6318).

Hadrian's Wall

ROME'S FINAL FRONTIER

Of all Britain's Roman ruins, Emperor Hadrian's 2nd-century wall, cutting across northern England from the Irish Sea to the North Sea, is by far the most spectacular; Unesco awarded it world cultural heritage status in 1987.

We've picked out the highlights, one of which is the prime remaining Roman fort on the wall, Housesteads, which we've reconstructed here.

Housesteads' granaries
Nothing like the clever underground ventilation system, which kept vital supplies of grain dry in Northumberland's damp and drizzly climate, would be seen again in these parts for 1500 years.

Milecastle

North Gate

Interval Tower

Birdoswald Roman Fort
Explore the longest intact stretch of the wall, scramble over the remains of a large fort then head indoors to wonder at a full-scale model of the wall at its zenith. Great fun for the kids.

Housesteads Roman Fort
See Illustration Right

Birdoswald Roman Fort · Harrow Scar Milecastle · Greenhead · Brampton · Irthing · Roman Army Museum · Once Brewed · Haltwhistle · South Tyne · Sewingshields · Housesteads Roman Fort & Museum · Hadrian's Wall · B6318 · Vindolanda Roman Fort & Museum · Bardon Mill · Haydon Bridge · A69 · Chesters Roman Fort & Museum · Chollerford · Low Brunton · Acomb · Hexham

0 — 10 km / 0 — 5 miles

Chesters Roman Fort
Built to keep watch over a bridge spanning the River North Tyne, Britain's best-preserved Roman cavalry fort has a terrific bathhouse, essential if you have months of nippy northern winter ahead.

Hexham Abbey
This may be the finest non-Roman sight near Hadrian's Wall, but the 7th-century parts of this magnificent church were built with stone quarried by the Romans for use in their forts.

Housesteads' hospital
Operations performed at the hospital would have been surprisingly effective, even without anaesthetics; religious rituals and prayers to Aesculapius, the Roman god of healing, were possibly less helpful for a hernia or appendicitis.

ALISON ROSCOE / GETTY ©

Housesteads' latrines
Communal toilets were the norm in Roman times and Housesteads' are remarkably well preserved – fortunately no traces remain of the vinegar-soaked sponges that were used instead of toilet paper.

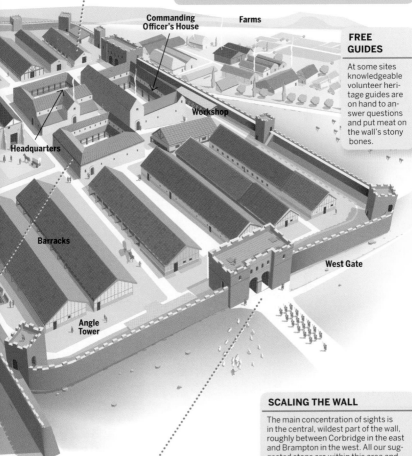

Commanding Officer's House

Farms

Workshop

Headquarters

Barracks

West Gate

Angle Tower

FREE GUIDES

At some sites knowledgeable volunteer heritage guides are on hand to answer questions and put meat on the wall's stony bones.

SCALING THE WALL

The main concentration of sights is in the central, wildest part of the wall, roughly between Corbridge in the east and Brampton in the west. All our suggested stops are within this area and follow an east–west route. The easiest way to travel is by car, scooting along the B6318, but special bus AD122 will also get you there. Hiking along the designated Hadrian's Wall Path (84 miles) allows you to appreciate the achievement up close.

Housesteads' gatehouses
Unusually at Housesteads neither of the gates faces the enemy, as was the norm at a Roman fort – builders aligned them east-west. Ruts worn by cart wheels are still visible in the stone.

Wales

Wales is a separate nation, with its own language and culture.

And you can feel the difference as soon as you cross the border. Although this ancient Celtic country was under English rule from around 1300, the flame of independence never died, and in 1998 Wales finally regained control of its own destiny.

So after centuries of oppression and decades in the doldrums, Wales is now rediscovering itself with energy and determination. Cultural landmarks across the country have been restored; the capital city of Cardiff has decorated the once-abandoned waterfront with stunning new buildings; and even the summit of Snowdon, the highest peak in the land, has received a 21st-century visitor centre. Whether you're marvelling at the medieval castles in the north, exploring pubs and shops in the south, or hiking airy clifftops in the west, you certainly won't regret spending some time in Wales.

St Davids Head coastal path
ANDREW BOXALL/GETTY IMAGES ©

Wales

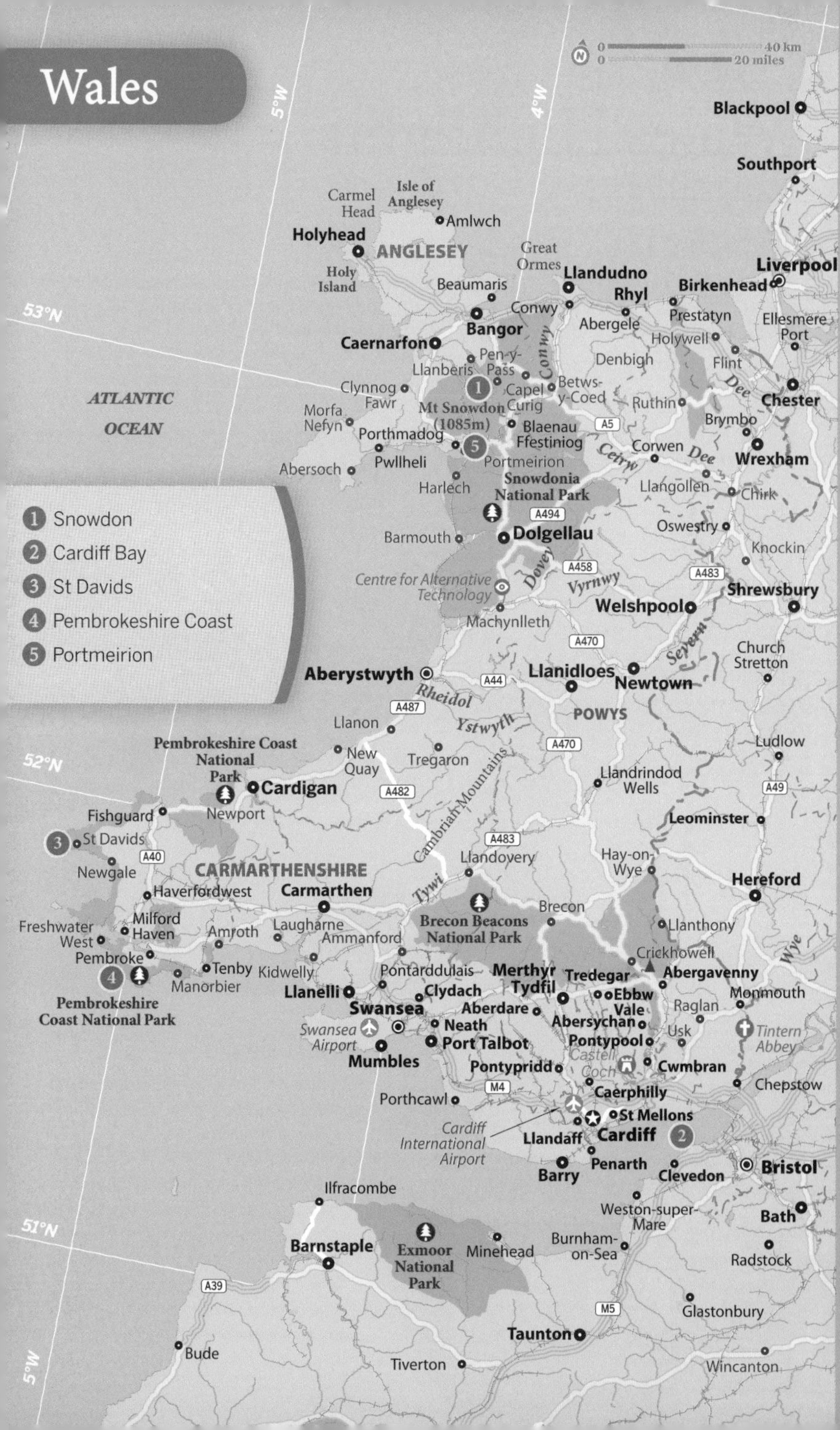
1 Snowdon
2 Cardiff Bay
3 St Davids
4 Pembrokeshire Coast
5 Portmeirion
0 40 km
0 20 miles
5°W
4°W
53°N
52°N
51°N
ATLANTIC OCEAN
Blackpool
Southport
Liverpool
Birkenhead
Isle of Anglesey
Carmel Head
Amlwch
Holyhead
ANGLESEY
Holy Island
Beaumaris
Great Ormes
Llandudno
Rhyl
Prestatyn
Conwy
Abergele
Bangor
Caernarfon
Holywell
Ellesmere Port
Pen-y-Pass
Llanberis
Denbigh
Flint
Chester
Clynnog Fawr
Capel Curig
Betws-y-Coed
Ruthin
Mt Snowdon (1085m)
Morfa Nefyn
Porthmadog
Blaenau Ffestiniog
A5
Brymbo
Wrexham
Pwllheli
Portmeirion
Corwen
Dee
Abersoch
Harlech
Snowdonia National Park
Llangollen
Chirk
Cetrw
A494
Oswestry
Barmouth
Dolgellau
Knockin
Dovey
A458
A483
Centre for Alternative Technology
Vyrnwy
Shrewsbury
Welshpool
Machynlleth
A470
Severn
Church Stretton
Aberystwyth
A44
Llanidloes
Newtown
Rheidol
A487
POWYS
Llanon
Ystwyth
Ludlow
Pembrokeshire Coast National Park
New Quay
Tregaron
A470
Cambrian Mountains
Llandrindod Wells
Cardigan
A482
A49
Fishguard
Newport
Leominster
St Davids
A483
A40
Llandovery
Hay-on-Wye
Newgale
CARMARTHENSHIRE
Haverfordwest
Carmarthen
Tywi
Hereford
Brecon
Freshwater West
Milford Haven
Amroth
Laugharne
Brecon Beacons National Park
Llanthony
Ammanford
Crickhowell
Wye
Pembroke
Pontarddulais
Merthyr Tydfil
Tredegar
Abergavenny
Tenby
Kidwelly
Manorbier
Llanelli
Clydach
Ebbw Vale
Monmouth
Pembrokeshire Coast National Park
Swansea
Aberdare
Raglan
Abersychan
Swansea Airport
Neath
Usk
Tintern Abbey
Port Talbot
Pontypool
Mumbles
Castell Coch
Pontypridd
Cwmbran
M4
Chepstow
Caerphilly
Porthcawl
St Mellons
Cardiff International Airport
Llandaff
Cardiff
Penarth
Barry
Clevedon
Bristol
Ilfracombe
Weston-super-Mare
Bath
Barnstaple
Exmoor National Park
Minehead
Burnham-on-Sea
Radstock
A39
M5
Glastonbury
Taunton
Bude
Tiverton
Wincanton

Wales Highlights

Snowdon

Dominating the map of North Wales is the spectacular mountainous landscape of Snowdonia (p277), much of it protected as a national park. The region gets its name from Snowdon, the highest peak in Wales and the most popular spot for visitors.

2 Cardiff Bay

The Welsh capital city is buzzing with confidence, and nowhere is this more apparent than the revitalised waterfront of Cardiff Bay (p265). Once a derelict dock now it's home to a collection of fascinating structures including the historic Pierhead building, the new Wales Millennium Centre and the Senedd (the Assembly Building for Wales's devolved government) – not to mention several film locations for *Dr Who*.

Pembrokeshire Coast

At the end of the peninsula that makes up the southwest part of Wales is the old county of Pembrokeshire, edged on two sides by the sea, and some of the most beautiful stretches of coastline in Britain. It's protected as a national park, and provides excellent hiking, surfing and wildlife-watching opportunities – as well as bucket-and-spade beaches perfect for family holidays.

St Davids

It's little more than a village but St Davids ranks as Britain's smallest city thanks to the presence of a magnificent 12th-century cathedral (p271) that marks the burial place of the nation's patron saint. The burial place has been a place of pilgrimage for some 1400 years, and today St Davids still attracts many visitors, as it makes a good base for exploring this beautiful corner of West Wales. St Davids Cathedral

Portmeirion

Perhaps the wackiest attraction in Wales is the seaside fantasy-land of Portmeirion (p286), an Italianate village perched above the sea, created by the eccentric architect Sir Clough Williams-Ellis in the early 20th century. Brimming with follies, colonnades, pastel-coloured palaces and other architectural oddities, it provided the perfect setting for the classic cult TV series *The Prisoner* in the 1960s.

Wales' Best…

Castles

○ **Cardiff Castle** Roman foundations, Norman additions, Victorian frills – the capital's stronghold has a chequered past (p264)

○ **Conwy Castle** Part of the English 'iron ring' that controlled North Wales for centuries (p275)

○ **Caernarfon Castle** Yet another 'magnificent badge of our subjection', as Welsh writer Thomas Pennant put it (p282)

○ **Beaumaris Castle** Moody fortress situated on the island of Anglesey, which once guarded the Welsh coastline (p275)

Architecture

○ **Cardiff Bay** Victorian Gothic splendour at the Pierhead and modernist style at the Millennium Centre (p265)

○ **Portmeirion** Bizarre fantasy land of follies, colonnades and architectural oddities (p286)

○ **St Davids Cathedral** Small maybe, but one of the loveliest cathedrals in Wales (p271)

○ **Castell Coch** Near-Disneyesque Victorian-medieval flight of fancy (p269)

Culture Spots

○ **Hay-on-Wye** Self-proclaimed second-hand bookshop capital of the world, and home of the Hay Literary Festival (p275)

○ **Wales Millennium Centre, Cardiff** The capital's stunning centre for music and the performing arts (p268)

○ **Tintern Abbey** Evocative ruins in the Wye Valley, and the inspiration for poets and artists through the centuries (p269)

○ **Laugharne** Visit the ramshackle hut where Dylan Thomas penned some of his finest poems (p270)

Natural Beauty

○ **Pembrokeshire** In the far west of Wales, a beautiful rural area with a dramatic coastline (p271)

○ **Snowdonia** The largest national park in Wales, home to the mighty peak of Mt Snowdon (277)

○ **Gower Peninsula** This sea-fringed headland makes a lovely detour from Cardiff (p270)

○ **Ramsey Island** Wildlife-spotting opportunities aplenty on this island near St Davids (p272)

Need to Know

ADVANCE PLANNING

○ **Six months before** Make accommodation plans if you're interested in the Hay Literary Festival, the Eisteddfod or other major events.

○ **Two months before** Book long-distance train and bus tickets for the best deals.

○ **Two weeks before** Confirm opening times and prices for the major sights.

RESOURCES

○ **Wales** (www.visitwales.co.uk)

○ **Cardiff** (www.visitcardiff.com)

○ **Snowdonia** (www.visitsnowdonia.info)

○ **Snowdonia National Park** (www.eryri-npa.co.uk)

○ **Pembrokeshire** (www.visitpembrokeshire.com)

GETTING AROUND

○ **Bus** Long-distance buses between main centres are good; local buses are infrequent in some rural areas.

○ **Train** Wales has useful railways through the south and north of the country, plus a number of scenic branch lines.

○ **Car** Gives you maximum freedom, but many roads are narrow and twisting; don't aim on getting anywhere in a hurry.

BE FOREWARNED

○ **Festivals** Accommodation is practically impossible to find during major events such as the Eisteddfod and the Hay Festival. If you're not coming for the festivals, you're better off avoiding these towns at these times.

○ **Welsh** In some parts of Wales (but not all) the first language is Welsh. Trying a few words can help break the ice, but remember not everyone's a Welsh speaker! Try: *sut mae* (pronounced 'sit mai') – hello; *bore da* ('boray da') – good morning; *diolch* ('dee-olkh') – thanks and *hwyl fawr* ('hueyl vowrr') – goodbye.

Left: A book shop sign, Hay-on-Wye (p275); **Above:** Dylan Thomas Boathouse, Laugharne (p270)

Wales Itineraries

Our three-day trip runs along the southern edge of Wales, while the five-day option heads up through the borders to the mountains and castles of the north. The routes intersect at Cardiff.

3 DAYS

BRISTOL TO ST DAVIDS
CITY TO COAST

From southwest England's largest city, ❶ **Bristol**, head across the Severn Bridge into Wales and start your tour with a visit to the Wye Valley and the romantic ruins of ❷ **Tintern Abbey**, immortalised in a William Wordsworth poem.

Continue west to ❸ **Cardiff**, the dynamic Welsh capital. The city has plenty of diversions, especially around revitalised Cardiff Bay, which is home to the Wales Millennium Centre and the Welsh Parliament building. Rugby fans may want to visit the Millennium Stadium in the city centre, and everyone should catch the sunset from Cardiff Castle.

After the city, head out along the south coast into the national park of the ❹ **Pembrokeshire Coast**, known for its stunning coastal scenery, clifftop walks and world-class surf. Wind your way along the coast all the way to the tiny city of ❺ **St Davids** and its fine cathedral.

Top Left: Tenby, Pembrokeshire (p271);
Top Right: Caernarfon Castle (p282)

5 DAYS

CARDIFF TO CAERNARFON

WELSH WONDERS

Start your tour in ❶**Cardiff**, the capital of Wales. On day two head north via the impressive monuments of ❷**Caerphilly** and ❸**Castell Coch**, both awash with local history. A little further north is the eccentric border town of ❹**Hay-on-Wye**, famous for its population of over 30 secondhand bookshops, and its celebrated annual literary festival.

Next stop is the coastal town of Machynlleth and the nearby ❺**Centre for Alternative Technology**, where you can check out a selection of ingenious solutions tackling our future energy needs. Then it's on into the mountainous landscape of Snowdonia National Park, centring on the windswept peak of ❻**Snowdon**, where you'll find hiking trails aplenty and a historic mountain railway.

On the edge of the park sit four sturdy fortresses, together forming a World Heritage Site. Base yourself in ❼**Caernarfon**, and make day trips to visit nearby Conwy Castle and Harlech Castle. Finish up with some more outlandish architecture at ❽**Portmeirion**, a fantasy land of turrets, follies and multicoloured buildings made famous by *The Prisoner*.

Discover Wales

Gower Peninsula (p270)
THOMAS STANKIEWICZ/GETTY IMAGES ©

CARDIFF (CAERDYDD)

POP 447,000

The capital of Wales since only 1955, Cardiff has embraced its new role with vigour, emerging as one of Britain's leading urban centres in the 21st century. Caught between an ancient fort and an ultramodern waterfront, this compact city seems to have surprised even itself with how interesting it has become. This new-found confidence is infectious; people now travel to Cardiff for a good night out, bringing with them a buzz that reverberates through the streets.

◎ Sights

CENTRAL CARDIFF

Cardiff Castle   Castle
(www.cardiffcastle.com; Castle St; adult/child £12/9, incl guided tour £15/11; ⊙9am-5pm) Cardiff Castle is, quite rightly, the city's leading attraction. There's a medieval keep at its heart, but it's the later additions that capture the imagination of many visitors: during the Victorian era extravagant mock-Gothic features were grafted onto this relic, including a clock tower and a lavish banqueting hall.

National Museum Cardiff   Museum
(www.museumwales.ac.uk; Gorsedd Gardens Rd; ⊙10am-5pm Tue-Sun) **FREE** Devoted mainly to natural history and art, this grand neoclassical building is the centrepiece of the seven institutions dotted around the country that together form the Welsh National Museum. It's one of Britain's best museums; you'll need at least three hours to do it justice, but it could easily consume the best part of a rainy day. The excellent art collection's treasures

include a trio of Monet's *Water Lilies*, alongside his scenes of London, Rouen and Venice; Sisley's *The Cliff* at Penarth (the artist was married in Cardiff); Renoir's shimmering *La Parisienne*; and Van Gogh's anguished *Rain: Auvers*. Welsh artists such as Gwen and Augustus John, Richard Wilson, Thomas Jones, David Jones and Ceri Richards are well represented. A large new space is devoted to contemporary exhibitions.

Bute Park   Park

(☉7.30am-sunset) Flanked by the castle and the River Taff, Bute Park was donated to the city along with the castle in 1947. With Sophia Gardens, Pontcanna Fields and Llandaff Fields, it forms a green corridor that stretches northwest for 1½ miles to Llandaff. All were once part of the Bute's vast holdings.

Forming the park's southern edge, the **Animal Wall** is topped with stone figures of lions, seals, bears and other creatures. It was designed by castle architect William Burges but only completed in 1892 after his death, with more animals added in the 1920s. In the 1930s they were the subject of a newspaper cartoon strip and many Cardiff kids grew up thinking the animals came alive at night.

Millennium Stadium   Stadium

(☎029-2082 2228; www.millenniumstadium. com; Westgate St; tours adult/child £9.50/6) This spectacular stadium squats like a stranded spaceship on the River Taff's east bank. This 74,500-seat, £168-million, three-tiered stadium with sliding roof was completed in time to host the 1999 Rugby World Cup. Rugby is Wales' national game and when the crowd begins to sing at Millennium, the whole of Cardiff resonates. If you can't get tickets to a match, it's well worth taking a tour. Book online or at the **WRU Store** (8 Westgate St; ☉10am-5.30pm Mon-Sat, 11am-4pm Sun).

CARDIFF BAY

Lined with important national institutions such as the Senedd and the Millennium Centre, Cardiff Bay is where the modern Welsh nation is put on display in an archi-

tect's playground of interesting buildings, large open spaces and public art.

Doctor Who Experience   Exhibition

(☎0844 801 2279; www.doctorwhoexperience. com; Porth Teigr; adult/child £15/11; ☉10am-5pm (last admission 3.30pm) Wed-Mon, daily school holidays) The huge success of the reinvented classic TV series *Doctor Who*, produced by BBC Wales, has brought Cardiff to the attention of sci-fi fans worldwide. City locations have featured in many episodes; and the first two series of the spin-off *Torchwood* were also set in Cardiff Bay. Capitalising on Timelord tourism, this interactive exhibition is located right next to the BBC studios where the series is filmed – look out for the Tardis hovering outside.

Senedd   Notable Building

(National Assembly Building; ☎0845 010 5500; www.assemblywales.org; ☉10.30am-4.30pm) FREE Designed by Lord Richard Rogers (the architect behind London's Lloyd's Building and Millennium Dome and Paris' Pompidou Centre), the Senedd is a striking structure of concrete, slate, glass and steel, with an undulating canopy roof lined with red cedar. It has won awards for its environmentally friendly design, including a huge rotating cowl on the roof for power-free ventilation and a rainwater system for flushing the toilets.

🛏 Sleeping

Park Plaza   Hotel ££

(☎029-2011 1111; www.parkplazacardiff.com; Greyfriars Rd; r from £86; 🛜🏊) Luxurious without being remotely stuffy, the Plaza has all the five-star facilities you'd expect from an upmarket business-orientated hotel. The snug reception sets the scene, with a gas fire blazing along one wall and comfy wingback chairs. The rear rooms have leafy views over the Civic Centre.

St David's Hotel & Spa   Hotel ££

(☎029-2045 4045; www.thestdavidshotel.com; Havannah St; r from £119; @🛜🏊) A glittering, glassy tower topped with a sail-like flourish, St David's epitomises Cardiff Bay's transformation from wasteland to

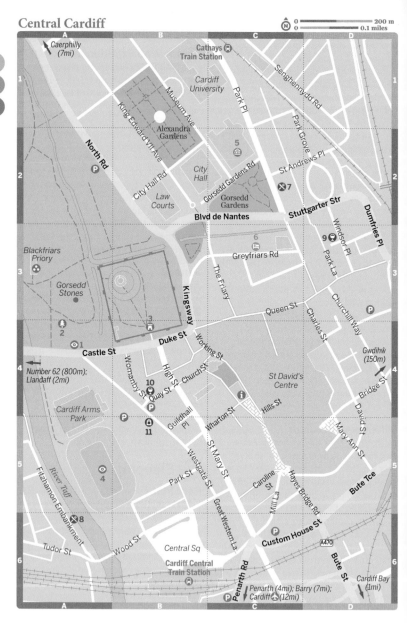

desirable address. Almost every room has a small private balcony with a bay view. The exterior is already showing signs of wear and tear, but the rooms have been recently renovated.

Number 62   Guesthouse ££

(07974 571348; www.number62.com; 62 Cathedral Rd; s/d from £49/65; @) The only thing stopping us calling Number 62 a B&B is that breakfast is only offered as an add-on. In all other respects it's very similar to the other converted town houses on this strip, although it does have one of the most lovingly tended front gardens. The cosy rooms are simply decorated.

Eating

Riverside Market — Market £
(www.riversidemarket.org.uk; Fitzhamon Embankment; ⊙10am-2pm Sun; ✔) What it lacks in size, Riverside Market makes up for in sheer yumminess, its stalls heaving with cooked meals, cakes, cheese, organic meat, charcuterie, bread, apple juice and real ale. There are lots of options for vegetarians and the Welsh cakes, hot off the griddle, are exceptional.

Ffresh — Modern Welsh ££
(☎029-2063 6465; www.ffresh.org.uk; Wales Millennium Centre; mains £14-18; ⊙noon-9.30pm Mon-Sat, to 5pm Sun) ✔ Overlooking the Senedd from the glassed-in end of the Millennium Centre, Ffresh has the Welshiest of settings and a menu to match. Local, seasonal produce features heavily in a creative menu that includes some traditional favourites, like lamb rack with faggots.

Park House — Modern British £££
(☎029-2022 4343; www.parkhouserestaurant. co.uk; 20 Park Pl; mains £26, 2-/3-course lunch

£16/21; ⊙11am-10pm Wed-Sat, to 6pm Sun) The ambience is rather stuffy, but the menu at this private members' club is anything but conservative, adding subtle Indian and Southeast Asian influences to classic European dishes. Dress up and push the buzzer for admittance.

Drinking

Gwdihŵ — Bar
(www.gwdihw.co.uk; 6 Guildford Cres; ⊙3pm-midnight Sun-Wed, noon-2am Thu-Sat) The last word in Cardiff hipsterdom, this cute little bar has an eclectic line-up of entertainment (comedy nights, markets and lots of live music, including microfestivals that spill over into the car park) but it's a completely charming place to stop for a drink at any time.

Buffalo Bar — Bar
(www.buffalocardiff.co.uk; 11 Windsor Pl; ⊙noon-3am) A haven for cool kids about town, the laid-back Buffalo features retro furniture, tasty food, life-affirming cocktails and alternative tunes. There's a small beer garden at the rear, while upstairs a roster of cutting-edge indie bands takes to the stage.

City Arms — Pub
(www.thecityarmscardiff.com; 10-12 Quay St; ⊙11am-11pm Mon-Wed, to 2am Thu-Sun; 🛜) What's affectionately known in these parts as an 'old man's pub' – despite it attracting just as many young geezers – the City Arms is an unpretentious, old-fashioned kind of place, its walls lined with rugby memorabilia and beer labels. It gets predictably packed out on rugby weekends (Millennium Stadium is right across the road), but on weekday afternoons it's a quiet place for a pint.

ⓘ Information

Cardiff Tourist Office (☎029-2087 3573; www.visitcardiff.com; Old Library, The Hayes; ⊙9.30am-5.30pm Mon-Sat, 10am-4pm Sun) Cardiff's main tourist office stocks Ordnance Survey maps and Welsh books, and offers an accommodation booking service and internet access.

ARCAID/GETTY IMAGES ©

⭐ Don't Miss
Wales Millennium Centre

The centrepiece and symbol of Cardiff Bay's regeneration is the superb Wales Millennium Centre, an architectural masterpiece of stacked Welsh slate in shades of purple, green and grey topped with an overarching bronzed steel shell. Designed by Welsh architect Jonathan Adams, it opened in 2004 as Wales' premier arts complex, housing major cultural organisations such as the Welsh National Opera, National Dance Company, National Orchestra, Literature Wales, HiJinx Theatre and Ty Cerdd (Music Centre of Wales).

The roof above the main entrance is pierced by 2m-high letter-shaped windows, spectacularly backlit at night, which spell out phrases from poet Gwyneth Lewis: 'Creu Gwir fel Gwydr o Ffwrnais Awen' (Creating truth like glass from inspiration's furnace) and 'In these stones horizons sing'.

You can wander through the large public lobby at will. Guided tours lead visitors behind the giant letters, onto the main stage and into the dressing rooms, depending on what shows are on.

NEED TO KNOW

📞 029-2063 6464; www.wmc.org.uk; Bute Pl; tours £6; 🕐 tours 11am & 2.30pm

ℹ️ Getting There & Away

Trains from major British cities arrive at Cardiff Central station, on the southern edge of the city centre. Direct services from Cardiff include London Paddington (£39, 2¼ hours), Bristol (£13, 35 minutes), Abergavenny (£13, 45 minutes), Cheltenham (£18, 1½ hours) and Birmingham (£26, two hours).

Around Cardiff

CASTELL COCH

Cardiff Castle's little brother is perched atop a thickly wooded crag on the northern fringes of the city. Fanciful **Castell Coch** (Cadw; 029-2081 0101; www.cadw.wales.gov.uk; adult/child £5.50/4.10; 10am-4pm) was the summer retreat of the third marquess of Bute and, like Cardiff Castle, was designed by William Burges in gaudy Victorian medieval style.

Raised on the ruins of Gilbert de Clare's 13th-century Castell Coch (Red Castle), the Butes' Disneyesque holiday home is a monument to high camp. Lady Bute's huge, circular bedroom is pure fantasy: her bed, with crystal globes on the bedposts, sits beneath an extravagantly decorated and mirrored cupola, with painted panels around the walls depicting monkeys (fashionable at the time, apparently; just plain weird now). The corbels are carved with images of birds nesting or feeding their young, and the washbasin is framed between two castle towers.

Lord Bute's bedroom is small and plain by comparison, but the octagonal drawing room is another hallucinogenic tour de force. Its walls are painted with scenes from Aesop's Fables, while the domed ceiling is a flurry of birds and stars. The tower to the right of the entrance has exhibits explaining the castle's history.

Stagecoach (www.stagecoachbus.com) buses 26 and 132 (27 minutes) stop at Tongwynlais, a 10-minute walk from the castle. Bus 26 continues to Caerphilly Castle, and the two can be combined in a day trip.

CAERPHILLY (CAERFFILI)

You could be forgiven for thinking that **Caerphilly Castle** (Cadw; 029-2088 3143; www.cadw.wales.gov.uk; adult/child £5.50/4.10; 9.30am-5pm), with its profusion of towers and crenellations reflected in a duck-filled lake, was a film set rather than an ancient monument. While it often is used as a film set, it is also one of Britain's finest examples of a 13th-century fortress with water defences.

Most of the construction was completed between 1268 and 1271 by the powerful English baron Gilbert de Clare, Lord Marcher of Glamorgan (1243–95), in response to the threat of attack by Prince Llywelyn ap Gruffydd, prince of Gwynedd (and the last Welsh Prince of Wales), who had already united most of the country under his control. In the 13th century Caerphilly was state of the art, one of the earliest castles to use lakes, bridges and a series of concentric fortifications for defence. To reach the inner court you had to overcome no fewer than three drawbridges, six portcullises and five sets of double gates. Much of what you see today is the result of restoration from 1928 to 1939 by the fourth marquess of Bute.

The easiest way to reach Caerphilly from Cardiff is by train (£4.20, 19 minutes).

SOUTH WALES

Tintern Abbey

The A466 road follows the snaking, steep-sided valley of the River Wye from Chepstow to Monmouth, passing through the straggling village of Tintern. It's a beautiful drive, rendered particularly mysterious when a twilight mist rises from the river and shrouds the illuminated ruins of **Tintern Abbey** (Cadw; www.cadw.wales.gov.uk; adult/child £4.50/3.40; 10am-4pm; P). The huge abbey church was built between 1269 and 1301, the stone shell of which remains surprisingly intact; the finest feature is tracery that once contained the magnificent west windows.

If you take the narrow country lane along the west bank of the Wye, a mile north of the turn-off where the A466 crosses the river into England, and 5 miles north of the abbey, you'll find the Michelin-starred **Crown at Whitebrook** (01600-860254; www.crownatwhitebrook.co.uk; Whitebrook; r £110-140). The food is

Detour:
Gower Peninsula (Y Gŵyr)

With its broad butterscotch beaches, pounding surf, precipitous clifftop walks and rugged, untamed uplands, the Gower Peninsula feels a million miles away from Swansea's urban bustle – yet it's just on the doorstep. This 15-mile-long thumb of land stretching west from Mumbles was designated the UK's first official Area of Outstanding Natural Beauty (AONB) in 1956. The National Trust (NT) owns about three-quarters of the coast, so access for walkers is good. The peninsula also has the best surfing in Wales outside Pembrokeshire.

The main family beaches, patrolled by lifeguards during the summer, are **Langland Bay**, **Caswell Bay** and **Port Eynon**.

astonishingly good – inventive, intricately crafted and delicious. If you don't fancy driving afterwards, or the romantic ambience has worked its magic, get a room (single/double from £100/145).

Laugharne (Talacharn)

POP 817

Sleepy little Laugharne (pronounced 'larn') sits above the tide-washed shores of the Taf Estuary, overlooked by a Norman castle. Dylan Thomas, one of Wales' greatest writers, spent the last four years of his life here, during which he produced some of his most inspired work, including *Under Milk Wood;* the town is one of the inspirations for the play's fictional village of Llareggub (spell it backwards and you'll get the gist).

 Sights

Dylan Thomas Boathouse
Museum

(www.dylanthomasboathouse.com; Dylan's Walk; adult/child £4.20/3.20; ⊙10am-5.30pm May-Oct, 10.30am-3.30pm Nov-Apr) Except at high tide, you can follow a path along the shoreline below the castle, then up some stairs to a lane that leads to the boathouse where the poet lived from 1949 to 1953 with his wife Caitlin and their three children. It's a beautiful setting, looking out over the estuary with its 'heron-priested shore', silent except for the long, liquid call of the curlew and the urgent 'pleep pleep pleep' of the oystercatcher, birds that appear in Thomas' poetry of that time.

The parlour of the Boathouse has been restored to its 1950s appearance, with the desk that once belonged to Thomas' schoolmaster father and recordings of the poet reading his own works. Upstairs are photographs, manuscripts, a short video about his life, and his death mask, which once belonged to Richard Burton; downstairs is a coffee shop.

Along the lane from the Boathouse is the old shed where Thomas did most of his writing. It looks as if he has just popped out, with screwed-up pieces of paper littered around, a curiously prominent copy of *Lives of the Great Poisoners* and, facing out to sea, the table where he wrote *Under Milk Wood* and poems such as *Over Sir John's Hill* (which describes the view).

 Sleeping & Eating

Boat House
B&B ££

(☎01994-427263; www.theboathousebnb.co.uk; 1 Gosport St; s/d £60/80; ⊛) Friendly, homey and tastefully decorated, the blue-painted Boat House is the smartest B&B in town, with four superior rooms. The building was formerly the Corporation Arms pub, where Dylan Thomas told stories in exchange for free drinks. The great home-cooked breakfasts would assuage even Thomas' legendary hangovers.

Cors
Modern British £££

(☎01994-427219; www.thecors.co.uk; Newbridge Rd; mains £19-27, s/d £50/80; ☺7pm-midnight Thu-Sat; 📶) A colourful, stylish and pleasantly eccentric restaurant that serves excellent local seasonal food such as salt marsh lamb. It is just off the main street, and has a beautiful bog garden ('cors' means bog). Just be aware of the limited opening hours.

PEMBROKESHIRE COAST NATIONAL PARK

Established in 1952, Pembrokeshire Coast National Park (Parc Cenedlaethol Arfordir Sir Benfro) takes in almost the entire coast and its offshore islands, as well as the Preseli Hills in the north and the inland waters of the Cleddau rivers near Milford Haven. Pembrokeshire's sea cliffs and islands support huge breeding populations of seabirds, while seals, dolphins, porpoises and whales are frequently spotted in coastal waters.

The **Pembrokeshire Coast Path** (www.pcnpa.org.uk) is one of the most spectacular long-distance hiking trails in Britain. Established in 1970, it meanders along 186 miles of Britain's most dramatic coastal scenery running from Amroth to St Dogmaels. Short stretches make for excellent day or half-day walks.

St Davids (Tyddewi)
POP 1840

Charismatic St Davids is Britain's smallest 'city', its status ensured by the magnificent 12th-century cathedral that marks Wales' holiest site. The birth and burial place of the nation's patron saint, St Davids has been a place of pilgrimage for more than 1500 years.

◎ Sights & Activities

St Davids Cathedral
Cathedral

(www.stdavidscathedral.org.uk; suggested donation £3, tours £4; ☺8.30am-6pm Mon-Sat, 12.45-5.30pm Sun) Hidden in a hollow and behind high walls, St Davids Cathedral is intentionally unassuming. The valley site was chosen in the vain hope that the church would be overlooked by Viking raiders, but it was ransacked at least

St Davids Cathedral

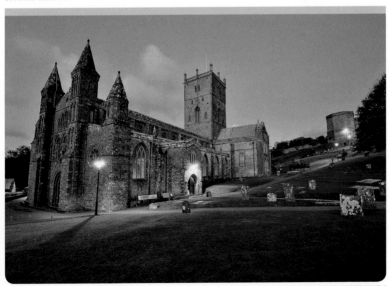

seven times. Built on the site of a 6th-century chapel, the building dates mainly from the 12th to the 14th centuries.

Bishop's Palace   Ruin
(Cadw; www.cadw.wales.gov.uk; adult/child £3.50/2.65; ☉10am-4pm) Across the river from the cathedral, this atmospheric ruined palace, run by Cadw (the Welsh historic monuments agency), was begun at the same time as the cathedral, but its final, imposing form owes most to Henry de Gower, bishop from 1327 to 1347.

Ramsey Island   Wildlife Reserve
🐾 Ramsey Island lies off the headland to the west of St Davids, ringed by dramatic sea cliffs and an offshore armada of rocky islets and reefs. The island is a reserve, run by the Royal Society for the Protection of Birds, famous for its large breeding population of choughs – members of the crow family with glossy black feathers and distinctive red bills and legs – and for its grey seals. You can reach the island by boat from the tiny harbour at St Justinian's, 2 miles west of St Davids. Longer boat trips run up to 20 miles offshore, to the edge of the Celtic Deep, to spot whales, porpoises and dolphins. What you'll see depends on the weather and the time of year: July to September are the best months. Porpoises are seen on most trips, dolphins on four out of five, and there's a 40% chance of seeing whales. The most common species is the minke, but pilot whales, fin whales and orcas have also been spotted.

Thousand Islands Expeditions (☎01437-721721; www.thousandislands.co.uk; Cross Sq) is the only operator permitted to land day trippers on the island(adult/child £15/7.50). It has a range of other boat trips, including 2½-hour whale- and dolphin-spotting cruises (£55/30) and one-hour jet-boat trips (£24/12).

Voyages of Discovery (☎01437-721911; www.ramseyisland.co.uk; 1 High St; ☉Apr-Oct) and **Aquaphobia** (☎01437-720471; www. aquaphobiaramseyisland.co.uk; Grove Hotel, High St) offer a similar selection of cruises.

 ## Sleeping

Ramsey House
B&B ££

(☏01437-720321; www.ramseyhouse.co.uk; Lower Moor; r £105-115; P 🛜) The young owners have created a fashionable boutique-style B&B from their new house on the outskirts of St Davids, which is still only a short stroll from the town centre. The six rooms are all different but feature bold wallpapers, contemporary chandeliers, silky throws and goose down duvets, as well as stylish bathrooms.

Coach House
B&B ££

(☏01437-720632; www.thecoachhouse.biz; 15 High St; s/d from £55/80; 🛜) The bright, simple rooms at the Coach House are just part of its appeal. Friendly and helpful hosts, excellent breakfasts and its central location all conspire to make it one of St Davids' better options. There's also a small cottage at the back sleeping up to five people, which makes a good base for families.

Eating & Drinking

Sampler
Cafe £

(www.sampler-tearoom.co.uk; 17 Nun St; cakes £2-3; ⏰10.30am-5pm Mon-Wed Mar-Nov) Named after the embroidery samples blanketing the walls, this may be the perfect exemplar of the traditional Welsh tearoom. Pembrokeshire Clotted Cream Tea comes served with freshly baked scones and *bara brith* (a rich, fruit tea loaf), and there are Welsh cheese platters, jacket potatoes, soups and sandwiches.

Cwtch
Modern Welsh £££

(☏01437-720491; www.cwtchrestaurant. co.uk; 22 High St; 2/3 courses £22/26; ⏰6-9.30pm Wed-Sat, noon-2.30pm Sun, daily high season, closed Jan-mid-Feb) Stone walls and wooden beams mark this out as a sense-of-occasion place, yet there's a snugness that lives up to its name (*cwtch* means 'a cosy place' or 'a cuddle'). There's an

273

emphasis on local produce, so expect plenty of fresh seafood on the menu.

Farmer's Arms   Pub

(www.farmersstdavids.co.uk; 14 Goat St; ⏱4pm-midnight Mon-Fri, 11.30am-midnight Sat & Sun) Even though St Davids is a bit of a tourist trap, you'd be hard-pressed finding a more authentic country pub than the Farmer's Arms. There's real ale and Guinness on tap, and it's the place to be when the rugby's playing. The beer garden out the back is a pleasant place to watch the sun go down on a summer's evening.

❶ Information

National Trust Visitor Centre (📞01437-720385; High St; ⏱10am-5pm daily Apr-Dec, Mon-Sat Jan-Mar) Sells local-interest books and guides to NT properties in Pembrokeshire.

Preseli Hills

The only upland area in the Pembrokeshire Coast National Park is the Preseli Hills (Mynydd Preseli), rising to 536m at Foel Cwmcerwyn. These hills are at the centre of a fascinating prehistoric landscape, scattered with hill forts, standing stones and burial chambers, and are famous as the source of the mysterious bluestones of Stonehenge. An ancient track called the **Golden Road**, once part of a 5000-year-old trade route between Wessex and Ireland, runs along the crest of the hills, passing prehistoric cairns and the stone circle of **Bedd Arthur**.

The largest dolmen in Wales, **Pentre Ifan**, is a 4500-year-old neolithic burial chamber set on a remote hillside three miles southeast of Newport, signposted from the A487. The huge, 5m-long capstone, weighing more than 16 tonnes, is delicately poised on three upright bluestones.

MID WALES

Brecon Beacons National Park

Rippling dramatically for 45 miles from Llandeilo in the west all the way to the English border, Brecon Beacons

Hay Bluff, near Hay-on-Wye

MICHAEL ROBERTS/GETTY IMAGES ©

National Park (Parc Cenedlaethol Bannau Brycheiniog) encompasses some of the finest scenery in Mid Wales. High mountain plateaus of grass and heather, their northern rims scalloped with glacier-scoured hollows, rise above wooded, waterfall-splashed valleys and green, rural landscapes. It couldn't be more different than rock-strewn Snowdonia to the north, but it offers comparable thrills.

There are hundreds of walking routes in the park, ranging from gentle strolls to strenuous climbs. The park's staff organise guided walks and other active events throughout summer. A set of six Walk Cards (£1 each) is available from the town tourist offices in and around the park, as well as the national park visitor centre near Libanus.

ℹ️ Information

National Park Visitor Centre (📞01874-623366; www.breconbeacons.org; Libanus; ⏰9.30am-5pm) The park's main visitor centre has full details of walks, hiking and biking trails, outdoor activities, wildlife and geology. It's located off the A470 road, 5 miles southwest of Brecon and 15 miles north of Merthyr Tydfil. Any of the buses on the Merthyr Tydfil–Brecon route stop at Libanus village, a 1.25-mile walk away.

Hay-on-Wye (Y Gelli Gandryll)

POP 1600

This pretty little town on the banks of the River Wye, just inside the Welsh border, has developed a reputation disproportionate to its size. Since the 1960s it's become the world's secondhand book capital, and now hosts the UK's largest and most prestigious literary festival in late May. The small town centre is made up of narrow sloping lanes, generously peppered with interesting shops, and peopled by the differing types that such individuality and so many books tend to attract.

❤️ If You Like…
Welsh Castles

After visiting Caerphilly (p269) and Caernarfon (p282), there are plenty more fantastic fortresses to explore around Wales.

1 **CONWY CASTLE**
(Cadw; 📞01492-592358; www.cadw.wales.gov.uk; Castle Sq; adult/child £5.75/4.35; ⏰9.30am-5pm; P) The most stunning of Edward I's Welsh fortresses, built between 1277 and 1307, Conwy Castle rises from a rocky outcrop with commanding views across the estuary and Snowdonia National Park.

2 **HARLECH CASTLE**
(Cadw; www.cadw.wales.gov.uk; Castle St; adult/child £4.25/3.20; ⏰9.30am-5pm) Edward I finished this intimidating building in 1289, the southernmost of his 'iron ring' of fortresses. Despite its might, the storybook fortress has been called the 'Castle of Lost Causes' because it has been lucklessly defended so many times.

3 **CARREG CENNEN**
(Cadw; www.carregcennencastle.com; adult/child £4/3.50; ⏰9.30am-5.30pm) Perched atop a steep limestone crag high above the River Cennen is Wales' ultimate romantic ruined castle, visible for miles in every direction. It's signposted from the A483, heading south from Llandeilo.

4 **BEAUMARIS CASTLE**
(Cadw; www.cadw.wales.gov.uk; Castle St; adult/child £5.25/3.90; ⏰9.30am-5pm) Sited on the island of Anglesey and a World Heritage site, Beaumaris Castle is another of Edward I's coastal fortresses, and with its stout walls and arrow slits definitely has the 'wow' factor. Anglesey is easily reached from nearby Bangor.

🛏️ Sleeping & Eating

Bear B&B ££
(📞01497-821302; www.thebearhay.com; 2 Bear St; s £55, d £75-95; P 📶) Homey and rustic with exposed stone walls and original beams, plus a liberal sprinkling of books,

Detour:
Centre for Alternative Technology

Founded in 1974, the **Centre for Alternative Technology** (Canolfan y Dechnoleg Amgen; ☏01654-705950; www.cat.org.uk; Pantperthog; adult/child £8.50/4; ◷10am-5pm; P ♿) ✐ is an education and visitor centre that demonstrates practical solutions for sustainability. There are more than 3 hectares of displays dealing with topics such as composting, organic gardening, environmentally friendly construction, renewable energy sources and sewage treatment and recycling. To explore the whole site takes about two hours – take rainwear as it's primarily outdoors. Kids love the interactive displays and adventure playground and there's a great organic wholefood restaurant.

The visit starts with a 60m ride up the side of an old quarry in an ingenious water-balanced cable car (closed in winter to save water). A drum beneath the top car fills with stored rainwater and is then drawn down while the bottom car is hauled up. At the top you disembark by a small lake with great views across the Dyfi Valley.

There are workshops and games for children during the main school holidays and an extensive program of residential courses for adults throughout the year (day courses start from around £50). A new purpose-built education centre also offers postgraduate programmes on sustainability, renewable energy and sustainable architecture. Volunteer helpers are welcome, but you'll need to apply.

The site is about 3 miles from the village of Machynlleth.

this former coaching inn (1590) is an excellent choice. It has three rooms, all beautifully decorated with bright Welsh blankets and retro furniture.

Old Black Lion
Pub ££

(☏01497-820841; www.oldblacklion.co.uk; Lion St; s/d £55/99; P) As traditional and atmospheric as they come, this inn looks 17th century but parts of it date from the 13th; expect low ceilings and uneven floors. Staff cheerfully carry the accumulated weight of centuries of hospitality.

Hay Stables
B&B ££

(☏01497-820008; www.haystables.co.uk; Oxford Rd; s/d £40/60; ⧇ ♿) Three modern, homey en suite twins and doubles, decked out in neutral tones, welcome you at this friendly guesthouse. There's a common area for guests and a large, fully equipped guest kitchen; breakfast is a self-serve affair but ingredients are provided and the owners are very accommodating.

St John's Place
Modern Welsh ££

(☏07855 783799; stjohnsplacehay.tumblr.com; Lion St; mains £12-16; ◷6-10pm Thu-Sat) The menu at this low-key spot is limited, but each of the three unusual starters, mains and desserts is conceived and executed with imagination and flair. Expect the likes of brown shrimp with duck egg, palm sugar and chilli, mackerel with samphire and date and pecan tart.

🔒 Shopping

There are 26 secondhand and antiquarian bookshops in Hay, with hundreds of thousands of tomes stacked floor to ceiling across town.

Richard Booth's Bookshop
Books

(www.boothbooks.co.uk; 44 Lion St; ◷9.30am-5.30pm Mon-Sat, 11am-5pm Sun) The most famous, and still the best; has a sizeable Anglo-Welsh literature section, and a Wales travel section.

Information

Tourist Office (☎ 01497-820144; www.hay-on-wye.co.uk; Oxford Rd; ⏰ 10am-1pm & 2-5pm) This office stocks a free guide and map showing all of Hay's bookshops (most bookshops have the map, too). You can also access the internet here (around £1 per 30 minutes).

SNOWDONIA NATIONAL PARK

Snowdonia National Park (Parc Cenedlaethol Eryri; www.eryri-npa.gov.uk) was founded in 1951 (making it Wales' first national park) and it's Wales' best known and most heavily used slice of nature. The busiest part, around Snowdon (1085m) itself, attracts around 350,000 people who climb, walk or take the train to the summit each year.

The Welsh name for Snowdonia is Eryri (eh-*ruh*-ree), meaning highlands. The Welsh call Snowdon itself Yr Wyddfa (uhr-*with*-vuh), meaning Great Tomb – according to legend a giant called Rita Gawr was slain here by King Arthur and is buried at the summit.

....

Betws-y-Coed

POP 2253

If you're looking for a base with an Alpine feel from which to explore Snowdonia National Park, the bustling little stone village of Betws-y-Coed (*bet-us-ee-koyd*) stands out as a natural option.

◉ Sights & Activities

Gwydyr Forest
Forest

The 28-sq-mile Gwydyr Forest, planted since the 1920s with oak, beech and larch, encircles Betws-y-Coed and is scattered with the remnants of lead and zinc mine workings. It's ideal for a day's walking, though it gets very muddy in wet weather. *Walks Around Betws-y-Coyd* (£5), available from the National Park Information Centre, details several circular forest walks.

Swallow Falls
Waterfall

(Rhaeadr Ewynnol; admission £1.50) Betws-y-Coed's main natural tourist trap is located 2 miles west of town alongside the A5. It's a beautiful spot, with the torrent weaving through the rocks into a green pool below. Outside of seasonal opening hours, bring a £1 coin for the turnstile.

Go Below Underground Adventures
Adventure Tour

(☎ 01690-710108; www.go-below.co.uk; adult/child from £49/39) Head into the depths of an old slate mine and try your hand zip-lining across lakes and abseiling down shafts. It's based on the A5 south of Betws at the turn-off to Penmachno.

Sleeping & Eating

Tŷ Gwyn Hotel
Historic Hotel ££

(☎ 01690-710383; www.tygwynhotel.co.uk; A5; r £60-140; P 🛜 👪) This atmospheric ex–coaching house has been welcoming guests since 1636, its venerable age borne out by misshapen rooms, low ceilings and exposed beams. Not all rooms have en suites, but all are attractively decorated; one has a four-poster.

Afon Gwyn
B&B £££

(☎ 01690-710442; www.guest-house-betws-y-coed.com; A470, Coed-y-Celyn; r £176-256; P 🛜 👪) Down in the valley, this old stone house has been skilfully converted into a grand boutique guesthouse. The decor is faultlessly tasteful, with hushed tones, white-painted wood panelling, glittering chandeliers, and bathrooms bedecked in Italian tiles and marble. While all the rooms are spacious, the Alice Suite is massive.

Bistro Betws-y-Coed
Welsh ££

(☎ 01690-710328; www.bistrobetws-y-coed.com; Holyhead Rd; lunch £6-9, dinner £13-20; ⏰ noon-3pm & 6.30-9.30pm Jun-Sep, closed Mon & Tue Oct-May) This cottage-style eatery's statement of intent is 'modern and traditional Welsh', and the menu features some interesting adaptations of Welsh recipes from the 18th and 19th centuries. It gets absolutely packed in summer; book ahead.

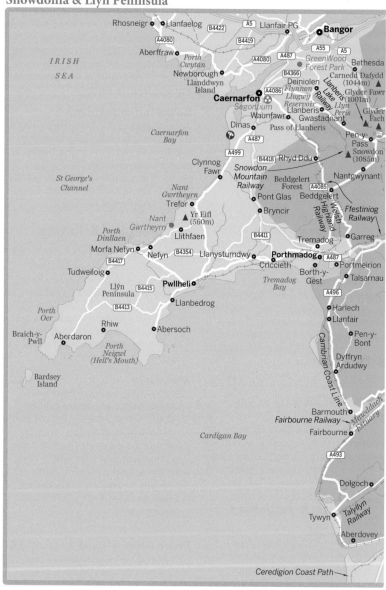

❶ Information

Tourist Office (📞01690-710426; www.
eryri-npa.gov.uk; Royal Oak Stables; 🕙9.30am-
5.30pm) Sells books, maps and local craft, and
is a good source of information about walking
trails and mountain conditions.

❶ Getting There & Away

Betws-y-Coed is on the Conwy Valley Line, with
six daily services (three on Sunday) to Llandudno
(£5.60, 52 minutes) and Blaenau Ffestiniog
(£4.50, 27 minutes).

and has long been a magnet for walkers, climbers and other outdoor junkies. The village spreads out along the A5, but the main hub of activity is at the intersection of the A4086.

Plas y Brenin (☎01690-720214; www.pyb. co.uk; A4086), at the western edge of the village, is a multiactivity centre offering an array of year-round courses on both land and water, ranging from basic rock climbing and summer and winter mountaineering to kayaking, canoeing and abseiling. Taster days for youngsters available throughout the school holidays.

Snowdon

No Snowdonia experience is complete without coming face-to-face with Snowdon (1085m), one of Britain's most awe-inspiring mountains and the highest summit in Wales (it's actually the 61st highest in Britain, with the higher 60 all in Scotland). On a clear day the views stretch to Ireland and the Isle of Man over Snowdon's fine jagged ridges, which drop away in great swoops to sheltered cwms (valleys) and deep lakes. Even on a gloomy day you could find yourself above the clouds. Thanks to the Snowdon Mountain Railway it's extremely accessible – the summit and some of the tracks can get frustratingly crowded.

◉ Sights & Activities

Snowdon Trails   Hiking

Six paths of varying length and difficulty lead to the summit, all taking around six hours return. Just because Snowdon has a train station and a cafe on its summit, doesn't mean you should underestimate it. No route is completely safe, especially in winter. People regularly come unstuck here and many have died over the years, including experienced climbers.

The most straightforward route to the summit is the **Llanberis Path** (9 miles return) running beside the train line. The two paths starting from Pen-y-Pass require the least amount of ascent but are nevertheless tougher walks: the **Miner's Track** (8 miles return) starts off wide and

Capel Curig

POP 206

Tiny Capel Curig, 5 miles west of Betws-y-Coed and ringed by looming mountains, is one of Snowdonia's oldest hill stations,

gentle but gets steep beyond Llyn Llydaw; and the more interesting **Pyg Track** (7 miles return) is more rugged still.

Snowdon Mountain Railway
Heritage Railway

(☑ 0844 493 8120; www.snowdonrailway.co.uk; return diesel adult/child £27/18, steam £35/25; ☺ 9am-5pm mid-Mar–Oct) If you're not physically able to climb a mountain, short on time or just plain lazy, those industrious, railway-obsessed Victorians have gifted you an alternative. Opened in 1896, the Snowdon Mountain Railway is the UK's highest and its only public rack-and-pinion railway. Vintage steam and modern diesel locomotives haul carriages from Llanberis up to Snowdon's very summit in an hour.

🛏 Sleeping

Pen-y-Gwryd
Hotel ££

(☑ 01286-870211; www.pyg.co.uk; Nant Gwynant; s/d £43/86; P 🔊 ⛑ 😺) Eccentric but full of atmosphere, Pen-y-Gwryd was used as a training base by the 1953 Everest team, and memorabilia from their stay includes signatures on the restaurant ceiling. TV, wi-fi and mobile phone signals don't penetrate here. Instead, there's a comfy games room, sauna and a lake for bathing. You'll find the hotel below Pen-y-Pass, at the junction of the A498 and A4086.

ℹ Information

Hafod Eryri (☺ 10am to 20min before last train departure; 🔊) Just below the cairn that marks Snowdon's summit, this striking piece of architecture opened in 2009 to replace the dilapidated 1930s visitor centre which Prince Charles famously labelled 'the highest slum in Europe'. Clad in granite and curved to blend into the mountain, it's a wonderful building, housing a cafe, toilets and ambient interpretative elements built into the structure itself. A wall of picture windows gazes down towards the west, while a small row faces the cairn. The centre (including the toilets) closes in the winter or if the weather's terrible; it's open whenever the train is running.

ℹ Getting There & Away

The **Welsh Highland Railway** (☑ 01766-516000; www.festrail.co.uk; adult/child return £35/31.50) stops at the trailhead of the Rhyd Ddu Path, and

Snowdon, seen from Llyn Llydaw

there is a request stop (Snowdon Ranger Halt) where you can alight for the Snowdon Ranger path.

Dolgellau

POP 2688

The seat of Owain Glyndwr's Welsh Parliament, a safe haven for Quakers, even a gold rush town: the charming little market town of Dolgellau has worn many hats over the centuries. The prosperous wool industry that ruled the town in the 18th and early 19th centuries is responsible for the highest concentration of listed buildings in Wales.

Sleeping

Bryn Mair House
B&B ££

(☏ 01341-422640; www.brynmairbedandbreakfast.co.uk; Love Lane; s £75-85, d £95-105; P 🛜) This impressive stone house – a former Georgian rectory no less – sits among gardens on wistfully monikered Love Lane. Its three luxurious B&B rooms are all kitted out with Egyptian cotton sheets, DVD players and iPod docks; Room 1 has sublime mountain views.

Ffynnon
B&B £££

(☏ 01341-421774; www.ffynnontownhouse.com; Love Lane; s £100, d £150-215; P 🛜) With a keen eye for contemporary design and a super-friendly welcome, this first-rate boutique B&B feels both homey and stylish. French antiques are mixed in with modern chandeliers, claw-foot tubs and electronic gadgets, and each room has a seating area so you can admire the views in comfort. There's even an outdoor hot tub.

Eating

TH Roberts
Cafe £

(Parliament House, Glyndŵr St; mains £4.50-7; ⏰ 9.30am-5.30pm Mon-Sat; 🛜) It's easy to walk past this atmospheric Grade II-listed cafe as it still looks exactly like the ironmonger's shop that it once was, with its original counter, glass cabinets, wooden drawers and other fittings. It's a favourite

Local Knowledge

Snowdon

RECOMMENDATIONS FROM SAM ROBERTS, SENIOR WARDEN (RETIRED) OF SNOWDONIA NATIONAL PARK

1 HIKE TO SNOWDON'S SUMMIT

I've lived in this area all my life, and as a Welshman I'm naturally proud of my homeland. My favourite hike up to Snowdon's summit is the Rhyd-Ddu Path; it's on the western side of the mountain which sees fewer visitors. Alternatively, take the Snowdon Sherpa bus to Pen-y-Pass, reach the summit from there and descend on the Llanberis Path.

2 LLANBERIS PATH

This is one of the most popular walking trails up the mountain, starting from Llanberis. You can stroll up just for a short distance, or it's easy enough to go all the way to the summit. On your way back down the Llanberis Path, enjoy a drink and a warm welcome at my favourite cafe, Penceunant Tearoom.

3 SNOWDON MOUNTAIN RAILWAY

If you can't hike up to the summit, or haven't got time, you can take a ride on the unique Snowdon Mountain Railway, built in the 19th century for Victorian tourists and still working today. Be aware that queues at the ticket office in Llanberis can be long on sunny days in the summer, so I recommend booking ahead if you can.

4 HAFOD ERYRI

Not only does a railway run up Snowdon, you can get a cup of tea at the top as well! Hafod Eryri was built in 2009 and is the highest cafe in Wales. It can be very busy, but to escape the crowds you need walk only a short distance back down the mountain. If you get a return ticket on the train, the half-hour allowed at the top is not really enough; I recommend train up, walk down.

with locals, with jolly, if haphazard, service, light meals (soup, rarebit, sandwiches, cakes), newspapers and books to browse, and a good wi-fi connection.

Mawddach Restaurant
Modern Welsh **££**

(Bwyty Mawddach; ☎ 01341-421752; www.mawddach.com; Llanelltyd; mains £14-21; ⊗ noon-2.30pm & 6-9.30pm Wed-Sat, noon-3.30pm Sun) Located 2 miles west of Dolgellau on the A496, Mawddach brings a touch of urban style to what was once a barn. Slate floors, leather seats and panoramic views across to Cader Idris set the scene. The food is equally impressive: meat straight from nearby farms, fresh local fish specials and traditional Sunday roasts (two/three courses £18/20).

❶ Information

Tourist Office (☎ 01341-422888; www.eryri-npa.gov.uk; Eldon Sq; ⊗ 9.30am-5pm) Sells maps, local history books and trail leaflets for climbing Cader Idris. Downstairs there's a free video about the national park, while upstairs there's a permanent exhibition on the region's Quaker heritage.

NORTH WALES

Caernarfon
POP 9493

Wedged between the gleaming Menai Strait and the deep-purple mountains of Snowdonia, Caernarfon is home to a fantastical castle, its main claim to fame.

◉ Sights & Activities

Caernarfon Castle Castle, Museum
(Cadw; www.cadw.wales.gov.uk; adult/child £6.75/5.10; ⊗ 9.30am-5pm) Majestic Caernarfon Castle was built between 1283 and 1330 as a military stronghold, a seat of government and a royal palace. Like the other royal strongholds of the time, it was designed and mainly supervised by Master James of St George, from Savoy, but the brief and scale were extraordinary. Inspired by the dream of Macsen Wledig recounted in the *Mabinogion*, Caernarfon echoes the 5th-century walls of Constantinople, with colour-banded masonry and polygonal towers, instead of the traditional round towers and turrets.

Caernarfon Castle

Despite its fairy-tale aspect it is thoroughly fortified with a series of murder holes and a sophisticated arrangement of multiple arrow slits. It repelled Owain Glyndŵr's army in 1404 with a garrison of only 28 men, and resisted three sieges during the English Civil War before surrender to Cromwell's army in 1646. There is an exhibition on the Princes of Wales in the **North East Tower**, including video footage of the 1969 investiture of Prince Charles in that role. In the **Queen's Tower** (named after Edward I's wife Eleanor) is the **Regimental Museum of the Royal Welch Fusiliers**, which is filled with medals, uniforms and weapons.

Segontium Roman Fort   Ruin
(Cadw; www.cadw.wales.gov.uk; Ffordd Cwstenin; ◷10am-4pm Tue, Wed & Sat Apr-Oct) FREE
Just east of the town centre, these low stone foundations represent the western-most legionary fort of the Roman Empire. The fort dates back to AD 77, when General Gnaeus Julius Agricola completed the Roman conquest of Wales by capturing the Isle of Anglesey. Sadly the on-site museum is closed for the foreseeable future and the only interpretive sign is on the side of the building. The site is about half a mile along the A4085 (to Beddgelert), which crosses through the middle of it.

🛏 Sleeping & Eating

Caer Menai   B&B £
(☎01286-672612; www.caermenai.co.uk; 15 Church St; s/d/f from £45/57/78; @🤝) A former school (1894), this elegant building is on a quiet street nestling against the western town wall. The seven renovated rooms are fresh, clean and snug; number seven has sunset sea views.

Victoria House   B&B ££
(☎01286-678263; www.thevictoriahouse.co.uk; Church St; r £75-80; @🤝) Victoria House is an exceptional four-bedroom guesthouse with a homey feel, spacious modern rooms and some nice touches, such as an impressive selection of free toiletries and a DVD on the town's history in each room. Breakfast is a joy.

Blas   Modern Welsh ££
(☎01286-677707; www.blascaernarfon.co.uk; 23-25 Hole in the Wall St; mains lunch £7-16, dinner £13-18; ◷noon-2.30pm & 6.30-11pm) The chef must be some kind of mad genius, pairing wood pigeon with rhubarb and smoked salmon with tangy horseradish ice, but the flavours come together seamlessly and each of the dishes on the short menu really makes your taste buds sing. The setting is intimate, the service efficient and friendly and the food's the best in town.

ℹ Information

Tourist Office (☎01286-672232; www.visitsnowdonia.info; Castle St; ◷9.30am-4.30pm; 🛜) Opposite the castle's main entrance. It incorporates the Pendeitsh Gallery, which hosts art exhibitions and a permanent display on Caernarfon's history.

ℹ Getting There & Away

The northern terminus of the Welsh Highland Railway (p280) is on St Helen's Rd. Trains run to Porthmadog (£35 return, 2½ hours) via Dinas, Waunfawr, Rhyd Ddu and Beddgelert.

Porthmadog & Around
POP 2981

Busy little Portmadog (port-mad-uk) was founded by (and named after) reforming landowner William Alexander Madocks, who went to work on a grand scale, laying down the mile-long Cob causeway, draining some 400 hectares of wetland habitat, and creating a brand-new harbour. After his death, the causeway became the route for the new Ffestiniog Railway: at its 1873 peak, it transported over 116,000 tons of slate from the mines to the harbour.

Today Porthmadog is railway buff heaven, with no less than two of Wales' finest narrow-gauge train journeys, run by the oldest independent railway company in the world, departing from its Harbour Station in pungent puffs of smoke.

Sights & Activities

The **Ffestiniog Railway** (Rheilffordd Ffestiniog; ☏ 01766-516024; www.festrail.co.uk; adult/child return £20.20/18.20) is Wales' most spectacular and beautiful narrow-gauge journey, a twisting and precipitous line built between 1832 and 1836 to haul slate down to Porthmadog from the mines at Blaenau Ffestiniog, 13 ½ miles away. Steam locomotives took over from horses in the 1860s and the line opened to passengers in the 1920s. Views are best on the right-hand side as the steam engines chug their way up through the lush, green valley to the slate-strewn final terminus.

The Welsh Highland Railway (p280) is an amalgamation of several late-19th-century slate railways that runs for 25 miles through lovely landscapes to Caernarfon via Beddgelert. En route it passes through the splendid Aberglaslyn Gorge and between Beddgelert and Caernarfon it chugs along Snowdon's south flank, rising steeply to its highest point of 198m. Walkers can hop off at either Rhyd Ddu (£23/20.70) station or the Snowdon Ranger request stop to follow paths up Snowdon.

Sleeping & Eating

Yr Hen Fecws
B&B ££
(☏ 01766-514625; www.henfecws.com; 16 Lombard St; s/d from £65/80; P 🛜) This stylishly restored stone cottage has seven simply decorated en suite rooms with exposed-slate walls and fireplaces. Breakfast is served within the marigold walls and exposed beams of the cosy cafe downstairs (mains £4 to £10; open 8am to 4pm Monday to Saturday).

Golden Fleece Inn
Pub ££
(☏ 01766-512421; www.goldenfleeceinn.com; Market Sq, Tremadog; s/d from £60/75; P 🛜) Hop flowers hang from the ceiling of this inviting and friendly old inn, which offers real ales, pub grub, an open fire on cold nights and live acoustic music on Tuesdays. The rooms above the pub are comfortable and atmospheric but noisy until closing. Enquire about quieter rooms in neighbouring buildings.

Hotel Portmeirion & Castell Deudraeth
Hotel, Cottage £££
(☏ 01766-770000; www.portmeirion-village.com; Portmeirion; hotel s/d £204/219, castle & village s/d from £145/179; P 🏊 🐾) You can live the fantasy and stay within the famous fairy-tale village itself in one of 17 whimsical cottages. Down by the water, the over-the-top Hotel Portmeirion (1926) has elegant rooms while up the drive, storybook Castell Deudraeth is, perversely, a more modern alternative, despite its Victorian provenance. Prices drop considerably in low season.

Welsh Highland Railway (p280)
GRAHAM BELL/GETTY IMAGES ©

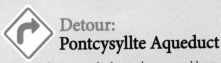

Detour:
Pontcysyllte Aqueduct

In the 18th century the horse-drawn canal barge was the most efficient way of hauling goods over long distances but, with the advent of the railway, most of them fell into disrepair. The Llangollen Canal fared better than most because it was used, for years more, to carry drinking water from the River Dee to the Hurleston Reservoir in Cheshire. Today it's again in use, carrying visitors up and down the Vale of Llangollen. In addition, the old towpaths offer miles of peaceful, traffic-free walking. And the canal itself is part of the attraction, thanks to the work of the great civil engineer Thomas Telford (1757–1834).

However, Thomas Telford's real masterpiece is the Pontcysyllte Aqueduct, completed in 1805 to carry the canal over the River Dee. At 307m long, 3.6m wide, 1.7m deep and 38m high, it is the most spectacular piece of engineering on the entire UK canal system and the highest canal aqueduct ever built. In recognition of this, the aqueduct and an 11-mile stretch of the canal have been declared a Unesco World Heritage Site.

The small visitor centre at the aqueduct runs guided tours (call ahead for times), while canal boats offer trips along the 'stream in the sky' from the nearby quay and from Llangollen wharf. Otherwise you can simply stroll across, free of charge. Whichever way you choose, you'll need a head for heights.

ⓘ Information

Porthmadog Tourist Office (☏01766-512981; www.visitsnowdonia.info; High St; ⏱9.30am-5pm daily Easter-Oct, 10am-3.30pm Mon-Sat Nov-Easter; 🛜)

ⓘ Getting There & Away

A daily National Express coach heads to London (£35, 10 hours), via Caernarfon (£7.60, 45 minutes), Llandudno (£8.30, 1¾ hour) and Birmingham (£29.60, 6¾ hours).

See the Ffestiniog Railway and Welsh Highland Railway for steam services to Blaenau Ffestiniog, the Snowdon trailheads and Caernarfon.

Llandudno

POP 15,371

Llandudno is a master of reinvention. Backed against an enormous limestone headland, this formerly upmarket Victorian holiday town retains much of its 19th-century grandeur, yet continues to find new fans with its booming boutique accommodation, Welsh art scene and varied dining options.

◎ Sights & Activities

Great Orme   Headland

(Y Gogarth) From sea level it's difficult to gauge the sheer scale of the Great Orme, yet it stretches for around 2 miles and rises to a height of 207m. Named after a Norse word for worm or sea serpent, this gentle giant looms benevolently over the town. Designated a Site of Special Scientific Interest (SSSI), the headland is home to a cornucopia of flowers, butterflies and sea birds; a herd of around 150 wild Kashmir mountain goats; three waymarked summit trails (of which the Haulfre Gardens Trail is the easiest to negotiate); a neolithic burial chamber; a Bronze Age mine; the remains of an Iron Age fort; and an ancient church dedicated to Llandudno's namesake, St Tudno. At the summit there's a cafe, bar, gift shop and various amusements, as well as the **Great Orme Country Park Visitor Centre** (www.conwy.gov.uk/greatorme; ⏱10am-5.30pm Easter-Oct), which has lots of fascinating displays including a 15-minute video.

JOHN FREEMAN/GETTY IMAGES ©

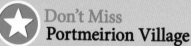

Don't Miss
Portmeirion Village

Set on its own tranquil peninsula reaching into the estuary, Portmeirion Village is an oddball, gingerbread collection of colourful buildings with a heavy Italian influence, masterminded by the Welsh architect Sir Clough Williams-Ellis. Starting in 1925, Clough collected bits and pieces from disintegrating stately mansions and set them alongside his own creations to create this weird and wonderful seaside utopia. Fifty years later, and at the ripe old age of 90, Sir Clough deemed the village to be complete. Today the buildings are all heritage-listed and the site is a conservation area.

It's really more like a stage set than an actual village and, indeed, it formed the ideally surreal set for cult TV series, *The Prisoner,* which was filmed here from 1966 to 1967. It still draws fans of the show in droves, with rival Prisoner conventions held annually in March and April. The giant plaster of Paris Buddha, just off the piazza, also featured in the 1958 film, *The Inn of the Sixth Happiness, s*tarring Ingrid Bergman.

Portmeirion is 2 miles east of Porthmadog; public transport isn't great, so if you don't fancy the walk, you're best to catch a taxi. Half-price admission is offered after 3.30pm.

NEED TO KNOW

www.portmeirion-village.com; adult/child £10/6.50; ⏱9.30am-7.30pm; P

Llandudno Promenade & Pier
Waterfront

(⏱pier 9am-6pm) A trip to Llandudno isn't complete until you've strolled along the majestic sweep of the promenade, eating ice cream and shooing away seagulls. Queen Victoria herself watched **Professor Codman's Punch & Judy Show** (www.

punchandjudy.com/codgal.htm; The Promenade; ⏰2pm & 4pm Sat & Sun plus school holidays Easter–mid-Sep), performed by the same family since 1860 – we hope she was amused. Mr Punch's iconic red-and-white-striped tent sits by the entrance to the 1878-built Victorian pier, the longest in Wales at 670m. A small amusement hall at the far end contains slot machines and twopenny-falls.

Sleeping

Clontarf Hotel Hotel **££**
(☎01492-877621; www.clontarf.co.uk; 2 Great Ormes Rd; s £45, d £65-88; P 🛜) The nine individually styled rooms at this small, friendly hotel come with luxurious touches: sophisticated showers in three of the rooms, a four-poster bed and whirlpool bath in the Romantic room. All rooms look out either onto the sea or the Great Orme, a small bar contributes to evening relaxation and the friendly proprietress cooks up delicious breakfasts.

Osborne House Hotel **£££**
(☎01492-860330; www.osbornehouse.co.uk; 17 North Pde; ste £145-176; P @) All marble, antique furniture and fancy drapes, the lavish Osborne House takes a classical approach to aesthetics and the results are impressive. The best suites are on the 1st floor with Victorian-style sitting rooms and sea views. Guests have use of the spa and swimming pools at nearby sister property, the Empire Hotel.

Eating & Drinking

Characters Cafe **£**
(www.charactersllandudno.com; 11 Llewelyn Ave; lunch £4-6, dinner £14-16; ⏰11am-5pm Mon-Sat, 6-8pm Fri & Sat;) If you're wondering whether it's the place that's full of character or the people running it, it's both. Llandudno's hippest tearoom serves wonderful cream teas (£4) and three-tiered high teas (£7), along with light lunches of sandwiches, soup and jacket potatoes; avoid the coffee. Weekends sizzle with hot-stone dinners.

Fish Tram Chips Fish & Chips **£**
(www.fishtramchipsllandudno.co.uk; 22-24 Old Rd; mains £7-10; ⏰noon-2pm & 5-9pm Tue-Sat, noon-2.30pm Sun) Low on thrills but big on tasty, fresh fish and homemade side dishes, this is where the locals head for good-value fish meals. It's probably the best bargain in the resort town.

Carmel Bistro Modern Welsh **££**
(☎01492-877643; www.carmelbistro.co.uk; 17 Craig y Don Pde; 2-course menu £18.50; ⏰6.45pm-late Tue-Sat) With its short but sweet menu and an emphasis on fresh local ingredients, this is the place for the discerning carnivore. Choose one of three starters and then have your mature Welsh rump steak cooked one of five different ways, or else sink your teeth into some slow-grilled lamb chops. A couple of fishy options also available. Book ahead.

Seahorse Seafood **£££**
(☎01492-875315; 7 Church Walks; mains £15-23; ⏰4.30pm-late Tue-Sat) Puzzlingly for a coastal resort, this is Llandudno's only proper seafood restaurant. Thankfully it's a good 'un! The chef is a keen fisherman, and the menu reflects his passion for the local catch (although there are meat and veggie options too). The restaurant is a split-level affair: upstairs is decorated with large murals, while the more intimate cellar room has a cosier feel.

 # Information

Llandudno Tourist Office (☎01492-577577; www.visitllandudno.org.uk; Mostyn St; ⏰9.30am-5pm Apr-Oct, closed Sun Nov-Mar) In the library building, with helpful staff and an accommodation booking service.

 # Getting There & Away

Direct services head to/from Betws-y-Coed (£5.90, 48 minutes), Blaenau Ffestiniog (£8.10, 1¼ hours), Chester (£18, one hour) and Manchester Piccadilly (£30, 2¼ hours); for other destinations you'll need to change at Llandudno Junction (£2.60, eight minutes).

Edinburgh & Central Scotland

Every visit to Scotland simply has to begin in Edinburgh, the elegant capital. Packed with more history and heritage per square inch than any other Scottish city, it's a place that rewards leisurely wandering – a stroll along the famous Royal Mile, a shopping spree on Princes St, a wander around the smart streets and Georgian squares of the New Town, and a picnic on the grassy lawns of Holyrood Park. And Edinburgh's pubs and restaurants are among the best in the country.

Then it's time to leave the city behind and venture out to Central Scotland's other sights. The neighbouring city of Glasgow offers quirky museums and sublime art-nouveau architecture. Stirling tempts with a castle to rival Edinburgh's, while Loch Lomond and the Trossachs serve up lake and mountain scenery.

For a final flourish there's St Andrews, the home of golf; Balmoral Castle, the holiday retreat of British monarchs since Victorian times; and glorious Speyside, dotted with dozens of whisky distilleries.

View over Edinburgh (p298)
JOHN AND TINA REID/GETTY IMAGES ©

Statue of Robert the Bruce, Stirling Castle (p322)

Edinburgh & Central Scotland

1 Edinburgh Castle
2 Speyside
3 Stirling Castle
4 Palace of Holyroodhouse
5 Glasgow

Edinburgh & Central Scotland Highlights

Edinburgh Castle

The brooding, black crags of Castle Rock are the very reason for Edinburgh's existence – it was the most easily defended hilltop on the invasion route from England. Crowning the crag with a profusion of battlements, Edinburgh Castle (p308) is now Scotland's most popular pay-to-enter tourist attraction.

Speyside Whisky Trail

No trip to Scotland is complete without visiting a whisky distillery, and the Speyside region (p331) is the heartland of Scotch whisky, with no fewer than 50 distilleries. Dufftown lies at the middle of it all, within easy reach of seven distilleries, and sporting its own whisky museum.

WILL ROBB/GETTY IMAGES ©

Stirling Castle

While Edinburgh Castle tops the visitor stakes, in terms of history and heritage its sister fortress at Stirling (p324) is arguably more rewarding.

This sturdy bastion has played a pivotal role in many key events of Scottish history, and was once a residence of the Stuart monarchs. Highlights include the Great Hall, the largest medieval banqueting hall ever built in Scotland.

Palace of Holyroodhouse

This Edinburgh palace is Her Majesty the Queen's official residence (p303) in Scotland, but the building is better known for its association with Mary, Queen of Scots, who spent six eventful years (1561–67) living here. As well as Mary's private bedchamber, the palace brims with fascinating antiques and artworks, and after your visit you can wander around Holyrood Park.

Glasgow

Scotland's second city is often eclipsed by the capital, but it's well worthy of a visit in its own right, with a wealth of wonderful museums, galleries and buildings – many of which were designed by Scotland's most gifted designer, Charles Rennie Mackintosh. Don't miss a visit to the Kelvingrove Art Gallery & Museum (p317), a treasure trove of quirky Victoriana. Detail of a Charles Rennie Mackintosh design

293

Edinburgh & Central Scotland's Best...

Cultural Experiences

o **Scottish National Gallery** Scotland's foremost repository of art (p300)

o **Royal Yacht Britannia** Wander the decks of the Queen's own holiday boat (p302)

o **Kelvingrove Art Gallery & Museum** Weird and wonderful exhibits at Glasgow's top museum (p317)

o **Mackintosh House** Marvel at the decorative detail in this reconstruction of Charles Rennie Mackintosh's Glasgow home (p316)

Castles & Palaces

o **Edinburgh Castle** Icon of the capital and home to the Stone of Destiny (p308)

o **Stirling Castle** Always in the shadow of Edinburgh, but can be a more rewarding visit (p324)

o **Culzean Castle** Stately castle surrounded by a landscaped park and wraparound views (p321)

o **Glamis Castle** Moody and marvellous, this is one of the region's most photogenic castles (p330)

Historic Sites

o **Palace of Holyroodhouse** The British monarch's official residence in Scotland, also a former home of Mary, Queen of Scots (p303)

o **Scott Monument** Lofty perch with stunning views of Edinburgh's Old Town skyline (p299)

o **Scone Palace** Where generations of Scottish kings were crowned (p325)

o **National Wallace Monument** Follow in the footsteps of the real-life Braveheart (p324)

o **Bannockburn Heritage Centre** Battlefield where Scotland triumphed over England in 1314 (p325)

Natural Beauty

○ **Holyrood Park, Edinburgh** Unexpected touch of the wilds and great viewpoint in the heart of the city (p303)

○ **Loch Lomond** Beautiful loch immortalised in song, easily reached from Edinburgh or Glasgow (p327)

○ **Speyside** Valley of the 'slivery Spey' and the heartland of Scotch whisky (p331)

○ **The Trossachs** Craggy hills and scenic lochs; often described as 'the Highlands in miniature' (p326)

Need to Know

ADVANCE PLANNING

○ **Six months before** Reserve a tee time for playing golf on St Andrews Old Course. Book accommodation in Edinburgh if you plan to visit during festival time (August) or Hogmanay (New Year).

○ **One month before** Reserve accommodation for any other time of year.

○ **One week before** Book for Speyside distillery tours, Edinburgh Castle and other big sights.

RESOURCES

○ **Edinburgh** (www.edinburgh.org)

○ **Edinburgh Museums & Galleries** (www.edinburghmuseums.org.uk)

○ **Edinburgh Festivals** (www.edinburghfestivals.co.uk)

○ **Glasgow** (peoplemakeglasgow.com)

○ **Speyside** (www.greaterspeyside.com; www.maltwhiskytrail.com)

○ **Loch Lomond & the Trossachs National Park** (www.lochlomond-trossachs.org)

○ **St Andrews** (www.visitstandrews.com)

GETTING AROUND

○ **Bus** Edinburgh and Glasgow have good bus networks.

○ **Car** The most time-efficient way to get around. Parking in Edinburgh city centre is difficult, so avoid bringing a car if you can.

○ **Train** Good for reaching major towns, but less useful for day-to-day getting around – the train lines skirt the region to the east and west.

BE FOREWARNED

○ **Crowds** Edinburgh is swamped by crowds during festival season in August.

○ **Weather** Scotland is notoriously wet, so come prepared with waterproofs and an umbrella.

○ **Golf** Accommodation is impossible to find when St Andrews hosts the Open Championships.

Left: Highland cow, near Loch Lomond (p327);
Above: Looking towards the Cairngorms from Glenfeshie, Speyside (p331)

Edinburgh & Central Scotland Itineraries

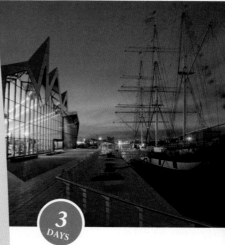

Do a three-day loop and explore the best of the capital and surrounds. The five-day trip leads further north, into the central Scottish heartland.

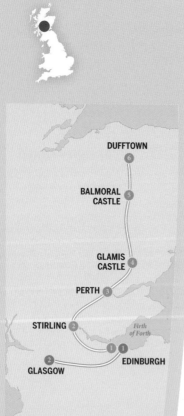

EDINBURGH TO GLASGOW

A TALE OF TWO CITIES

Spend a day getting to know **❶ Edinburgh** beginning with the Royal Mile and the Old Town, a visit to the underground chambers of Real Mary King's Close, and an afternoon at Edinburgh Castle. On day two, focus on the New Town and Princes St, and spend the afternoon exploring the Palace of Holyroodhouse.

On day three, head west to **❷ Glasgow**, where the main highlights include the artnouveau work of Charles Rennie Mackintosh and the excellent Kelvingrove Art Gallery & Museum and Hunterian Museum.

3 DAYS

DUFFTOWN ❻

BALMORAL CASTLE ❺

GLAMIS CASTLE ❹

PERTH ❸

STIRLING ❷

Firth of Forth

❶ ❶ EDINBURGH

❷ GLASGOW

Top Left: Riverside Museum (p316), Glasgow;
Top Right: Balmoral Castle (p331)

5 DAYS

EDINBURGH TO DUFFTOWN
CASTLE COUNTRY

Spend your first day or two in **①Edinburgh**) then it's a short journey to **②Stirling**, where visiting the castle and the nearby Wallace Monument will take the best part of the day. Head east to Perth for a visit to the **③Scone Palace**, where Scottish kings were once crowned. If you have time, a detour to the notoriously haunted castle at **④Glamis** is well worth it.

The scenery gets wilder as you drive further north towards Braemar and Royal Deeside. Stop in for a visit to **⑤Balmoral Castle**, the royal family's holiday home (they usually visit in August, when the castle is closed to the public). Then it's on into the Spey Valley, the spiritual home of Scottish Whisky, centring on **⑥Dufftown**. There are lots of high-profile distilleries nearby where you can sample some of the good stuff before continuing west to **⑦Inverness**, the start of our Highlands itinerary.

Discover Edinburgh & Central Scotland

EDINBURGH

POP 460,400

Edinburgh is a city that begs to be explored. From the vaults and wynds that riddle the Old Town to the urban villages of Stockbridge and Cramond, it's filled with quirky come-hither nooks that tempt you to walk just a little bit further. And every corner turned reveals sudden views and unexpected vistas – green sunlit hills, a glimpse of rust-red crags, a blue flash of distant sea.

All these superlatives come together in August at festival time, when it seems as if half the world descends on Edinburgh for one enormous party.

◎ Sights

Edinburgh's main attractions are concentrated in the city centre – on and around the Old Town's Royal Mile between the castle and Holyrood, and in New Town. A major exception is the Royal Yacht *Britannia*, which is in the redeveloped docklands district of Leith, 2 miles northeast of the centre.

OLD TOWN

The Royal Mile

Scotch Whisky Experience Exhibition
(www.scotchwhiskyexperience.co.uk; 354 Castlehill; adult/child incl tour & tasting £13.50/6.75; ☉10am-6.30pm Jun-Aug, to 6pm Sep-May; 🚌 2, 23, 27, 41, 42, 45) A former school houses this multimedia centre explaining the making of whisky from barley to bottle in a series of exhibits, demonstrations and tours that combine sight, sound and smell, including the world's largest collection of malt whiskies; look out for Peat the distillery cat! More expensive tours

St Giles Cathedral
CHRIS HEPBURN/GETTY IMAGES ©

include more extensive whisky tastings and samples of Scottish cuisine. There's also a **restaurant** (☏0131-477 8477; www.amber-restaurant.co.uk; 354 Castlehill; mains £12-20; ⊘10am-7.30pm Sun-Thu, to 9pm Fri & Sat; ☐23, 27, 41, 42) that serves traditional Scottish dishes with, where possible, a dash of whisky thrown in.

Camera Obscura   Exhibition

(www.camera-obscura.co.uk; Castlehill; adult/child £12.95/9.50; ⊘9.30am-9pm Jul & Aug, to 7pm Apr-Jun & Sep-Oct, 10am-6pm Nov-Mar; ☐2, 23, 27, 42) Edinburgh's camera obscura is a curious 19th-century device – in constant use since 1853 – that uses lenses and mirrors to throw a live image of the city onto a large horizontal screen. The accompanying commentary is entertaining and the whole experience has a quirky charm, complemented by an intriguing exhibition dedicated to illusions of all kinds. Stairs lead up through various displays to the **Outlook Tower**, which offers great views over the city.

St Giles Cathedral   Church

(www.stgilescathedral.org.uk; High St; suggested donation £3; ⊘9am-7pm Mon-Fri, to 5pm Sat, 1-5pm Sun May-Sep, 9am-5pm Mon-Sat, 1-5pm Sun Oct-Apr; ☐23, 27, 41, 42) The great grey bulk of St Giles Cathedral dominates Edinburgh's High St. Properly called the High Kirk of Edinburgh (it was only a true cathedral – the seat of a bishop – from 1633 to 1638 and from 1661 to 1689), the church was named after the patron saint of cripples and beggars. The present building dates largely from the 15th century – the beautiful crown spire was completed in 1495 – but much of it was restored in the 19th century.

Real Mary King's
Close   Historic Building

(☏0845 070 6244; www.realmarykingsclose.com; 2 Warriston's Close, High St; adult/child £12.95/7.45; ⊘10am-9pm daily Apr-Oct, to 11pm Aug, 10am-5pm Sun-Thu, 10am-9pm Fri & Sat Nov-Mar; ☐23, 27, 41, 42) Edinburgh's 18th-century City Chambers were built over the sealed-off remains of Mary King's Close, and the lower levels of this medieval Old Town alley have survived almost

unchanged amid the foundations for 250 years. Now open to the public, this spooky, subterranean labyrinth gives a fascinating insight into the everyday life of 17th-century Edinburgh. Costumed characters lead tours through a 16th-century town house and the plague-stricken home of a 17th-century gravedigger. Advance booking recommended.

Museum of Edinburgh   Museum

(www.edinburghmuseums.org.uk; 142 Canongate; ⊘10am-5pm Mon-Sat year-round, noon-5pm Sun Aug; ☐35) **FREE** You can't miss the colourful facade of Huntly House, brightly renovated in red and yellow ochre, opposite the Tolbooth clock on the Royal Mile. Built in 1570, it houses a museum covering Edinburgh from its prehistory to the present. Exhibits of national importance include an original copy of the National Covenant of 1638, but the big crowd-pleaser is the dog collar and feeding bowl that once belonged to Greyfriars Bobby, the city's most famous canine citizen.

NEW TOWN

Edinburgh's New Town lies north of the Old Town, on a ridge running parallel to the Royal Mile and separated from it by the valley of Princes Street Gardens. Its regular grid of elegant, neoclassical terraces is the world's most complete and unspoilt example of Georgian architecture and town planning. Along with the Old Town, it was declared a Unesco World Heritage Site in 1995.

Princes Street

Scott Monument   Monument

(www.edinburghmuseums.org.uk; East Princes Street Gardens; admission £4; ⊘10am-7pm Apr-Sep, 10am-4pm Oct-Mar; ☐all Princes St buses) The eastern half of Princes Street Gardens is dominated by the massive Gothic spire of the Scott Monument, built by public subscription in memory of the novelist Sir Walter Scott after his death in 1832. The exterior is decorated with carvings of characters from his novels; inside you can see an exhibition on Scott's life, and climb the 287 steps to the top for a superb view of the city.

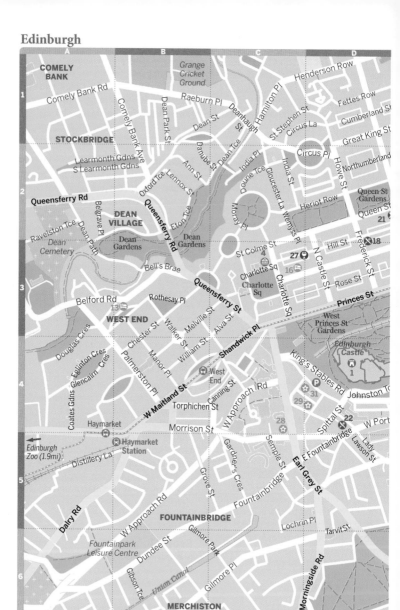

Scottish National Gallery Gallery
(www.nationalgalleries.org; The Mound; fee for
special exhibitions; ⏱10am-5pm Fri-Wed, to 7pm
Thu; 🚌all Princes St buses) FREE Designed
by William Playfair, this imposing classical
building with its Ionic porticoes dates
from the 1850s. Its octagonal rooms, lit
by skylights, have been restored to their
original Victorian decor of deep-green
carpets and dark-red walls. The gallery
houses an important collection of European art from the Renaissance to post-

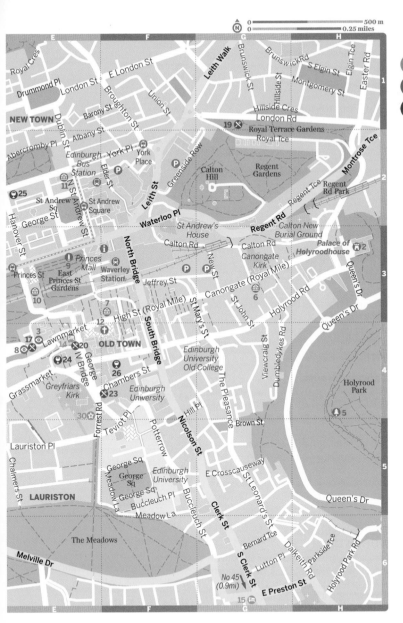

Impressionism, with works by Verrocchio (Leonardo da Vinci's teacher), Tintoretto, Titian, Holbein, Rubens, Van Dyck, Vermeer, El Greco, Poussin, Rembrandt, Gainsborough, Turner, Constable, Monet, Pissarro, Gauguin and Cézanne.

George Street & Around

Until the 1990s George St – the major axis of New Town – was the centre of Edinburgh's financial industry and Scotland's equivalent of Wall St. Today the big

Edinburgh

financial firms have moved to premises in the Exchange office district west of Lothian Rd, and George St's former banks and offices house upmarket shops, pubs and restaurants.

Georgian House   Historic Building

(NTS; www.nts.org.uk; 7 Charlotte Sq; adult/child £6.50/5; ◎10am-6pm Jul & Aug, 10am-5pm Apr-Jun & Sep-Oct, 11am-4pm Mar, 11am-3pm Nov; 🚌47) The National Trust for Scotland's Georgian House has been beautifully restored and furnished to show how Edinburgh's wealthy elite lived at the end of the 18th century. The walls are decorated with paintings by Allan Ramsay, Sir Henry Raeburn and Sir Joshua Reynolds.

Scottish National
Portrait Gallery   Gallery

(www.nationalgalleries.org; 1 Queen St; ◎10am-5pm Fri-Wed, to 7pm Thu) FREE The Venetian Gothic palace of the Scottish National Portrait Gallery reopened its doors in 2011 after a two-year renovation, emerging as one of the city's top attractions. Its galleries illustrate Scottish history through paintings, photographs and sculptures, putting faces to famous names from Scotland's past and present, from Robert Burns, Mary, Queen of Scots and Bonnie

Prince Charlie to Sean Connery, Billy Connolly and poet Jackie Kay.

LEITH

Royal Yacht Britannia   Ship

(www.royalyachtbritannia.co.uk; Ocean Terminal; adult/child £12.75/7.75; ◎9.30am-6pm Jul-Sep, to 5.30pm Apr-Jun & Oct, 10am-5pm Nov-Mar, last admission 90min before closing; 🚌11, 22, 34, 35, 36) Built on Clydeside, the former Royal Yacht Britannia was the British royal family's floating holiday home during their foreign travels from the time of her launch in 1953 until her decommissioning in 1997, and is now moored permanently in front of Ocean Terminal. The tour, which you take at your own pace with an audioguide (included in admission fee and available in 20 languages), lifts the curtain on the everyday lives of the royals, and gives an intriguing insight into the Queen's private tastes.

GREATER EDINBURGH

Edinburgh Zoo   Zoo

(www.edinburghzoo.org.uk; 134 Corstorphine Rd; adult/child £16.50/12; ◎9am-6pm Apr-Sep, to 5pm Oct & Mar, to 4.30pm Nov-Feb) Opened in 1913, Edinburgh Zoo is one of the world's leading conservation zoos. Edinburgh's captive breeding program has helped

continued on page 306

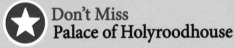

Don't Miss
Palace of Holyroodhouse

This palace is the royal family's official residence in Scotland, but is more famous as the 16th-century home of the ill-fated Mary, Queen of Scots. The highlight of the tour is **Mary's Bed Chamber**, home to the unfortunate queen from 1561 to 1567. It was here that her jealous first husband, Lord Darnley, restrained the pregnant queen while his henchmen murdered her secretary – and favourite – David Rizzio. A plaque in the neighbouring room marks the spot where he bled to death.

The palace developed from a guesthouse, attached to Holyrood Abbey, which was extended by King James IV in 1501. The oldest surviving part of the building, the northwestern tower, was built in 1529 as a royal apartment for James V and his wife, Mary of Guise. Mary, Queen of Scots spent six turbulent years here, during which time she debated with John Knox, married both her first and second husbands, and witnessed the murder of Rizzio.

The self-guided audio tour leads you through a series of impressive royal apartments, culminating in the **Great Gallery**. The 89 portraits of Scottish kings were commissioned by Charles II and supposedly record his unbroken lineage from Scota, the Egyptian pharaoh's daughter who discovered the infant Moses in a reed basket on the banks of the Nile. The tour continues to the oldest part of the palace, which contains Mary's Bed Chamber, connected by a secret stairway to her husband's bedroom, and ends with the ruins of Holyrood Abbey. Save time to explore Holyrood Park.

NEED TO KNOW
www.royalcollection.org.uk; Horse Wynd; adult/child £11.30/6.80; ⊗9.30am-6pm Apr-Oct, to 4.30pm Nov-Mar; 🚌35, 36

Royal Mile

A GRAND DAY OUT

Planning your own procession along the Royal Mile involves some tough decisions – it would be impossible to see everything in a single day, so it's wise to decide in advance what you don't want to miss and shape your visit around that. Remember to leave time for lunch, for exploring some of the Mile's countless side alleys and, during festival time, for enjoying the street theatre that is bound to be happening in High St.

The most pleasant way to reach the Castle Esplanade at the start of the Royal Mile is to hike up the zigzag path from the footbridge behind the Ross Bandstand in Princes Street Gardens (in springtime you'll be knee-deep in daffodils). Starting at **Edinburgh Castle** ❶ means that the rest of your walk is downhill. For a superb view up and down the length of the Mile, climb the **Camera Obscura's Outlook Tower** ❷ before visiting **Gladstone's**

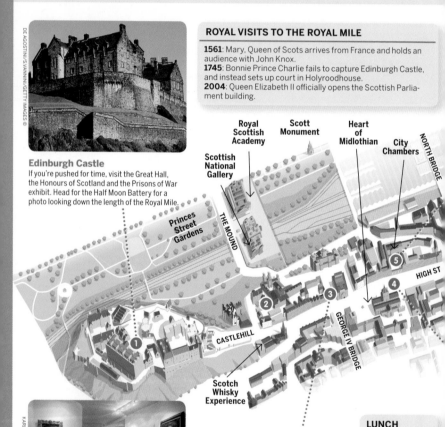

ROYAL VISITS TO THE ROYAL MILE

1561: Mary, Queen of Scots arrives from France and holds an audience with John Knox.
1745: Bonnie Prince Charlie fails to capture Edinburgh Castle, and instead sets up court in Holyroodhouse.
2004: Queen Elizabeth II officially opens the Scottish Parliament building.

DE AGOSTINI/S.VANNINI/GETTY IMAGES ©

Edinburgh Castle
If you're pushed for time, visit the Great Hall, the Honours of Scotland and the Prisons of War exhibit. Head for the Half Moon Battery for a photo looking down the length of the Royal Mile.

Royal Scottish Academy

Scott Monument

Heart of Midlothian

City Chambers

NORTH BRIDGE

Scottish National Gallery

Princes Street Gardens

THE MOUND

HIGH ST

CASTLEHILL

GEORGE IV BRIDGE

Scotch Whisky Experience

KARL BLACKWELL/GETTY IMAGES ©

Gladstone's Land
The 1st floor houses a faithful recreation of how a wealthy Edinburgh merchant lived in the 17th century. Check out the beautiful Painted Bedchamber, with its ornately decorated walls and wooden ceilings.

LUNCH BREAK

Burger and a beer at **Holyrood 9A**; steak and chips at **Maxie's Bistro**; slap-up seafood at **Ondine**.

Land ❸ and **St Giles Cathedral** ❹. If history's your thing, you'll want to add **Real Mary King's Close** ❺, **John Knox House** ❻ and the **Museum of Edinburgh** ❼ to your must-see list.

At the foot of the mile, choose between modern and ancient seats of power – the **Scottish Parliament** ❽ or the **Palace of Holyroodhouse** ❾. Round off the day with an evening ascent of Arthur's Seat or, slightly less strenuously, Calton Hill. Both make great sunset viewpoints.

TAKING YOUR TIME

Minimum time needed for each attraction:

» **Edinburgh Castle**: two hours
» **Gladstone's Land**: 45 minutes
» **St Giles Cathedral**: 30 minutes
» **Real Mary King's Close**: one hour (tour)
» **Scottish Parliament**: one hour (tour)
» **Palace of Holyroodhouse**: one hour

Real Mary King's Close
The guided tour is heavy on ghost stories, but a highlight is standing in an original 17th-century room with tufts of horsehair poking from the crumbling plaster, and breathing in the ancient scent of stone, dust and history.

Canongate Kirk

❾

❽

❼

CANONGATE

❻

ST MARY'S ST

Our Dynamic Earth

SOUTH BRIDGE

Tron Kirk

Scottish Parliament
Don't have time for the guided tour? Pick up a 'Discover the Scottish Parliament Building' leaflet from reception and take a self-guided tour of the exterior, then hike up to Salisbury Crags for a great view of the complex.

Palace of Holyroodhouse
Find the secret staircase joining Mary, Queen of Scots' bedchamber with that of her husband, Lord Darnley, who restrained the queen while his henchmen stabbed to death her secretary (and possible lover), David Rizzio.

St Giles Cathedral
Look out for the Burne-Jones stained-glass window (1873) at the west end, showing the crossing of the River Jordan, and the bronze memorial to Robert Louis Stevenson in the Moray Aisle.

continued from page 302

save many endangered species, including Siberian tigers, pygmy hippos and red pandas. The main attractions are the two **giant pandas**, Tian Tian and Yang Guang, who arrived in December 2011; the **penguin parade** (the zoo's penguins go for a walk every day at 2.15pm), and the **sea lion** training session (daily at 11.15am).

Rosslyn Chapel   Church

(Collegiate Church of St Matthew; www.rosslyn chapel.org.uk; Chapel Loan, Roslin; adult/child £9/free; ⏱9.30am-5pm Mon-Sat, noon-4.45pm Sun) The success of Dan Brown's novel *The Da Vinci Code* and the subsequent Hollywood film has seen a flood of visitors descend on Scotland's most beautiful and enigmatic church – Rosslyn Chapel. The chapel was built in the mid-15th century for William St Clair, third earl of Orkney, and the ornately carved interior – at odds with the architectural fashion of its time – is a monument to the mason's art, rich in symbolic imagery.

As well as flowers, vines, angels and biblical figures, the carved stones include many examples of the pagan 'Green Man'; other figures are associated with Freemasonry and the Knights Templar. Intriguingly, there are also carvings of plants from the Americas that predate Columbus' voyage of discovery. The symbolism of these images has led some researchers to conclude that Rosslyn is some kind of secret Templar repository, and it has been claimed that hidden vaults beneath the chapel could conceal anything from the Holy Grail or the head of John the Baptist to the body of Christ himself.

The chapel is on the eastern edge of the village of Roslin, 7 miles south of Edinburgh's centre. Lothian Bus 15 (not 15A) runs from the west end of Princes St in Edinburgh to Roslin (£1.40, 30 minutes, every 30 minutes).

Tours

City of the Dead Tours
Walking Tour

(www.cityofthedeadtours.com; adult/concession £10/8) This tour of Greyfriars Kirkyard is probably the scariest of Edinburgh's 'ghost' tours. Many people have reported encounters with the 'Mackenzie Poltergeist', the ghost of a 17th-century judge who persecuted the Covenanters, and now haunts their former prison in a corner of the kirkyard. Not suitable for young children.

Edinburgh Literary Pub Tour
Walking Tour

(www.edinburghliterarypubtour.co.uk; adult/student £14/10) An enlightening two-hour trawl through Edinburgh's literary history – and its associated howffs (pubs) – in the entertaining company of Messrs Clart and McBrain. One of the city's best walking tours.

Majestic Tour
Bus Tour

(www.edinburghtour.com; adult/child £13/6; ⏰daily year-round except 25 Dec) Hop on-hop off tour departing every 15 to 20 minutes from Waverley Bridge to the Royal Yacht *Britannia* at Ocean Terminal via the New Town, Royal Botanic Garden and Newhaven, returning via Leith Walk, Holyrood and the Royal Mile.

🛏 Sleeping

Edinburgh is not short of accommodation, but you can guarantee the city will be packed to the gills during the festival period (August) and over Hogmanay (New Year).

OLD TOWN

Hotel Missoni
Boutique Hotel £££

(☏0131-220 6666; www.hotelmissoni.com; 1 George IV Bridge; r £125-290; 📶) The Italian fashion house has established a style icon

307

Don't Miss
Edinburgh Castle

Edinburgh Castle has played a pivotal role in Scottish history, both as a royal residence and as a military stronghold. The castle last saw military action in 1745; from then until the 1920s it served as the British army's main base in Scotland. Today it is one of Scotland's most atmospheric and most popular tourist attractions.

www.edinburghcastle.gov.uk

adult/child incl audioguide £16/9.60

⊙9.30am-6pm Apr-Sep, to 5pm Oct-Mar, last admission 45min before closing

🚌23, 27, 41, 42

One O'Clock Gun

The Entrance Gateway, flanked by statues of Robert the Bruce and William Wallace, opens to a cobbled lane that leads up beneath the 16th-century Portcullis Gate to the cannons ranged along the Argyle and Mills Mount batteries. The battlements here have great views over New Town to the Firth of Forth.

At the far end of Mills Mount Battery is the famous One O'Clock Gun, where crowds gather to watch a gleaming WWII 25-pounder fire an ear-splitting time signal at exactly 1pm (every day except Sunday, Christmas Day and Good Friday).

National War Memorial

The main group of buildings on the summit of Castle Rock is ranged around Crown Sq, dominated by the shrine of the Scottish National War Memorial. Opposite is the Great Hall, built for James IV (r 1488–1513) as a ceremonial hall and used as a meeting place for the Scottish parliament until 1639. Its most remarkable feature is the original, 16th-century hammerbeam roof.

Royal Palace

On the eastern side of the square is the Royal Palace, built during the 15th and 16th centuries, where a series of historical tableaux leads to the highlight of the castle – a strongroom housing the Honours of Scotland (the Scottish crown jewels), the oldest surviving crown jewels in Europe. Locked away in a chest following the Act of Union in 1707, the crown (made in 1540 from the gold of Robert the Bruce's 14th-century coronet), sword and sceptre lay forgotten until they were unearthed at the instigation of the novelist Sir Walter Scott in 1818. Also on display here is the Stone of Destiny.

Among the neighbouring Royal Apartments is the bedchamber where Mary, Queen of Scots gave birth to her son James VI, who was to unite the crowns of Scotland and England in 1603.

> **Local Knowledge**

Edinburgh Castle

BY PETER YEOMAN, HEAD OF CULTURAL HERITAGE AT HISTORIC SCOTLAND

1 HONOURS OF SCOTLAND
The crown, sceptre and sword of state are glittering symbols of our nationhood. They were first used at the coronation of Mary, Queen of Scots in 1543 when she was only nine months old. The centuries-old regalia are displayed in the Royal Palace alongside the Stone of Destiny.

2 ST MARGARET'S CHAPEL
The oldest building in the castle is a wee gem, possibly part of a tower keep built in the early 1100s to commemorate Scotland's royal saint, who died in the castle in 1093. The chapel is delightfully decorated inside with fine Romanesque architecture.

3 MONS MEG
Step outside the chapel and you are confronted by the great bombard Mons Meg, gifted to James II in 1457. This is a great vantage point for the firing of the one o'clock gun (fired daily except Sunday), causing many visitors to jump out of their skins! The views from here across the Georgian New Town to the Forth Estuary are truly magnificent.

4 DAVID'S TOWER
Deep beneath the Half Moon Battery lies David's Tower, built as a fancy residence for David II in 1371. Badly damaged in the siege of 1573, the tower became hidden in the foundations for the new battery, and was only rediscovered in 1912. The Honours of Scotland spent much of WWII here, hidden down a medieval loo!

5 CASTLE VAULTS
In 1720 21 pirates captured in Argyll were thrown into the castle dungeons. The following decades saw a busy time for this State Prison, stuffed full of prisoners from the wars with America and France. The reconstructed cells allow you to experience something of the squalor!

in the heart of the medieval Old Town with this bold statement of a hotel – modernistic architecture, black-and-white decor with well-judged splashes of colour, impeccably mannered staff and, most importantly, very comfortable bedrooms and bathrooms with lots of nice little touches, from fresh milk in the minibar to plush bathrobes.

NEW TOWN & AROUND

B+B Edinburgh
Hotel ££

(☎ 0131-225 5084; www.bb-edinburgh.com; 3 Rothesay Tce; d/ste from £110/170; 🛜📶) Built in 1883 as a grand home for the proprietor of the *Scotsman* newspaper, this Victorian extravaganza of carved oak, parquet floors, stained glass and elaborate fireplaces was given a designer makeover in 2011 to create a striking contemporary hotel. Rooms on the 2nd floor are the most spacious, but the smaller top-floor rooms enjoy the finest views.

Tigerlily
Boutique Hotel £££

(☎ 0131-225 5005; www.tigerlilyedinburgh. co.uk; 125 George St; r from £210; 🛜) Georgian meets gorgeous at this glamorous, glittering boutique hotel (complete with its own nightclub) decked out in mirror mosaics, beaded curtains, swirling Timorous Beasties textiles and wall coverings, and atmospheric pink uplighting. Book the Georgian Suite (from £410) for a truly special romantic getaway.

SOUTH EDINBURGH

Southside Guest House
B&B ££

(☎ 0131-668 4422; www.southsideguesthouse. co.uk; 8 Newington Rd; s/d £75/95; 🛜) Though set in a typical Victorian terrace, the Southside transcends the traditional guesthouse category and feels more like a modern boutique hotel. Its eight stylish rooms ooze interior design, standing out from other Newington B&Bs through the clever use of bold colours and modern furniture. Breakfast is an event, with Bucks Fizz (champagne mixed with orange juice) on offer to smooth the rough edges off your hangover!

No 45
B&B ££

(☎ 0131-667 3536; www.edinburghbedbreakfast.com; 45 Gilmour Rd; s/d £70/140; 🛜) A peaceful setting, large garden and friendly owners contribute to the appeal of this Victorian terraced house, which overlooks

Bow Bar

the local bowling green. The decor is a blend of 19th- and 20th-century, with bold Victorian reds, pine floors and period fireplace in the lounge, a rocking horse and art-nouveau lamp in the hallway, and a 1930s vibe in the three spacious bedrooms.

Eating

OLD TOWN

Timberyard   Scottish ££
(✆0131-221 1222; www.timberyard.co; 10 Lady Lawson St; mains £16-21; ⏲noon-9.30pm Tue-Sat; ☎; ▣2, 35) 🍴 Ancient worn floorboards, cast-iron pillars, exposed joists and tables made from slabs of old mahogany create a rustic, retro atmosphere in this slow-food restaurant where the accent is on locally sourced produce from artisan growers and foragers. Typical dishes include seared scallop with apple, Jerusalem artichoke and sorrel; and juniper-smoked pigeon with wild garlic flowers and beetroot.

Ondine   Seafood £££
(✆0131-226 1888; www.ondinerestaurant.co.uk; 2 George IV Bridge; mains £14-39, 2-/3-course lunch £22/25; ⏲noon-3pm & 5.30-10pm Mon-Sat; ▣23, 27, 41, 42) Ondine is one of Edinburgh's finest seafood restaurants, with a menu based on sustainably sourced fish. Take a seat at the curved Oyster Bar and tuck into oysters Kilpatrick, lobster thermidor, a roast shellfish platter or just good old haddock and chips (with minted pea purée, just to keep things posh).

Tower   Scottish £££
(✆0131-225 3003; www.tower-restaurant.com; National Museum of Scotland, Chambers St; mains £18-39, 2-course lunch & pretheatre menu £19, afternoon tea £19; ⏲10am-11pm; ▣23, 27, 41, 42) Chic and sleek, with a great view of the castle, Tower is perched in a turret atop the National Museum of Scotland building. A star-studded guest list of celebrities has enjoyed its menu of quality Scottish food, simply prepared – try half a dozen oysters followed by roast loin of venison. Afternoon tea (£18) is served from 2.30pm to 5.30pm.

NEW TOWN

Gardener's Cottage   Scottish ££
(✆0131-558 1221; www.thegardenerscottage. co; 1 Royal Terrace Gardens, London Rd; lunch mains £16-17, dinner set menu £30; ⏲noon-2.30pm & 5-10pm Thu-Mon, 10am-2pm Sat & Sun; ▣all London Rd buses) 🍴 This country cottage in the heart of the city, bedecked with flowers and fairy lights, offers one of Edinburgh's most interesting dining experiences – two tiny rooms with communal tables made of salvaged timber, and a set menu based on fresh local produce (most of the vegetables and fruit are grown in an organic garden in the city suburbs). Booking essential.

The Dogs   British ££
(✆0131-220 1208; www.thedogsonline.co.uk; 110 Hanover St; mains £10-15; ⏲noon-4pm & 5-10pm; ▣23, 27) 🍴 One of the coolest tables in town, this bistro-style place uses cheaper cuts of meat and less-well-known, more-sustainable species of fish to create hearty, no-nonsense dishes such as lamb sweetbreads on toast, baked coley with *skirlie* (fried oatmeal and onion), and devilled liver with bacon and onions.

Café Marlayne   French ££
(✆0131-226 2230; www.cafemarlayne.com; 76 Thistle St; mains £12-15; ⏲noon-10pm; ▣24, 29, 42) All weathered wood and candlelit tables, Café Marlayne is a cosy nook offering French farmhouse cooking – *brandade de morue* (salt cod) with green salad, slow-roast rack of lamb, *boudin noir* (black pudding) with scallops and sautéed potato – at very reasonable prices. Booking recommended.

Drinking

OLD TOWN

Bow Bar   Pub
(80 West Bow; ▣23, 27, 41, 42) One of the city's best traditional-style pubs (it's not as old as it looks), serving a range of excellent real ales and a vast selection of malt whiskies. The Bow Bar often has standing-room only on Friday and Saturday evenings.

BrewDog
Bar

(www.brewdog.com; 143 Cowgate; 📶; 🚌36)
The Edinburgh outpost of Scotland's self-styled 'punk brewery', BrewDog stands out among the grimy, sticky-floored dives that line the Cowgate, with its cool, industrial-chic designer look. As well as its own highly rated beers, there's a choice of four guest real ales.

NEW TOWN

Oxford Bar
Pub

(www.oxfordbar.co.uk; 8 Young St; 🚌19, 36, 37, 41, 47) The Oxford is that rarest of things: a real pub for real people, with no 'theme', no music, no frills and no pretensions. 'The Ox' has been immortalised by Ian Rankin, author of the Inspector Rebus novels, whose fictional detective is a regular here.

Bramble
Cocktail Bar

(www.bramblebar.co.uk; 16a Queen St; 🚌23, 27) One of those places that easily earns the sobriquet 'best-kept secret', Bramble is an unmarked cellar bar where a maze of stone and brick hideaways conceals what is arguably the city's best cocktail venue. No beer taps, no fuss, just expertly mixed drinks.

⭐ Entertainment

The comprehensive source for what's-on info is **The List** (www.list.co.uk), an excellent listings magazine covering both Edinburgh and Glasgow. It's available from most newsagents, and is published fortnightly on a Thursday.

Sandy Bell's
Folk

(www.sandybellsedinburgh.co.uk; 25 Forrest Rd) This unassuming pub is a stalwart of the traditional music scene (the founder's wife sang with The Corries). There's music almost every evening at 9pm, and from 3pm Saturday and Sunday, plus lots of impromptu sessions.

Henry's Cellar Bar
Rock, Blues

(www.henryscellarbar.com; 16 Morrison St; admission free–£5) One of Edinburgh's most eclectic live-music venues, Henry's has something going on most nights of the week, from rock and indie to 'Balkan-inspired folk', funk to hip-hop to hard-core, staging both local bands and acts from around the world. Open till 3am at weekends.

Royal Lyceum Theatre
Theatre, Music

(www.lyceum.org.uk; 30b Grindlay St; 🕐box office 10am-6pm Mon-Sat, to 8pm show nights; ♿) A grand Victorian theatre located beside the Usher Hall, the Lyceum stages drama, concerts, musicals and ballet.

Traverse Theatre
Theatre, Dance

(www.traverse.co.uk; 10 Cambridge St; 🕐box office 10am-6pm Mon-Sat, to 8pm show nights) The Traverse is the main focus for new Scottish writing and stages an adventurous program of contemporary drama and dance. The box office is only open on Sunday (from 4pm) when there's a show on.

ℹ Information

Edinburgh Information Centre (📞0131-473 3868; www.edinburgh.org; Princes Mall, 3 Princes St; 🕐9am-9pm Mon-Sat, 10am-8pm Sun Jul & Aug, 9am-7pm Mon-Sat, 10am-7pm Sun May-Jun & Sep, 9am-5pm Mon-Wed, to 6pm Thu-Sun Oct-Apr) Includes an accommodation booking service, currency exchange, gift and bookshop, internet access and counters selling tickets for Edinburgh city tours and Scottish Citylink bus services.

ℹ Getting There & Away

Air

Edinburgh Airport (📞0844 448 8833; www.edinburghairport.com) Eight miles west of the city; has numerous flights to other parts of Scotland and the UK, Ireland and mainland Europe.

Train

The main terminus in Edinburgh is Waverley train station, located in the heart of the city.

You can buy tickets, make reservations and get travel information at the **Edinburgh Rail Travel Centre** (🕐4.45am-12.30am Mon-Sat, 7am-12.30am Sun) in Waverley station.

First ScotRail operates a regular shuttle service between Edinburgh and Glasgow (£13.20, 50 minutes, every 15 minutes), and frequent daily services to all Scottish cities, including Aberdeen (£34, 2½ hours), Dundee (£17.30, 1¼ hours) and Inverness (£72, 3½ hours).

GLASGOW

POP 595,100

Disarmingly blending sophistication and earthiness, Scotland's biggest city has evolved over the last couple of decades to become one of Britain's most intriguing metropolises.

Its shopping – whether you're looking for Italian fashion or pre-loved denim – is famous and there are top-drawer museums and galleries. Charles Rennie Mackintosh's sublime designs dot the city, which – always proud of its working-class background – also innovatively displays its industrial heritage. The River Clyde, traditionally associated with Glasgow's earthier side, is now a symbol of the city's renaissance.

Sights

CITY CENTRE

Glasgow School of Art
Historic Building

(0141-353 4526; www.gsa.ac.uk/tours; 167 Renfrew St; adult/child £9.75/4.75; 9.30am-6.30pm Mar-Oct, 10am-5pm Nov-Feb) Charles Rennie Mackintosh's greatest building – extensively damaged by fire in 2014, so access may be limited by renovation works – still fulfils its original function, so just follow the steady stream of eclectically dressed students up the hill to find it. Visits are by excellent hour-long guided tours (roughly hourly in summer, 11am, 1pm and 3pm in winter, multilingual translations available) run by architecture students. These leave from the new building; book online or by phone at busy times.

Willow Tea Rooms
Historic Building

(www.willowtearooms.co.uk; 217 Sauchiehall St; 9am-5pm Mon-Sat, 11am-5pm Sun) **FREE** Admirers of the great Charles Rennie Mackintosh will love the Willow Tea Rooms, an authentic reconstruction of tea rooms

The Willow Tea Rooms

VISITBRITAIN/BRITAIN ON VIEW/GETTY IMAGES ©

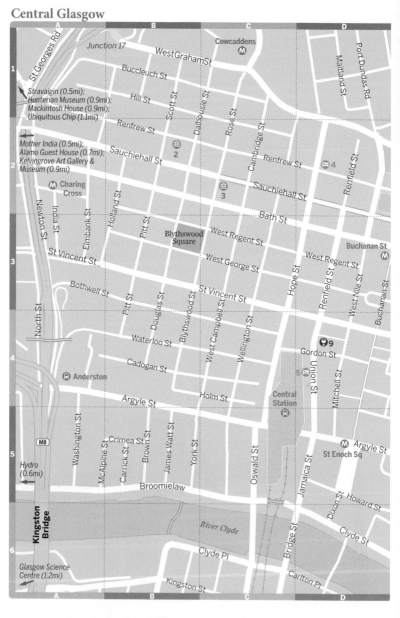

Mackintosh designed and furnished in the early 20th century for restaurateur Kate Cranston. You can relive the original splendour of this unique tearoom while admiring the architect's distinctive touch in just about every element.

EAST END

Glasgow Cathedral · Church

(HS; www.historic-scotland.gov.uk; Cathedral Sq; ⊙9.30am-5.30pm Mon-Sat, 1-5pm Sun Apr-Sep, closes 4.30pm Oct-Mar) FREE Glasgow

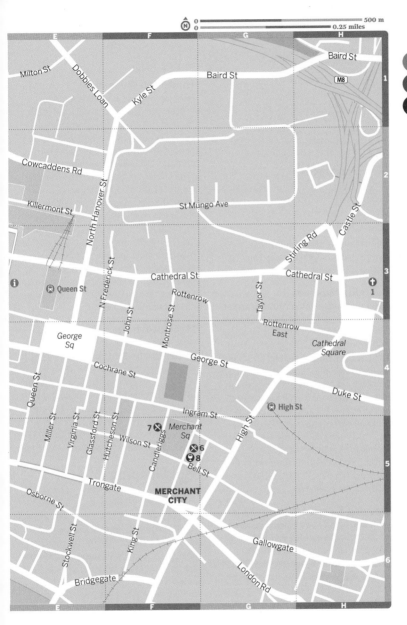

EDINBURGH & CENTRAL SCOTLAND GLASGOW

Cathedral has a rare timelessness. The dark, imposing interior conjures up medieval might and can send a shiver down the spine. It's a shining example of Gothic architecture, and, unlike nearly all of Scotland's cathedrals, survived the turmoil of the Reformation mobs almost intact. Most of the current building dates from the 15th century.

Central Glasgow

⊙ Sights

THE CLYDE

Once a thriving shipbuilding area, the Clyde sank into dereliction during the postwar era, but is being rejuvenated.

Riverside Museum   Museum

(www.glasgowmuseums.com; 100 Pointhouse Pl; ⊙10am-5pm Mon-Thu & Sat, 11am-5pm Fri & Sun; 👶) **FREE** This visually impressive modern museum at Glasgow Harbour (west of the centre – get bus 100 from the north side of George Sq, or the Clyde Cruises boat service) owes its striking curved forms to British-Iraqi architect Zaha Hadid. A transport museum forms the main part of the collection, featuring a fascinating series of cars made in Scotland, plus assorted railway locos, trams, bikes (including the world's first pedal-powered bicycle from 1847) and model Clyde-built ships.

Glasgow Science Centre   Museum

(☎0141-420 5000; www.glasgowsciencecentre. org; 50 Pacific Quay; adult/child £10.50/8.50, IMAX, tower or planetarium extra £2.50; ⊙10am-5pm Wed-Sun Nov-Mar, 10am-5pm daily Apr-Oct; 👶) This ultramodern science museum will keep the kids entertained for hours (that's middle-aged kids, too!). It brings science and technology alive through hundreds of interactive exhibits on four floors: a bounty of discovery for inquisitive minds. There's also an **IMAX theatre** (see www.cineworld.com for current screenings), a rotating 127m high **observation tower**, a planetarium,

and a **Science Theatre**, with live science demonstrations. To get here, take bus 89 or 90 from Union St.

WEST END

Hunterian Museum   Museum

(www.hunterian.gla.ac.uk; University Ave; ⊙10am-5pm Tue-Sat, 11am-4pm Sun) **FREE** Housed in the glorious sandstone university building, which is in itself reason enough to pay a visit, this quirky museum contains the collection of renowned one-time student of the university, William Hunter (1718–83). Hunter was primarily an anatomist and physician but, as one of those gloriously well-rounded Enlightenment figures, he interested himself in everything the world had to offer. Pickled organs in glass jars take their place alongside geological phenomena, potsherds gleaned from ancient brochs (defensive towers), dinosaur skeletons and a creepy case of deformed animals.

Mackintosh House   Historic Building

(www.hunterian.gla.ac.uk; 82 Hillhead St; ⊙10am-5pm Tue-Sat, 11am-4pm Sun) **FREE** Attached to the Hunterian Art Gallery, this is a reconstruction of the first home that Charles Rennie Mackintosh bought with his wife, noted designer/artist Margaret Macdonald. It's fair to say that interior decoration was one of their strong points; Mackintosh House is startling even today.

🛏 Sleeping

CITY CENTRE

Citizen M   Hotel ££

(☎0141-404 9485; www.citizenm.com; 60 Renfrew St; r £75-105; @ 📶) This modern chain does away with some normal hotel accoutrements in favour of self-check-in terminals and minimalist, plasticky modern rooms with just two features: a big, comfortable king-sized bed and a decent shower with mood lighting. The idea is that guests make liberal use of the public areas, and why wouldn't you, with upbeat and super-comfortable designer furniture, a 24-hour cafe and a table full of iMacs.

ART WORK: FLOATING HEADS BY SOPHY CAVE
PHOTOGRAPH: VISITBRITAIN/BRITAIN ON VIEW/GETTY IMAGES ©

 Don't Miss
Kelvingrove Art Gallery & Museum

A magnificent stone building, this grand Victorian cathedral of culture is a fascinating and unusual museum, with a bewildering variety of exhibits. You'll find fine art alongside stuffed animals, and Micronesian shark-tooth swords alongside a Spitfire plane, but it's not mix 'n' match: rooms are carefully and thoughtfully themed, and the collection is a manageable size. There's an excellent room of Scottish art, a room of fine French Impressionist works, and quality Renaissance paintings from Italy and Flanders.

Salvador Dalí's superb *Christ of St John of the Cross* is also here. Best of all, nearly everything, including the paintings, has an easy-reading paragraph of interpretation. You can learn a lot about art here, and it's excellent for children, with plenty to do and displays aimed at a variety of ages. Free hour-long guided tours begin at 11am and 2.30pm. Bus 17, among many others, runs here from Renfield St.

NEED TO KNOW

www.glasgowmuseums.com; Argyle St; ◷10am-5pm Mon-Thu & Sat, 11am-5pm Fri & Sun

Grasshoppers Hotel £££

(☎0141-222 2666; www.grasshoppersglasgow. com; 87 Union St; r £85-115; ☎) Discreetly hidden atop a timeworn railway administration building right alongside Glasgow Central, this small, well-priced hotel is a modern, upbeat surprise. Rooms are compact – a few larger ones are available – but well-appointed, with unusual views over the station roof's glass sea. Numerous nice touches: friendly staff, interesting art, proper in-room coffee, free cupcakes, and weeknight suppers available make this one of the centre's homeliest choices.

There's a very good deal available (£6 per day) at a car park a block away.

WEST END

Alamo Guest House
B&B ££

(☎ 0141-339 2395; www.alamoguesthouse.com; 46 Gray St; basic/superior d £89/149, s/d without bathroom £49/59; @ 🛜) The Alamo may not sound a peaceful spot, but that's exactly what this great place is. Opposite Kelvingrove Park, it feels miles from the city's hustle, but several of the best museums and restaurants in town are very close by. The decor is an enchanting mixture of antique furnishings and modern design, with excellent bathrooms, and the owners will make you very welcome.

Embassy Apartments
Apartments ££

(☎ 0141-946 6698; www.glasgowhotelsand-apartments.co.uk; 8 Kelvin Dr; 1-/2-/4-person apt £60/80/99; P 🛜) This elegant self-catering place offers both facilities and location. Situated on a quiet, exclusive street right on the edge of the Botanical Gardens, the studio-style apartments sleep one to seven, have fully-equipped

kitchens and are sparkling clean. They're a particularly good option for couples and families with older kids. Available by the day, but prices drop for longer rentals and vary extensively by demand.

Eating

CITY CENTRE

Café Gandolfi
Cafe, Bistro ££

(☎ 0141-552 6813; 64 Albion St; mains £9-15; ⏰ 8am-11.30pm Mon-Sat, 9am-11.30pm Sun; 🛜) In Merchant City, this cafe was once part of the old cheese market. It's been pulling in the punters for years and attracts an interesting mix of die-hard Gandolfers, the upwardly mobile and tourists. It covers all the bases with excellent breakfasts and coffee, an enticing upstairs bar, and top-notch bistro food, covering Scottish and Continental bases in an atmospheric medieval-like setting. There's an expansion, specialising in fish, next door, with a takeaway outlet.

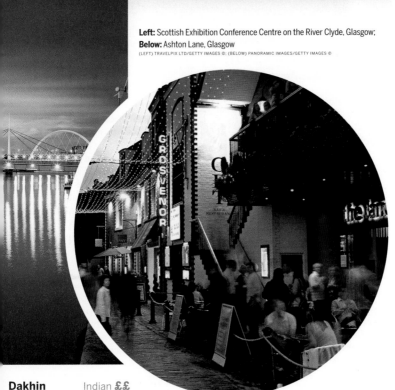

Dakhin
Indian ££

(0141-553 2585; www.
dakhin.com; 89 Candleriggs; mains £10-19;
noon-2pm & 5-11pm Mon-Fri, 1-11pm Sat &
Sun;) This south Indian restaurant
breathes some fresh air into the city's
curry scene. Dishes are from all over the
south, and include dosas (thin rice-based
crêpes) and a yummy variety of fragrant
coconut-based curries. If you're really
hungry, try a thali: an assortment of
Indian 'tapas'.

WEST END

Stravaigin
Scottish ££

(0141-334 2665; www.stravaigin.co.uk; 28
Gibson St; mains £10-18; 9am-11pm;)
Stravaigin is a serious foodie's delight,
with a menu constantly pushing the
boundaries of originality and offering
creative culinary excellence. The cool
contemporary dining space in the basement has booth seating, and helpful, laid-
back waiting staff to assist in deciphering
the audacious menu. Entry-level has a
buzzing bar; you can also eat here. There

are always plenty of menu deals and
special culinary nights.

Mother India
Indian ££

(0141-221 1663; www.motherindia.co.uk; 28
Westminster Tce, Sauchiehall St; mains £9-15;
5.30-10.30pm Mon-Thu, noon-11pm Fri,
1-11pm Sat, 1-10pm Sun;) Glasgow
curry buffs forever debate the merits
of the city's numerous excellent south
Asian restaurants; this features in every
discussion. It may lack the trendiness of
some of the up-and-comers but it's been
a stalwart for years, and the quality and
innovation on show is superb. The three
separate dining areas are all attractive
and they make an effort for kids, with a
separate menu.

Ubiquitous Chip
Scottish £££

(0141-334 5007; www.ubiquitouschip.co.uk;
12 Ashton Lane; 2-/3-course lunch £16/20, mains
£23-27, brasserie mains £9-14; noon-2.30pm
& 5-11pm;) The original champion of

319

The Genius of Charles Rennie Mackintosh

Great cities have great artists, designers and architects contributing to the cultural and historical roots of their urban environment while expressing its soul and individuality. Charles Rennie Mackintosh was all of these. His quirky, linear and geometric designs have had almost as much influence on the city as have Gaudí's on Barcelona. Many of the buildings Mackintosh designed in Glasgow are open to the public, and you'll see his tall, thin, art-nouveau typeface repeatedly reproduced.

If you're planning to go CRM crazy, the **Mackintosh Trail ticket** (£10), available at the tourist office or any Mackintosh building, gives you a day's free or discounted admission to patrticipating attractions as well as unlimited bus and subway travel.

Scottish produce, this is legendary for its unparalleled Scottish cuisine and lengthy wine list. Named to poke fun at Scotland's culinary reputation, it offers a French touch but resolutely Scottish ingredients, carefully selected and following sustainable principles. The elegant courtyard space offers some of Glasgow's highest-quality dining, while above the cheaper brasserie menu offers exceptional value for money.

🍷 Drinking & Entertainment

Artà — Bar, Club
(www.arta.co.uk; 62 Albion St; ☺5pm-3am Thu-Sat; 🛜) This extraordinary place is so baroque that when you hear a Mozart concerto over the sound system, it wouldn't surprise you to see the man himself at the other end of the bar. Set in a former cheese market, it really does have to be seen to be believed. Despite the luxury, it's got a relaxed, chilled vibe. The big cocktails are great.

Horse Shoe — Pub
(www.horseshoebar.co.uk; 17 Drury St; ☺10am-midnight Mon-Sat, 11am-midnight Sun) This legendary city pub and popular meeting place dates from the late 19th century and is largely unchanged. It's a picturesque spot, with the longest continuous bar in the UK, but its main attraction is what's served over it – real ale and good cheer. Upstairs in the lounge is some of the best-value pub food (three-course lunch £4.50) in town.

Hydro — Auditorium
(📞0141-248 3000; www.thessehydro.com; Finnieston Quay) Another spectacular modern building to keep the adjacent 'Armadillo' company, the Hydro amphitheatre is a phenomenally popular venue for big-name concerts and shows, and also hosted gymnastics and netball in the 2014 Commonwealth Games.

ℹ Information

The List (www.list.co.uk), available from newsagents, is Glasgow and Edinburgh's invaluable fortnightly guide to films, theatre, cabaret, music, clubs – the works.

Tourist Information

Glasgow Information Centre (📞0845 225 5121; www.visitscotland.com; 170 Buchanan St; ☺9am-6pm Mon-Sat, noon-4pm or 10am-5pm Sun; 🛜) In the heart of the shopping area.

ℹ Getting There & Away

Air

Ten miles west of the city, **Glasgow International Airport** (GLA; 📞0844 481 5555; www.glasgowairport.com) handles domestic traffic and international flights. **Glasgow Prestwick Airport** (PIK; 📞0871 223 0700; www.glasgowprestwick.com), 30 miles southwest of Glasgow, is used by Ryanair and some other budget airlines, with many connections to the rest of Britain and Europe.

Train

As a general rule, Glasgow Central station serves southern Scotland, England and Wales, and Queen St station serves the north and east. There are buses every 10 minutes between them.

Destinations include: Edinburgh (£12.50, 50 minutes, every 15 minutes), Oban (£23.10, three hours, three to six daily), Fort William (£28.20, 3¾ hours, four to five daily), Dundee (£21.30, 1½ hours, hourly), Aberdeen (£38.20, 2½ hours, hourly) and Inverness (£84.70, 3½ hours, 10 daily, four on Sunday).

CULZEAN CASTLE & COUNTRY PARK

The Scottish National Trust's flag-ship property, magnificent **Culzean Castle** (NTS; ☑01655-884400; www.culzeanexperience.org; castle adult/child/family £15.50/11.50/38; ☉castle 10.30am-5pm Apr-Oct, last entry 4pm, park 9.30am-sunset year-round) is one of the most impressive of Scotland's great stately homes. The entrance to Culzean (kull-*ane*) is a converted viaduct, and on approach the castle appears like a mirage, floating into view. Designed by Robert Adam, who was encouraged to exercise his romantic genius in its design, this 18th-century mansion is perched dramatically on the edge of the cliffs. Robert Adam was the most influential architect of his time, renowned for his meticulous attention to detail and the elegant classical embellishments with which he decorated his ceilings and fireplaces.

Culzean is 12 miles south of Ayr.

STIRLING

POP 36,150

With an utterly impregnable position atop a mighty wooded crag (the plug of an extinct volcano), Stirling's beautifully preserved Old Town is a treasure trove of noble buildings and cobbled streets winding up to the ramparts of its dominant castle, which offer views for miles around. Clearly visible is the brooding Wallace Monument, a strange Victorian Gothic creation honouring the legendary freedom fighter of *Braveheart* fame. Nearby is Bannockburn, scene of Robert the Bruce's major triumph over the English.

Stone Bridge, Stirling

Stirling Castle

PLANNING YOUR ATTACK

Stirling's a sizeable fortress, but not so huge that you'll have to decide what to leave out – there's time to see it all. Unless you've got a working knowledge of Scottish monarchs, head to the **Castle Exhibition** ❶ first: it'll help you sort one James from another. That done, take on the sights at leisure. First, stop and look around you from the **ramparts** ❷; the views high over this flat valley, a key strategic point in Scotland's history, are magnificent.

Track back towards the citadel's heart, stopping for a quick tour through the **Great Kitchens** ❸; looking at all that fake food might make you seriously hungry, though. Then enter the main courtyard. Around you are the principal castle buildings. During summer there are events (such as Renaissance dancing) in the **Great Hall** ❹ – get details at the entrance. The **Museum of the Argyll & Sutherland Highlanders** ❺ is a treasure trove if you're interested in regimental history, but missable if you're not. Leave the best for last – crowds thin in the afternoon – and enter the sumptuous **Royal Palace** ❻.

Take time to admire the beautiful **Stirling Tapestries** ❼, skillfully woven by hand on-site between 2001-2014.

THE WAY UP & DOWN

If you have time, take the atmospheric Back Walk, a peaceful, shady stroll around the Old Town's fortifications and up to the castle's imposing crag-top position. Afterwards, wander down through the Old Town to admire its facades.

DAVID ROBERTSON/ALAMY ©

Museum of the Argyll & Sutherland Highlanders
The history of one of Scotland's legendary regiments – now subsumed into the Royal Regiment of Scotland – is on display here, featuring memorabilia, weapons and uniforms.

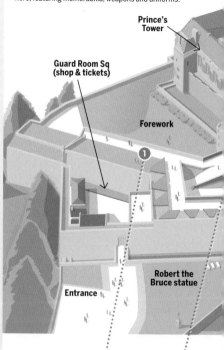

Prince's Tower

Guard Room Sq (shop & tickets)

Forework

Robert the Bruce statue

Entrance

TOP TIPS

» **Admission** Entrance is free for Historic Scotland members. If you'll be visiting several Historic Scotland sites a membership will save you plenty.

» **Vital Statistics** First constructed: before 1110; number of sieges: at least nine; last besieger: Bonnie Prince Charlie (unsuccessful); money spent refurbishing the Royal Palace: £12 million.

Castle Exhibition
A great overview of the Stewart dynasty here will get your facts straight, and also offers the latest archaeological titbits from the ongoing excavations under the citadel. Analysis of skeletons has revealed surprising amounts of biographical data.

Royal Palace
The impressive new highlight of a visit to the castle is this recreation of the royal lodgings originally built by James V. The finely worked ceiling, ornate furniture and sumptuous unicorn tapestries dazzle.

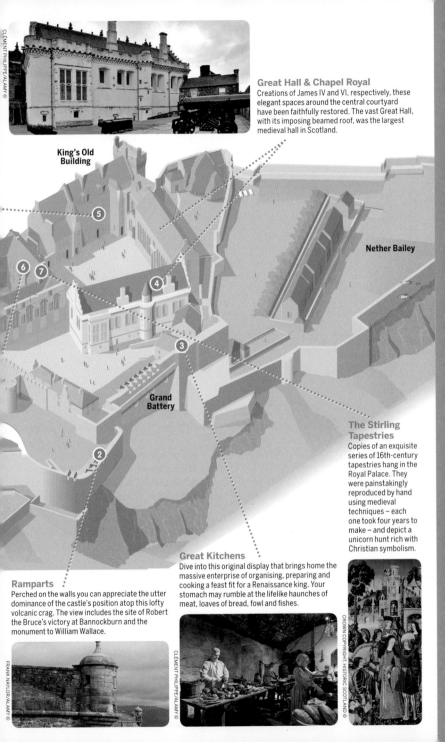

Great Hall & Chapel Royal
Creations of James IV and VI, respectively, these elegant spaces around the central courtyard have been faithfully restored. The vast Great Hall, with its imposing beamed roof, was the largest medieval hall in Scotland.

King's Old Building

Nether Bailey

⑤

⑥ ⑦

④

③

Grand Battery

②

The Stirling Tapestries
Copies of an exquisite series of 16th-century tapestries hang in the Royal Palace. They were painstakingly reproduced by hand using medieval techniques – each one took four years to make – and depict a unicorn hunt rich with Christian symbolism.

Great Kitchens
Dive into this original display that brings home the massive enterprise of organising, preparing and cooking a feast fit for a Renaissance king. Your stomach may rumble at the lifelike haunches of meat, loaves of bread, fowl and fishes.

Ramparts
Perched on the walls you can appreciate the utter dominance of the castle's position atop this lofty volcanic crag. The view includes the site of Robert the Bruce's victory at Bannockburn and the monument to William Wallace.

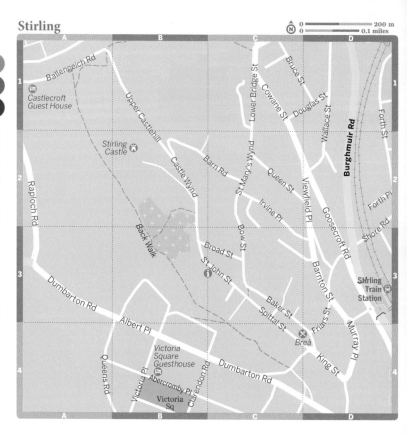

Ⓝ 0 ——————— 200 m
  0 ——————— 0.1 miles

◎ Sights

Stirling Castle
Castle

(HS; www.stirlingcastle.gov.uk; adult/child £14/7.50; ⏰9.30am-6pm Apr-Sep, to 5pm Oct-Mar) Hold Stirling and you control Scotland. This maxim has ensured that a fortress of some kind has existed here since prehistoric times. You cannot help drawing parallels with Edinburgh Castle, but many find Stirling's fortress more atmospheric – the location, architecture, historical significance and commanding views combine to make it a grand and memorable sight. It's best to visit in the afternoon; many tourists come on day trips, so you may have the castle almost to yourself by about 4pm.

National Wallace Monument
Monument

(www.nationalwallacemonument.com; adult/child £9.50/5.90; ⏰10am-5pm Apr-Jun, Sep & Oct, to 6pm Jul & Aug, 10.30am-4pm Nov-Mar) Perched high on a crag above the floodplain of the River Forth, this Victorian monument is so Gothic it deserves circling bats and croaking ravens. In the shape of a medieval tower, it commemorates William Wallace, the hero of the bid for Scottish independence depicted in the film *Braveheart*. The view from the top over the flat, green gorgeousness of the Forth Valley, including the site of Wallace's 1297 victory over the English at Stirling Bridge, almost justifies the steep entry fee.

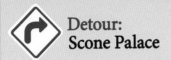

Detour:
Scone Palace

Scone Palace (www.scone-palace.co.uk; adult/child/family £10.50/7.60/33; ⊗palace & grounds 9.30am-5pm Apr-Oct, grounds only 10am-4pm Fri-Sun Nov-Mar) 'So thanks to all at once and to each one, whom we invite to see us crowned at Scone.' This line from *Macbeth* indicates the importance of Scone (pronounced 'skoon') as the coronation place of Scottish monarchs. The original palace of 1580, built on a site intrinsic to Scottish history, was rebuilt in the early 19th century as a Georgian mansion of extreme elegance and luxury. The visit takes you through a succession of sumptuous rooms filled with fine French furniture and noble portraits. Ancient kings were crowned on **Moot Hill**, now topped by a chapel next to the palace. It's said that the hill was created by bootfuls of earth, brought by nobles attending the coronations as an acknowledgement of the king's rights over their lands, although it's more likely the site of an ancient motte-and-bailey castle. Here in 838, Kenneth MacAlpin became the first king of a united Scotland and brought to Scone the **Stone of Destiny**, on which Scottish kings were ceremonially invested. In 1296 Edward I of England carted this talisman off to Westminster Abbey, where it remained for 700 years before being returned to Scotland in 1997.

Scone Palace is 2 miles north of Perth.

Bannockburn Heritage Centre
Interpretation Centre

(NTS; battleofbannockburn.com; Glasgow Rd; adult/child/family £11/8/30; ⊗10am-5.30pm Mar-Oct, to 5pm Nov-Feb) The Bannockburn Heritage Centre uses animated films, 3D imagery and interactive technology in an attempt to bring the battle to life – great fun for kids, a little naff for history buffs. The highlight is a digital projection of the battlefield onto a 3D landscape that shows the progress of the battle and the movements of infantry and cavalry.

 **Sleeping & Eating**

Castlecroft Guest House
B&B ££

(☏01786-474933; www.castlecroft-uk.com; Ballengeich Rd; s/d £50/65; P@⊗) Nestling into the hillside under the back of the castle, this hideaway feels like a rural retreat but is a short, spectacular walk from the heart of Stirling. The lounge and deck enjoy views over green fields to the nearby hills, the rooms have excellent modern bathrooms and the welcome couldn't be more hospitable. Breakfast has homemade bread, among other delights.

Victoria Square Guesthouse
B&B ££

(☏01786-473920; www.victoriasquareguesthouse.com; 12 Victoria Sq; s/d £70/105; ⊗) Though close to the centre of town, Victoria Sq is a quiet oasis with elegant Victorian buildings surrounding a verdant swath of lawn. This luxury guest house's huge rooms, bay windows and period features make it a winner – there's a great four-poster room for romantic getaways, and some bedrooms have views to the castle towering above. No children.

Breá
Cafe ££

(www.breastirling.com; 5 Baker St; mains £9-18; ⊗10am-9.30pm Tue-Sun; ⛄) ✒ Bringing a bohemian touch to central Stirling, this busy bistro has pared-back contemporary decor and a short menu showcasing carefully sourced Scottish produce, including Brewdog beers. Best in show is perhaps the pork burger with apple and black pudding – a huge thing served with homemade bread.

ℹ Information

Stirling Tourist Office (☎ 01786-475019; www.visitstirling.org; Old Town Jail, St John St; ⏰10am-5pm) Accommodation booking and internet access.

ℹ Getting There & Away

First ScotRail (www.scotrail.co.uk) has services to/from a number of destinations, including the following:

Aberdeen £32, 2¼ hours, hourly weekdays, every two hours Sunday

Edinburgh £8.30, one hour, twice hourly Monday to Saturday, hourly Sunday

Glasgow £8.60, 50 minutes, twice hourly Monday to Saturday, hourly Sunday

THE TROSSACHS

The Trossachs region has long been a favourite weekend getaway, offering outstanding natural beauty and excellent walking and cycling routes within easy reach of the southern population centres.

With thickly forested hills, romantic lochs and an increasingly interesting selection of places to stay and eat, its popularity is sure to continue, protected by its national park status.

In summer the Trossachs can be overburdened with coach tours, but many of these are day trippers – peaceful, long evenings gazing at the reflections in the nearest loch are still possible. It's worth timing your visit to avoid a weekend.

Loch Katrine

This rugged area, 6 miles north of Aberfoyle and 10 miles west of Callander, is the heart of the Trossachs. From April to October two **boats** (☎ 01877-376315; www.lochkatrine.com; Trossachs Pier; 1hr cruise adult/child £13/8; ⏰Easter-Oct) run cruises from Trossachs Pier at the eastern tip of Loch Katrine. One of these is the fabulous centenarian **steamship Sir Walter Scott**; check the website to see which boats depart when.

Left: Loch Arklet, the Trossachs; **Below:** Old Course (p328), St Andrews

(LEFT) THOMAS DICKSON/GETTY IMAGES ©; (BELOW) ANDREA PISTOLESI/GETTY IMAGES ©

LOCH LOMOND & AROUND

The 'bonnie banks' and 'bonnie braes' of Loch Lomond have long been Glasgow's rural retreat – a scenic region of hills, lochs and healthy fresh air within easy reach of Scotland's largest city. The main tourist focus is along the A82 on the loch's western shore, and at the southern end, around Balloch, which can occasionally be a nightmare of jet skis and motorboats. The eastern shore, which is followed by the West Highland Way long-distance footpath, is a little quieter.

 Activities

The main centre for boat trips is Balloch, where **Sweeney's Cruises** (☏ 01389-752376; www.sweeneyscruises.com; Balloch Rd, Balloch) offers a range of trips including a one-hour cruise to Inchmurrin and back (adult/child £8.50/5, departs hourly).

Cruise Loch Lomond (☏ 01301-702356; www.cruiselochlomond.co.uk; Tarbet/Luss;

⏱ 8.30am-5.30pm early Apr-late Oct) is based in Tarbet and offers trips to Inversnaid and Rob Roy MacGregor's Cave. You can also be dropped off at Rowardennan and picked up at Inversnaid after a 9-mile hike along the West Highland Way (£14.50).

ℹ Information

National Park Gateway Centre (☏ 01389-751035; www.lochlomondshores.com; Loch Lomond Shores, Balloch; ⏱ 10am-6pm Apr-Sep, 10am-5pm Oct-Mar; ☏) Crowded information desk with shop and cafe.

ℹ Getting There & Away

Train

Glasgow–Balloch £5.10, 45 minutes, every 30 minutes

327

Glasgow–Arrochar & Tarbet £11.40, 1¼ hours, three or four daily

Glasgow–Ardlui £14.90, 1½ hours, three or four daily, continuing to Oban and Fort William

ST ANDREWS

POP 16,900

For a small place, St Andrews made a big name for itself, firstly as a religious centre, then as Scotland's oldest university town. But its status as the home of golf has propelled it to even greater fame, and today's pilgrims arrive with a set of clubs.

The **Old Course** (www.standrews. uk; Golf Pl), the world's most famous golf course, has a striking seaside location at the western end of town. It's a thrilling experience to stroll the hallowed turf.

You'll need to book in advance to play via **St Andrews Links Trust** (01334-466666; www.standrews.org.uk). Reservations open on the first Wednesday in September the year before you wish to play. No bookings are taken for Saturdays or the month of September.

Unless you've booked months in advance, getting a tee-off time is literally a lottery; enter the ballot at the **caddie pavilion** (01334-466666; West Sands Rd) before 2pm two days before you wish to play (there's no Sunday play). Be warned that applications by ballot are normally heavily oversubscribed, and green fees are £160 in summer.

◎ Sights

St Andrews Cathedral   Ruin

(HS; www.historic-scotland.gov.uk; The Pends; adult/child £4.50/2.70, incl castle £7.20/4.40; ⊘9.30am-5.30pm Apr-Sep, to 4.30pm Oct-Mar) The ruins of this cathedral are all that's left of one of Britain's most magnificent medieval buildings. You can appreciate the scale and majesty of the edifice from the small sections that remain standing. Although founded in 1160, it was not consecrated until 1318. It stood as the focus of this important pilgrimage centre until 1559, when it was pillaged during the Reformation.

St Andrews Castle   Castle

(HS; www.historic-scotland.gov.uk; The Scores; adult/child £5.50/3.30, incl cathedral £7.20/4.40; ⊘9.30am-5.30pm Apr-Sep, to 4.30pm Oct-Mar) The town's castle is mainly in ruins, but the site itself is evocative and has dramatic coastline views. It was founded around 1200 as a fortified home for the bishop of St Andrews. After the execution of Protestant reformers in 1545, other reformers retaliated by murdering Cardinal Beaton and taking over the castle. They spent almost a year holed up, during which they and their attackers dug a complex of **siege tunnels**; you can walk (or stoop) along their damp mossy lengths.

🛏 Sleeping

Five Pilmour Place   B&B ££

(01334-478665; www.5pilmourplace.com; 5 Pilmour Pl; s/d from £75/110; @ 🛜) Just around the corner from the Old Course, this luxurious and intimate spot offers stylish, compact rooms with an eclectic range of styles as well as modern conveniences such as flatscreen TV and DVD player. The king-size beds are especially comfortable, and the lounge area is a stylish treat.

Fairways of St Andrews   B&B £££

(01334-479513; www.fairwaysofstandrews. co.uk; 8a Golf Pl; d £130-170; 🛜) Just a few paces from golf's most famous 18th green, this is more of a boutique hotel than a B&B, despite its small size. There are just three super-stylish rooms; the

St Andrews

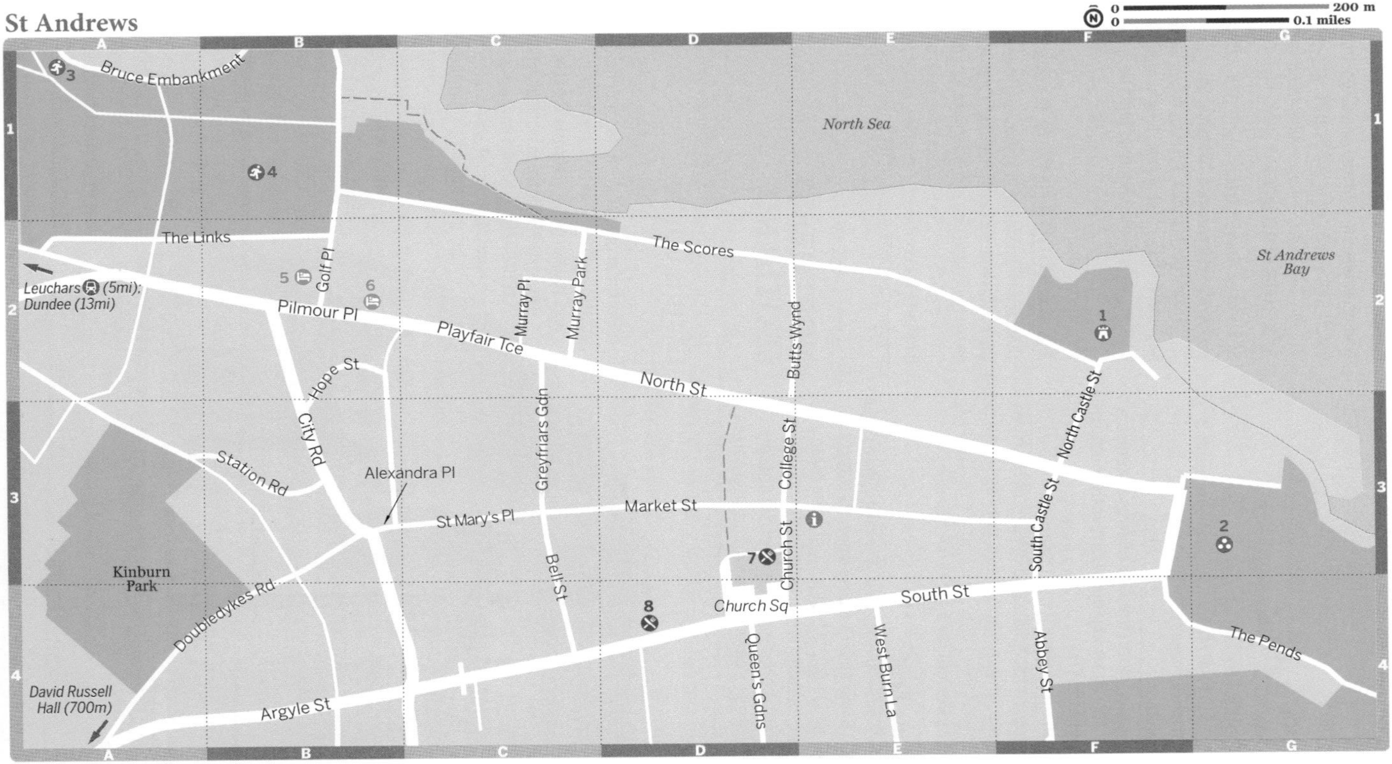

St Andrews Bay

St. Andrews Bay

North Sea

The Pends

North Castle St

South Castle St

Abbey St

South St

West Burn La

Butts Wynd

College St

Church St

Church Sq

Queen's Gdns

The Scores

North St

Market St

Bell St

Greyfriars Gdn

Murray Park

Murray Pl

Playfair Tce

St Mary's Pl

Alexandra Pl

Hope St

City Rd

Station Rd

Doubledykes Rd

Argyle St

Golf Pl

Pilmour Pl

The Links

Bruce Embankment

Kinburn Park

David Russell Hall (700m)

Leuchars (5mi); Dundee (13mi)

200 m
0.1 miles

329

best on the top floor is huge and has its own balcony with views over the Old Course.

Eating

Doll's House   Scottish ££
(☎01334-477422; www.dolls-house.co.uk; 3 Church Sq; mains £12-18; ♿) With its high-backed chairs, bright colours and creaky wooden floor, the Doll's House blends a Victorian child's bedroom with modern stylings. The result is a surprising warmth and no pretensions. The menu makes the most of local fish and other Scottish produce, and the £6.95 two-course lunch is unbeatable value. The early evening two-course deal for £11.95 isn't bad, either.

Vine Leaf   Scottish £££
(☎01334-477497; www.vineleafstandrews.co.uk; 131 South St; 2-/3-course dinner £27/30; ⏰6-10pm Tue-Sat; 🖋) Classy, comfortable and well established, the friendly Vine Leaf offers a changing menu of sumptuous Scottish seafood, game and vegetarian dishes. There's a huge selection within the set-price menu, all well presented, and an interesting, mostly old-world wine list. It's down a close off South St.

ℹ Information

St Andrews Tourist Office (☎01334-472021; www.visitstandrews.com; 70 Market St; ⏰9.15am-6pm Mon-Sat, 10am-5pm Sun Jul & Aug, shorter hourr rest of year) Helpful staff with good knowledge of St Andrews and Fife.

ℹ Getting There & Away

There is no train station in St Andrews itself, but you can take a train from Edinburgh (grab a seat on the right-hand side of the carriage for great firth views) to Leuchars (£13.50, one hour, hourly), 5 miles to the northwest. From here, buses leave regularly for St Andrews (£2.75, 10 minutes).

NORTHEAST SCOTLAND

Glamis Castle

Looking every inch the archetypal Scottish Baronial castle, with its roofline sprouting a forest of pointed turrets and battlements, **Glamis Castle** (www.glamis-castle.co.uk; adult/child £10.90/8; ⏰10am-6pm Apr-Oct, last entry 4.30pm; P ♿) claims to be the legendary setting for Shakespeare's *Macbeth* (his character is the Thane of Glamis at the start of the play). A royal residence since 1372, it is the family home of the earls of Strathmore and Kinghorne: the Queen Mother (born Elizabeth Bowes-Lyon; 1900–2002) spent her childhood at Glamis (pronounced 'glams') and Princess Margaret

Glamis Castle
IVAN VDOVIN/GETTY IMAGES ©

(the Queen's sister; 1930–2002) was born here. The one-hour guided tours depart every 15 minutes (last tour at 4.30pm, or 3.30pm in winter).

Glamis Castle is 12 miles north of Dundee.

Balmoral Castle

Eight miles west of Ballater lies **Balmoral Castle** (☏01339-742334; www.balmoral-castle.com; adult/child £11/5; ⊙10am-5pm Apr-Jul, last admission 4.30pm), the Queen's Highland holiday home, screened from the road by a thick curtain of trees. Built for Queen Victoria in 1855 as a private residence for the royal family, it kicked off the revival of the Scottish Baronial style of architecture that characterises so many of Scotland's 19th-century country houses.

The admission fee includes an interesting and well-thought-out audioguide, but the tour is very much an outdoor one through garden and grounds; as for the castle itself, only the ballroom, which displays a collection of Landseer paintings and royal silver, is open to the public. Don't expect to see the Queen's private quarters!

Balmoral is beside the A93 at Crathie and can be reached on the Aberdeen to Braemar bus.

Speyside

Rome may be built on seven hills, but **Dufftown**'s built on seven stills, say the locals. Founded in 1817 by James Duff, 4th Earl of Fife, Dufftown is 17 miles south of Elgin and lies at the heart of the Speyside whisky-distilling region. With seven working distilleries nearby, Dufftown has been dubbed Scotland's malt-whisky capital and is host to the biannual **Spirit of Speyside** (www.spiritof-speyside.com) whisky festival. Ask at the whisky museum about the **Malt Whisky Trail** (www.maltwhiskytrail.com), a self-guided tour around the local distilleries.

Local Knowledge

Speyside
BY IAN LOGAN, BRAND AMBASSADOR, CHIVAS BROTHERS

1 **THE GLENLIVET DISTILLERY**
The home of the most iconic single malt whisky in the world, the Glenlivet offers a great mix of old and new, and a chance to see how modern technology has been adapted to work alongside traditional techniques. It's at Ballindalloch, 10 miles west of Dufftown.

2 **SPEYSIDE COOPERAGE**
The Speyside Cooperage gives you a chance to watch a craft that has changed little over the centuries – the quality of the cask is one of the biggest contributing factors to the flavour of a single malt. The team here supply barrels to distilleries all over the world and share with the distillers the passion of creating the finest whiskies in the world.

3 **GORDON & MACPHAIL**
The most famous whisky shop in the world, Gordon & MacPhail in the town of Elgin, is home to some of the oldest whiskies including a 70-year-old Mortlach. The owners have played an important part in making single malt whisky what it is today, bottling these whiskies long before the distillers ever did.

4 **CORGARFF CASTLE**
The impressive and remote Corgarff Castle was once home to the redcoats whose job it was to chase down illegal distillers in the early 19th century. The castle is near Cockbridge, 30 miles south of Dufftown on the road to Ballater.

5 **GROUSE INN**
Set deep in the heart of the old smuggling country, this remote pub at Cabrach, in the hills 10 miles south of Dufftown, has nearly 250 single malts on optic with many more on display around the bar, a collection that is home to several rare and unique bottlings.

If You Like...
Whisky Distilleries

Visiting a distillery can be memorable, but only hardcore malthounds will want to go to more than two or three. Some are great to visit; others are depressingly corporate. Here are some of our favourites.

1 ABERLOUR DISTILLERY

(☎01340-881249; www.aberlour.com; tours from £14; ☺10am & 2pm daily Apr-Oct, by appointment Mon-Fri Nov-Mar) This distillery has an excellent, detailed tour with a proper tasting session. It's on the main street in Aberlour.

2 GLENFARCLAS DISTILLERY

(☎01807-500257; www.glenfarclas.co.uk; admission £5; ☺10am-4pm Mon-Fri Oct-Mar, to 5pm Mon-Fri Apr-Sep, plus to 4pm Sat Jul-Sep) Small, friendly and independent, Glenfarclas is 5 miles south of Aberlour on the Grantown road. The last tour leaves 90 minutes before closing.

3 GLENFIDDICH DISTILLERY VISITOR CENTRE

(☎01340-820373; www.glenfiddich.co.uk; admission free; ☺9.30am-4.30pm Mon-Sat, from noon Sun Easter–mid-Oct, 9.30am-4.30pm Mon-Fri mid-Oct–Easter) The Glenfiddich distillery is big and busy, but the handiest for Dufftown, and foreign languages are available. The standard tour starts with an overblown video, but it's fun, informative and free.

4 MACALLAN DISTILLERY

(☎01340-872280; www.themacallan.com; tours £15; ☺9.30am-6pm Mon-Sat Easter-Oct, 9.30am-5pm Mon-Fri Nov-Mar) Macallan makes an excellent sherry-casked malt. The 2¼-hour tours (maximum group of 10) should be prebooked. Lovely location 2 miles northwest of Craigellachie.

Five miles to the northwest, **Aberlour** (www.aboutaberlour.co.uk) – or Charlestown of Aberlour, to give it its full name – is prettier than Dufftown, straggling along the banks of the River Spey. It is famous as the home of Walkers Shortbread, and has Aberlour Distillery right on the main street. Attractions include salmon fishing, and some lovely walks along the Speyside Way.

◉ Sights

Whisky Museum Museum
(☎01340-821097; www.dufftown.co.uk; 12 Conval St; ☺1-4pm Mon-Fri May-Sep) FREE As well as housing a selection of distillery memorabilia (try saying that after a few drams), the Whisky Museum holds 'nosing and tasting evenings' in the Commercial Hotel where you can learn what to look for in a fine single malt (£10 per person; 8pm Wednesday in July and August).

🛏 Sleeping & Eating

Mash Tun B&B ££
(☎01340-881771; www.mashtun-aberlour.com; 8 Broomfield Sq; s/d from £65/100; 🛜🚹) Housed in a stone building made for a sea captain in the shape of a ship, this luxurious B&B is famous for its whisky bar – a place of pilgrimage for whisky enthusiasts – which has a collection of old and rare single malts. There's also an excellent restaurant (mains £10-20, lunch and dinner daily) that specialises in modern Scottish cuisine.

La Faisanderie Scottish £££
(☎01340-821273; The Square; mains £19-23; ☺noon-1.30pm & 6-8.30pm, closed Mon-Thu Nov-Mar) 🍽 This is a great place to eat, run by a local chef who shoots much of

Glenfiddich Distillery, Dufftown

PAUL HARRIS/GETTY IMAGES ©

his own game. The interior is decorated in French *auberge* style with a cheerful mural and pheasants hiding in every corner. The three-course early-bird dinner menu (£19.50, from 5.30pm to 7pm) won't disappoint, but you can order à la carte as well.

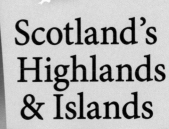

Scotland's Highlands & Islands

The Highlands are clear testimony to the sculpting power of ice and weather. From the subarctic plateau of the Cairngorms to the rocky summit of Ben Nevis, here the Scottish landscape is at its grandest, with high peaks bounded by wooded glens, deep lochs and rushing waterfalls.

Glen Coe and Fort William draw hordes of hill walkers in summer and skiers in winter, while Inverness, the Highland capital, provides urban rest and relaxation. Not far away, Loch Ness and its elusive monster add a hint of mystery.

To the west are Scotland's many off-shore islands, including major highlights such as Skye and Mull. Even further off the track, beyond the mainland to the north sits another island group, the Orkneys, where intrepid travellers can admire some of the finest prehistoric sites in the whole of Britain.

Eilean Donan Castle (p354)

Scotland's Highlands & Islands

1 Loch Ness
2 Isle of Skye
3 Isle of Mull
4 Glen Coe
5 Eilean Donan Castle

To Shetland
Islands
(see insert)

59°N

4°W
5°W
6°W

NORTH
SEA

**ORKNEY
ISLANDS**

North
Ronaldsay
Firth

The North
Sound

Northwall
Whitehall

Rapness
Balfour
Kirkwall Skaill

Birsay Rousay Mainland Burwick

Stromness
Rackwick Hoy Lyness Duncansby
Head

**John
O'Groats** **Wick**

Castletown Achavanich Lybster

Dunnet
Head
Thurso Dunbeath

Scrabster
Melvich

Bettyhill Sutherland
Mountains Kinbrace **Helmsdale**

Tongue A9 **Brora**

▲ Ben Hope
(927m)

Durness Croick Lairg Dornoch

A838 Portmahomack

Inchnadamph Moray
Firth
▲ Ben More Findhorn
Assynt Tain Lossiemouth
(998m)

Tarbet A835 **Bonar Cromarty Fort George Elgin**
Bridge
Invergordon **Culloden**
Point Dundonnell **Ullapool** Black
of Stoer **Dingwall** Isle
Garve Beauly **Inverness**
Clachtoll Croick Muir of Ord

Achiltibuie Drumchork Achnasheen A9 A96
Garrinin
Ruadh Lower A890 Aberlour Dufftown
Reidh **Gairloch** Diabaig Strathcarron

Redpoint Torridon

ATLANTIC
OCEAN

The Minch Brochel
Port of
Ness Uig A87 Portree

Port nan The Little
Gizran Minch
Stornoway Drinishader A87

Lewis Carnach
Leumrabhagh Dunvegan 2 Portree
Harris Rodel Borraig

Husinish Cladach

OUTER
HEBRIDES North
Uist
Port nan
Long Balivanich
(Baile a'Mhanaich)
Geirrinis

58°N
8°W

HIGHLANDS

Fraserburgh
A90
Pennan
Boddam
Banff
Portknockie Aberchirder Maud
Portsoy Keith
A951
A835

Shetland

20 km
10 miles

Herma
Ness
Sand
Wick
Ulsta Housay
North
Sea
**Ronas
Hill** Bard
Head
ATLANTIC
OCEAN **Lerwick**
Fitful
Head Sumburgh
Head

60°N
1°W
2°W

---

0 60 km
0 30 miles

Scotland's Highlands & Islands Highlights

Loch Ness

Stretching along the glacier-gouged trench of the Great Glen, 23-mile-long Loch Ness (p345) contains more water than all the lakes in England and Wales combined. Its peaty depths conceal the mystery of its legendary monster, and thousands flock here each year in hope of catching a glimpse.

Glen Coe

If you only have time to visit one Highland glen, make it this one. Glen Coe (p347) sums up the lonely grandeur and windswept majesty of the Scottish landscape. Catch it on a clear summer day and you'll be treated to non-stop mountain views; come in midwinter an you'll likely be stuck in a wraparound white-out. Either way, be sure to keep your camera handy. Red deer

Isle of Mull

Even without being immortalised in legend and song, Mull (p353) would still be a must-see for any visit to the Highlands. Ringed by miles of white sand and dotted with rugged hills, it's known for its stirring views and fantastic wildlife-watching – if you're lucky, you'll have the chance to spot seabirds, sea eagles or even a pod of dolphins. Common dolphin

Isle of Skye

Along with Edinburgh and Loch Ness, Skye (p355) is one of Scotland's top-three tourist destinations. The stunning scenery is the main attraction, from the jagged peaks of the Cuillin Hills and the otherworldly pinnacles and breathtaking sea cliffs of Trotternish. Come prepared for changeable weather: when it's fine it's very fine indeed, but when the mist closes in there are plenty of castles and cosy pubs to retire to. Cuillin Hills (p357)

Eilean Donan Castle

Perched on a tiny island linked to the shore by a picturesque arched bridge, Eilean Donan (p354) is perhaps the most picturesque of Scottish castles. Its image has graced everything from postcards to shortbread tins, and has appeared in many movies including *Highlander* and *The World Is Not Enough*. Despite its venerable appearance, it is actually a relatively modern restoration, dating from the early 20th century.

Scotland's Highlands & Islands' Best...

Scenic Drives

● **Loch Ness** Classic loch views from Fort Augustus and Urquhart Castle (p345)

● **Glen Coe** Brooding mountain scenery looms over a narrow glen (p347)

● **The Road to the Isles** From Fort William to Mallaig (p351)

● **Glen Etive** This beautiful glen makes an ideal detour from Glen Coe (p359)

Historic Sites

● **Urquhart Castle** Impressive medieval castle overlooking the shores of Loch Ness (p346)

● **Eilean Donan Castle** This archetypal Scottish fortress is scenically backed by sea and mountains (p354)

● **Glen Coe** Site of one of Scotland's most notorious massacres (p347)

● **Skara Brae** Wander through Britain's best-preserved ancient settlement (p361)

Outdoor Experiences

● **Conquering Ben Nevis** The Scottish hike to top them all (p350)

● **Watching wildlife on Mull** Spot Mull's wildlife, either onshore or by boat (p354)

● **Cruising Loch Ness** Keep your eyes peeled for Nessie (p347)

● **Walking on Skye** Strap on your boots and explore Skye's hilly scenery (p355)

Need to Know

Islands

○ **Mull** This large island boasts mountains, beaches, castles and even a railway (p353)

○ **Skye** Sail over the sea to the best known of all Scottish islands (p355)

○ **Iona** Tiny sacred island with a spiritual atmosphere (p356)

○ **Orkney Islands** Rocky archipelago off Scotland's north coast, with many prehistoric remains (p360)

ADVANCE PLANNING

○ **One month before** Book accommodation if visiting in summer, especially for popular spots such as Mull and Skye.

○ **Two weeks before** If travelling by car, make reservations for any ferry crossings – as early as possible in summer.

○ **One week before** Make bookings for wildlife-spotting boat trips.

RESOURCES

○ **Highlands** (www.visithighlands.com)

○ **Loch Ness** (www.visitlochness.com)

○ **Fort William** (www.visit-fortwilliam.co.uk)

○ **Skye** (www.skye.co.uk)

○ **Caledonian Macbrayne** (www.calmac.co.uk)

GETTING AROUND

○ **Bus** Run between major towns, but travel times can be long. Most islands have a limited bus network.

○ **Car** The best way to explore the more remote glens and islands – but car ferry services to the more popular islands are best booked at least a few days in advance.

○ **Ferry** Frequent services from Oban to Mull year-round; for Skye there's a ferry from Mallaig and a bridge at Kyle of Lochalsh.

○ **Train** Scenic lines from Edinburgh or Glasgow to Inverness, Fort William, Oban, Mallaig or Kyle of Lochalsh.

BE FOREWARNED

○ **Midges** These tiny biting flies are a pest from June to September, especially in still weather around dawn and dusk; bring insect repellent and wear long-sleeved clothing.

○ **Weather** Always unpredictable on the west coast; be prepared for wet and windy days, even in the middle of summer.

Left: Ring of Brodgar (p361); **Above:** Sheep grazing on the Isle of Skye (p355)
(LEFT) BILL HEINSOHN/GETTY IMAGES ©; (ABOVE) JAMES P. BLAIR/ GETTY IMAGES ©

Scotland's Highlands & Islands Itineraries

The three-day trip takes in some big-name locations,
while the five-day trip combines highlands with islands.
The routes intersect at Fort William.

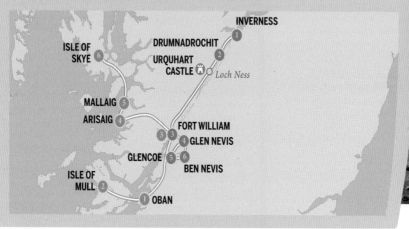

INVERNESS TO BEN NEVIS
SCOTTISH ICONS

Start your tour in ❶ **Inverness**, capital of the Highlands, then head south on the A82 along the west bank of legendary Loch Ness. Stop at ❷ **Drumnadrochit** to visit the monster exhibitions and Urquhart Castle, and perhaps take a cruise on the loch.

On day two, continue south via ❸ **Fort William**, the self-proclaimed 'Outdoor Capital of the UK'. If the weather is good, get your boots on and go for a hike; if not, hop in the car and explore a few of the nearby

glens, such as ❹ **Glen Nevis** or ❺ **Glen Coe** a bit further afield.

On day three, hopefully the weather will be good enough for you to tackle Scotland's highest mountain, ❻ **Ben Nevis**; if not, you could get an early start and head down the scenic coast road to Oban, the pretty coastal village which marks the departure point for ferries to the Isle of Mull.

OBAN TO SKYE
HIGHLAND & ISLAND HOPPING

5 DAYS

Our longer tour begins in ❶ **Oban**, the 'gateway to the isles'. Take a day trip out to the smaller islands of Lismore or Kerrera, and in the evening walk up to McCaig's Tower.

The second day begins with the ferry ride across to the ❷ **Isle of Mull**. Spend a day or two here, touring the island; options include the holy islet of Iona and the colourful island capital of Tobermory. The roads are narrow and the scenery stunning at every turn – two good reasons for allowing plenty of time.

Return to Oban and travel up the A828 towards ❸ **Fort William**. Turn west along the A830, the famous 'Road to the Isles'. Leave the main road at ❹ **Arisaig**, signposted 'Alternative Coastal Route' for the best views. From the fishing harbour of ❺ **Mallaig** take the ferry across to Armadale on the ❻ **Isle of Skye**.

Spend the final day or two exploring Skye. Follow the scenic roads to Portree, the capital, via a stop at Sligachan for views of the Cuillin ridge. Return to the mainland via the Skye Bridge.

Sgurr Nan Gillean, Cuillin Hills, Isle of Skye (p355)
CHRIS HEPBURN/GETTY IMAGES ©

Discover Scotland's Highlands & Islands

At a Glance

○ **Inverness** (p344) The main launchpad for the Highlands.

○ **Loch Ness** (p345) Home to the mysterious monster – perhaps.

○ **Glen Coe** (p347) The classic Scottish valley, overlooked by towering peaks.

○ **Fort William** (p349) Dubbed the outdoor capital of the UK.

○ **Isle of Skye** (p355) Misty, mountainous island of legend and song.

INVERNESS

POP 61,235

Inverness, one of the fastest-growing towns in Britain, is the capital of the Highlands. It's a transport hub and jumping-off point for the central, western and northern Highlands, the Moray Firth coast and the Great Glen.

◉ Sights

Ness Islands Park

The main attraction in Inverness is a leisurely stroll along the river to the Ness Islands. Planted with mature Scots pine, fir, beech and sycamore, and linked to the river banks and each other by elegant Victorian footbridges, the islands make an appealing picnic spot. They're a 20-minute walk south of the castle; head upstream on either side of the river (the start of the Great Glen Way), and return on the opposite bank.

On the way you'll pass the red-sandstone towers of **St Andrew's Cathedral** (11 Ardross St), dating from 1869, and the modern **Eden Court Theatre** (☎01463-234234; www.eden-court.co.uk; Bishop's Rd), which hosts regular art exhibits, both on the west bank.

Tours

Jacobite Cruises Boat Tour

(☎01463-233999; www.jacobite.co.uk; Glenurquhart Rd; adult/child £31.50/25; ☉daily Apr-Sep) Boats depart from Tomnahurich Bridge at 2pm for a 1½-hour 'Discovery' cruise along Loch Ness, followed by a visit to Urquhart Castle and a return to Inverness by coach. You can buy tickets at the tourist office and catch a free minibus to the boat.

Old Man of Storr, Trotternish Peninsula (p359)
DAVID C TOMLINSON/GETTY IMAGES ©

Other cruises and combined cruise/coach tours, from one to 6½ hours, are also available.

Sleeping

Trafford Bank
B&B ££

(☏01463-241414; www.traffordbankguesthouse.co.uk; 96 Fairfield Rd; d £120-132; P ☏) Lots of word-of-mouth rave reviews for this elegant Victorian villa, which was once home to a bishop, just a mitre-toss from the Caledonian Canal and 10 minutes' walk west from the city centre. The luxurious rooms include fresh flowers and fruit, bathrobes and fluffy towels – ask for the Tartan Room, which has a wrought-iron king-size bed and Victorian roll-top bath.

Rocpool Reserve
Boutique Hotel £££

(☏01463-240089; www.rocpool.com; Culduthel Rd; s/d from £185/220; P ☏) Boutique chic meets the Highlands in this slick and sophisticated little hotel, where an elegant Georgian exterior conceals an oasis of contemporary cool. A gleaming white entrance hall lined with red carpet and contemporary art leads to designer rooms in shades of chocolate, cream and gold; a restaurant by Albert Roux completes the luxury package.

Eating

Café 1
Bistro ££

(☏01463-226200; www.cafe1.net; 75 Castle St; mains £10-24; ☺noon-2.30pm & 5-9.30pm Mon-Fri, noon-2.30pm & 6-9.30pm Sat) 🗲 Café 1 is a friendly and appealing bistro with candlelit tables amid elegant blonde-wood and wrought-iron decor. There is an international menu based on quality Scottish produce, from Aberdeen Angus steaks to crisp pan-fried sea bass and meltingly tender pork belly. The set lunch menu (two courses for £8) is served noon to 2.30pm Monday to Saturday.

Joy of Taste
British ££

(☏01463-241459; www.thejoyoftaste.co.uk; 25 Church St; mains £15-19; ☺noon-3pm & 5.30-10.30pm Mon-Sat, 5.30-9.30pm Sun) 🗲 Here's a novel concept – a restaurant run by a head chef and 25 volunteers who work a shift a week just for 'the love of creating a beautiful restaurant' (plus a share of the profits). And a very good job they have made of it, with a menu of classic British cuisine and a growing fan club of satisfied customers.

ℹ Information

Inverness Tourist Office (☏01463-252401; www.visithighlands.com; Castle Wynd; internet access per 20min £1; ☺9am-6pm Mon-Sat, 9.30am-5pm Sun Jul & Aug, 9am-5pm Mon-Sat, 10am-4pm Sun Jun, Sep & Oct, 9am-5pm Mon-Sat Apr & May) Bureau de change and accommodation booking service; also sells tickets for tours and cruises. Opening hours limited November to March.

ℹ Getting There & Away

Air

Inverness Airport (INV; ☏01667-464000; www.hial.co.uk/inverness-airport) At Dalcross, 10 miles east of the city, off the A96 towards Aberdeen. There are scheduled flights to Amsterdam, London, Manchester, Orkney, Shetland and the Outer Hebrides, as well as other places in the British Isles.

Train

Edinburgh £41, 3½ hours, eight daily

Glasgow £41, 3½ hours, eight daily

Kyle of Lochalsh £22, 2½ hours, four daily Monday to Saturday, two Sunday; one of Britain's great scenic train journeys

London £100, eight to nine hours, one daily direct; others require a change at Edinburgh

LOCH NESS

Deep, dark and narrow, Loch Ness stretches for 23 miles between Inverness and Fort Augustus. Its bitterly cold waters have been extensively explored in search of Nessie, the elusive Loch Ness monster, but most visitors see her only in cardboard-cutout form at the monster exhibitions. A complete circuit of the loch is about 70 miles – travel anticlockwise for the best views.

The Legend of Nessie

Highland folklore is filled with tales of strange creatures living in lochs and rivers, notably the kelpie (water horse) that lures unwary travellers to their doom. The use of the term 'monster', however, is a relatively recent phenomenon whose origins lie in an article published in the *Inverness Courier* on 2 May 1933, entitled 'Strange Spectacle on Loch Ness'.

The article recounted the sighting of a disturbance in the loch by Mrs Aldie Mackay and her husband: 'There the creature disported itself, rolling and plunging for fully a minute, its body resembling that of a whale, and the water cascading and churning like a simmering cauldron'.

In December 1933 the *Daily Mail* sent Marmaduke Wetherall, a film director and big-game hunter, to Loch Ness to track down the beast. Within days he found 'reptilian' footprints in the shoreline mud (soon revealed to have been made with a stuffed hippopotamus foot, possibly an umbrella stand). Then in April 1934 came the famous 'long-necked monster' photograph taken by the seemingly reputable Harley St surgeon Colonel Kenneth Wilson. The press went mad and the rest, as they say, is history.

In 1994, however, Christian Spurling – Wetherall's stepson, by then 90 years old – revealed that the most famous photo of Nessie ever taken was in fact a hoax, perpetrated by his stepfather with Wilson's help.

Drumnadrochit

POP 1100

Seized by monster madness, its gift shops bulging with Nessie cuddly toys, Drumnadrochit is a hotbed of beastie fever, with two monster exhibitions battling it out for the tourist dollar.

⊙ Sights & Activities

Urquhart Castle　　　　　Castle

(HS; ☑01456-450551; adult/child £7.90/4.80; ◷9.30am-6pm Apr-Sep, to 5pm Oct, to 4.30pm Nov-Mar; P) Commanding a brilliant location 1.5 miles east of Drumnadrochit, with outstanding views (on a clear day), Urquhart Castle is a popular Nessie-watching hotspot. A huge visitor centre (most of which is beneath ground level) includes a video theatre (with a dramatic 'unveiling' of the castle at the end of the film) and displays of medieval items discovered in the castle.

The castle was repeatedly sacked and rebuilt (and sacked and rebuilt) over the centuries; in 1692 it was blown up to prevent the Jacobites from using it. The five-storey tower house at the northern point is the most impressive remaining fragment and offers wonderful views across the water. The site includes a huge gift shop and a restaurant, and is often very crowded in summer.

**Loch Ness Centre
& Exhibition**　　Interpretation Centre

(☑01456-450573; www.lochness.com; adult/child £7.45/4.95; ◷9.30am-6pm Jul & Aug, to 5pm Easter-Jun, Sep & Oct, 10am-3.30pm Nov-Easter; P) This Nessie-themed attraction adopts a scientific approach that allows you to weigh the evidence for yourself. Exhibits include the original equipment – sonar survey vessels, miniature submarines, cameras and sediment coring tools – used in various monster hunts, as well as original photographs and film footage of sightings. You'll find out about hoaxes and optical illusions, as well as learning a lot about the ecology of Loch Ness – is there enough food in the loch to support even one 'monster', let alone a breeding population?

Nessie Hunter
Boat Tour

(📞01456-450395; www.lochness-cruises.com; adult/child £15/10; 🕐Easter-Oct) One-hour monster-hunting cruises, complete with sonar and underwater cameras. Cruises depart from Drumnadrochit hourly (except 1pm) from 9am to 6pm daily.

 ## Sleeping & Eating

Loch Ness Inn
Inn ££

(📞01456-450991; www.staylochness.co.uk; Lewiston; d/f £90/120; P🅿🛜🧺) The Loch Ness Inn ticks all the weary traveller's boxes, with comfortable bedrooms (the family suite sleeps two adults and two children), a cosy bar pouring real ales from the Cairngorm and Isle of Skye breweries, and a rustic restaurant (mains £9 to £19) serving hearty, wholesome fare such as whisky-flambéed haggis, and roast rump of Scottish lamb.

Drumbuie Farm
B&B ££

(📞01456-450634; www.loch-ness-farm.co.uk; Drumnadrochit; s/d from £44/68; P) Drumbuie is a B&B in a modern house on a working farm – the surrounding fields are full of sheep and highland cattle – with views over Urquhart Castle and Loch Ness. Walkers and cyclists are welcome.

ℹ Getting There & Away

Scottish Citylink and Stagecoach buses from Inverness to Fort William run along the shores of Loch Ness (six to eight daily, five on Sunday); those headed for Skye turn off at Invermoriston. There are bus stops at Drumnadrochit (£3.20, 30 minutes) and Urquhart Castle (£3.50, 35 minutes).

GLEN COE

Scotland's most famous glen is also one of the grandest and, in bad weather, the grimmest. The southern side is dominated by three massive, brooding spurs, known as the **Three Sisters**, while the northern side is enclosed by the continuous steep wall of the knife-edged

Loch Ness

RECOMMENDATIONS FROM ADRIAN SHINE, LEADER OF THE LOCH NESS PROJECT

1 LOCH NESS EXHIBITION CENTRE

I designed this exhibition myself, presenting the results of eight decades of research. The collection has everything from one-man submarines to the ROSETTA apparatus that opened the 10,000-year-old time capsule concealed within the loch's sediment layers. The exhibition does not have all the answers and it will certainly not try to sell you a monster. Instead, it places the mystery in its proper context, which is the environment of Loch Ness.

2 URQUHART CASTLE

If, having learned some of the inner secrets of the loch, you want to see it through new eyes, you cannot do better than visit Urquhart Castle. Perched on a rocky promontory jutting into Loch Ness, its exhibits recount the castle's history from a vitrified Pictish fort to its role in the Scottish Wars of Independence. The view from the Grant Tower is truly breathtaking.

3 FORT AUGUSTUS LOCKS

At the southern end of the loch there is a flight of locks on the Caledonian Canal, built by the great engineer Thomas Telford. It is always interesting to watch vessels being worked up this 'staircase' of water. British Waterways has a fascinating exhibition halfway up.

4 CRUISING THE LOCH

Venturing onto the water puts the seemingly tiny trunk road and Urquhart Castle into a new perspective. The Deepscan cruise boat runs from the Loch Ness Centre; I use this boat for my research and the skipper will tell you about his experiences. There are other cruise boats operating from Drumnadrochit, and the larger Jacobite vessels depart from Inverness.

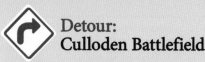

Detour:
Culloden Battlefield

The Battle of Culloden in 1746, the last pitched battle ever fought on British soil, saw the defeat of Bonnie Prince Charlie and the end of the Jacobite dream when 1200 Highlanders were slaughtered by government forces in a 68-minute rout. The duke of Cumberland, son of the reigning king George II and leader of the Hanoverian army, earned the nickname 'Butcher' for his brutal treatment of the defeated Scottish forces. The battle sounded the death knell for the old clan system, and the horrors of the Clearances soon followed. The sombre moor where the conflict took place has scarcely changed in the ensuing 260 years.

The impressive new **visitor centre** (NTS; www.nts.org.uk/culloden; adult/child £11/8.50; ☉9am-6pm Jun-Aug, to 5.30pm Apr, May, Sep & Oct, 10am-4pm Nov-Mar) presents detailed information about the battle, including the lead-up and the aftermath, with perspectives from both sides. An innovative film puts you on the battlefield in the middle of the mayhem, and a wealth of other audio presentations must have kept Inverness' entire acting community in business for weeks. The admission fee includes an audioguide for a self-guided tour of the battlefield itself.

Culloden is 6 miles east of Inverness. Bus 1 runs from Queensgate in Inverness to Culloden battlefield (30 minutes, hourly).

Aonach Eagach ridge. The main road threads its way through the middle of all this grandeur, past deep gorges and crashing waterfalls, to the more pastoral lower reaches of the glen around Loch Achtriochtan and Glencoe village. Glencoe was written into the history books in 1692 when the resident MacDonalds were murdered by Campbell soldiers in what became known as the Glencoe Massacre.

👁 Sights

Glencoe Folk Museum   Museum
(☎01855-811664; www.glencoemuseum.com; adult/child £3/free; ☉10am-4.30pm Mon-Sat Easter-Oct) This small, thatched museum houses a varied collection of military memorabilia, farm equipment, and tools of the woodworking, blacksmithing and slate-quarrying trades.

Glencoe Visitor
Centre   Interpretation Centre
(NTS; ☎01855-811307; www.glencoe-nts.org.uk; adult/child £6.25/5; ☉9.30am-5.30pm Easter-Oct, 10am-4pm Thu-Sun Nov-Easter; P) The

centre provides comprehensive information on the geological, environmental and cultural history of Glencoe via high-tech interactive and audiovisual displays, charts the history of mountaineering in the glen, and tells the story of the Glencoe Massacre in all its gory detail. It's 1.5 miles east of Glencoe village.

🛏 Sleeping & Eating

Clachaig Inn   Hotel ££
(☎01855-811252; www.clachaig.com; r per person from £51; P 🛜 ♿) The Clachaig has long been a favourite haunt of hill walkers and climbers. As well as comfortable en suite accommodation, there's a wood-panelled lounge bar with lots of sofas and armchairs, mountaineering photos, and climbing magazines to leaf through.

Glencoe Café   Cafe £
(☎01855-811168; www.glencoecafe.com; mains £4-8; ☉10am-4pm, to 5pm May-Sep, closed Nov) This friendly cafe is the hub of Glencoe village, serving breakfast fry-ups till 11.30am (including vegetarian versions),

light lunches based around local produce (think Cullen skink, smoked salmon quiche, venison burgers), and the best cappuccino in the glen.

ℹ️ Getting There & Away

Scottish Citylink (📞0871 266 3333; www. citylink.co.uk) buses run between Fort William and Glencoe (£7.80, 30 minutes, eight daily) and from Glencoe to Glasgow (£21, 2½ hours, eight daily). Buses stop at Glencoe village, Glencoe Visitor Centre and Glencoe Mountain Resort.

Stagecoach (www.stagecoachbus.com) bus 44 links Glencoe village with Fort William (£3.70, 35 minutes, hourly Monday to Saturday, three on Sunday) and Kinlochleven (£2, 25 minutes).

FORT WILLIAM

POP 9900

Basking on the shores of Loch Linnhe amid magnificent mountain scenery, Fort William has one of the most enviable settings in the whole of Scotland. If it wasn't for the busy dual carriageway crammed between the town centre and the loch, and one of the highest rainfall records in the country, it would be almost idyllic.

◎ Sights

Jacobite Steam Train   Heritage Railway

(📞0844 850 4685; www.westcoastrailways. co.uk; day return adult/child £34/19; ⏱daily Jul & Aug, Mon-Fri mid-May–Jun & Sep-Oct) The Jacobite Steam Train, hauled by a former LNER K1 or LMS Class 5MT locomotive, travels the scenic two-hour run between Fort William and Mallaig. Classed as one of the great railway journeys of the world, the route crosses the historic Glenfinnan Viaduct, made famous in the Harry Potter films – the Jacobite's owners supplied the steam locomotive and rolling stock used in the film.

Trains depart from Fort William train station in the morning and return from Mallaig in the afternoon. There's a brief stop at Glenfinnan station, and you get 1½ hours in Mallaig.

West Highland Museum   Museum

(📞01397-702169; www.westhighlandmuseum. org.uk; Cameron Sq; ⏱10am-5pm Mon-Sat Apr-Oct, to 4pm Mar & Nov-Dec, closed Jan & Feb) **FREE** This small but fascinating museum is packed with all manner of Highland

Ben Nevis (p350) and the Caledonian Canal

BRIAN LAWRENCE/GETTY IMAGES ©

Climbing Ben Nevis

As the highest peak in the British Isles, Ben Nevis (1344m) attracts many would-be hikers who would not normally think of climbing a Scottish mountain – a staggering (often literally) 100,000 people reach the summit each year.

Although anyone who is reasonably fit should have no problem climbing Ben Nevis on a fine summer's day, an ascent should not be undertaken lightly. Every year people have to be rescued from the mountain. You will need proper walking boots (the path is rough and stony, and there may be snow on the summit), warm clothing, waterproofs, a map and compass, and plenty of food and water. And don't forget to check the weather forecast (see www.bennevisweather.co.uk).

There are three possible starting points for the tourist track ascent – Achintee Farm; the footbridge at Glen Nevis SYHA; and, if you have a car, the car park at Glen Nevis Visitor Centre. The total distance to the summit and back is 8 miles; allow at least four or five hours to reach the top, and another 2½ to three hours for the descent.

---

memorabilia. Look out for the secret portrait of Bonnie Prince Charlie – after the Jacobite rebellions all things Highland were banned, including pictures of the exiled leader, and this tiny painting looks like nothing more than a smear of paint until viewed in a cylindrical mirror, which reflects a credible likeness of the prince.

Sleeping

Grange
B&B ££

(01397-705516; www.grangefortwilliam.com; Grange Rd; r per person £65-70; P) An exceptional 19th-century villa set in its own landscaped grounds, the Grange is crammed with antiques and fitted with log fires, chaise longues and Victorian roll-top baths. The Turret Room, with its window seat in the turret overlooking Loch Linnhe, is our favourite. It's 500m southwest of the town centre. No children.

Lime Tree
Hotel ££

(01397-701806; www.limetreefortwilliam. co.uk; Achintore Rd; s/d from £100/110; P) Much more interesting than your average guesthouse, this former Victorian manse overlooking Loch Linnhe is an 'art gallery with rooms', decorated throughout with

the artist-owner's atmospheric Highland landscapes. Foodies rave about the restaurant, and the gallery space – a triumph of sensitive design – stages everything from serious exhibitions (works by David Hockney and Andy Goldsworthy have appeared) to folk concerts.

Eating

Crannog Seafood Restaurant
Seafood ££

(01397-705589; www.crannog.net; Town Pier; mains £15-20, 2-course lunches £15; noon-2.30pm & 6-9pm) The Crannog wins the prize for best location in town – perched on the Town Pier, giving window-table diners an uninterrupted view down Loch Linnhe. Informal and unfussy, it specialises in fresh local fish – there are three or four daily fish specials plus the main menu – though there are lamb, venison and vegetarian dishes, too. Two-course lunch £15.

Lime Tree
Scottish £££

(01397-701806; www.limetreefortwilliam. co.uk; Achintore Rd; mains £14-23; 6.30-9.30pm) Fort William is not over-endowed with great places to eat, but the restaurant at this small hotel and art gallery has put the UK's Outdoor Capital on the gastronomic map. The chef turns out delicious dishes built around fresh Scottish produce, ranging from partan bree (crab soup) to roast cod to venison sausage.

ℹ Information

Fort William Tourist Office (☎01397-703781; www.visithighlands.com; 15 High St; internet per 20min £1; ☺9am-6pm Mon-Sat, 10am-5pm Sun Apr-Sep, limited hours Oct-Mar) Internet access.

ℹ Getting There & Away

Train

The spectacular West Highland line runs from Glasgow to Mallaig via Fort William. The overnight **Caledonian Sleeper** (www.scotrail.co.uk/sleeper) service connects Fort William and London Euston (from £113 sharing a twin-berth cabin, 13 hours).

Edinburgh £42, five hours; change at Glasgow's Queen St station, three daily, two on Sunday

Glasgow £28, 3¾ hours, three daily, two on Sunday

Mallaig £11.80, 1½ hours, four daily, three on Sunday

THE ROAD TO THE ISLES

The 46-mile A830 road from Fort William to Mallaig is traditionally known as the Road to the Isles, as it leads to the jumping-off point for ferries to the Small Isles and Skye, itself a stepping stone to the Outer Hebrides. This is a region steeped in Jacobite history, having witnessed both the beginning and the end of Bonnie Prince Charlie's doomed attempt to regain the British throne in 1745–46; the **Glenfinnan Visitor Centre** (NTS; adult/child £3.50/2.50; ☺9.30am-5pm Jul & Aug, 10am-5pm Easter-Jun, Sep & Oct) at Loch Shiel tells the whole story.

The final section of this scenic route, between Arisaig and Mallaig, has been upgraded to a fast straight road. Unless you're in a hurry, opt instead for the more scenic old road (signposted Alternative Coastal Route).

OBAN

POP 8600

Oban, main gateway to many of the Hebridean islands, is a peaceful waterfront town on a delightful bay, with sweeping views to Kerrera and Mull. OK, that first bit about peaceful is true only in winter; in summer the town centre is jammed with traffic and crowded with holiday-makers and travellers headed for the islands. But the setting is still lovely, and Oban's brilliant seafood restaurants are marvellous places to be as the sun sets over the bay.

🛏 Sleeping

Old Manse Guest House B&B ££ (☎01631-564886; www.obanguesthouse.co.uk; Dalriach Rd; s/d £65/90; Ⓟ🛜♿) Set on the hillside above town, this commands

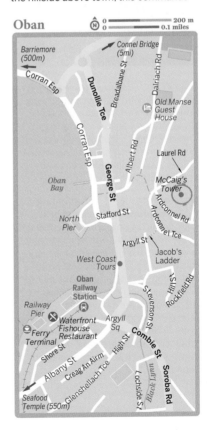

Oban

magnificent views over to Kerrera and Mull. It's run with genuine enthusiasm, and the owners are constantly adding thoughtful new features to the bright, cheerful rooms – think binoculars, DVDs, poetry, corkscrews and tartan hot water bottles – and breakfast menus, with special diets catered for.

Barriemore
Guesthouse ££

(01631-566356; www.barriemore-hotel. co.uk; Corran Esplanade; s from £70, d £99-119; Mar-Nov; P) With a grand location overlooking the entrance to Oban Bay, this offers top-notch hospitality with tartan carpets on the stairs and plump Loch Fyne kippers on the breakfast menu. Rooms are all spacious, recently refurbished and full of features. The front ones – pricier but enormous – have fabulous vistas; there's also a great family suite up the back and solicitous service.

Eating

Waterfront Fishhouse Restaurant
Seafood ££

(01631-563110; www.waterfrontoban.co.uk; Railway Pier; mains £12-20; noon-2.15pm & 5.30-9.30pm Sun-Fri, noon-9.30pm Sat;) Housed on the top floor of a converted seamen's mission, the Waterfront's stylish, unfussy decor in burgundy and brown, with dark wooden furniture, does little to distract from the superb seafood freshly landed at the quay just a few metres away. The menu ranges from classic haddock and chips to fresh oysters, scallops and langoustines. Best to book for dinner.

Seafood Temple
Seafood £££

(01631-566000; www.obanseafood.com; Gallanach Rd; mains £16-25; 6.15-8.30pm Apr-Sep, 6.15-8.30pm Wed-Sat Oct-Dec, Feb & Mar) Locally sourced seafood is the god that's worshipped at this tiny temple – a former park pavilion with glorious views

over the bay. Oban's smallest restaurant serves up whole lobster cooked to order, baked crab, plump langoustines, and a seafood platter (£75 for two), which offers a taste of everything. Dinner is in two sittings, at 6.15pm and 8.30pm; bookings essential.

ⓘ Getting There & Away

Boat

CalMac (☏0800 066 5000; www.calmac.co.uk) ferries link Oban with the islands of Mull, Coll, Tiree, Lismore, Colonsay, Barra and Lochboisdale (South Uist).

Train

Oban is at the terminus of a scenic route that branches off the West Highland line at Crianlarich. The train isn't much use for travelling north – to reach Fort William requires a long detour (3¾ hours). Take the bus instead.

Glasgow £22, three hours, three daily

ISLE OF MULL

POP 2600

From the rugged ridges of Ben More and the black basalt crags of Burg to the blinding white sand, rose-pink granite and emerald waters that fringe the Ross, Mull can lay claim to some of the finest and most varied scenery in the Inner Hebrides. Noble birds of prey soar over mountain and coast, while the western waters provide good whale-watching. Add a lovely waterfront 'capital', an impressive castle, the sacred island of Iona and easy access from Oban, and you can see why it's sometimes impossible to find a spare bed on the island.

👉 Tours

West Coast Tours   Coach Tour
(☏01631-566809; www.westcoasttours.co.uk; 1 Queens Park Pl; ☺Apr-Oct) Offers a Three Isles day trip (adult/child £60/30, 10

353

MACIEJ NOSKOWSKI/GETTY IMAGES ©

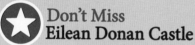

Don't Miss
Eilean Donan Castle

Photogenically sited at the entrance to Loch Duich, near Dornie village, **Eilean Donan Castle** (☎01599-555202; www.eileandonancastle.com; adult/child/family £6.50/5.50/16; ⏲10am-6pm Feb-Dec, from 9am Jul & Aug) is one of Scotland's most evocative castles, and must be represented in millions of photo albums. It's on an offshore islet, magically linked to the mainland by an elegant, stone-arched bridge. Keep an eye out for the photos of castle scenes from the movie *Highlander*. There's also a sword used at the battle of Culloden in 1746. The castle was ruined in 1719 after Spanish Jacobite forces were defeated at the Battle of Glenshiel, and it was rebuilt between 1912 and 1932.

Citylink buses from Fort William and Inverness to Portree will stop at the castle.

hours, daily) from Oban that visits Mull, Iona and Staffa. The crossing to Staffa is weather dependent. Without Staffa, the trip is £40/20 and takes eight hours. Also runs various trips on Mull.

Mull Wildlife Expeditions   Wildlife Watching
(☎01688-500121; www.scotlandwildlife.com; Ulva Ferry) Full-day Land Rover tours of the island with the chance of spotting red deer, golden eagles, peregrine falcons, white-tailed sea eagles, hen harriers, otters and perhaps dolphins and porpoises. Cost includes pick-up from

accommodation or ferry, picnic lunch and binoculars. Can be a day trip from Oban.

Sea Life Surveys   Wildlife Watching
(☎01688-302916; www.sealifesurveys.com; Ledaig) Whale-watching trips head from Tobermory harbour to the waters north and west of Mull. An all-day whale-watch gives up to seven hours at sea (£80), and has a 95% success rate for sightings. The four-hour Wildlife Adventure cruise (adult/child £50/40) is better for young kids. Shorter seal-spotting excursions are also available.

 Sleeping & Eating

Tobermory has the best choice of accommodation.

Sonas House
B&B ££

(☏01688-302304; www.sonashouse.co.uk; The Fairways, Erray Rd; s/d £110/125, apt from £90; P 🛜 🏊) Here's a first – a B&B with a heated, indoor 10m swimming pool! Sonas is a large, modern house – follow signs to the golf course – offering luxury B&B in a beautiful setting with superb views over Tobermory Bay; ask for the 'Blue Poppy' bedroom, which has its own balcony. There's also a self-contained studio apartment with double bed.

Highland Cottage
Hotel £££

(☏01688-302030; www.highlandcottage.co.uk; Breadalbane St; d £150-165; ⌚Apr–mid-Oct; P 🛜 🐾) Antique furniture, four-poster beds, embroidered bedspreads, fresh flowers and candlelight lend this small hotel (only six rooms) an appealingly old-fashioned cottage atmosphere, but with all mod cons including cable TV, full-size baths and room service. There's also an excellent restaurant here (dinner £39.50).

Café Fish
Seafood ££

(☏01688-301253; www.thecafefish.com; The Pier; mains £13-24; ⌚11am-3pm & 5.30-9.30pm mid-Mar–Oct) Seafood doesn't come much fresher than that served at this warm and welcoming little restaurant overlooking Tobermory harbour – as its motto says, 'The only thing frozen here is the fisherman'! Langoustines and squat lobsters go straight from boat to kitchen to join rich Tuscan-style seafood stew, fat scallops, fish pie and catch-of-the-day on the daily-changing menu, where confident use of Asian ingredients adds an extra dimension.

❶ Getting There & Away

Three **CalMac** (www.calmac.co.uk) car ferries link Mull with the mainland.

Oban to Craignure (passenger/car £5.55/49.50, 40 minutes, every two hours) The busiest route – booking advised for cars.

Lochaline to Fishnish (£3.30/14.45, 15 minutes, at least hourly) On Mull's east coast.

Tobermory to Kilchoan (£5.30/27.50, 35 minutes, seven daily Monday to Saturday, plus five Sunday May to August) Links to the Ardnamurchan peninsula.

ISLE OF SKYE

POP 10,000

The Isle of Skye (an t-Eilean Sgiathanach in Gaelic) takes its name from the old Norse *sky-a*, meaning 'cloud island', a Viking reference to the often mist-enshrouded Cuillin Hills. It's the second-largest of Scotland's islands, a 50-mile-long patchwork of velvet moors, jagged mountains, sparkling lochs and towering sea cliffs.

❶ Information

Portree Tourist Office (☏01478-612137; Bayfield Rd, Portree; internet per 20min £1; ⌚9am-6pm Mon-Sat, 10am-4pm Sun Jun-Aug, 9am-5pm Mon-Fri, 10am-4pm Sat Apr, May & Sep, shorter hours Oct-Mar) The only tourist office on the island; provides internet access (£1 per 20 minutes) and currency exchange.

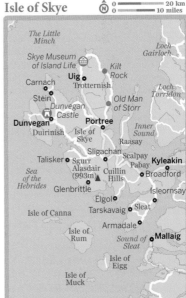

Isle of Skye

B. KIM BARNES/GETTY IMAGES ©

 Don't Miss
Isle of Iona

Like an emerald teardrop off Mull's western shore, enchanting, idyllic Iona, holy island and burial ground of kings, is a magical place that lives up to its lofty reputation. From the moment you embark on the ferry towards its sandy shores and green fields, you'll notice something different about it. To appreciate its charms, spend the night: there are some excellent places to do it. Iona has declared itself a fair-trade island and actively promotes ecotourism.

Iona's ancient but heavily reconstructed **abbey** (HS; ☎01681-700512; adult/child £7.10/4.30; ⏰9.30am-5.30pm Apr-Sep, to 4.30pm Oct-Mar) is the spiritual heart of the island. The spectacular nave, dominated by Romanesque and early Gothic vaults and columns is a powerful space; a door on the left leads to the beautiful cloister, where medieval grave slabs sit alongside modern religious sculptures. Out the back, the new museum displays fabulous carved high crosses and other inscribed stones, along with lots of background information. A replica of the intricately carved St John's Cross stands outside the abbey.

The passenger ferry from Fionnphort to Iona (£5.10 return, five minutes, hourly) runs daily. There are also various day trips available from Oban to Iona.

ⓘ Getting There & Away

Boat

Despite there being a bridge, there are still a couple of ferry links between Skye and the mainland.

Mallaig–Armadale CalMac operates the Mallaig to Armadale **ferry** (www.calmac.co.uk; per person/car £4.65/23.90). It's very popular in July and August, so book ahead if you're travelling by car.

Glenelg–Kylerhea Skye Ferry (www.skyeferry. com; foot passenger/bike/car with passengers £3/4/15; ⏰10am-6pm Easter–mid-Oct) runs a tiny vessel (six cars only) on the very worthwhile Glenelg to Kylerhea crossing.

Car & Motorcycle

The Isle of Skye became permanently tethered to the Scottish mainland when the Skye Bridge opened in 1995.

There are petrol stations at Broadford (open 24 hours), Armadale, Portree, Dunvegan and Uig.

Cuillin Hills

The Cuillin Hills are Britain's most spectacular mountain range. Though small in stature (**Sgurr Alasdair**, the highest summit, is only 993m), the peaks are near-alpine in character, with knife-edge ridges, jagged pinnacles, scree-filled gullies and acres of naked rock. While they are a paradise for experienced mountaineers, the higher reaches of the Cuillin are off limits to the majority of walkers.

The good news is that there are also plenty of good, low-level hikes within the ability of most. One of the best (on a fine day) is the steep climb from Glenbrittle camping ground to **Coire Lagan** (6 miles round trip; allow at least three hours).

 Sleeping

Sligachan Hotel
Hotel £££

(☎ 01478-650204; www.sligachan.co.uk; Sligachan; r per person £68-78; P @ 🛜 👶)
The Slig, as it has been known to generations of climbers, is a near village in itself, encompassing a comfortable hotel, a microbrewery, self-catering cottages, a small mountaineering museum, a big barn of a pub – **Seamus's Bar** (Sligachan Hotel; mains £8-13; ⏱ food served 11am-9.30pm; 🛜 👶) – and an adventure playground.

ℹ **Getting There & Away**

Bus 53 runs five times a day Monday to Friday (once on Saturday) from Portree to Carbost via Sligachan (50 minutes); for Glenbrittle, you'll have to hitch or walk the remaining 8 miles.

Portree (Port Righ)
POP 2300

Portree is Skye's largest and liveliest town. It has a pretty harbour lined with brightly painted houses, and there are great views of the surrounding hills.

Cuillin Hills

JULIAN ELLIOTT/GETTY IMAGES ©

Sleeping

Ben Tianavaig B&B
B&B ££

(☏01478-612152; www.ben-tianavaig.co.uk; 5 Bosville Tce; r £75-88; P🛜) ✐ A warm welcome awaits from the Irish-Welsh couple who run this appealing B&B bang in the centre of town. All four bedrooms have a view across the harbour to the hill that gives the house its name and breakfasts include free-range eggs and vegetables grown in the garden. Two-night minimum stay April to October; no credit cards.

Cuillin Hills Hotel
Hotel £££

(☏01478-612003; www.cuillinhills-hotel-skye.co.uk; Scorrybreac Rd; r £210-310; P🛜) Located on the eastern fringes of Portree, this luxury hotel enjoys a superb outlook across the harbour towards the Cuillin mountains. The more expensive rooms cosset guests with four-poster beds and panoramic views, but everyone can enjoy the scenery from the glass-fronted restaurant and well-stocked whisky bar.

✗ Eating

Café Arriba
Cafe £

(☏01478-611830; www.cafearriba.co.uk; Quay Brae; mains £5-10; ⊙7am-6pm daily May-Sep, 8am-5pm Thu-Sat Oct-Apr; 🖉) ✐ Arriba is a funky little cafe, brightly decked out in primary colours and offering delicious flatbread melts (bacon, leek and cheese is our favourite) as well as the best choice of vegetarian grub on the island, ranging from a veggie breakfast fry-up to falafel wraps with hummus and chilli sauce. Also serves excellent coffee.

Harbour View Seafood Restaurant
Seafood ££

(☏01478-612069; www.harbourviewskye.co.uk; 7 Bosville Tce; mains £14-19; ⊙noon-3pm & 5.30-11pm Tue-Sun) ✐ The Harbour View is Portree's most congenial place to eat. It has a homely dining room with a log fire in winter, books on the mantelpiece and bric-a-brac on the shelves. And on the table, superb Scottish seafood such as fresh Skye oysters, seafood chowder, king scallops, langoustines and lobster.

❶ Getting There & Around

The main bus stop is in Somerled Sq. There are six Scottish Citylink buses every day from Kyle of Lochalsh to Portree (£6.50, one hour) continuing to Uig.

Local buses (mostly six to eight Monday to Saturday, three on Sunday) run from Portree to:

Armadale (£6.80, 1¼ hours) Connecting with the ferry to Mallaig

Dunvegan Castle (£4.65, 40 minutes, one daily) There are also three buses a day on a circular route around Trotternish (in both directions), taking in Flodigarry (£4.65, 45 minutes), Kilmuir (£4.65, 45 minutes) and Uig (£3.50, 30 minutes).

Old Man of Storr, Trotternish Peninsula
JOE CORNISH/GETTY IMAGES ©

Dunvegan (Dun Bheagain) & Around

Skye's most famous historic building, and one of its most popular tourist attractions, is **Dunvegan Castle** (☏01470-521206; www.dunvegancastle.com; adult/child £10/7; ⏰10am-5.30pm Apr–mid-Oct; P), seat of the chief of Clan MacLeod. The oldest parts are the 14th-century keep and dungeon but most of it dates from the 17th to 19th centuries.

Sleeping & Eating

Three Chimneys

Modern Scottish £££

(☏01470-511258; www.threechimneys.co.uk; Colbost; 3-course lunch/dinner £37/60; ⏰12.15-1.45pm Mon-Sat mid-Mar–Oct, plus Sun Easter-Sep, 6.15-9pm daily year-round) ✦ Halfway between Dunvegan and Waterstein, the Three Chimneys is a superb romantic retreat combining a gourmet restaurant in a candlelit crofter's cottage with sumptuous five-star rooms (double £345) in the modern house next door. Book well in advance, and note that children are not welcome in the restaurant in the evenings.

Trotternish

The Trotternish Peninsula to the north of Portree has some of Skye's most beautiful – and bizarre – scenery. On the eastern coast, the 50m-high, pot-bellied pinnacle of crumbling basalt known as the **Old Man of Storr** is prominent above the road 6 miles north of Portree. North again is spectacular **Kilt Rock**, a stupendous cliff of columnar basalt whose vertical ribbing is fancifully compared to the pleats of a kilt, and the Quiraing, an impressive land-slipped escarpment bristling with crags and pinnacles.

On the western side of the peninsula, the peat-reek of crofting life in the 18th and 19th centuries is preserved in

 If You Like...
Scenic Glens

It's hard to beat Glen Coe in the scenery stakes, but the Highlands are riven with many other glorious glens.

1 GLEN NEVIS
Magical Glen Nevis begins near Fort William and wraps itself around the southern flanks of Ben Nevis (1344m). Its amazing scenery makes it popular with movie makers – parts of *Braveheart*, *Rob Roy* and the Harry Potter movies were filmed there.

2 GLEN AFFRIC
Glen Affric is one of the most beautiful glens in Scotland, extending deep into the hills beyond Cannich, 13 miles west of Drumnadrochit. It's a wonderland of shimmering lochs, rugged mountains and rare native wildlife.

3 GLEN ETIVE
At the eastern end of Glen Coe, a minor road leads south along this peaceful and beautiful glen. On a warm summer's day, there are many tempting pools to swim in and plentiful picnic sites.

4 GLEN TORRIDON
The drive along Glen Torridon is one of the most breathtaking in Scotland, overlooked by mighty, brooding mountains that tower over a winding, single-track road. The glen runs southwest from Kinlochewe and Loch Maree, about 50 miles west of Inverness.

thatched cottages at **Skye Museum of Island Life** (☏01470-552206; www.skyemuseum.co.uk; adult/child £2.50/50p; ⏰9.30am-5pm Mon-Sat Easter-Oct; P). Behind the museum is Kilmuir Cemetery, where a tall Celtic cross marks the grave of Flora MacDonald.

Whichever way you arrive at **Uig** (oo-ig), the picture-perfect bay, ringed by steep hills, rarely fails to impress.

JOHN O'GROATS

POP 300

Though it's not the northernmost point of the British mainland (that's Dunnet Head), John O'Groats still serves as the end-point of the mammoth cross-country trek from Land's End in Cornwall, a popular if arduous route for cyclists and walkers, many of whom raise money for charitable causes.

Two miles east, **Duncansby Head** provides a more solemn end-of-Britain moment with a small lighthouse and 60m cliffs sheltering nesting fulmars. From here a 15-minute walk through a sheep paddock yields spectacular views of the sea-surrounded monoliths known as **Duncansby Stacks**.

From May to September, a **passenger ferry** (☏01955-611353; www.jogferry.co.uk; single £15, incl bus to Kirkwall £17; ☺May-Sep) shuttles across to Burwick in Orkney. Ninety-minute wildlife cruises to the island of Stroma or Duncansby Head cost £17 (late June to August).

ORKNEY ISLANDS

There's a magic to the Orkney Islands that you'll begin to feel as soon as the Scottish mainland slips away astern. Consisting of 70 flat, green-topped islands stripped bare of trees by the wind, it's a place of ancient standing stones and prehistoric villages, an archipelago of old-style hospitality and Viking heritage narrated in the *Orkneyinga Saga* and still strong today, a region whose ports tell of lives led with the blessings and rough moods of the sea, and a destination where seekers can find melancholy wrecks of warships and the salty clamour of remote seabird colonies.

Tours

John O'Groats Ferries   Bus Tour
(☏01955-611353; www.jogferry.co.uk; ☺May-Sep) For the hurried; runs a one-day tour of the main sites for £58, including the ferry from John O'Groats. You can do the whole thing as a long day trip from Inverness.

Skara Brae

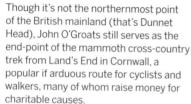

Maes Howe

Egypt has the pyramids, Scotland has **Maes Howe** (HS; ☎01856-761606; www.historic-scotland.gov.uk; adult/child £5.50/3.30; ⊙tours hourly 10am-4pm). Constructed about 5000 years ago, it's an extraordinary place, a Stone Age tomb built from enormous sandstone blocks, some of which weighed many tons and were brought from several miles away. Entry is by 45-minute guided tours that leave on the hour. Be sure to reserve your tour slot ahead by phone.

Ring of Brodgar

A mile north of Stenness is this wide circle of **standing stones** (HS; www.historic-scotland.gov.uk; ⊙24hr) FREE, some over 5m tall. They were the last of the three Stenness monuments to be built (2500–2000 BC). Free guided tours leave from the carpark at 1pm from June to August (Thursdays only during the rest of the year).

Skara Brae

A visit to extraordinary **Skara Brae** (HS; www.historic-scotland.gov.uk; joint ticket with Skaill House adult/child £7.10/4.30; ⊙9.30am-5.30pm Apr-Sep, to 4.30pm Oct-Mar), one of the world's most evocative prehistoric sites, offers the best opportunity in Scotland for a glimpse of Stone Age life. Idyllically situated by a sandy bay 8 miles north of Stromness, and predating Stonehenge and the pyramids of Giza, Skara Brae is northern Europe's best-preserved prehistoric village.

❶ Getting There & Away

Air

Flybe (☎0871 700 2000; www.flybe.com) flies daily from Kirkwall to Aberdeen, Edinburgh, Glasgow, Inverness and Sumburgh (Shetland). Most summers it also serves Bergen (Norway).

Boat

Northlink Ferries (☎0845 6000 449; www.northlinkferries.co.uk) operates ferries from Scrabster to Stromness (passenger/car £19.15/58, 1½ hours, two to three daily), from Aberdeen to Kirkwall (passenger/car £31/110, six hours, three or four weekly) and from Kirkwall to Lerwick (passenger/car £24.30/101, six to eight hours, three or four weekly) on Shetland. Fares are up to 30% lower off-season.

From May to September, John O'Groats Ferries (p360) operates a passenger-only service from John O'Groats to Burwick, on the southern tip of South Ronaldsay. A bus to Kirkwall meets the ferry. There are two to three departures daily.

Great Britain
In Focus

Westminster Abbey (p60)
CHRISTOPHER HOPE-FITCH/GETTY IMAGES ©

Great Britain Today

Changing of the Guard, Buckingham Palace (p61)

> *questioning the balance of power has led to a reassessment of what it actually means to be British*

belief systems
(% of population)

59	25	•	•	●
		5	4	7
Christian	No Religion	Muslim	Other	Not Stated

if Britain were 100 people

85 would be Caucasian
4 would be South Asian
2 would be African & Afro Caribbean
9 would be other

population per sq km

♦ ≈ 30 people

BRITAIN   USA   FRANCE

The End of the UK?

Where once the United Kingdom of Great Britain and Northern Ireland was a single political entity, it's now anything but united. From 1999 onwards, the process of devolution has seen the nations of Scotland, Wales, and Northern Ireland get their own ruling bodies – the Scottish Parliament in Edinburgh, the Welsh Assembly in Cardiff, and the Northern Ireland Assembly in Belfast – with power over domestic affairs such as health and education.

However, when the Scottish National Party won a surprise majority in the Scottish Parliament elections of 2011 they went further, and pledged to hold a referendum on full Scottish independence in 2014. The implications of Scotland breaking away from the UK were hotly debated. Would an independent Scotland need a new currency, or continue using the pound? Would there be border controls with England? Would Scotland be able to remain in the EU? Would the Queen still be head of state?

PAWEL LIBERA/GETTY IMAGES ©

smaller nations, have always been more aware of the institutions that bind the countries together – and the tensions that threaten to drive them apart – the English are now having to confront the questions of what Britain actually represents.

The Rise of UKIP

Although British politics since 2010 has been dominated by austerity measures supposed to combat the impact of the global financial crisis, by the start of 2014 the economy had been joined by immigration as the issue of most concern. The same year saw the rise to prominence of UKIP (the United Kingdom Independence Party), a right-wing, libertarian party whose flagship policies include cutting back on immigration and taking Britain out of the European Union.

UKIP took first place in the European elections of May 2014 with 27.5% of the vote (on a turnout of 34%) – the first time any party other than Labour or Conservative had come first in a UK-wide election since 1906. The result threw Britain into a spin. Did this herald a fundamental change in the direction of British politics? Or was it a protest vote from an electorate fed up with Westminster politicians?

Opinion polls suggesting that UKIP might win a couple of Westminster seats in the 2015 election saw both Labour and the Conservatives harden their positions on immigration, while the Tory leader David Cameron pledged that he would offer the country a referendum on whether to stay in the EU if he remained as prime minister after 2015.

The referendum took place on 18 September 2014, posing the question: 'Should Scotland be an independent country?'. The result was that 55% voted to maintain the status quo (with a turnout of 85%). What this means for the future of Scotland – and of Britain – remains unclear. Will there be increased powers for the Scottish Parliament? Will there be increased devolution to the English regions? Will the UK become a federal state?

What Does It Mean to be British?

This questioning of the balance of power across Britain has led to a reassessment – both by politicians and the people themselves – of what it actually means to be British. This has occurred especially in England where for centuries 'British' and 'English' have meant essentially the same thing. While Wales and Scotland, as

Hadrian's Wall (p250)

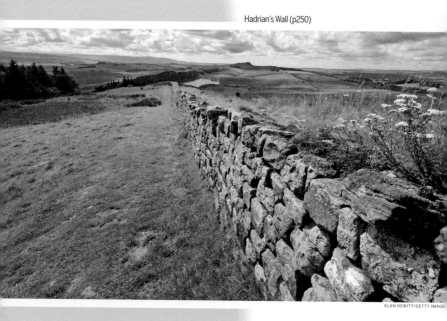

ALAN HEWITT/GETTY IMAGE

It may be a small island on the edge of Europe, but Britain has never been on the sidelines of history. For centuries, invaders and incomers have made their mark – Celts, Romans, Vikings, Anglo-Saxons, Normans – and the result is a fascinating mix of culture and language, a dynamic pattern that has shaped the nation and continues to evolve today.

First Arrivals

Stone tools discovered in eastern England show that human habitation in Britain stretches back at least 700,000 years, but the first structural signs of settlements emerge around 4000 BC, when early peoples constructed massive burial mounds and stone circles, most famously at Stonehenge.

3500 BC
First period of construction at Stonehenge begins.

Celts & Romans

By around 500 BC, the Celts had settled across much of the island of Britain, and a Celtic-British population – sometimes known as the 'ancient Britons' – developed. The next arrivals were the Romans, colonising the island they called Britannia from around AD 43.

Early England, Wales & Scotland

When the power of the Romans faded around AD 410, the province of Britannia went into decline, and a new wave of invaders – Angles and Saxons – crossed from the European mainland, setting the foundation for the English language and culture. Meanwhile the Celts were pushed to the island's fringes (especially present-day Wales and Scotland), in the process creating their own distinct cultures.

The Best...
Ancient Sites

1 Stonehenge (p192)

2 Avebury (p196)

3 Skara Brae (p361)

4 Hadrian's Wall (p250)

5 Bath's Roman Baths (p177)

IN FOCUS HISTORY

The Viking Era

Just as the new territories of England, Wales and Scotland were becoming established, Britain was again invaded – this time by Scandinavian Vikings, who conquered northeast England and made York their capital. Their advance south was halted by Alfred the Great, who brought the disparate Anglo-Saxon armies under one leader for the first time in history. His grandson, Athelstan, became the first King of England in 925.

1066 & All That

The next major landmark in Britain's history was the 1066 Battle of Hastings, when the Norman king William led an invading army into southern England. The Saxons were defeated, and William became king of England, earning himself the prestigious epithet of Conqueror.

Royal & Holy Squabbling

The early 12th century was marked by tension between church and state, culminating in Henry II's murder of 'turbulent priest' Thomas Becket at Canterbury Cathedral in 1170.

AD 43
Emperor Claudius orders the Roman invasion of Britannia.

5th–7th centuries
Anglo-Saxons migrate to England and expand across the country.

1066
Norman French armies defeat the English at the Battle of Hastings.

The next king, Richard I (aka the Lionheart), headed off to the Middle East on a series of Crusades, leaving his brother John to rule in his stead. According to legend, it was during this time that Robert of Loxley, better known as Robin Hood, hid in Sherwood Forest and engaged in a spot of wealth redistribution.

Edward I in Wales & Scotland

By 1272 England was ruled by Edward I, an ambitious leader and skilled general. First he invaded Wales, building massive castles at places like Caernarfon and Conwy, that are still impressive today. Then Edward I was invited to choose a new Scottish king. Disputes arose from this decision and Edward I seized the opportunity to invade the country, forcing clan leaders to swear allegiance. In a final blow to Scottish pride, Edward removed the Stone of Scone, on which the kings of Scotland had been crowned for centuries. Edward's bloody suppression of the Scots inspired not obedience, but rebellion, and in 1297 at the Battle of Stirling Bridge, the English were defeated by a Scottish army under William Wallace (an episode which inspired the film *Braveheart*).

Robert the Bruce

The English soon reasserted themselves in Scotland. Edward II came to the throne, but lacked the military success of his forebear. Meanwhile, Robert the Bruce had crowned himself King of Scotland, and after a series of setbacks, decisively defeated the English at the Battle of Bannockburn in 1314, another milestone in Scotland's long struggle to remain independent.

The House of Lancaster

The year 1399 was another major milestone in Britain's history: King Richard II of England was ousted by a powerful baron called Henry Bolingbroke, who became King Henry IV – the first monarch of the House of Lancaster. His son Henry V led his forces to a famous defeat of France at the Battle of Agincourt, while his grandson Henry VI oversaw the building of several great houses of worship, including King's College Chapel in Cambridge and Eton Chapel near Windsor.

Henry VIII vs the Church

Of all the Henrys, the last is undoubtedly the most notorious. Henry VIII's main problem was fathering a male heir – hence the famous six wives. The pope's disapproval of Henry's divorce from his first wife, Catherine of Aragon, lead Henry to split from the Catholic Church and found the Church of England. The so-called Reformation sowed the seeds of division between Protestants and Catholics that still endures in some corners of Britain. In 1536 Henry 'dissolved' nearly all of the monasteries in England and Wales, and now only their ruins remain.

1459–87
The Wars of the Roses between the Houses of Lancaster and York.

1536 & 1543
Henry VIII signs the Acts of Union, formally uniting England and Wales. Henry VIII, by Hans Holbein the Younger

As if that wasn't enough, Henry VIII's other great contribution to British history was signing the Acts of Union (1536 and 1543), formally uniting England and Wales for the first time.

The Elizabethan Age

Henry VIII died in 1547 and, shortly after, his daughter became Elizabeth I (sometimes known as the 'Virgin Queen', since she never married). Her 45-year reign heralded a golden period for England: explorer Francis Drake circumnavigated the globe, Walter Raleigh led expeditions to the New World, and William Shakespeare penned some of the greatest plays ever written. But perhaps Elizabeth's greatest achievement was her defeat of the mighty Spanish Armada, allowing England to retain her independence and build on her growing global power.

The Best...
Historic Cities

1 London

2 York

3 Edinburgh

4 Oxford

5 Bath

IN FOCUS HISTORY

Mary, Queen of Scots

Meanwhile, things were afoot up north. Elizabeth's cousin Mary had become Queen of the Scots aged just six years old, following the death of her father James V in 1542. Having married the Dauphin of France, Mary later returned to claim the English throne on the grounds that Elizabeth was illegitimate.

Mary's plans failed. She was forced to abdicate from the Scottish throne and was held under house arrest for 19 years, before involving herself in a plot to overthrow Elizabeth, for which she was executed in 1587.

United Britain

The Virgin Queen never provided an heir, so in 1603 she was succeeded by her closest relative, the Scottish King James VI, son of the executed Mary. He became James I of England, the first king of the House of Stuart – but more importantly, he united England, Wales and Scotland under one monarch for the first time in history.

The War of Three Kingdoms

During the reign of Charles I (1625-49), a power struggle between king and parliament eventually degenerated into the War of the Three Kingdoms. The antiroyalist forces were led by Oliver Cromwell, a Puritan who preached against the excesses of the monarch and established church. After a long and bloody struggle, his parliamentarian (or Roundhead) army eventually defeated the king's forces (the

---

1642–49
English Civil War results in the execution of Charles I, and exile of Charles II.

1666
Great Fire of London burns much of the city to the ground.

1707
The Act of Union links England, Wales and Scotland under one parliament.

What's in a Name?

Visitors are often confused about the difference between England and Britain. But it's actually simple – England is just one of the three countries (along with Wales and Scotland) which collectively make up Great Britain. To complicate things official documents often refer to the United Kingdom which is a political state that also includes Northern Ireland. Clear enough? Don't worry – many British people aren't 100% sure of the difference either.

Cavaliers). The king was executed and England was declared a republic – with Cromwell hailed as 'Lord Protector', allowing him to enforce a raft of dictatorial (and hugely unpopular) laws.

Two years after Cromwell's death in 1658, parliament decided to re-establish the monarchy. Charles II, the exiled son of Charles I, returned to the throne, marking the beginning of the period known as the Restoration.

Age of Empire

In 1707, the Act of Union was passed, bringing an end to the independent Scottish Parliament, and finally linking the countries of England, Wales and Scotland under one parliament.

Stronger control over the British Isles was mirrored by even greater expansion abroad. The British Empire continued to grow in America, Canada and India, and laid claim to the newly discovered country of Australia following James Cook's epic voyage in 1768.

The empire's first major reverse came when the American colonies won the War of Independence (1776–83). Another challenge arose some time later, when French forces under Napoleon threatened to invade Britain and its territories, but were ultimately defeated by the heroic duo of Viscount Horatio Nelson and the Duke of Wellington, who won landmark victories at the Battles of Trafalgar (1805) and Waterloo (1815).

The Industrial Age

While the empire expanded, at home Britain had become the crucible of the Industrial Revolution. Steam power (patented by James Watt in 1781) and steam trains (launched by George Stephenson in 1825) transformed methods of production and transport, and the towns of the English Midlands became the world's first industrial cities. Huge numbers of people migrated from the countryside to work in the rapidly-expanding cities – a mass migration that was mirrored north of the Scottish border, when landowners expelled whole communities to make way for more profitable sheep farms, an event now known as the Highland Clearances.

1799–1815
Napoleon threatens invasion but is defeated at Trafalgar and Waterloo.

1837–1901
Under the reign of Queen Victoria, the British Empire expands its influence across the globe.

1914
The assassination of Archduke Franz Ferdinand of Austria leads to the outbreak of WWI.

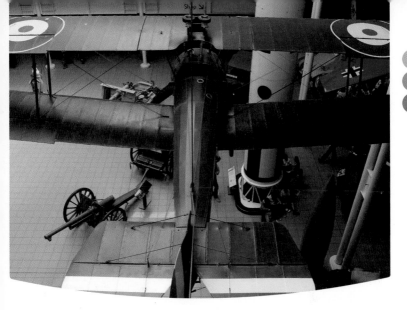

By the time Queen Victoria took the throne in 1837, Britain's colonies covered almost a quarter of the world's surface, and her factories and fleets dominated world trade. But her reign also marked an era of new social conscience: education became universal, trade unions were legalised, environmental laws were enacted, and the right to vote was extended to those lower down the social and economic ladder (well, to more adult males – women didn't get the vote until the efforts of the Suffragettes were successful a few decades later).

WWI

When Queen Victoria died in 1901, it seemed that Britain's energy fizzled out. In Continental Europe, other states were more active: the military powers of Russia, Austro-Hungary, Turkey and Germany were sabre-rattling in the Balkan states, a dispute that eventually culminated in WWI. When German forces entered Belgium on their way to invade France, Britain was drawn into the conflict. The next four years witnessed the emergence of 'trench warfare' and slaughter on a truly horrific scale; by the war's end in 1918, over a million Britons had died, not to mention millions more from the Commonwealth.

Biplane, Imperial War Museum (p73)

LONELY PLANET/GETTY IMAGES ©

1939–45

WWII: Britain and its allies from America and the Commonwealth defeat Germany.

1953

The coronation of Queen Elizabeth II takes place in Westminster Abbey.

1979

Margaret Thatcher's Conservative Party wins the general election.

Disillusion & Depression

For soldiers who did return from WWI, disillusion led to questioning of the social order. Many supported the ideals of a new political force – the Labour Party, representing the working class – upsetting the balance long enjoyed by the Liberal and Conservative Parties.

The Labour Party was elected to government for the first time in 1923, in coalition with the Liberals, with James Ramsay MacDonald as prime minister. In the 1930s the world economy slumped and the Great Depression took hold. Even the royal family took a knock when Edward VIII abdicated in 1936 so he could marry a woman who was twice divorced and – horror of horrors – American.

The throne was taken by Edward's less-than-charismatic brother George VI and Britain dithered through the rest of the decade, with mediocre government failing to confront the country's deep-set social and economic problems.

WWII

Meanwhile, on mainland Europe, Germany saw the rise of Adolf Hitler, leader of the Nazi party. Many feared another war, but Prime Minister Neville Chamberlain met the German leader in 1938 and promised Britain 'peace for our time'. He was wrong. The following year Hitler invaded Poland, and two days later Britain was once again at war with Germany.

Chamberlain, reviled for his policy of 'appeasement', stood aside for a new prime minister, Winston Churchill. The war exacted a heavy toll on Britain – most notably during the Blitz, when much of London was levelled by the Luftwaffe, a phenomenon mirrored in many other British cities. By the time the war came to a close in 1945, Britain was utterly broke and facing a bleak future.

Swinging & Sliding

Seeking a new direction, the postwar years saw the rise of the socialist Labour Party, and the dawn of the 'welfare state'. The National Health Service was founded, providing free health care for all, and key industries (such as steel, coal and railways) were nationalised. In 1952, Elizabeth II came to the throne, and stayed there for six decades and counting.

During the Swinging Sixties, Britain became the centre of a new explosion in youth culture, but by the 1970s economic decline had set in once again, and the rest of the decade was marked by strikes, disputes and a general sense of discontent. Into the fray stepped an Iron Lady by the name of Margaret Thatcher, whose election in 1979 heralded a new but equally turbulent era.

1997

The Labour Party wins the general election with a record-breaking majority.

1999

Devolution leads to the formation of the Scottish Parliament and Welsh Assembly.

2007

Tony Blair resigns, and Gordon Brown takes over as Britain's prime minister.

The Thatcher Years

Love her or loathe her, no one could argue that Thatcher feared a fight. The nationalised industries were sold off, leading to widespread strikes and industrial disputes; the banks were deregulated, leading to a huge boom in London's financial district; and in 1982 the faraway Falkland Islands were regained by force following their invasion by Argentina. But ultimately Thatcher became a victim of her own conviction: her refusal to scrap the hugely unpopular 'poll tax' sparked nationwide riots, and ultimately led to her being booted from power in 1990.

New Labour, New Millennium

In the elections of 1997, the now rebranded 'New' Labour swept to power under fresh-faced leader Tony Blair. Among a host of other reforms, Mr Blair's government established devolved parliaments in Scotland and Wales, granting both countries limited control over their own taxation and public policy – something they hadn't enjoyed since the Act of Union in 1707.

Tony Blair and New Labour enjoyed an extended honeymoon period, and the next election (in 2001) was another walkover. Despite his controversial decision to participate in the wars in Afghanistan and Iraq, Labour won a historic third term in 2005, and Blair became the longest-serving Labour prime minister in British history. He finally resigned in June 2007, allowing Gordon Brown, the Chancellor of the Exchequer (the British term for Minister of Finance), to get the top job.

Unfortunately Brown's long-awaited leadership descended into disaster following the worldwide financial crisis in 2008. In the general election of 2010, a record 13 years of Labour rule came to an end, and a coalition between the Conservatives and the Liberal Democrats formed a new government, with David Cameron as prime minister.

The Best...
History Museums

1 Ironbridge Gorge (p155)

2 SS *Great Britain* (p185)

3 Imperial War Museum (p73)

4 Greenwich Royal, Observatory (p 82)

5 Jorvik (p221)

IN FOCUS HISTORY

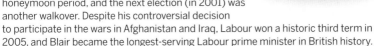

2010
A coalition between Conservatives and Liberal-Democrats wins the election.

2012
London hosts the Olympic Games and the Queen celebrates her Diamond Jubilee.
Olympic Stadium

MARK CHIVERS/GETTY IMAGES ©

Family Travel

Eden Project (p207), Cornwall

NIGEL HICKS/GETTY IMAGES

Britain is great for travel with children because it's compact, with a lot of attractions in a small area. So when the kids in the back of the car say 'are we nearly there yet?', your answer can often be 'yes'. With a bit of planning ahead, and some online research to get the best bargains, having the kids on board can make a trip around Britain even more enjoyable.

Attractions

Many places of interest in Britain cater for kids as much as adults. At the country's historic castles, for example, mum and dad can admire the medieval architecture, while the kids can stomp off round the battlements. In the same way, many national parks and holiday resorts organise specific activities for children. It goes without saying that everything ramps up (both in prices and visitor congestion) during the school holidays.

Most visitor attractions offer family tickets (usually two adults plus two children) which offer a discount on individual entrance charges. Most offer cheaper rates for solo parents and kids too. Be sure to ask, as these are not always clearly displayed.

On the Road

If you're going by public transport, trains are great for families: intercity services have plenty of room for luggage and extra stuff like buggies (pushers), and the kids can move about a bit when bored. In contrast, they need to stay in their seats on long-distance coaches.

If you're hiring a car, most (but not all) rental firms can provide child seats – but you'll need to check this in advance. Most will not actually fit the child seats; you need to do that yourself, for insurance reasons.

There are usually hefty child discounts available on most forms of public transport, too.

Accommodation

It's worth checking in advance that the place you're planning on staying at is happy to accept children. Some places are thoroughly child-friendly and will be able to provide cots, toys and babysitting services. Others (especially at the boutique end) prefer to maintain an adult atmosphere and consequently don't accept kids.

Many places also quote prices per person, so you might find yourself having to pay extra (albeit at a reduced rate) even if the kids share your room. Some B&Bs and hotels offer 'family suites' of two adjoining bedrooms with a shared bathroom.

Renting a self-catering cottage can be a good way to economise for family travellers, although obviously it means you'll be rooted to one particular area. Popular spots such as the Lake District, Devon, Cornwall and the Cotswolds have a particularly good selection to choose from.

Dining Out

Most cafes and teashops are child friendly. Restaurants are mixed: some offer high-chairs and kiddy portions; others firmly say 'no children after 6pm'.

Children under 18 are usually not allowed in pubs serving just alcohol. Pubs serving meals usually allow children of any age (with their parents) in England and Wales, but in Scotland they must be over 14 and must leave by 8pm. If in doubt, ask the bar staff.

Breastfeeding in public remains mildly controversial, but if done discreetly, will rarely attract comment.

All Change

On the sticky topic of dealing with nappies (diapers), most museums and other attractions in Britain usually have good baby-changing facilities.

Elsewhere, some city-centre public toilets have baby-changing areas, although these can be a bit grimy; your best bet for clean facilities is an upmarket department store.

On the road, baby-changing facilities are usually bearable at motorway service stations and OK at out-of-town supermarkets.

The Best...
Children's Attractions

1 Warwick Castle (p149)

2 Science Museum, London (p76)

3 Ironbridge (p155)

4 Eden Project, Cornwall (p207)

5 Jorvik Viking Centre, York (p221)

6 Natural History Museum, London (p73)

IN FOCUS FAMILY TRAVEL

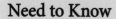

Need to Know

Changing facilities In most large shopping centres, museums and attractions

Cots Usually available at hotels, less common in B&Bs – ask in advance

Health Just do as you'd do back home

Highchairs Common in specific family-friendly restaurants

Nappies (diapers) Sold in every supermarket

Transport Look out for kids' discounts on trains and long-distance buses. Children under five usually travel free (but must give up the seat to paying passengers if transport is full).

Holiday Times

The best time for families to visit Britain is pretty much the best time for everyone else – from April/May to the end of September. It's worth avoiding August – the heart of school summer holidays – when prices go up and roads are busy, especially near the coast. Other school holidays are two weeks around Easter Sunday, and mid-December to early January, plus three week-long 'half-term' breaks – usually late February (or early March), late May and late October.

Information

Tourist offices are a great source of information for kids' activities – the shelves are usually loaded with leaflets advertising kid-friendly attractions in the local area. Ask at national park information centres too about activities for children. Many holiday resort towns also organise activities for children, especially during school-holiday periods.

Some handy websites:

Baby Goes 2 (www.babygoes2.com) Advice, tips and encouragement (and a stack of advertisements).

Mums Net (www.mumsnet.com) No-nonsense advice on travel and more from a gang of UK mothers.

Travel for Kids (www.travelforkids.com) Straightforward advice on kid-friendly places to visit.

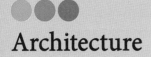

Architecture

Chatsworth House (p161)

DAVE PORTER PETERBOROUGH UK/GETTY IMAGES ©

One of the highlights of visiting Britain is the chance to explore its architectural heritage – encompassing everything from 5000-year-old stone circles to medieval cathedrals, thatched cottages and stunning stately homes. But don't make the mistake of thinking Britain is just one big museum piece. Landmark new buildings have sprung up in many major cities in recent years, demonstrating that Britain is still capable of mustering up a spirit of architectural adventure.

Early Foundations

The oldest 'buildings' in Britain are the grass-covered earth-mounds called 'barrows' (or 'tumuli') used as burial sites by Britain's prehistoric residents, but it's the country's many menhirs (standing stones) and stone circles which are the most obvious architectural legacy of the prehistoric past. No-one's quite sure what purpose they served, although they seem to have served some kind of sacred function. Famous examples include Stonehenge and Avebury in Wiltshire, and the Ring of Brodgar in the Orkney Islands.

Bronze Age & Iron Age

During these periods the architecture is on a more domestic scale. Hut circles can still be seen in several parts of Britain, most notably on Dartmoor in Devon and the stone village of Skara Brae on the Orkney Islands.

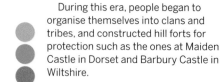

During this era, people began to organise themselves into clans and tribes, and constructed hill forts for protection such as the ones at Maiden Castle in Dorset and Barbury Castle in Wiltshire.

The Roman Era

Roman remains are found in many towns and cities, mostly in England and Wales, as the Romans never colonised Scotland. There are impressive remains in Chester, Exeter and St Albans, and some in York, as well as the lavish Roman spa and bathing complex in Bath. But Britain's largest and most impressive Roman relic is the 73-mile sweep of Hadrian's Wall, built in the 2nd century AD as a defensive line stretching coast-to-coast across the country, for over 300 years marking the northern limit of the Roman Empire.

Chalk Figures

As you travel around Britain, look out for the chalk figures gracing many of the country's hilltops. They're made by cutting through the turf to reveal the white chalk soil below, so obviously are found in chalk areas – most notably in southwest England, especially the counties of Dorset and Wiltshire. Some figures, such as the Uffington White Horse, date from the Bronze Age, but most are more recent; the formidably endowed Cerne Abbas Giant is often thought to be an ancient pagan figure, although recent research suggests it was etched sometime in the 17th century.

Medieval Cathedrals & Castles

In the centuries following the Norman invasion of 1066, Britain saw an explosion of architecture inspired by the two most pressing concerns of the day: worship and defence. Many landmark cathedrals were constructed during the early Middle Ages, including Salisbury, Winchester, Wells, Glasgow, St David's and Canterbury, plus York Minster, one of the finest cathedrals in all of Europe.

Alongside the churches and cathedrals, many abbeys and monasteries were built in Britain during the medieval period – nearly all of which were destroyed under the orders of Henry VIII between 1536 and 1540 as part of his dispute with the Catholic Church, or, in the case of Scotland, by Protestants during the Reformation that took place there. The period is now known as the 'dissolution of the monasteries' and the legacy today is picturesque ruins such as Melrose, Tintern, Fountains, Glastonbury, St Andrews and Rievaulx.

As for castles in Britain, you're spoilt for choice, ranging from atmospheric ruins like Tintagel to well-preserved structures like Warwick, Conwy, Stirling and Edinburgh. And then there's the most impressive of them all – the Tower of London, guardian of the capital for around 950 years.

Stately Homes

By the 17th century life had became more settled, and the nobility increasingly began to convert their draughty castles into lavish homes: Hardwick Hall and Burghley House are good examples of this fortress-to-finery process. Other nobles simply started from scratch on brand new stately homes, many of which were designed by the most famous architects of the day. Among the most extravagant are Chatsworth House, Stourhead and Blenheim Palace.

Sometimes, these improvements took place on a citywide scale: many of Britain's cities were heavily redeveloped during the Georgian era, including London, Edinburgh, Glasgow and the famous crescents and terraces of Bath.

Victoriana

The Victorian era – mainly the 19th century – was a time of great national confidence in Britain, reflected in a period of great building. A style called Victorian-Gothic developed, echoing the towers and spires that were such a feature of the original Gothic cathedrals. The best-known example of this style is the Palace of Westminster, better known as the Houses of Parliament and the tower of Big Ben, in London. Other highlights in the capital include London's Natural History Museum and St Pancras Train Station. The style was copied around the country, especially for civic buildings – the finest examples including Manchester Town Hall and Glasgow City Chambers.

The Industrial Era

Through the late 19th and early 20th century, as Britain's cities grew in size and stature, the newly moneyed middle classes built streets and squares of smart town houses.

During the Industrial Revolution, town planners oversaw the construction of endless terraces of 'back-to-back' and 'two-up-two-down' houses to accommodate the massive influx of workers needed to run the country's factories. In South Wales, similar houses – though often single storey – were built for the burgeoning numbers of coal miners, while the industrial areas of Scotland saw the rise of tenements, usually three or four storeys high, with a central communal staircase and two dwellings on each floor.

Postwar

During WWII many of Britain's cities were damaged by bombing, and the rebuilding that followed showed scant regard for the overall aesthetic of the cities, or for the lives of the people who lived in them. The rows of terraces were swept away in favour of high-rise tower blocks, while the 'brutalist' architects of the 1950s and '60s employed the modern and efficient materials of steel and concrete, leaving legacies such as London's South Bank Centre.

Perhaps this is why, on the whole, the British people are conservative in their architectural tastes, and often unhappy with experimental designs, especially when they're applied to public buildings. But a familiar pattern often unfolds: after a few years of resentment, first comes a nickname, then grudging acceptance, and finally – once the locals have become used to it – comes pride and affection for the new building. The Brits just don't like to be rushed, that's all.

21st Century

Over the last couple of decades, British architecture has started to redeem itself, and many big cities now have contemporary buildings their residents can rightly be proud of. Others, such as the much-criticised Scottish Parliament in Edinburgh, are still dividing opinion.

A new fashion for skyscrapers has recently taken hold in many cities, a trend perhaps started by London's cone-shaped Swiss Re building (now forever known as 'The Gherkin'). Leeds, Manchester, Brighton and Birmingham have all announced plans for new buildings over 200m high, while several more have recently been added to the London skyline, each with their own inevitable nickname (the Walkie Talkie, the Cheese Grater and so on). Tallest of all is 'The Shard', which opened in 2013 and at 309m is now one of Europe's tallest structures.

Writers & Artists

Dove Cottage (p247), Grasmere

PAUL THOMPSON/GETTY IMAGES

The roots of Britain's literary heritage stretch back to Early English epics such as Beowulf. As the English language spread around the world, so too did English literature, such that writers like Shakespeare and Austen are well known far from their homeland. Britain's visual art scene is equally rich, and as you travel around the region you'll see vistas you may recognise from classic paintings.

Literature

First Stars

Modern English literature starts around 1387 with Geoffrey Chaucer's bawdy, allegorical *Canterbury Tales*, a mammoth poem based around fables, stories and morality tales, each told by one of the travelling pilgrims.

The next big name came two centuries later, when William Shakespeare entered the stage and penned his pantheon of histories, comedies and tragedies. It's still possible to visit various sites linked to Shakespeare in his birthplace of Stratford-upon-Avon, where you can also catch a play courtesy of the Royal Shakespeare Company – but for the authentic Elizabethan experience, you'll need to head for the reconstructed Globe Theatre on London's South Bank.

17th & 18th Centuries

The early 17th century saw the rise of the metaphysical poets, including John Donne and Andrew Marvell. Their vivid imagery and far-fetched 'conceits', or comparisons, daringly pushed the boundaries. In 'A Valediction: Forbidding Mourning', for instance, Donne compares the points of a compass with a pair of conjoined lovers. Racy stuff in its day.

The 18th century saw the birth of Scotland's best-loved lyricist and poet Robert Burns, whose work is still celebrated across the nation on Burns' Night, held on 25 January every year.

The Romantics

As the Industrial Revolution gathered steam in the late 18th and early 19th century, many writers increasingly turned towards the natural world and the power of imagination (in many cases helped along by a healthy dose of laudanum). Leading lights of the Romantic movement, as it became known, were William Blake, John Keats, Percy Bysshe Shelley, Lord Byron, Samuel Taylor Coleridge and William Wordsworth, whose most famous lines from *Daffodils*, 'I wandered lonely as a cloud', were inspired by a hike in the Lake District.

At around the same time, Sir Walter Scott produced his well-known novels such as *Waverley* and *Rob Roy*, both partly set in the Scottish Highlands.

Jane Austen

Almost two centuries after her death, Jane Austen is still one of Britain's best-known novelists, thanks to her exquisite observations of English class, society, love, friendship and buttoned-up passion – helped along by an endless stream of film and TV adaptations of her work. The city most associated with Austen is Bath; although she only lived there from 1801 to 1806, the city's Georgian streets and squares conjure an inescapably Austenesque atmosphere, and an intriguing museum commemorates her life and work.

Victoriana

Next came the reign of Queen Victoria and the era of industrial expansion. Novels increasingly began to explore social and political themes, epitomised by the work of Charles Dickens: in *Oliver Twist*, he captures the lives of young thieves in the London slums, while *Bleak House* critiqued the English legal system and *Hard Times* decried the excesses of capitalism.

Meanwhile, Thomas Hardy's works often dealt with the changing face of rural England; all his novels are based in the fictionalised county of Wessex, based on Dorset and the surrounding counties. Also popular during this period were two Scottish novelists: Robert Louis Stevenson, best known for his children's book *Treasure Island*, and Sir Arthur Conan Doyle, creator of detective Sherlock Holmes.

20th Century

The ideological chaos and social disruption of the postwar period fed into the fractured narratives of modernism. Perhaps the greatest British novelist of the interwar period is DH Lawrence, particularly known for his multi-generational family saga *Sons and Lovers*, and his controversial exploration of sexuality in *Lady Chatterley's Lover*.

Other landmark novels of the modern period include EM Forster's *A Passage to India*, about the hopelessness of British colonial rule, and the politically charged works of George Orwell such as *1984* and *Animal Farm*. Evelyn Waugh often dealt with the changing nature of British society – particularly the decline of the aristocracy, as

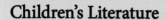

Children's Literature

British writers have produced some of the great works of children's fiction of the last century, from Charles Dodgson's mind-bending *Alice in Wonderland* through to Roald Dahl's mischievous tales and J.K. Rowling's mega-selling *Harry Potter* novels. A few classics that are particularly worth seeking out are *The Railway Children* by the children's writer E. Nesbit; Beatrix Potter's anthropomorphic *Tales* and Arthur Ransome's *Swallows and Amazons*, both of which were largely inspired by the scenery of the Lake District; and *The Wind in the Willows* by Kenneth Grahame, set on a stretch of the River Thames.

Oxford has particularly strong links with children's fiction: CS Lewis and JRR Tolkien both lived and worked here, while a fantastical version of the city features heavily in Philip Pullman's *His Dark Materials*.

examined in *Brideshead Revisited*. The Cold War era spawned many great novels by writers such as Graham Greene and John Le Carré, and also inspired Ian Fleming to create the archetypal British hero, James Bond.

The 20th century was also a great time for poets. Major names such as WH Auden, Stephen Spender and TS Eliot (an American by birth but a lifelong Anglophile) broke new poetic ground during the first half of the century, followed by modern poets including Ted Hughes and Philip Larkin. Wales also produced an iconic poet in Dylan Thomas, whose most famous work is *Under Milk Wood* (1954), examining the tensions and peculiarities of Welsh village life.

New Millennium

As the 20th century came to a close, the nature of multicultural Britain proved a rich inspiration for contemporary novelists. Hanif Kureishi sowed the seeds with his ground-breaking 1990 novel *The Buddha of Suburbia,* examining the hopes and fears of a group of suburban Anglo-Asians in London, while the magical realist novels of Salman Rushdie attracted huge sales (and worldwide notoriety in the wake of his most controversial novel, *The Satanic Verses*).

Other big beasts of the British literary establishment include names such as Martin Amis, Ian McEwan, the late Iain Banks, Kazuo Ishiguro and David Mitchell, whose century-spanning work *Cloud Atlas* has had a Hollywood blockbuster treatment. Don't overlook Britain's 'popular' writers, who specialise in crime fiction or fantasy: the *Inspector Rebus* novels of Ian Rankin and the *Discworld* novels of Terry Pratchett attract huge sales.

The biggest event of the literary world is the Man Booker Prize (www.theman bookerprize.com), awarded to the year's best new novel written in English. Hilary Mantel, author of *Wolf Hall*, recently made history by winning the prize for the second time for her latest tale of Tudor intrigue, *Bring Up the Bodies*.

Painting & Sculpture

Early Days

For many centuries, Continental Europe – especially Holland, Spain, France and Italy – set the artistic agenda. The first artist with a truly British style and sensibility was arguably William Hogarth, whose riotous canvases exposed the vice and corruption of 18th-century London. His most celebrated work is *A Rake's Progress*.

While Hogarth was busy satirising society, other artists were hard at work showing it in its best light. The leading figures of 18th-century British portraiture were Sir Joshua Reynolds, Thomas Gainsborough and George Stubbs, the latter known for his intricate studies of animals (particularly horses). Most of these artists are represented at Tate Britain or the National Gallery in London.

19th Century

In the 19th century leading painters favoured images of the landscape. John Constable's idyllic depictions of the Suffolk countryside are summed up in *The Haywain* (National Gallery), while JMW Turner was fascinated by the effects of light and colour, with his works becoming almost entirely abstract by the 1840s.

The Pre-Raphaelite movement of the mid- to late 19th century explored the Victorian taste for myths and fairy tales. Key members of the movement included John Everett Millais; his *Ophelia* is an excellent example of their style, and can be seen at the Tate Britain gallery.

A good friend of the Pre-Raphaelites was William Morris; he saw late 19th-century furniture and interior design as increasingly vulgar, and with Dante Gabriel Rossetti and Edward Burne-Jones founded the Arts and Crafts movement to encourage the revival of a decorative approach to design. A close contemporary was Charles Rennie Mackintosh, who became one of the stars of the art-nouveau movement; his designs still grace many of Glasgow's buildings.

Early 20th Century

In the tumultuous 20th century, British art became increasingly experimental. Its place on the international stage was ensured by the monumental sculptures of Henry Moore and Barbara Hepworth (whose work can be seen at St Ives in Cornwall); the contorted paintings of Francis Bacon and the works of the Scottish Colourists – Francis Cadell, SJ Peploe, Leslie Hunter and JD Ferguson – have turned into the type of prints and postcards favoured by souvenir shops.

Postwar

The mid-1950s and early '60s saw an explosion of British artists plundering television, music, advertising and popular culture for inspiration. Leaders of this new 'pop-art' movement included David Hockney, who used bold colours and simple lines to depict his dachshunds and swimming pools; and Peter Blake, who designed the collage cover for The Beatles' landmark *Sgt. Pepper's* album.

The 1990s

The next big explosion in British art came in the 1990s; it was called 'Britart', and key figures included Damien Hirst and Tracy Emin. Another key artist of the period – and still going strong today – is the sculptor Antony Gormley, whose *Angel of the North*, a massive steel human figure with outstretched wings, was initially derided by the locals but is now an instantly recognised symbol of northeast England.

New Millennium

In 2008 a contest was announced to create a huge outdoor sculpture in Kent to counterbalance the Angel of the North. Mark Wallinger's 50m-high White Horse of Ebbsfleet would have been visible from the train line between London and Paris – a 'Welcome to Britain' sign for the 21st century. The project stalled through lack of funding, but in Scotland 2014 saw the unveiling of a pair of stunning equine statues known as The Kelpies. Named after mythical Scottish water-creatures, the two 30m-tall horse's heads are clearly visible from the M9 motorway between Edinburgh and Stirling.

Music

Royal Albert Hall (p98)

DAVID BANK/GETTY IMAGES

If there's one thing Britain has given the world, it's great music. Ever since the days of the Fab Four and the Swinging Sixties this musical island has been producing world-beating bands, and it's a process that continues to this day. The Brits love their music.

Pop & Rock

Pioneers & Punks

Britain's brought pop to the world ever since The Beatles, The Rolling Stones, The Who, Cream, and The Kinks spear-headed the 'British Invasion' of the 1960s.

Glam rock swaggered in to replace peace and love in the early 1970s, with Marc Bolan and David Bowie donning spandex in a variety of chameleonic guises, succeeded by art-rockers Roxy Music and anthemic popsters Queen and Elton John. Meanwhile Led Zeppelin laid down the blueprint for heavy metal and hard rock, and 1960s psychedelia morphed into the spacey noodlings of prog rock, epitomised by Pink Floyd, Genesis and Yes.

By the late '70s the prog bands were looking out of touch and punk exploded onto the scene, with nihilistic lyrics and short, sharp, three-chord tunes. The Sex Pistols produced one landmark album *(Never Mind the Bollocks: Here's the Sex Pistols)*, a clutch of (mostly banned) singles and a storm of controversy, ably assisted by The Clash, The Damned, The Buzzcocks and The Stranglers.

While punk burned itself out in a blaze of squealing guitars, New Wave musicians including The Jam and Elvis Costello took up the torch, blending spiky tunes and sharp lyrics into a poppier, more radio-friendly sound.

Ravers & New Romantics

The 1980s was mostly dominated by big pop bands with big egos and equally big hair, including acts such as Duran Duran, Wham and Culture Club, known for their flamboyant costumes and synthesised sounds. Meanwhile the Smiths took an entirely different direction based around Johnny Marr's guitars and Morrissey's arch (and often existentially bleak) lyrics.

Live Music

Most cities have at least one concert hall regularly hosting big acts, as well as smaller venues where lesser-known acts strut their stuff. Bands large and small are pretty much guaranteed to play in London, but often tour extensively to major cities (Cardiff, Liverpool, Manchester and Glasgow usually feature).

For tickets and listings, agencies include **See** (www.seetickets.com) and **Ticketmaster** (www.ticketmaster.co.uk), or **Gigs in Scotland** (www.gigsinscotland.com) for info north of the border.

The beats and bleeps of 1980s electronica fuelled the burgeoning dance-music scene of the early '90s. Pioneering artists such as New Order (risen from the ashes of Joy Division) used synthesised sounds to inspire the soundtrack for the ecstasy-fuelled rave culture, centred on famous clubs like Manchester's Haçienda and London's Ministry of Sound.

By the mid-1990s, Manchester was a focus for the burgeoning British indie scene, driven by guitar-based bands such as the Charlatans, the Stone Roses, James, Happy Mondays and Manchester's most famous musical export, Oasis. Such was the atmosphere and energy that the city was dubbed 'Madchester', and the whole world, it seemed, was 'up for it'. In the late 1990s indie segued into Britpop, a catch-all term covering bands Pulp and Blur (much to their distain, Oasis came under the banner too), all part of the short-lived phenomenon of 'Cool Britannia'.

New Millennium

The new millennium saw no let up in the British music scene's continual shifting and reinventing. Jazz, soul, R&B and hip-hop beats fused into a new 'urban' sound epitomised by artists like Jamelia, The Streets and Dizzee Rascal.

On the pop side, singer-songwriters are enjoying a renaissance thanks to multi-Grammy-winning Adele and contemporaries such as Ed Sheeran, Emeli Sandé and the late Amy Winehouse. The spirit of British indie has been kept alive by new bands (especially the all-conquering Coldplay), while traces of punk and postpunk live on in the music of artists such as Franz Ferdinand, The Arctic Monkeys, Muse and others.

Pop Today, Gone Tomorrow

Today's music scene is as fast-moving and varied as ever – trying to keep up with the latest acts is the main challenge. By the time you read this, half of the 'great new bands' of last year will have sunk without trace, and a fresh batch of unknowns will have risen to dominate the airwaves and download sites. This is true of the latest stars of reality

TV shows such as *The X-Factor*, who tend to produce a single or two and then disappear into obscurity.

A good place to check out who's hot are the UK's wealth of outdoor summer festivals. The original (and still the biggest) is held near Glastonbury in Somerset, but there are many more: Reading, Leeds and Hyde Park host their own major festivals, while other big names such as Latitude, Truck, Green Man and Bestival follow the Glastonbury tradition and are held out in the great British countryside.

Another good guide is the annual Mercury Music Prize (www.mercuryprize.com), awarded to the best British album of the last year.

Traditional & Folk Music

Scotland, England and Wales all have long histories of traditional folk music, each with its own distinctive styles and melodies. Well-known native instruments include the bagpipes in Scotland and the harp in Wales, while Wales also has a strong tradition of poetry and song (although perhaps the best-known genre – male voice choirs – is a relatively recent phenomenon). These days, the term 'folk music' generally refers to singers and musicians perform-ing traditional (or traditional-style) songs accompanied by instruments such as guitar, fiddle and penny whistle.

British folk music mines a rich seam of regional culture, from the rhythmic 'waulking songs' of the tweed weavers of the Outer Hebrides to the jaunty melodies that accompany England's morris dancers. Local history plays its part too – many Welsh folk songs recall Owain Glyndŵr's battles against English domination, while English folk lyrics range from memories of the Tolpuddle Martyrs to sea shanties sung by Liverpool sailors. In Scotland, the Jacobite rebellion of 1745 was a rich source of traditional songs, while *Flower of Scotland* – written in 1967 by popular folk duo the Corries, and today the unofficial Scottish national anthem – harks back to the Battle of Bannockburn in 1314.

In the last decade or so, thanks largely to the rise in interest in world music, the folk music of Britain has enjoyed its biggest revival since the 1960s. Leading exponents include Eliza Carthy, Kate Rusby and Bellowhead, as well as Mumford & Sons, whose latest album became one of the fastest selling in history when it was released in 2012.

You can see traditional and folk music at informal gigs or jam sessions in pubs (notably in Edinburgh), or at events such as the annual folk festivals in Sidmouth and Cambridge, and cultural festivals such as the National Eisteddfod in Wales and the Mòd in Scotland.

Classical Music

Britain has 13 symphony orchestras, as well as dozens of amateur and youth orches-tras, who stage concerts throughout the year. The biggest classical event of all is The Proms, one of the world's greatest music festivals, which takes place from July to September at London's Royal Albert Hall.

Well-known British composers include Edward Elgar, famous for his *Enigma Variations*; Gustav Holtz, who wrote *The Planets*; Benjamin Britten, particularly known for his two operas *Peter Grimes* and *The Turn of the Screw*; and Vaughan Williams whose well-known *A London Symphony* ends with chimes of Big Ben.

The Best...
Music Venues

1 Royal Albert Hall (p98)

2 Wales Millennium Centre (p268)

3 Ronnie Scott's (p98)

4 The Roundhouse (p98)

5 The Hydro(p320)

Sport

United Trinity sculpture by Philip Jackson, Old Trafford football stadium (p233)

PETER RICHARDSON/GETTY IMAGES ©

If you want a short cut into the heart of British culture, watch the British at play. They're passionate about their sport – as participants or spectators. Every weekend thousands of people turn out to cheer their favourite team, and sporting highlights such as Wimbledon keep the entire nation enthralled. The biggest sporting event of all – the Olympic Games – came to London in 2012, focusing the world's attention on this sports-mad nation.

Football (Soccer)

Despite what the fans may say in Madrid or Milan, the English football league has some of the finest – and richest – teams and players in the world. The Premier League is for the country's top 20 clubs, including internationally famous Arsenal, Liverpool and Manchester United, while 72 other teams from England and Wales play in the three divisions called the Championship, League One and League Two. In addition to the various leagues, there are also several cup competitions – the most famous of which is the knock-out FA Cup, which culminates in May at Wembley Stadium.

Many cities have a couple of major teams – Manchester United and Manchester City, or Liverpool and Everton, for example. When they play each other (usually twice a season) these games are known as 'local derbies', and the rivalry is especially intense.

The football season lasts from August to May, but tickets for the big games in the upper division are like gold dust, and cost £30 to £70, even if you're lucky enough to find one.

Rugby

A popular witticism holds that football is a gentlemen's game played by hooligans, while rugby is the other way around. There are two variants of the game: rugby union is played in southern England, Wales and Scotland; rugby league is the main sport in northern England, although there is crossover. Many rules and tactics of both codes are similar, but in league there are 13 players in each team (ostensibly making the game faster), while rugby union sides have 15 players each. Wales has a particularly special relationship with rugby – it's considered the national game, and for many Welsh people, football pales into insignificance in comparison.

The main season for club matches is roughly September to Easter, while the international rugby union calendar is dominated by the annual Six Nations Championship (England, Scotland, Wales, Ireland, France and Italy) between January and April. It's usual for the Scots to support Wales, or vice versa, when either team is playing the 'old enemy', England.

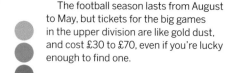

London's Olympic Legacy

London's stint as host for the 2012 Olympics brought the city to the world's attention, and despite plenty of the inevitable British cynicism prior to the event, it was generally deemed a great success. Most of the major events took place around Stratford in London's East End; since the Olympics, the site has been renamed the Queen Elizabeth Olympic Park. You can enjoy a variety of parks, walks and landscaped areas alongside the sporting venues, as well as Anish Kapoor's helter-skelter style tower, the **ArcelorMittal Orbit**, which provides great views over the park.

Cricket

Cricket has its origins in southeast England, with the earliest written record dating to 1598. It became an international game during Britain's colonial era, when it was exported to the countries of the Commonwealth. There are a number of different formats: one-day and Twenty20 matches last one day, while test matches usually stretch out over five days. Cricket's rules and terminology are infamously arcane, but for aficionados, it isn't just a sport – it's a way of life.

County cricket is the mainstay of the domestic game, while international one-day games and five-day test matches are played against sides such as Australia and the West Indies at landmark grounds like Lords in London and Headingley in Leeds. Test match tickets cost from £30 to well over £200 and tend to sell fast. County championships usually charge £5 to £25, and rarely sell out. Twenty20 cricket is a TV-friendly short form of the game encouraging big scores; it's more interesting to watch, but decried by purists.

To catch a game, the easiest option of all – and often the most enjoyable – is stumbling across a local match on a village green as you travel around the country. There's no charge for spectators, and no one will mind if you nip to the pub during a quiet period. If you're lucky, the locals might even try and explain the rules.

Golf

Golf is a very popular sport in Britain, with millions taking to the fairways every week. The main golfing tournament for spectators is the Open Championship, often referred to simply as The Open (or the 'British Open' outside the UK). It's the oldest of professional golf's major championships (dating back to 1860) and the only one held outside the USA. It is usually played over the third weekend in July and the location changes each year, using nine courses around the country.

Perhaps the UK's most famous golfing destination is the Old Course at St Andrews, often dubbed the 'home of golf' as it was one of the first places the sport was played, all the way back in the early 1400s. Playing here is almost a spiritual experience for golf enthusiasts, but you'll need to plan well ahead to get a game.

If you fancy a round as part of your visit to Britain, there are around 2000 private and public golf courses to choose from, with 500 in Scotland alone. (There are more golf courses per capita in Scotland than in any other country in the world.) Some private clubs admit only members or golfers with a handicap certificate, but most welcome visitors. Public golf courses are open to anyone. A round costs around £10 to £30 on a public course, and up to £200 on private courses.

Tennis

Tennis is widely played in Britain, but the most famous tournament is the All England Lawn Tennis Championships – more commonly known as Wimbledon – when tennis fever sweeps through the country for the last week of June and the first week of July. In between matches, the crowds traditionally feast on strawberries and cream – that's 28 tonnes of strawberries and 7000L of cream annually, to be precise.

Demand for seats at Wimbledon (www.wimbledon.org) always outstrips supply, but to give everyone an equal chance the tickets are sold through a public ballot. You can also take your chance on the spot: about 6000 tickets are sold each day (but not on the last four days) and queuing at dawn should get you into the ground.

The Best...
Sporting Locations

1 St Andrews (p328)

2 Millennium Stadium, Cardiff (p265)

3 Old Trafford, Manchester (p233)

4 Wimbledon, London (p43)

Food & Drink

Fish and chips

VISITBRITAIN/MARTIN BRENT/GETTY IMAGES

Britain once had a reputation for bad food, but the nation has enjoyed something of a culinary revolution over the last few years. London is recognised as having one of the best collections of restaurants in the world, while all across the country stylish eateries and gourmet gastropubs are springing up practically everywhere you look.

British Classics

One foodie phenomenon you'll definitely encounter is the 'full English breakfast' (just 'full breakfast' in Wales and Scotland), more colloquially known as a 'fry-up', consisting of bacon, sausage, egg, mushrooms, fried tomatoes, baked beans and a choice of white or brown toast. Sometimes you'll also be offered black pudding – known in other countries as 'blood sausage' – and fried bread. It's fine to ask for just the bits you want (just bacon and egg, for example).

Some B&Bs offer other alternatives, such as kippers (smoked fish) – especially in Scotland – or a 'continental breakfast', which omits the cooked stuff and may even add something exotic like croissants.

Moving on to lunch, one of the many great inventions that Britain gave the world is the sandwich, supposedly invented in the 18th century by the aristocratic Earl of

Sandwich. Another classic – especially in pubs – is the ploughman's lunch. Basically it's bread and cheese, usually accompanied by a spicy pickle, salad and some onions, although you'll also find other variations, such as farmer's lunch (bread and chicken), stockman's lunch (bread and ham) and so on.

When it comes to main meals, a classic British dinner is roast beef. The most famous beef comes from Scotland's Aberdeen Angus cattle, while the best-known food from Wales is lamb. Venison – usually from red deer – is readily available in Scotland, as well as in parts of Wales and England, most notably in the New Forest.

The traditional accompaniment for British beef is Yorkshire pudding. It's simply roasted batter, but very tasty when properly cooked. Bring sausages and Yorkshire 'pud' together and you have another favourite dish: toad-in-the-hole.

But perhaps the best-known classic British staple is fish and chips, often bought as a takeaway. Sometimes the fish can be tasteless (especially when eaten far from the sea), but in towns with salt in the air this deep-fried delight is always worth trying.

Thanks to its colonial past, Britain has also become a nation of curry-lovers: a recent poll suggested that the Brits' favourite dish was actually chicken tikka masala. You'll find at least one curry house in most British towns – ask around for a local recommendation, as standards vary.

The Best...
Local Classics

1 Fish and chips

2 Yorkshire pudding

3 Welsh rarebit

4 Cullen skink

5 A pint of bitter

6 A dram of whisky

Regional Specialities

Seafood is a highlight in this island nation, especially in Scotland, West Wales and southwest England. Scottish salmon is also well known, and available everywhere in Britain smoked or poached, but there's a big difference between the fatty version from fish farms and the tastier wild variety. Other British seafood includes herring, trout and haddock; in Scotland the latter is best enjoyed with potato and cream in the old-style soup called cullen skink.

Treats in northern England include Cumberland sausage, a tasty mix of minced pork and herbs so large it has to be spiralled to fit on your plate. In Scotland, the most famous meaty speciality is haggis, a large sausage made from a sheep's stomach filled with minced meat and oatmeal.

For a snack in central England, try Melton Mowbray pork pies, cooked ham compressed in a casing of pastry. A legal victory in 2005 ensured that only pies made in the eponymous Midlands town could carry the Melton Mowbray moniker – in the same way that fizzy wine from regions outside Champagne can't claim that name.

Another British speciality that enjoys the same protection is Stilton – a strong white cheese, either plain or in a blue-vein variety. Only five dairies in the country are allowed to produce cheese with this name.

A couple of other regional classics to look out for are Welsh rarebit – really just a sophisticated variation of cheese on toast, seasoned and flavoured with butter, milk and sometimes beer – and Scotch broth, a thick soup of barley, lentils and mutton stock.

British Beer

Among alcoholic drinks, Britain is best known for its beer. Typically ranging from dark brown to bright orange in colour, technically it is called 'ale', and is more commonly called 'bitter' in England and Wales. Traditionally made and stored beer is called 'real ale' and, for the unwary, the first sip may come as a shock – a warm, flat shock. It's an acquired taste, but the trick is to focus on the flavour: this beer doesn't need to be chilled or fizzed to make it palatable.

Whisky

The spirit most visitors associate with Britain – and especially Scotland – is whisky. (Note the spelling – it's *Irish* whiskey that has an 'e'.) More than 2000 brands are produced, but the two main kinds are single malt, made from malted barley, and blended whisky, made from unmalted grain blended with malts. Single malts are rarer and more expensive. When ordering a 'dram' in Scotland remember to ask for whisky – only the English and other foreigners say 'Scotch'.

Testing whisky in a distillery
LEON HARRIS/GETTY IMAGES ©

Survival Guide

Leeds Castle (p110)
PHOTOGRAPHER: VISITBRITAIN/BRITAIN ON VIEW/GETTY IMAGES ©

A-Z
Directory

● ● ●

Accommodation

Accommodation in Britain is as varied as the sights you visit. From hip hotels to basic barns, the wide choice is all part of the attraction.

B&Bs

The B&B (bed and breakfast) is a great British institution. At smaller places it's pretty much a room in somebody's house; larger places may be called a 'guesthouse' (halfway between a B&B and a full hotel).

When booking, check where your B&B actually is. In country areas, postal addresses include the nearest town, which may be 20 miles away – important if you're walking! Some B&B owners will pick you up by car for a small charge.

Prices Usually quoted per person, based on two people sharing a room. Single rooms for solo travellers are harder to find, and attract a 20% to 50% premium. Some B&Bs simply won't take single people (unless you pay the full double-room price), especially in summer.

Booking Advance reservations are preferred at B&Bs and are essential during popular periods. You can book many B&Bs via online agencies but rates may be cheaper if you book direct. If you haven't booked in advance, most towns have a main drag of B&Bs; those with spare rooms hang up a 'Vacancies' sign. Many B&Bs require a minimum two-night stay at weekends. Some places reduce rates for longer stays (two or three nights) mid-week. If a B&B is full, owners may recommend another place nearby (possibly a private house taking occasional guests, not in tourist listings).

Food Most B&Bs serve enormous breakfasts; some offer packed lunches (around £6) and evening meals (around £15 to £20).

Hotels

There's a massive choice of hotels in Britain, from small town houses to grand country mansions, from no-frills locations to boutique hideaways. At the bargain end, single/double rooms cost from £40/50. Move up the scale and you'll pay £100/150 or beyond.

If all you want is a place to put your head down, budget chain hotels can be a good option. Most are lacking in ambience, but who cares? You'll only be there for 12 hours, and eight of them you'll be asleep. Prices vary on demand: at quiet times twin-bed rooms start from £30; at the height of the tourist season you'll pay £60 or more. Options include:

○ **Ibis Hotels** (www.ibis.com)

○ **Premier Inn** (www.premierinn.com)

○ **Travelodge** (www.travelodge.co.uk)

Pubs & Inns

As well as selling drinks, many pubs and inns offer lodging, particularly in country areas. For bed and breakfast, you'll pay around £25 per person for a basic room, around £40 for something better. An advantage for solo tourists: pubs often have single rooms.

Sleeping Price Ranges

Reviews of places to stay use the following price ranges, all based on double room with private bathroom in high season. Hotels in London are more expensive than the rest of the country, so have different price ranges.

	LONDON	ELSEWHERE
£	<£100	<£65
££	£100–180	£65–130
£££	>£180	>£130

Book Your Stay Online

For more accommodation reviews by Lonely Planet authors, check out http://hotels.lonelyplanet.com. You'll find independent reviews, as well as recommendations on the best places to stay. Best of all, you can book online.

Customs Regulations

Travellers arriving in the UK from EU countries don't have to pay tax or duty on goods for personal use, and can bring in as much EU duty-paid alcohol and tobacco as they like. However, if you bring in more than the following, you'll probably be asked some questions:

- 800 cigarettes
- 1kg of tobacco
- 10L of spirits
- 90L of wine
- 110L of beer.

Travellers from outside the EU can bring in, duty-free:

- 200 cigarettes *or* 100 cigarillos *or* 50 cigars *or* 250g of tobacco
- 16L of beer
- 4L of non-sparkling wine
- 1L of spirits *or* 2L of fortified wine or sparkling wine
- £390 worth of all other goods, including perfume, gifts and souvenirs.

Anything over this limit must be declared to customs officers on arrival. Check www.hmrc.gov.uk/customs for further details, and for information on reclaiming VAT on items purchased in the UK by non-EU residents.

Electricity

230V/50Hz

Gay & Lesbian Travellers

Britain is a generally tolerant place for gays and lesbians. London, Manchester and Brighton have flourishing gay scenes, and in other sizeable cities (even some small towns) you'll find communities not entirely in the closet. That said, you'll still find pockets of homophobic hostility in some areas. Resources include the following:

- Diva (www.divamag.co.uk)
- Gay Times (www.gaytimes.co.uk)
- London Lesbian & Gay Switchboard (www.llgs.org.uk)

Health

- If you're an EU citizen, a European Health Insurance Card (EHIC) – available from health centres or, in the UK, post offices – covers you for most medical care. An EHIC will not cover you for non-urgent cases, or emergency repatriation.
- Citizens from non-EU countries should find out if there is a reciprocal arrangement for free medical care between their country and the UK.
- If you do need health insurance, make sure you get a policy that covers you for the worst possible scenarios, including emergency flights home.
- No jabs (vaccinations) are required to travel to Britain. For more information, check with your medical provider in your own country before you travel.
- Chemists (pharmacies) can advise on minor ailments such as sore throats and earaches. In large cities, there's always at least one 24-hour chemist.

Insurance

Although everyone receives free emergency treatment, regardless of nationality, travel insurance is still highly recommended. It will usually

Eating Price Ranges

In reviews, the following price ranges refer to a main dish.

£ less than £10

££ £10 to £20

£££ more than £20

cover medical and dental consultation and treatment at private clinics, which can be quicker than NHS places – as well as the cost of any emergency flights – plus all the usual stuff like loss of baggage.

Worldwide travel insurance is available at www.lonelyplanet.com/bookings. You can buy, extend and claim online anytime, even if you're already on the road.

Internet Access

◦ 3G and 4G mobile broadband coverage is good in large population centres, but limited or nonexistent in rural areas. However, beware high charges for data roaming – check with your mobile/cellphone provider before travelling.

◦ Most hotels, B&Bs, hostels, stations and coffee shops (even some trains and buses) have wi-fi access, charging anything from nothing to £6 per hour.

◦ Internet cafes are surprisingly rare in Britain, especially away from big cities and tourist spots. Most charge from £1 per hour, but out in the sticks you can pay £5 per hour.

◦ Public libraries often have computers with free internet access, but only for 30-minute slots, and demand is high. All the usual warnings apply about keystroke-capturing software and other security risks.

◦ We've indicated accommodation and eating and drinking options that have wi-fi with the 🛜 symbol in the text. Wi-fi is often free, but some places (usually upmarket hotels) charge.

◦ If you see the @ symbol, then the place has an internet terminal.

Climate

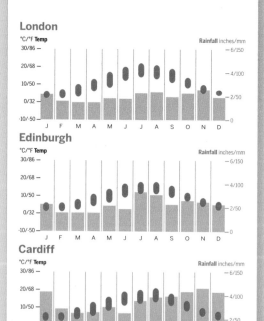

London
°C/°F **Temp**   **Rainfall** inches/mm

Edinburgh
°C/°F **Temp**   **Rainfall** inches/mm

Cardiff
°C/°F **Temp**   **Rainfall** inches/mm

Legal Matters

◦ Police have the power to detain, for up to six hours, anyone suspected of having committed an offence punishable by imprisonment (including drugs offences). Police have the right to search anyone they suspect of possessing drugs.

◦ You must be over 18 to buy alcohol and cigarettes. You usually have to be 18 to enter a pub or bar, although rules are different for under-18s if eating. Some bars and clubs are over-21 only.

o Illegal drugs are widely available, especially in clubs. Cannabis possession is a criminal offence; punishment for carrying a small amount may be a warning, a fine or imprisonment. Dealers face stiffer penalties, as do people caught with other drugs.

o On buses and trains (including the London Underground), people without a valid ticket are fined on the spot – usually around £20.

Money

The currency of Britain is the pound sterling (£). Paper money ('notes') comes in £5, £10, £20 and £50 denominations. Some shops don't accept £50 notes because fakes circulate.

ATMs

ATMs (usually called 'cash machines' in Britain) are common in cities and even small towns. Cash withdrawals from some ATMs may be subject to a small charge, but most are free. If you're not from the UK, your home bank will likely charge you for withdrawing money overseas. Watch out for tampered ATMs; a common ruse is to attach a card-reader or minicamera.

Credit & Debit Cards

Visa and MasterCard credit and debit cards are widely accepted in Britain. Most businesses will assume your card is 'Chip and PIN' enabled (using a PIN instead of signing). If it isn't, you should be able to sign instead, but some

places may not accept your card. Some smaller country B&Bs don't take cards, so you'll need to pay with cash.

Moneychangers

Cities and larger towns have banks and exchange bureaux for changing your money into pounds. Check rates first; some bureaux offer poor rates or levy outrageous commissions. You can also change money at some post offices – very handy in country areas, and exchange rates are fair.

Opening Hours

Banks

o 9.30am to 4pm or 5pm Monday to Friday

o Main branches 9.30am to 1pm Saturday

Bars, Pubs & Clubs

o Standard hours for pubs: 11am to 11pm Monday to Sunday. Some pubs shut from 3pm to 6pm; some open to midnight or 1am Friday and Saturday.

o Standard hours for bars: 11am to midnight, often later, especially at weekends.

o Clubs open any time from 8pm to 11pm, until 2am or beyond.

Cafes & Restaurants

o Standard hours for cafes: 9am to 5pm. Most cafes open daily.

o Standard hours for restaurants: lunch noon to 3pm, dinner 6pm to 11pm (to

midnight or later in cities). Most restaurants open daily; some close Sunday evening or all day Monday.

Museums & Sights

o Large museums and sights usually open daily.

o Some smaller places open Saturday and Sunday but close Monday and/or Tuesday.

o Smaller places open daily in high season but operate weekends only or completely close in low season.

Post Offices

o 9am to 5pm (5.30pm or 6pm in cities) Monday to Friday

o 9am to 12.30pm Saturday; main branches to 5pm

Shops

o 9am to 5pm (5.30pm or 6pm in cities) Monday to Friday

School Holidays

Roads get busy and hotel prices go up during school holidays. Exact dates vary from year to year and region to region, but are roughly as follows:

Easter Holiday Week before and week after Easter

Summer Holiday Third week of July to first week of September

Christmas Holiday Mid-December to first week of January

There are also three week-long 'half-term' school holidays – usually late February (or early March), late May and late October. These vary between Scotland, England and Wales.

○ 9am to 5pm Saturday

○ larger shops open 10am to 4pm Sunday. London and other cities have convenience stores open 24/7.

○ In smaller towns and country areas shops often shut for lunch (normally 1pm to 2pm) and on Wednesday or Thursday afternoon.

●●● Public Holidays

Holidays for the whole of Britain:

New Year's Day 1 January (plus 2 January in Scotland)

Easter March/April (Good Friday to Easter Monday inclusive)

May Day First Monday in May

Spring Bank Holiday Last Monday in May

Summer Bank Holiday Last Monday in August

Christmas Day 25 December

Boxing Day 26 December

If a public holiday falls on a weekend, the nearest Monday is usually taken instead. In England and Wales most businesses and banks close on official public holidays (hence the quaint term 'bank holiday'). In Scotland, bank holidays are just for the banks, and many businesses stay open. Many Scottish towns normally have a spring and autumn holiday, but the dates vary.

On public holidays, some small museums and places of interest close, but larger attractions have their busiest times. If a place closes on Sunday, it'll probably be shut on bank holidays as well.

Virtually everything – attractions, shops, banks, offices – closes on Christmas Day, although pubs are open at lunchtime. There's usually no public transport on Christmas Day, and a very minimal service on Boxing Day.

●●● Safe Travel

Britain is a remarkably safe country, but crime is not unknown in London and other cities.

○ Watch out for pickpockets and hustlers in crowded areas popular with tourists such as around Westminster Bridge in London.

○ When travelling by tube, tram or urban train services at night, choose a carriage containing other people.

○ Many town centres can be rowdy on Friday and Saturday nights when the pubs and clubs are emptying

○ Unlicensed minicabs – a bloke with a car earning money on the side – operate in large cities, and are worth avoiding unless you know what you're doing.

●●● Telephone

Mobile Phones

The UK uses the GSM 900/1800 network, which covers the rest of Europe, Australia and New Zealand, but isn't compatible with the North American GSM 1900. Most modern mobiles can function on both networks – but check before you leave home just in case.

Though roaming charges within the EU are due to be entirely eliminated in December 2015, other international roaming charges can be prohibitively high, and you'll probably find it cheaper to get a UK number. This is easily done by buying a SIM card (around £10 including calling credit) and sticking it in your phone. Your phone may be locked to your home network, however, so you'll have to either get it unlocked, or buy a pay-as-you-go phone along with your SIM card (around £50).

Pay-as-you-go phones can be recharged by buying vouchers from shops.

Phone Codes

Dialling into the UK Dial your country's international access code then 44 (the UK country code), then the area code (dropping the first 0) followed by the telephone number.

Dialling out of the UK The international access code is 00; dial this, then add the code of the country you wish to dial.

Making a reverse-charge (collect) international call Dial 155 for the operator. It's an expensive option, but not for the caller.

Area codes in the UK No standard format or length, eg Edinburgh 0131, London 020, Ambleside 015394.

Directory Assistance A host of agencies compete for your business and charge from 10p to 40p; numbers include 118 192, 118 118, 118 500 and 118 811.

Mobile phones Codes usually begin with 07.

Free calls Numbers starting with 0800 are free; calls to 0845 numbers are charged at local rates.

National operator 100

International operator 155

Emergency (police, fire, ambulance, mountain rescue, coastguard) 999

Time

Britain is on GMT/UTC. The clocks go forward for 'summer time' one hour at the end of March, and go back at the end of October. The 24-hour clock is used for transport timetables.

Tourist Information

Most British cities and towns, and some villages, have a tourist information centre or visitor information centre – for ease we've called all these places 'tourist offices'. Such places have helpful staff, books and maps for sale, leaflets to give away, and advice

---

Heritage Organisations

A highlight of a journey through Britain is visiting the numerous castles and historic sites that pepper the country. Membership of a heritage organisation gets you free admission (usually a good saving) as well as information handbooks and so on.

National Trust (NT; www.nationaltrust.org.uk) A charity protecting historic buildings and land with scenic importance across England and Wales. Annual membership £58 (discounts for under-26s and families). A Touring Pass allows free entry to NT properties for one/two weeks (£25/30 per person); families and couples get cheaper rates. The **National Trust for Scotland** (NTS; www.nts.org.uk) is a similar organisation in Scotland; annual membership £52.

English Heritage (EH; www.english-heritage.org.uk) State-funded organisation responsible for numerous historic sites. Annual membership £49 (couples and seniors get discounts). An Overseas Visitors Pass allows free entry to most sites for nine/16 days for £25/30 (cheaper rates for couples and families). In Wales and Scotland the equivalent organisations are **Cadw** (www.cadw.wales.gov.uk) and **Historic Scotland** (HS; www.historic-scotland.gov.uk).

You can join at the first site you visit. If you join an English heritage organisation, it covers you for Wales and Scotland, and vice versa.

Practicalities

○ **Newspapers** Tabloids include the *Sun* and *Mirror*, and *Daily Record* (in Scotland); quality 'broadsheets' include (from right to left, politically) the *Telegraph*, *Times*, *Independent* and *Guardian*.

○ **TV** All TV in the UK is digital. Leading broadcasters include BBC, ITV and Channel 4. Satellite and cable TV providers include Sky and Virgin Media.

○ **Radio** Main BBC stations and wavelengths are Radio 1 (98–99.6MHz FM), Radio 2 (88–92MHz FM), Radio 3 (90–92.2 MHz FM), Radio 4 (92–94.4MHz FM) and Radio 5 Live (909 or 693 AM). National commercial stations include Virgin Radio (1215Hz MW) and non-highbrow classical specialist Classic FM (100–102MHz FM). All are available on digital.

○ **DVD** PAL format (incompatible with NTSC and Secam).

○ **Weights & Measures** Britain uses a mix of metric and imperial measures (eg petrol is sold by the litre but beer by the pint; mountain heights are in metres but road distances in miles).

on things to see or do. Some can also assist with booking accommodation. Some are run by national parks and often have small exhibits about the area. Most tourist offices keep regular business hours; in quiet areas they close from October to March, while in popular areas they open daily year-round. Recent cost-cutting has closed many smaller tourist offices. Before leaving home, check the website of Britain's official tourist board, **Visit Britain** (www.visitbritain.com), covering all national tourism, with links to numerous other sites.

Travellers with Disabilities

All new buildings have wheelchair access, and even hotels in grand old country houses often have lifts, ramps and other facilities. Hotels and B&Bs in historic buildings are often harder to adapt, so you'll have less choice here.

Modern city buses and trams have low floors for easy access, but few have conductors who can lend a hand when you're getting on or off. Many taxis take wheelchairs, or just have more room in the back.

For long-distance travel, coaches may present problems but the main operator, National Express (p402) has wheelchair-friendly coaches on many routes. For details, see the website or ring the dedicated Disabled Passenger Travel Helpline on ☎08717 81 81 79.

On most intercity trains there's more room and better facilities, compared with travel by coach, and usually station staff

around to help. A **Disabled Person's Railcard** (www.disabledpersons-railcard.co.uk) costs £20 and gets you 33% off most train fares.

Useful resources include **Disability Rights UK** (whose services include a key for 7000 public disabled toilets across the UK and who publish a Holiday Guide), **Good Access Guide** and **Tourism for All**

Visas

○ If you're a citizen of the EEA (European Economic Area) nations or Switzerland, you don't need a visa to enter or work in Britain – enter using your national identity card.

○ Visa regulations are always subject to change, and immigration restriction is currently big news in Britain, so it's essential to check with your local British embassy, high commission or consulate before leaving home.

○ Currently, if you're a citizen of Australia, Canada, New Zealand, Japan, Israel, the USA and several other countries, you can stay for up to six months (no visa required), but are not allowed to work.

○ Nationals of many countries, including South Africa, will need to obtain a visa: for more info, see www.ukvisas.gov.uk.

○ British immigration authorities have always been tough; dress neatly and carry proof that you have sufficient funds with which to support yourself. A credit card and/or an onward ticket will help.

Transport

●●●

Getting There & Away

Most visitors reach Britain by air. As London is a global transport hub, it's easy to fly to Britain from just about anywhere. In recent years, the massive growth of budget ('no-frills') airlines has increased the number of routes – and reduced the fares – between Britain and other countries in Europe.

International trains are a comfortable and a 'green' option; the Channel Tunnel allows direct rail services between Britain, France and Belgium, with onward connections to many other European destinations.

Flights, cars and rail tickets can be booked online at lonelyplanet.com/bookings.

 Air

London Airports

For details of getting from the airports into the city, see p104.

Heathrow (LHR; www. heathrowairport.com) Britain's main airport for international flights. About 15 miles west of central London.

Gatwick (LGW; www. gatwickairport.com) Britain's number-two airport, mainly for international flights, 30 miles south of central London.

Stansted (STN; www. stanstedairport.com) About 35 miles northeast of central London, mainly handling charter and budget European flights.

Luton (LTN; www.london-luton.co.uk) Some 35 miles north of central London, well known as a holiday-flight airport.

London City (LCY; www. londoncityairport.com) A few miles east of central London, specialising in flights to/from European and other UK airports.

Regional Airports

Some European and long-haul routes avoid London and use major regional airports including Manchester and Glasgow. Smaller airports such as Southampton, Cardiff and Birmingham have flights to/from Europe and Ireland.

 Train

Channel Tunnel Passenger Service

High-speed **Eurostar** (www. eurostar.com) passenger services shuttle at least 10 times daily between London and Paris (2½ hours) or Brussels (two hours). Buy tickets from travel agencies, major train stations or the Eurostar website. The normal one-way fare

Climate Change & Travel

Every form of transport that relies on carbon-based fuel generates CO_2, the main cause of human-induced climate change. Modern travel is dependent on planes which might use less fuel per kilometre per person than most cars but travel much greater distances. The altitude at which aircraft emit gases (including CO_2) and particles also contributes to their climate change impact. Many websites offer 'carbon calculators' that allow people to estimate the carbon emissions generated by their journey and, for those who wish to do so, to offset the impact of the greenhouse gases emitted with contributions to portfolios of climate-friendly initiatives throughout the world. Lonely Planet offsets the carbon footprint of all staff and author travel.

between London and Paris/Brussels costs £140 to £180; advance booking and off-peak travel gets cheaper fares as low as £39 one-way.

Channel Tunnel Car Service

Drivers use **Eurotunnel** (www. eurotunnel.com). At Folkestone in England or Calais in France, you drive onto a train, get carried through the tunnel and drive off at the other end. Trains run about four times an hour from 6am to 10pm, hourly through the night. Loading and unloading takes an hour; the journey lasts 35 minutes.

Book in advance online or pay on the spot. The one-way

Train & Ferry Connections

As well as Eurostar, many 'normal' trains run between Britain and mainland Europe. You buy one ticket, but get off the train at the port, walk onto a ferry, then get another train on the other side. Routes include Amsterdam–London (via Hook of Holland and Harwich). Travelling between Ireland and Britain, the main train-ferry-train route is Dublin to London, via Dun Laoghaire and Holyhead. Ferries also run between Rosslare and Fishguard or Pembroke (Wales), with train connections on either side.

cost for a car and passengers is between £75 and £165 depending on time of day; promotional fares often bring it down to £55.

Getting Around

For getting around Britain your first big decision is to travel by car or public transport.

Having your own car makes the best use of time, and helps reach remote places, but rental, fuel and parking costs can be expensive and traffic jams frustrating – public transport is often the better choice. As long as you have time, using a mix of train, bus, taxi, walking or hiring a bike, you can get almost anywhere in Britain without having to drive.

The main public transport options are train and long-distance bus. Services between major towns and cities are generally good, although at peak times you must book in advance to be sure of getting a ticket. If you book ahead early or travel at off-peak periods – ideally both – train and coach tickets can be very cheap.

 Air

Britain's domestic airline companies include British Airways, FlyBe/Loganair, EasyJet and Ryanair. If you're really pushed for time, flights on longer routes across Britain (eg Exeter or Southampton to Newcastle, Edinburgh or Inverness), or to the Scottish islands, are handy, although you miss the glorious scenery in between. On some shorter routes (eg London to Newcastle, or Manchester to Newquay) trains compare favourably with planes on time, once airport downtime is factored in. On costs, you might get a bargain airfare, but trains can be cheaper if you buy tickets in advance.

Bicycle

Hiring a bike – for an hour or two, or a week or longer – is a great way to really see the country if you've got time.

Rental in London

London is famous for its Barclays Cycle Hire Scheme, known as 'Boris' bikes' after the mayor that introduced them to the city. Bikes can be hired on the spot from automatic docking stations.

For more information visit the **Transport for London** (www.tfl.gov.uk) website. Other rental options in the capital are listed at www.lcc.org.uk.

Rental Elsewhere

The **nextbike** (www.nextbike.co.uk) bike sharing scheme currently has stations in Glasgow, Stirling and Bath, while tourist towns such as Oxford and Cambridge have plentiful bike rental options. Bikes can also be hired in national parks or forestry sites and in some areas disused railway lines are now bike routes. Rental rates start at about £10 per day, or £20 for something half decent.

Bus & Coach

Long-distance buses (called coaches in Britain) are nearly always the cheapest way to get around, although they're also the slowest – sometimes by a considerable margin. Many towns have separate stations for local buses and long-distance coaches; make sure you go to the right one!

National Express (www.nationalexpress.com) is the main coach operator, with a wide network and frequent services between main centres. North of the border, services tie in with those of **Scottish Citylink** (☎ 0871 266 3333; www.citylink.co.uk), Scotland's leading coach company. Fares vary: they're cheaper if you book in advance and travel at quieter times, and more expensive if you buy your ticket on the spot and it's Friday afternoon. As a guide, a 200-mile trip (eg London to York) will cost £15 to £30 if you book a few days in advance.

Megabus (www.megabus.com) operates a budget

coach service between about 30 destinations around the country.

Car & Motorcycle

Car Rental

Compared with many countries (especially the USA), hire rates are expensive in Britain; the smallest cars start from about £120 per week, and it's around £250 per week for a medium car. All rates include insurance and unlimited mileage, and can rise at busy times (or drop at quiet times).

Some main players:

o **Avis** (www.avis.co.uk)

o **Budget** (www.budget.co.uk)

o **Europcar** (www.europcar.co.uk)

o **Sixt** (www.sixt.co.uk)

o **Thrifty** (www.thrifty.co.uk)

Another option is to look online for small local car-hire companies in Britain that can undercut the international franchises. Generally those in cities are cheaper than in rural areas. Using a rental-broker or comparison site such as **UK Car Hire** (www.ukcarhire.net) or Kayak can also help find bargains.

Insurance

It's illegal to drive a car or motorbike in Britain without (at least) third-party insurance. This will be included with all rental cars. If you're bringing a car from Europe you'll need to arrange it.

Parking

Many cities have short-stay and long-stay car parks; the latter are cheaper though may be less convenient. 'Park & Ride' systems allow you to park on the edge of the city then ride to the centre on frequent nonstop buses for an all-in-one price.

Yellow lines (single or double) along the edge of the road indicate restrictions. Nearby signs spell out when you can and can't park. In London and other big cities, traffic wardens operate with efficiency; if you park on the yellow lines at the wrong time, your car will be clamped or towed away, and it'll cost you £100 or more to get driving again. In some cities there are also red lines, which mean no stopping at all. Ever.

Roads

Motorways and main A-roads deliver you quickly from one end of the country to another. Lesser A-roads, B-roads and minor roads are much more scenic – ideal for car or motorcycle touring. You can't travel fast, but you won't care.

Speed limits are usually 30mph (48km/h) in built-up areas, 60mph (96km/h) on main roads and 70mph (112km/h) on motorways and most (but not all) dual carriageways.

Road Rules

o A foreign driving licence is valid in Britain for up to 12 months

o Drink driving is taken very seriously; you're allowed a maximum blood-alcohol level of 80mg/100mL (0.08%).

o drive on the left

o wear fitted seat belts in cars

o wear helmets on motorcycles

> ## Passport Check
>
> Travelling between Britain's three nations of England, Scotland and Wales is easy. The bus and train systems are fully integrated and in most cases you won't even know you've crossed the border; passports are not required.

o give way to your right at junctions and roundabouts

o always use the left lane on motorways and dual carriageways unless overtaking (although so many people ignore this rule, you'd think it didn't exist)

o don't use a mobile phone while driving unless it's fully hands-free (another rule frequently flouted)

Local Transport

Local Bus

There are good local bus networks year-round in cities and towns. Buses also run in some rural areas year-round, although timetables are designed to serve schools and businesses, so there aren't many midday and weekend services (and they may stop running during school holidays), or buses may link local villages to a market town on only one day each week.

In tourist areas (especially national parks), there are frequent services from Easter to September. However, it's always worth double-checking

How Much To…?

When travelling by long-distance bus, coach or train in Britain, it's important to realise that there's no such thing as a standard fare. Prices vary according to demand and when you buy your ticket. Book long in advance and travel on Tuesday mid-morning and it's cheap. Buy your ticket on the spot late Friday afternoon and it'll be a lot more expensive. Ferries use similar systems. We have quoted sample fares somewhere in between the very cheapest and most expensive options. The price you pay will almost certainly be different.

at a tourist office before planning your day's activities around a bus that may not actually be running.

Along with the local bus route number, frequency and duration we have provided indicative fares.

Local Bus Passes

If you're taking a few local bus rides in one area, day passes (with names like Day Rover, Wayfarer or Explorer) are cheaper than buying several single tickets. Often they can be bought on your first bus, and may include local rail services.

Taxi

There are two sorts of taxi in Britain: those with meters that can be hailed in the street; and minicabs, which are cheaper but can only be called by phone. Unlicensed minicabs operate in some cities.

In London, most taxis are the famous 'black cabs' (some with advertising livery in other colours) which charge by distance and time. Depending on the time of day, a 1-mile journey takes five to 10 minutes and cost £6 to £9. Longer journeys are proportionally cheaper.

Black cabs also operate in

some other large cities around Britain, with rates usually lower than in London.

In London, taxis are best flagged down in the street; a 'for hire' light on the roof indicates availability. In other cities, you can flag down a cab if you see one, but it's usually easier to go to a taxi rank.

In rural areas, taxis need to be called by phone; the best place to find the local taxi's phone number is the local pub. Fares are £2 to £4 per mile.

Train-Taxi is a portal site that helps 'bridge the final gap' between the train station and your hotel or other final destination.

🚆 Train

For long-distance travel around Britain, trains are generally faster and more comfortable than coaches but can be more expensive, although with discount tickets they're competitive – and often take you through beautiful countryside. The British like to moan about their trains, but around 85% run on time. The other 15% that get delayed or cancelled mostly impact commuter services rather than long-distance journeys.

Information

Your first stop should be **National Rail Enquiries** (📞 08457 48 49 50; www.nationalrail.co.uk), the nationwide timetable and fare information service. Its website advertises special offers and has real-time links to station departure boards and downloadable maps of the rail network.

Operators

About 20 different companies operate train services in Britain, while Network Rail operates track and stations. For some passengers this system can be confusing at first, but information and ticket-buying services are mostly centralised. If you have to change trains, or use two or more train operators, you still buy one ticket – valid for the whole journey. The main railcards and passes are also accepted by all train operators.

Where more than one train operator services the same route, eg York to Edinburgh, a ticket purchased from one company may not be valid on trains run by another. So if you miss the train you originally booked, it's worth checking which later services your ticket will be valid for.

Buying Tickets

Once you've found the journey you need on the National Rail Enquiries website, links take you to the relevant train operator to buy the ticket. This can be mailed to you (UK addresses only) or collected at the station on the day of travel from automatic machines. There's usually no booking fee on top of the ticket price.

You can also use a centralised ticketing service

to buy your train ticket. These cover all train services in a single site, and make a small booking fee on top of every ticket price. The main players:

○ **QJump** (www.qjump.co.uk)

○ **Rail Easy** (www.raileasy.co.uk)

○ **Train Line** (www.thetrainline.com)

To use operator or centralised ticketing websites, you always have to state a preferred time and day of travel, even if you don't mind when you go, but you can change it as you go through the process, and with a little delving around you can find some real bargains. You can also buy train tickets on the spot at stations for short journeys (under about 50 miles), but discount tickets for longer trips are usually not available and must be bought in advance by phone or online.

Costs

For longer journeys, on-the-spot fares are always available, but tickets are much cheaper if bought in advance. The earlier you book, the cheaper it gets. You can also save if you travel off-peak. Advance purchase usually gets a reserved seat.

Whichever operator you travel with and wherever you buy tickets, there are three main fare types:

Anytime Buy anytime, travel anytime – usually the most expensive option.

Off-peak Buy ticket any time, travel off-peak (when is off-peak depends on the journey).

Advance Buy ticket in advance, travel only on specific trains – usually the cheapest.

For an idea of the price difference, an Anytime single ticket from London to York will cost £125 or more, an Off-peak around £95, with an Advance around £30 to £40, and possibly less if you book early enough or don't mind arriving at midnight.

The cheapest fares are nonrefundable, so if you miss your train you'll have to buy a new ticket.

Train Classes

There are two classes of rail travel: first and standard. First class costs around 50% more than standard fare (up to double at busy periods) and gets you bigger seats, more leg-room, and usually a more peaceful business-like atmosphere, plus extras such as complimentary drinks and newspapers. At weekends some train operators offer 'upgrades' to first class for an extra £5 to £25 on top of your standard class fare, payable on the spot.

Train Passes

If you're staying in Britain for a while, passes known as **Railcards** (www.railcard.co.uk) are available:

○ **16-25 Railcard** For those aged 16 to 25, or a full-time UK student.

○ **Senior Railcard** For anyone over 60.

○ **Family & Friends Railcard** Covers up to four adults and four children travelling together.

Railcards cost £30 (valid for one year, available from major stations or online) and get 33% discount on most train fares, except those already heavily discounted. With the Family card, adults get 33% and children get 60%

discounts, so the fee is easily repaid in a couple of journeys.

Local & Regional Passes

Local train passes usually cover rail networks around a city (many include bus travel too) and are detailed in the relevant sections throughout this guide.

If you're concentrating your travels on southeast England (eg London to Dover, Weymouth, Cambridge or Oxford), a **Network Railcard** (www.railcard.co.uk/network; per year £30) covers up to four adults and up to four children travelling together outside peak times.

National Passes

For country-wide travel, **BritRail** (www.britrail.net) passes are available for visitors from overseas. They must be bought in your country of origin (not in Britain) from a specialist travel agency. Available in seven different versions (eg England only; Scotland only; all Britain; UK and Ireland) for periods from four to 30 days.

Behind the Scenes

Author Thanks

Neil Wilson

Many thanks to all my co-authors and to the ever-helpful and patient editors and cartographers at Lonely Planet.

Acknowledgments

Climate map data adapted from Peel MC, Finlayson BL & McMahon TA (2007) 'Updated World Map of the Köppen-Geiger Climate Classification', *Hydrology and Earth System Sciences*, 11, 1633-44.

Illustrations: pp68-9, pp252-3 and pp322-3 by Javier Zarracina; pp74-5 by Javier Zarracina and Michael Weldon

Cover photographs: Front: Castle Howard, North Yorkshire, Granville Harris/Alamy ©; Back: Ring of Brodgar stone circle, Orkney Islands, Justin Foulkes/Lonely Planet ©

This Book

This 4th edition of Lonely Planet's *Discover Great Britain* guidebook was coordinated by Neil Wilson and researched and written by Oliver Berry, Fionn Davenport, Marc Di Duca, Belinda Dixon, Peter Dragicevich, Damian Harper, Anna Kaminski, Catherine Le Nevez and Andy Symington. This guidebook was produced by the following:

Destination Editor James Smart
Product Editors Martine Power, Tracy Whitmey
Senior Cartographer Mark Griffiths
Book Designers Wibowo Rusli, Wendy Wright
Assisting Editors Kate Mathews, Anne Mulvaney
Cover Researcher Naomi Parker
Thanks to Sasha Baskett, Ryan Evans, Andi Jones, Wayne Murphy, Tony Wheeler

Index

R

Radcliffe Camera 135
radio 400
Ramsey Island 272
Reading Festival 44
Regent's Park 77-8
religion 364
Ribblesdale 230
Richmond 230-2
Ring of Brodgar 361
River Thames 74-5
Riverside Museum 316
road rules 403
Road to the Isles 351
Roman Baths 170, 177
Roman sites 250
    Birdoswald Roman Fort 250
    Chesters Roman Fort & Museum 250
    Hadrian's Wall 21, 215, 250-3
    Housesteads 251, 252-3
    Roman Baths, Bath 170, 177
    Segontium Roman Fort 283
    Vindolanda Roman Fort & Museum 250
Rosslyn Chapel 306
Royal Ascot 43
Royal Crescent 176-7
Royal Mile 298-9, 304-5
Royal Pavilion 113
Royal Yacht *Britannia* 302
rugby 388
Rydal Mount 248

S

safety 103, 398
Salisbury 190-5, **191**
Salisbury Cathedral 190-1
Sandringham 146
school holidays 398
Science Museum 76
Scone Palace 325
Scotland 289-361

Scotland's Highlands & Islands 335-61, **336-7**
    activities 340
    itineraries 342-3
    planning 341
    scenic drives 340
    travel within 341
    websites 341
Scott Monument 299
Scottish independence referendum 364-5
Scottish National Gallery 300-1
Scottish National Portrait Gallery 302
sculpture 382-3
Segontium Roman Fort 283
Senedd 265
Sennen 208
Shakespeare, William 23, 129, 150, 380
    Anne Hathaway's Cottage 152
    Holy Trinity Church 152
    Mary Arden's Farm 152
    Royal Shakespeare Company 154
    Shakespeare's Birthplace 150
    Shakespeare's Globe 72
Shambles 221
Shangri-La at the Shard 46
Shard 72-3
Sherwood Forest National Nature Reserve 154
shopping, *see individual locations*
Sir John Soane's Museum 64
Skara Brae 361
Skye 27, 339, 355-9, **355**
Snowdon 258, 279-80, 281
Snowdonia National Park 15, 277-82, **278-9**
south Wales 269-71
southwest England 167-209, **168-9**
    cathedrals 172
    highlights 170-1

itineraries 174-5
    planning 173
    travel within 173
    websites 173
Speyside 25, 292, 331-3
sport 387-9
sporting events
    Cotswold Olimpicks 43
    Cowes Week 44
    Derby Week 43
    FA Cup Final 43
    Grand National 42-3
    Great North Run 44
    London Marathon 43
    Royal Ascot 43
    Royal Regatta 43
    Six Nations Rugby Championship 42
    University Boat Race 42
    Wimbledon Tennis 43
St Andrews 24, 328-30, **329**
St Davids 259, 271-4
St Giles Cathedral 299
St Ives 205-8
St Michael's Mount 208
St Paul's Cathedral 55, 65
stately homes 17, 31, 146, 158
    see also castles, palaces
Stirling 321-6, **324**
Stirling Castle 293, 322-3, 324
Stonehenge 11, 46, 170, 192-3
Stourhead 194
Stow-on-the-Wold 147
Stratford-upon-Avon 23, 129, 150-5, **151**
Studley Royal 228
Sulgrave Manor 158

T

Talacharn (Laugharne) 270-1
Tate Britain 73
Tate Liverpool 240
Tate Modern 54, 71-2
Tate St Ives 205
telephone services 398-9
tennis 43, 389

How to Use This Book

These symbols will help you find the listings you want:

◉ Sights
🏖 Beaches
⚡ Activities
🎓 Courses
🎫 Tours
🎉 Festivals & Events
🛏 Sleeping
🍴 Eating
🍷 Drinking
☆ Entertainment
🛍 Shopping
ℹ Information/ Transport

Look out for these icons:

FREE No payment required

🌿 A green or sustainable option

Our authors have nominated these places as demonstrating a strong commitment to sustainability – for example by supporting local communities and producers, operating in an environmentally friendly way, or supporting conservation projects.

These symbols give you the vital information for each listing:

☑ Telephone Numbers
☉ Opening Hours
Ⓟ Parking
☒ Nonsmoking
✳ Air-Conditioning
@ Internet Access
☎ Wi-Fi Access
☒ Swimming Pool
⚘ Vegetarian Selection
⬚ English-Language Menu
👪 Family-Friendly
🐾 Pet-Friendly
🚌 Bus
⛴ Ferry
Ⓜ Metro
Ⓢ Subway
Ⓔ London Tube
🚋 Tram
🚆 Train

Reviews are organised by author preference.

Map Legend

Sights
🏖 Beach
🪷 Buddhist
🏰 Castle
✝ Christian
🕉 Hindu
☪ Islamic
✡ Jewish
⬙ Monument
🏛 Museum/Gallery
⊙ Ruin
🍷 Winery/Vineyard
🐾 Zoo
◉ Other Sight

Activities, Courses & Tours
🤿 Diving/Snorkelling
🛶 Canoeing/Kayaking
⛷ Skiing
🏄 Surfing
🏊 Swimming/Pool
🚶 Walking
🏄 Windsurfing
⊕ Other Activity/ Course/Tour

Sleeping
🛏 Sleeping
⛺ Camping

Eating
🍴 Eating

Drinking
☕ Drinking
☕ Cafe

Entertainment
🎭 Entertainment

Shopping
🛍 Shopping

Information
✉ Post Office
ℹ Tourist Information

Transport
✈ Airport
⊗ Border Crossing
🚌 Bus
🚡 Cable Car/ Funicular
🚲 Cycling
⛴ Ferry
🚝 Monorail
Ⓟ Parking
Ⓢ S-Bahn
🚕 Taxi
🚉 Train/Railway
🚋 Tram
Ⓣ Tube Station
Ⓤ U-Bahn
Ⓜ Underground Train Station
• Other Transport

Routes
Tollway
Freeway
Primary
Secondary
Tertiary
Lane
Unsealed Road
Plaza/Mall
Steps
Tunnel
Pedestrian Overpass
Walking Tour
Walking Tour Detour
Path

Boundaries
International
State/Province
Disputed
Regional/Suburb
Marine Park
Cliff
Wall

Population
✪ Capital (National)
◉ Capital (State/Province)
● City/Large Town
○ Town/Village

Geographic
🏠 Hut/Shelter
🚩 Lighthouse
👁 Lookout
▲ Mountain/Volcano
🌴 Oasis
🌳 Park
)(Pass
🌲 Picnic Area
💦 Waterfall

Hydrography
River/Creek
Intermittent River
Swamp/Mangrove
Reef
Canal
Water
Dry/Salt/ Intermittent Lake
Glacier

Areas
Beach/Desert
Cemetery (Christian)
Cemetery (Other)
Park/Forest
Sportsground
Sight (Building)
Top Sight (Building)